T0185841

Interactive Object-Oriented Programming in Java

Learn and Test Your Programming Skills

Second Edition

Vaskaran Sarcar

Foreword by Avirup Mullick

APress®

Interactive Object-Oriented Programming in Java

Vaskaran Sarcar
Bangalore, Karnataka, India

ISBN-13 (pbk): 978-1-4842-5403-5   ISBN-13 (electronic): 978-1-4842-5404-2
https://doi.org/10.1007/978-1-4842-5404-2

Managing Director, Apress Media LLC: Welmoed Spahr
Acquisitions Editor: Celestin Suresh John
Development Editor: Mathew Moodie
Coordinating Editor: Divya Modi

Cover designed by eStudioCalamar

Cover image designed by Pixabay

Distributed to the book trade worldwide by Springer Science+Business Media New York, 233 Spring Street, 6th Floor, New York, NY 10013. Phone 1-800-SPRINGER, fax (201) 348-4505, email orders-ny@springer-sbm.com, or visit www.springeronline.com. Apress Media, LLC is a California LLC and the sole member (owner) is Springer Science + Business Media Finance Inc (SSBM Finance Inc). SSBM Finance Inc is a **Delaware** corporation.

For information on translations, please email rights@apress.com or visit http://www.apress.com/rights-permissions.

Apress titles may be purchased in bulk for academic, corporate, or promotional use. eBook versions and licenses are also available for most titles. For more information, reference our Print and eBook Bulk Sales web page at http://www.apress.com/bulk-sales.

Any source code or other supplementary material referenced by the author in this book is available to readers on GitHub via the book's product page, located at www.apress.com/978-1-4842-5403-5. For more detailed information, please visit http://www.apress.com/source-code.

Printed on acid-free paper

Dear Reader,

You motivate me with your nice and loving comments,
you hurt me with your extremely critical comments, but in the
end you help me to become a better person and a better author.
So, this *book is dedicated to you.*

Table of Contents

About the Author

 **Vaskaran Sarcar** obtained his Master of Engineering degree from Jadavpur University, Kolkata, India. He was a national Gate Scholar and has more than twelve years of experience in education and the IT industry. He worked as senior software engineer, specialist, and team lead in the R&D Hub at HP Inc. India until August 2019. He is an alumnus of prestigious institutions in India, such as Jadavpur University, Vidyasagar University, and Presidency University (formerly Presidency College). He loves to spend time with his kids and family members. Reading and learning new things are his passions. Other books by Vaskaran include the following:

- *Java Design Patterns*, Second Edition (Apress, 2018)

- *Design Patterns in C#* (Apress, 2018)

- *Interactive C#* (Apress, 2017)

- *Interactive Object-Oriented Programming in Java* (Apress, 2016)

- *Java Design Patterns*, First Edition (Apress, 2016)

- *C# Basics: Test Your Skill* (CreateSpace, 2015)

- *Operating System: Computer Science Interview Series* (CreateSpace, 2014)

About the Technical Reviewer

Yogesh Sharma is a full-stack engineer at Mphasis Pvt Ltd where he primarily focuses on modernising existing stacks with the help of containerisation, microservices and prevalent DevOps disciplines. With his recently discovered love for Infrastructure as Code and Adaptive Intelligence, he enjoys travelling, voluntary services and watching sitcoms. He would also like to take this opportunity to thank his wife, Akanksha for supporting him in all his endeavors.

Acknowledgments

At first, I thank the Almighty. I sincerely believe that with *his* blessings only, I completed this book. I also extend my deepest gratitude and thanks to the following:

Ratanlal Sarkar and **Manikuntala Sarkar**: My dear parents, with your blessings only, could I complete this work.

Indrani, my wife, and **Ambika**, my daughter: Sweethearts, once again, without your love I could not proceed at all. I know that we needed to limit many social gatherings and invitations so I could complete this work on time, and each time I promised you that I would take a long break and spend more time with you.

Sambaran, my brother: Thank you for your constant encouragement toward me.

Yogesh: You are technical advisor for this second edition. I know that whenever I was in need, your support was there. Thank you one more time.

Shekhar and **Anupam**: My friends and technical advisors in the previous edition of this book. Though this time you were not involved, I still acknowledge your support and help in the development of *Interactive Object-Oriented Programming in Java*, First Edition.

Avirup Mullick: I first met you in 1998. You were my college senior. A special thanks to you for taking time to write a foreword for my book. From the moment experts like you agreed to write for me, I got additional motivation to enhance the quality of my work.

Celestin: Thanks for giving me another opportunity to work with you and Apress.

April, **Nirmal**, **Arockia Rajan**, **Ramraj**, **Chinnaparaj**, and **Vinoth**: Thank you for your exceptional support to beautify my work.

Lastly, I extend my deepest gratitude to my publisher, the editorial board members, and everyone who directly or indirectly supported this book.

Preface

It is my privilege to present you with *Interactive Object-Oriented Programming in Java: Learn and Test Your Programming Skills* (Second Edition).

If you are curious about what the most important and unique characteristics of this book are, I would say that it is interactive and very simple. The goal was not to demonstrate typical and tough programs using all the latest features of Java. On the contrary, the true goal is to fuel your creativity by using the core constructs in Java. The word *core* is more important than *the latest* when you learn a new technology. Whatever is the latest today will be outdated tomorrow. But core concepts are evergreen.

This book focuses on the implementation of object-oriented programming concepts using the most basic features of Java so that you don't need to be familiar with advanced Java topics. The examples are simple and straightforward. I believe that these examples are written in such a way that even if you are familiar with another popular language, such as C#, C++, and so on, you can still easily grasp the concepts in this book.

You'll probably agree that when you travel an unknown path to a destination, it can help if you get a loving and caring guide. Learning a new programming language through a book is also a journey, a fact that was always on my mind as I wrote. So, in this book, I did not explain a topic in only an informative way. Instead, I made this book interactive, with one or more "Q&A Sessions" in each chapter. These sessions will not only assist you in your learning process, but can also act as a "doubt-clearing session" because they will feel like you are asking your guide some questions (or expressing your doubts) and that you are receiving the answers from him in a simple one-to-one communication. In addition to this, in most of the cases, you'll get a full demonstration of a program with output analysis so that you can get the maximum benefit.

In short, the aim of this book is to help you to get a feel of a Java classroom environment. I have been involved in teaching since 2005. I have taken classes in both engineering and non-engineering colleges. And, fortunately, most of my teaching involvement was based on Java and its advanced topics. That is the true motivation for why I wanted to introduce a book like this. Before you jump into the topics, let me highlight a few points about the book, its chapters' organization, and the intended readers.

The book has three major parts. The first nine chapters make up Part 1, in which you will see the discussion and implementation of object-oriented concepts in Java. Part 2 consists of five more chapters (from Chapter 10 to Chapter 14). In Part 2, you will explore something from "Advanced Java," where you will learn about exception handling, multi-thread programming, generic programming, and JDBC programming. In Chapter 14, you will get to know about the feature evolution path, where you will experiment with important features that come in different versions of Java. But I have picked only those features that enhance what you will learn in Part 1 of the book, so that you can understand how these upgraded features can make your programming life easier. Finally, in Part 3 of the book, you will learn about some real-world implementation using three important design patterns. Part 3 also consists of a chapter of FAQs, which is basically a subset of all the Q&A Sessions in this book. It can provide a quick review of all the topics that you learn in this book.

The target readers for this book are those who know the basic language constructs in Java and how to compile or run a simple Java application. This book does not invest time in topics that are easily available online, such as how to install Eclipse on your system, or how to write a "Hello World" program in Java, or how can you use an `if-else` statement or a `while` loop in your Java program and so forth. Instead, the book starts with a discussion in object-oriented programming. So, I expect that before you enter into Chapter 1, you will be familiar with simple Java programs and your coding environment is ready. My discussion with you starts with the object-oriented concepts you can use in Java. Here, I focus on the fundamental features of Java, and I also explain how these concepts can be learned and used effectively.

But do not worry! To assist you with asking/thinking better questions in doubt-clearing sessions, an entire section is added at the end of the book (Appendix A). This appendix discusses some key concepts in Java and helps you evaluate your skills in the language basics. You may need to come back to this section many times because it acts as a reference. Even if you do not know all of these topics, gradually, upon repeated practice, you will become familiar with them. So, if you are new to programming or if you have some idea about other programming languages, this section can assist you a lot. It can also help you prepare for a job interview or an examination by answering some tricky questions that may seem very easy at the beginning.

I said earlier that in this book each chapter contains one or more Q&A Sessions, which will give you a feel of learning in a classroom environment—where your teacher will discuss some problems or topics, ask you questions, and allow you to ask counter questions. If you are dedicated to this subject and think deeply about the questions and the corresponding answers, you will surely develop confidence in this language.

In a semester, you need to attend a certain number of lectures to complete the fundamental topics, and you know that learning is a continuous process. So, this book is not for those who want to learn Java in 24 hours or in 7 days. It is up to you only. I can only say that the book is designed for you in such a way that upon its completion, you will have developed an adequate knowledge of the topic, you will have learned the key features of this powerful language and object-oriented programming, and you will have learned how you should write programs in Java and, most important, how to go further.

I have taken care to provide codes that are compatible with all the latest versions of Java. Also, it is not mandatory for you to learn Eclipse. You can simply run these programs in your preferred IDE (integrated development environment). I have chosen Eclipse because it is widely used to develop Java applications.

Please remember that as you learn about these concepts, try writing your own code; only then will you master this area. You can always share your comments to truly complete this book and enhance your future work.

You will be able to download all the source code of the book from the publisher's website. I have a plan to maintain the "Errata" and, if required, I can also make some updates/announcements there. So, it is suggested that you visit those pages to receive the corrections or updates, if any.

Lastly, I hope that this enhanced edition can provide more help to you and that you will like the book.

Who Is This Book For?

In short, **you can pick** this book if the answer is "yes" to the following questions:

- Are you familiar with basic constructs in Java?

- Do you know how to set up your coding environment?

- Do you want to explore object-oriented programming step-by-step?

- Do you want to review your understanding of basic programming skills in Java?

- Do you want to explore something from advanced Java (for example, generic programming, JDBC Programming, multi-thread programming, etc.)?

- Are you interested to know about some real-world implementation techniques?

Probably you **shouldn't pick** this book if the answer is "yes" to any of the following questions:

- Are you totally new to Java?

- Are you looking for all the advanced concepts in Java in depth?

- Are you interested in exploring only the latest features of Java?

- Do you dislike a book that has an emphasis on Q&A sessions?

- "I do not like Windows and Eclipse. I want to learn Java without them." Is this statement true for you?

Guidelines for Using This Book

Here are some suggestions so you can use this book more effectively:

- If you are confident with the topics covered in Appendix A, you can start with Chapter 1 of the book. I suggest you go through the chapters sequentially. Some fundamental questions may be discussed in the Q&A Session of a previous chapter, and I have not repeated those in the later chapters.

- These programs are tested with Java 8 (update 172), and I have used Eclipse IDE in a Windows 10 environment. When I started the second edition of the book, Photon was the latest edition of Eclipse (released June 27, 2018), Java 8 was the long-term support (LTS) version, and Java 10 was the rapid-release version. Java 11 is the next LTS version after Java 8 and was planned for September 2018. But as it turned out, by the time I finished my work, Java 13 and Eclipse Java 2019-09 had been released. But all these versions' details should not matter to you, because I have used the most basic constructs of Java. So, I believe that these codes should execute smoothly in the upcoming versions of Java/Eclipse as well. To experiment with this, I tested some portions of these codes in different systems and different environments (including online editors), and I always received the expected output. With these experiments, I believe that the results should not vary in other environments as well, but you know the nature of software—they can misbehave and surprise you. So, I recommend that if you want to see the exact same outputs that are shown in the book, it will be better if you can mimic the same environment.

- There is an exception for Chapter 14 codes. Some of them use the latest Java features, and my Eclipse environment was not ready to accommodate the changes. So, I executed some programs with the latest features in a command-line environment. You can do the same.

- In some examples, to draw class diagrams, ObjectAid Uml Explorer is used in the Eclipse editor. It is a lightweight tool for Eclipse. At the time of this writing, it is free if you want to draw the class diagrams, but to draw the sequence diagrams, you will need to purchase a license. The online link http://www.objectaid.com/home can give you the details of these licenses and terms and conditions.

Conventions Used in This Book

All programs in this book are organized under package statements like the following:

package java2e.chapter2;

```
class ClassEx1 {
    // Field initialization is optional.
    // Here myInt is initialized with the value 25.
    public int myInt = 25;
    // In the following case, it will be initialized with default //value 0.
}
public class Demonstration1 {

    public static void main(String[] args) {
        System.out.println("***Demonstration-1. A class demo with 2
        objects ***");
        ClassEx1 obA = new ClassEx1();
        ClassEx1 obB = new ClassEx1();
        System.out.println("obA.myInt = " + obA.myInt);
        System.out.println("obB.myInt = " + obB.myInt);
    }
}
```

It simply says that there is folder classed `java2e`, inside which is another folder chapter2, and you are storing Demonstration1.java inside it. So, the Demonstration1.class and ClassEx1.class files should be available there. You'll learn about Java packages in Chapter 7. Once you're familiar with them, you'll acknowledge that it is always a better practice to organize your codes with packages.

But when you start learning the concepts, to compile and run the programs, *the package statements are NOT mandatory for you*. So, initially you can play with all these programs without the package statements. And, you may store your programs in your preferred location, so, at your end, you may need to modify the package statements when you use them.

All the outputs and codes of the book follow the same font and structure. To draw your attention, in some places, I have made them bold like the following:

Demonstration-17.A comparison study:Using a final class vs using a private constructor

Called the private constructor.
Setting the default the value x=10.
        Exit-private non-parameterized constructor.
Updating the default value of x.
        Exit-parameterised constructor.
        The parent.x=15
Called the private constructor.
Setting the default the value x=10.
        Exit-private non-parameterized constructor.
Updating the default value of x.
        Exit-parameterised constructor.
        The child.x=2
        The child.y=3

Foreword

It is an absolute honor and privilege to write this foreword for Vaskaran's latest book, *Interactive Object-Oriented Programming in Java: Learn and Test Your Programming Skills*.

I have known Vaskaran for many years now. From studying in the same institutions, such as Presidency University (formerly Presidency College) and Vidyasagar University, to working in the IT industry, we tread our own paths in our academic and professional careers, but he always found a way to give back to the community. This is a unique trait, and I admire him for that.

His passion for writing and his desire to share the knowledge he has acquired through his years of experience in the industry are reflected in this book, where the approach to learning is through clarifying theoretical concepts while testing one's programming skills. This practical approach will be invaluable to readers and will help them in real-life programming situations in their exams, interviews, or jobs.

This book discusses the fundamental concepts of object-oriented programming in depth, with examples in Java. It also covers some advance concepts, including design patterns in Java. It is an easy read, and each concept has been handled with precision: fundamentals have been clarified for in-depth knowledge building while demonstrations and examples have kept it interesting. Each chapter is augmented with a Q & A Session, which will be helpful in putting things in perspective or clearing one's doubts by understanding the pros and cons of each of these patterns. The "Test Your Skill in Language Basics" section will help readers review their understanding of the fundamentals of Java before advancing their expertise in the field.

The FAQ chapter at the end of the book is particularly helpful in refreshing one's knowledge and getting one in the mindset to crack those technical interviews with confidence.

This book is a must-read for Java developers or aspiring Java developers, as it will most certainly enhance one's object-oriented programming skills in Java to a great extent. For that matter, even developers from a non-Java background can benefit from the book.

I wish Vaskaran and this book all the success it deserves.

Avirup Mullick
Manager, Global Operations Center, Adobe Systems

PART I

Fundamentals of Object-Oriented Programming

CHAPTER 1

Object-Oriented Programming Concepts

Welcome to object-oriented programming (OOP). Before we start, let's discuss some fundamental questions and answers. For example, why do you need this kind of programming? How can these concepts make your life easier? If you know the answers to these questions, your learning path will be easy, and you will be able to relate to these concepts in various ways. But, before you start, there are two warning messages for you.

- Do not lose your motivation if you cannot understand everything after the first pass. In many cases, it may seem complicated, but gradually it will be easier for you.

- Many developers criticize the concepts of OOP. But please remember that each human mind tends to criticize new things. So, even if you want to criticize these concepts, I suggest that you first understand it properly, use the concepts in various applications, and then make your own decision about whether to appreciate or criticize.

Now, let us begin the journey . . .

Computer programming started with binary code, and mechanical switches were used to load the programs. It is easy to assume that a programmer's life was very challenging in those days. To make programmers' lives easy, some high-level programming languages were developed, and, in those languages, some simple English-like instructions were used. But you should not forget the fact that a computer can understand instructions only in a binary language. So, the compiler's primary job was to translate these English-like instructions into binaries, and eventually these high-level languages gained in popularity.

© Vaskaran Sarcar 2020
V. Sarcar, *Interactive Object-Oriented Programming in Java*, https://doi.org/10.1007/978-1-4842-5404-2_1

Over a period of time, computer capacity and capabilities increased a lot. Then, developers started developing complex applications. Unfortunately, none of the programming languages that were available at that time was mature enough to handle all of the applications effectively. Some of the primary concerns were as follows:

- How can I avoid duplicate efforts? Or, how can I reuse existing code?

- How can I control the use of global variables in a shared environment?

- How can I debug the code when too much jumping is occurring (for example, when you use the goto keyword in various places in an application)?

- How can I make a new engineer's life easier?

- How can I maintain a large code base in a better way?

To solve these problems, expert programmers started breaking the large problems into smaller problems. The idea behind this philosophy was very simple: *If you can solve these smaller problems, eventually you can solve the big problem*. So, they started portioning the big problems into small chunks, and the concept of functions (or procedures or subroutines) developed. Each function was dedicated to solve one small problem. So, managing these functions and the interactions among them became the key focus, and the concept of **structured programming** was created. Structured programming was a big hit because managing small functions is easy, and you can debug them easily. At the same time, developers also started limiting the use of global variables, which were replaced with local variables in the functions (in most of the cases).

Structured programming was popular for almost two decades. During this time, the capacity of hardware increased significantly. So, developers wanted to solve more-complex tasks, and, gradually, the limitations of structured programming became more prominent; for example, consider the following cases:

- Suppose, in your application, you have used a particular data type across multiple functions in an application. Later, you identified that you need to change the data type. As a result, you need to implement the changes across all functions across the application.

- It is difficult to model all real-world scenarios with the key components of structured programming (i.e., data and functions). In the real world, whenever you create a product, there are two areas you need to focus on:

  - *Purpose.* Why is the product needed?

  - *Behavior.* How can the product make your life easier?

Then the idea of objects came into existence. Alan Curtis Kay is widely considered one of the fathers of object-oriented programming, which he named, along with some colleagues, at the Palo Alto Research Center (PARC), formerly known as Xerox PARC.

POINTS TO REMEMBER

The fundamental difference between structured programming and object-oriented programming can be summarized as follows: *In object-oriented programming, instead of focusing on the operations on data, focus on the data itself.*

OOP focuses on some key principles. I'll cover them in detail in this book. In this chapter, you will get a brief introduction to each of them. You may not understand all the terms in the first read-through, so, it is recommended that you visit these topics again.

Class and Objects

These are at the core of OOP. A **class** is the blueprint or template for its objects. **Objects** are instances of a class. Each object has its own state, behavior, and identity. In simple language, you can say that in structured programming, you segregate the problem into small functions, and in OOP, you divide the problem into objects. You are familiar with data types like `int`, `double`, `float`, and so forth. You know that these are *built-in data types* or *primitive data types* because they are already defined in a computer language. But when you create your own data type, let's say, `Student`, you need to create a `Student` class. Just as when you need to create an integer variable, you mention the `int` first, similarly, when you need to create a `Student` object (e.g., `john`), you need to mention your `Student` class first. So, when you're familiar with OOP, you may say something like this: a dog is an object from a `Mammal` class, your car is an object from a `Vehicle` class, and so on.

Encapsulation

In object-oriented programming, you do not allow your data to flow freely inside the system. Instead, you wrap the data and functions into a single unit (i.e., in a class). The purpose of encapsulation is at least one of the following:

- Putting restrictions in place so that the components of an object cannot be accessed directly

- Binding the data with methods that will act on that data (i.e., forming a capsule)

In some OOP languages, the hiding of the information is not implemented by default. So, they come up with an additional term called *information hiding*.

Later, you will see that data encapsulation is one of the key features in a class. If you want to promote security, your data should not be visible to the outside world. Only through the methods defined inside the class can you access these data. Therefore, you can think of these methods as the interface between the objects' data and the outside world (i.e., your program).

In Java, you can implement encapsulation in various ways. For example, you can use the access specifiers (or modifiers) and getter-setter methods in this context.

Note   You will learn about access specifiers and getter-setter methods in Chapter 3.

Abstraction

The key purpose of abstraction is to show only the essential features and to hide the background details of implementation. Abstraction is also very much related to encapsulation, but the difference may be easily understood with a simple day-to-day scenario.

When you press a button on your remote control to switch on the TV, you do not care about the internal circuits of the TV or how the remote control controls the operation of the TV. You simply know that different buttons on the remote control have different functionalities, and as long as they work properly, you are happy. So, the user is isolated from the complex implementation details, which are *encapsulated* within the remote control (and TV). At the same time, the common operations that can be performed through the remote control can be thought of as an *abstraction*. A manufacturer can enhance this feature when the same remote can also perform on a different model or product. For example, a DVD player's remote control can also be used to control the volume of a TV.

Inheritance

Whenever we talk about reusability, we'll generally refer to inheritance, which is a process in which one object acquires the properties of another object. Consider this example. Bus is one type of Vehicle because it fulfills the basic criteria of a Vehicle that is used for transportation purposes. Similarly, Train is another type of Vehicle. And even though a GoodsTrain and a PassengerTrain are different, we can say that both inherit from the Train category (or class) because ultimately both of them fulfill the basic criteria of a Train, which in turn is a Vehicle. So, you can simply say that hierarchical classifications are supported with the concept of inheritance.

In the programming world, inheritance creates a new child class from an existing parent class. This parent class is sometimes known by different names. For example, in C#, you call this parent class the base class and in Java, you may refer to it as the super class. So, in simple words, a parent class is placed one level up in that hierarchical chain. Then you can add new functionalities (methods) or modify the super class functionalities (later you will call it overriding the functionalities) into the child class. You must remember that due to these modifications, the core architecture should not be affected. In other words, if you derive Bus class from Vehicle class, and add/ modify the functionalities in Bus class, those modifications will not impact the original functionalities that were described for the Vehicle class.

So, the key advantage is that you can avoid lots of duplicate code with this mechanism.

Polymorphism

Polymorphism is generally associated with *one name with many forms*. Consider the behavior of your pet dog. When it sees an unknown person, it is angry and starts barking a lot. But when it sees you, it makes different noises and behaves differently. In the coding world, you can also think of a common method, addition. With addition in the context of two integers, you expect to get a sum of the integers. But for string operands, you expect to get a concatenated string.

Polymorphism can be of two types:

- **_Compile-time polymorphism:_** The compiler can decide very early
  which method to invoke in which situation once the program is
  compiled. This is also known as static binding or early binding.

- **_Runtime polymorphism:_** The actual method calls are resolved at
  runtime. At compile time, you cannot predict which method will be
  invoked when the program runs (for example, the program may behave
  differently with different inputs). Consider the following case: suppose
  you want to generate a random number at the very first line when you
  execute a program. If the generated number is an even number, you
  will call a method, Method1( ), which prints "Hello"; otherwise, you'll
  call a method whose name is the same but prints "Hi." Now, you'll agree
  that after you execute the program, you can only see which method is
  invoked (i.e., the compiler cannot resolve the call at compile time). In
  a situation like this, you do not have any clue as to whether you will see
  "Hello" or "Hi" prior to the program's execution. Therefore, sometimes
  it is also termed dynamic binding or late binding. In Chapter 5, you'll
  see a detailed discussion on polymorphism, and you will experience the
  necessity of runtime polymorphism in detail.

Q&A Session

1.1 What are the key features of object-oriented programming?

The following are the key features of object-oriented programming:

- Encapsulation

- Abstraction

- Inheritance

- Polymorphism

1.2 How is an object different from a class?

Objects are made from a class. An object is an instance of a class, which is just a template
or a blueprint for your object. An object is a physical entity and can allocate memory in
the system, but class is a logical entity and does not allocate memory in the system.

1.3 How is abstraction different from encapsulation?

Abstraction focuses on the noticeable behavior of an object, and encapsulation focuses on the implementation part of that behavior. Encapsulation helps you to bundle your data, and at the same time it can hide some information that you do not want to disclose to the outside world.

1.4 What is the key advantage associated with the inheritance mechanism?

Reusing the existing code, you can save time and effort. At the same time, this mechanism helps you to avoid duplicate codes in your application.

1.5 What are the characteristics of object-oriented programming?

Here are some important characteristics:

- Your focus is on data, not on functions. So, you divide your program into objects, not functions.

- You do not allow data to flow freely. You use methods to access them.

- Your objects communicate through methods.

- The outside world should not access your data.

- Your application can adapt to new changes easily. At the same time, it is easy to maintain.

Summary

This chapter discussed the following topics:

- What is object-oriented programming?

- Why did it evolve?

- How is it different from structured programming?

- What are the key features of object-oriented programming?

CHAPTER 2

The Building Blocks: Class and Objects

Object-oriented programming (OOP) techniques primarily depend on two concepts—class and objects. In this chapter, we'll discuss these topics in detail.

Class

A class is a blueprint, template, or prototype. It can describe the behaviors of its objects and is the foundation for how the objects are built or instantiated.

Object

An object is an instance of a class.

If you are familiar with the game of football (or *soccer*, as it's known in the United States), you know the players who are participating in a game are selected for their skills in various positions. In addition to these skills, they need to have a minimum level of match fitness and some important athletic capabilities. So, when I say that Ronaldo is a footballer (a.k.a. soccer player), you can assume that Ronaldo has these basic abilities as well as some skills specific to football (even though Ronaldo is unknown to you).This is why you can simply say that Ronaldo is an object of a Footballer class.

Note   It may appear to you that it is a chicken-or-the-egg type of dilemma. You could argue that if I say, "X is playing like Ronaldo," then in that case, Ronaldo is acting like a class. However, in object-oriented design, you make things simple by deciding who comes first, and you decide that guy is the class in your application.

© Vaskaran Sarcar 2020
V. Sarcar, *Interactive Object-Oriented Programming in Java*, https://doi.org/10.1007/978-1-4842-5404-2_2

Consider another footballer, Beckham. You can assume again that if Beckham is a footballer, then Beckham must be excellent in many aspects of football. Also, he must possess a minimum fitness level to participate in a game.

Now, let's assume that Ronaldo and Beckham both are participating in the same match. It's not difficult to predict that although both Ronaldo and Beckham are footballers, their playing styles and performances will be different from each other in that match. In the same way, in the world of object-oriented programming, the performance of objects can be different from each other, even though they belong to the same class.

You can consider any domain. For example, you could say that your pet dogs or cats are objects of the Animal class. Similarly, your favorite car could be considered an object of the Vehicle class, your favorite novel could be considered an object of the Book class, and so on.

In a real-world scenario, each of the objects must have two basic characteristics: state and behavior. If you consider the objects—Ronaldo or Beckham from the Footballer class—you may notice that they have states like "playing" or "non-playing." In the playing state, they can show different skills (or behaviors)—they can run, they can kick, they can pass the ball, and so forth.

In a non-playing state, the behavior will also change. In this state, they can take a much-needed nap, or they can eat their meals, or they can simply relax by doing activities like reading a book, watching a movie, and so forth.

Similarly, a television in your home, at any moment, can be in either an "on" state or an "off" state. It can display different channels if, and only if, it is in "switched on" mode. It does not show anything if it is in "switched off" mode.

So, to begin with object-oriented programming, you can ask the following questions:

- What are the possible states of my objects?

- What are the different functions (behaviors) that they can perform in those states?

Once you get the answers to these questions, you are ready to proceed. Software objects follow the same pattern in any object-oriented program: their states are stored in fields (variables), and their capabilities (behaviors) are described through different methods (functions).

Let's do some programming exercises now. You are about to start an exciting journey. I will try to make things very simple. At the same time, I'll ignore some typical corner cases to make your journey smooth and easy.

You now understand that to create objects, you need to first decide in which class they will belong; that is, in general, if you want to create objects, you need to create a class first.

POINTS TO REMEMBER

- You start with the class, which is the architectural blueprint. A class defines the structure and behavior of the objects. From a single blueprint, you can construct multiple buildings. Similarly, from a single class, you can construct multiple objects (or instances). (As said before, typical corner cases are ignored when I make this statement. For example, a true singleton class cannot have multiple instances).

- With a class, you create a new data type, and objects are used to hold the data (fields) and methods. Object behavior can be exposed through these methods.

In Java, you create a class as follows:

```java
class A
{
//This is a single-line comment.

//Here is some data, for example,
  int a;

//Here is a method, for example,
void someMethod()
  {
    //Some code
  }
}
```

You can see that to create a class, you need to use the `class` keyword. (The single-line comments' `//` are used for better readability.) The class body is enclosed with curly braces—`{` and `}`. The data or variables inside a class are termed *instance* variables. You can have some methods in your class. Collectively, these data and methods are referred to as ***class members***.

Now, you have created a class called A. So, you can create an object from it. Let's say your object is obA, which can be created with the following statement:

```
A obA=new A();
```

You can split the preceding statement into the following two lines:

```
A obA;//Line-1
obA=new A();//Line-2
```

It is important to note that at the end of Line 1, obA is a ***reference***. Up to this point, no memory has been allocated, and obA contains `null`. But once the new operator comes into the picture, the memory is allocated for it. So, at the end of Line 2, the new operator allocates the memory for the physical object and assigns a reference to it to obA.

POINTS TO REMEMBER

A class is a logical entity. Once you instantiate a class, you create objects. These objects occupy memory in your system. So, objects are physical entities. In the preceding code snippet, the new operator is used to create an object of class A. It allocates memory to it and returns an object of the class A, whose reference is stored in the variable obA.

Constructor

If you look carefully, you will observe that after the new keyword, the class name is followed by a parenthesis. You use this approach to construct an object. These are ***constructors*** that are used to run initialization codes. Constructors can be both parameterized and non-parameterized. So, you can pass different arguments to them. In simple words, constructors can vary, with a different ***number*** of parameters or different ***types*** of parameters. In the following example, class A has four different constructors.

```
class A
{
        public A()
        {
                System.out.println("Constructor with no parameter");
        }
        public A(int a)
        {
                System.out.println("Constructor with one integer parameter");
        }
        public A(int a,int b)
        {
                System.out.println("Constructor with two integer parameter");
        }
        public A(double a)
        {
                System.out.println("Constructor with one double parameter");
        }
}
```

If you do not supply any constructor for your class, Java will supply a default one for you.

POINTS TO REMEMBER

The compiler supplies a no-argument default constructor if you do not include any constructor for your class. This default constructor actually calls the no-argument constructor of the superclass (if any). In this context, the compiler may complain if the superclass doesn't have any such constructor. If your class does not have any explicit superclass, then it has an implicit superclass Object that has a no-argument constructor. You may not be familiar with all these terms yet, but you will know about them shortly.

So, when you see something like the following, you can be sure that a parameterless constructor will be used:

```
A obA=new A();
```

But to know whether it is a user-defined constructor or was provided by Java (in other words, a default constructor), you need to examine the class body; for example, in a class definition, if you have code like

```
class A
{
 A()
        {
          //some code
        }
}
```

you can conclude that you have used the user-defined parameterless constructor. So, in this scenario, Java will not supply any default constructor on your behalf.

So far you understand that classes are simply the building blocks of your programs. You **encapsulate** the variables (also known as **fields**) and methods inside a class to make a single unit. These variables are called as instance variables because each instance of this class contains its own copies of these variables. (Later, you'll learn that fields can be any implicit data type, different class objects, and so forth). Methods, on the other hand, contain a block of code. This is nothing but a series of statements that perform specific actions. Instance variables are generally accessed through methods. As said before, collectively, these variables and methods are called class members.

Note   An instance is a unique copy of a class and is used to represent an object. I have used these terms interchangeably.

Static variables will be discussed in Chapter 8.

In general, you can place different things inside your class declaration. For example, you can put variables, methods, constructors, inner classes, initialization blocks, enums (these are also internally implemented as classes), and so on inside your class body. But, for simplicity, I have started the discussion with methods and fields, which are the most common. You'll see the other topics in their respective chapters in this book.

Fields and methods can be associated with different kinds of modifiers; for example, `public`, `private`, `protected`, `default`, etc. You will be familiar with modifiers shortly.

Demonstration 1

Consider a simple example. Here, I have a class called ClassEx1 and have encapsulated only one integer field, myInt, into it. I have also initialized the value 25 into that field. So, you can predict that whenever I create an object of this class, that object will have an integer named myInt in it, and the corresponding value will be 25.

For your ready reference, I have created two objects—obA and obB—from the class ClassEx1. I have tested the values of the variable myInt inside the objects. In the output, you can see that in both cases, I am getting the value 25.

Note   All programs in this book are organized under package statements. You'll learn about Java packages in Chapter 7. To compile and run these programs, the package statements are NOT mandatory for you. So, initially you can play with all these programs without the package statement.

```
package java2e.chapter2;

class ClassEx1 {
    // Field initialization is optional.
    // Here myInt is initialized with the value 25.
    public int myInt = 25;
    // In the following case, it will be initialized with default value 0.
    // public int myInt;
}

class Demonstration1 {

    public static void main(String[] args) {
        System.out.println("***Demonstration-1. A class demo with 2
        objects ***");
        ClassEx1 obA = new ClassEx1();
        ClassEx1 obB = new ClassEx1();
        System.out.println("obA.myInt = " + obA.myInt);
        System.out.println("obB.myInt = " + obB.myInt);
    }
}
```

Output:

```
***Demonstration-1.A class demo with 2 objects ***
obA.myInt = 25
obB.myInt = 25
```

Additional comments:

- As mentioned in the comment, it is not necessary to initialize the
  myInt in this way. You are just starting up with a very simple example.
  Field initialization is optional.

- If you do not supply any initialization for your field, it will take a
  default value. I'll cover those default values shortly.

- Suppose that in the preceding example, you did not initialize the
  field. Then your class would look like this:

```
class ClassEx1 {
    public int myInt;
}
```

Still, you can instantiate your object and then supply your intended value, like in the
following:

```
ClassEx1 obA = new ClassEx1();
obA.myInt=25;//setting 25 into myInt of obA
```

You must remember these key points about constructors:

- Constructors are used to initialize objects.

- The class name and the corresponding constructor's name(s) must
  be the same.

- Constructors do not have any return types.

- There are two types of constructors: parameterless constructors
  (sometimes referred to as constructors with no argument or
  default constructor) and constructors with parameter(s) (known as
  parameterized constructors).

- In general, the common tasks, like initialization of all the variables
  inside a class, are achieved through constructors.

Q&A Session

2.1 The constructors do not have any return type. With this statement, did you mean that their return type is void?

No. You should not forget that even void is considered a return type.

2.2 I am little bit confused about the use of a user-defined parameterless constructor versus a default constructor that is supplied by Java. Is there any key difference between them?

Sometimes both may appear to be the same. But it can be helpful to remember that with a user-defined constructor, you can have more control and flexibility. You can put in your own logic prior to object creation.

Demonstration 2

Consider the following example and analyze the output:

```
package java2e.chapter2;
class DefConsDemo
{
    public int myInt;
    public float myFloat;
    public double myDouble;
    public DefConsDemo()
    {
        System.out.println("I am initializing with my own choice.");
        myInt = 10;
        myFloat = 0.123456f;
        myDouble = 9.8765432;
    }
}

class DefaultConstructorCaseStudy {
    public static void main(String[] args) {
        System.out.println("***Demonstration-2.Comparison between user-
        defined and  Java-provided default constructors***\n");
        DefConsDemo ObDef = new DefConsDemo();
```

```
        System.out.println("myInt="+ ObDef.myInt);
        System.out.println("myFloat="+ ObDef.myFloat);
        System.out.println("myDouble="+ ObDef.myDouble);
    }
}
```

Output:

```
***Demonstration-2.Comparison between user-defined and  Java-provided
default constructors***

I am initializing with my own choice.
myInt=10
myFloat=0.123456
myDouble=9.8765432
```

Analysis

You can see that before I set the values to the variables, I printed one additional line saying, "I am initializing with my own choice."

But if you simply do not supply this parameterless constructor and want to use the Java-provided default constructor, you need to comment out or remove the constructor body in the preceding example. This time, you will get the following output:

```
***Demonstration-2.Comparison between user-defined and  Java provided
default constructors***

myInt=0
myFloat=0.0
myDouble=0.0
```

You can see that each of these values is initialized with the corresponding default values of that type.

Though you would not notice the default constructor in your source code, you can decompile the .class, in which case you will notice the presence of Java compiler-provided default constructor. Suppose you have compiled the following class:

```
class DefConsDemo
{
    public int myInt;
    public float myFloat;
    public double myDouble;
}
```

Now you can decompile the class file again to examine the working mechanism of the Java-provided default constructor. You can decompile the class file in various ways (also, there are various online tools available to serve this purpose). In this case, I have used the javap command, which is available at C:\Program Files\Java\jdk1.8.0_172\ bin in my system. I set my CLASSPATH environment variable with this path and decompiled the class file again using the javap command, like the following, to get the following output:

```
C:\TestClass>javap DefConsDemo.class
Compiled from "DefaultConstructorCaseStudy.java"
class java2e.chapter2.DefConsDemo {
  public int myInt;
  public float myFloat;
  public double myDouble;
  java2e.chapter2.DefConsDemo();
}
```

You can notice the Java-provided default constructor present in the decompiled file.

Note   You may take note of another important point. You can use your own access modifiers for user-defined constructors. So, if you provide your own parameterless constructor, you can make it non-public. For a Java-provided default constructor, it will have default visibility (package private).

2.3 I am seeing that the Java-provided default constructor is initializing the instance variables with some default values. What are the default values for other types?

In general, the default values are zero or null. You can refer to Table 2-1.

Table 2-1. *Datatypes with Default Values in Java*

Data Type	Default Values
byte, short, int	0
char	'\u0000'
float	0.0f
double	0.0d
long	0L
String	null
Any object	null
boolean	false

2.4 It appears to me that you can also invoke some methods to initialize those variables. Why do you need constructors?

If you think like this, then you must agree that to do that job, you need to call the method explicitly; that is, in simple language, that your call will not be automatic. But with constructors, you can perform automatic initialization each time you create objects.

2.5 Can you predict the output of the following?

```
package java2e.chapter2;

class ConEx2 {
    int i;

    public ConsEx2(int i) {
        this.i = i;
    }
    // public ConsEx2() { }
}
```

```
public class Quiz1 {

    public static void main(String[] args) {
            System.out.println("***Experiment with constructor***");
            ConEx2 ob = new ConEx2 ();
            //ConsEx2 ob = new ConsEx2(25);//Choice-3
    }
}
```

Output:

```
Compilation error: The constructor ConsEx2() is undefined
```

See the following Q&A for explanation. I'll discuss the keyword this shortly.

2.6 You should get a default constructor from Java in this case. Why is the compiler complaining about this code snippet?

You have learned that in Java, you can get a default parameterless constructor if, and only if, you do not provide any constructor. But, in this example, you already have a parameterized constructor. So, in this case, the compiler will not provide the default parameterless constructor for you.

If you want to remove this compilation error, you have the following choices:

- You can define one more custom constructor, like this:

  ```
  public ConsEx2() { }
  ```

- You can remove the custom constructor declaration (that you already defined but have not used) from this program.

- You can supply the necessary integer argument inside your main() method, like this:

  ```
  ConsEx2 ob = new ConsEx2(25);
  ```

2.7 Can I say that a class is a custom type?

In general, the answer is yes. But at the same time, you need to remember that Java also has many built-in classes (for example, Array, String, etc.). In our prior demonstrations, you have seen the use of our own classes, which are nothing but custom classes.

2.8 Can you elaborate on the concept of reference?

Suppose you have a simple class like the following:

```
class ClassA
{
//An instance variable
  int a;
//An instance method, for example:
  void someMethod()
  {
   //Some code
  }
}
```

When you write `ClassA obA=new ClassA();` an instance of `ClassA` will be created in memory, and it creates a reference to that instance and stores the result inside the `obA` variable. So, you can say objects in memory are referenced by an identifier called a reference.

In Java, more broadly, you will use two different kinds of variables—one is primitive and the other is an object reference. It is similar to a pointer or an address, but you do not know (or care) about what resides inside your reference variable.

Simply, a reference provides a way to access an object. When you write

```
ClassA obA;
```

`obA` refers to `null`. But when you write

```
ClassA obA=new ClassA();
```

`obA` is initialized with an object of `ClassA`, and you say that `obA` is a reference to an object of `ClassA`.

Then you use a dot operator on a reference variable to invoke something (say, a method or variable) from your intended class, like the following:

```
obA.someMethod();
```

It should be noted that you *can* call a method without a reference. And you can do that when you write something like the following:

```
new classA(). someMethod(); //Not a recommended practice
```

But as mentioned with the single-line comment, it is not a recommended practice for you at this moment.

When you learn about memory management, you'll learn that all objects reside in a place called the heap and that there is a garbage collector that works on that heap. A detailed discussion on this would be complicated at this moment. At this stage, you may simply assume the following figures for a better understanding of object reference variables. Notice the bold portions in each step.

Step 1:

```
ClassA obA= new ClassA();
```

JVM allocates a space for a reference variable obA of type ClassA.

ClassA

Step 2:

```
ClassA obA= new ClassA();
```

JVM allocates a space for the object of type ClassA. Assume that it is something like the following.

An object of ClassA

Step 3:

```
ClassA obA = new ClassA();
```

JVM connects the two (notice the = operator in bold).

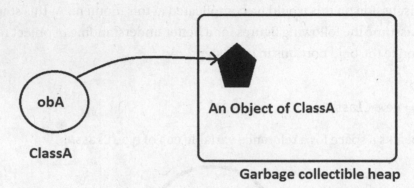

Garbage collectible heap

2.9 These references are similar to C/C++ pointers. Is this correct?

Nope. Java is different from C/C++. It may appear that references are a special kind of pointer. But you must note the key difference between these two. With a pointer, you can point to any address (basically, it is a number slot in the memory). So, it is quite possible that with a pointer, you will point to an invalid address, and then you may encounter unwanted outcomes during runtime. A reference variables can point either to valid addresses or to null. Also, you cannot do arithmetic on reference variables. It is also important how you interpret the word "point." For example, some developers prefer to use the word "refer" instead of "point" in a similar context.

2.10 Can I have multiple reference variables that refer the same object in memory?

Yes. The following type of declaration is perfectly fine:

```
ConsEx2 ob1 = new ConsEx2(25);
ConsEx2 ob2=ob1;
```

Demonstration 3

In the following example, I have created two objects of the same class, but the instance variable (i) is initialized with different values. To do this job, I have used a parameterized constructor that can accept one-integer argument.

```
package java2e.chapter2;
class ClassEx3
{
    public int i;
    public ClassEx3(int i)
    {
        this.i = i;
    }
}

class Demonstration3 {
    public static void main(String[] args) {
        System.out.println("***Demonstration-3.A class demo with 2
        objects ***");
                ClassEx3 obA = new ClassEx3(10);
                ClassEx3 obB = new ClassEx3(20);
                System.out.println("obA.i =" + obA.i);
                System.out.println("obB.i =" + obB.i);
        }
}
```

   Output:

```
***Demonstration-3.A class demo with 2 objects ***
obA.i =10
obB.i =20
```

2.11 What is the purpose of the **this** keyword?

Sometimes you need to refer to the current object, and to do that, you use the this keyword. In the preceding example, instead of using the this keyword, you could also write something like the following to achieve the same result:

```
class ClassEx3 {
    int i;// instance variable
    ClassEx3(int myInteger)// myInteger is a local variable
    {
        i = myInteger;
    }
}
```

As per Java's operator precedence table, the assignment operator (=) has associativity that runs right to left. (Associativity tells the direction of an operator's execution.) So, you are familiar with code like **a=25;** where you are assigning 25 to a. But are you familiar with code like **25=a;**? No. The compiler will raise an issue.

In the preceding example, **myInteger** was your *local variable* (seen inside methods, blocks, or constructors), and **i** was your *instance variable* (declared inside a class but outside a method, block, or constructor).

So, instead of myInteger, if you use i, you need to tell the compiler about your direction of assignment. It should not be confused with "which value is assigned where?" Here, you are assigning the value of the local variable to the instance variable, and the compiler should clearly understand your intention. With the statement **this.i=i;**, the compiler clearly understands that the instance variable i should be initialized with the value of the local variable i.

Also, consider this. Suppose, by mistake, you have written something like **i=i;** in the preceding scenario. There will be confusion from the compiler's point of view because it will see that you are dealing with two local variables that are the same. (Although your intention was different, and you meant that the i on the left side is the field and the other one is the method parameter.) Now, if you create an object, obA for ClassA, try to see the value of obA.i, with following code:

```
ClassEx3 obA = new ClassEx3(20);
System.out.println("obA.i =" + obA.i);
```

You will get obA.i=0 (the default value of an integer) in the output. So, your instance variable cannot get your intended value of 20. The Eclipse IDE also raises a warning in this case. See Figure 2-1.

The assignment to variable i has no effect

Figure 2-1. *The warning message for the statement i=i; in the constructor body of ClassEx3*

POINT TO REMEMBER

If your local variable has the same name as the instance variable, the local variable will hide the instance variable. In this type of scenario, the keyword `this` helps to resolve the namespace collision because it helps to identify which one is a local variable (method parameter) and which one is the instance variable (field). For your reference, the local variable and instance variable are marked with commented lines in the Q&A 2.11 code segment.

Demonstration 4

In the following demonstration, you will see the use of two different constructors. The user-defined parameterless constructor is always initializing the instance variable i with the value 5, but the parameterized constructor can initialize the instance variable with any integer value that you supply.

```
package java2e.chapter2;

//Constructor overloading example
class ClassEx4 {
    int i;

    ClassEx4() {
        this.i = 5;
    }

    public ClassEx4(int i) {
        this.i = i;
    }
}

class Demonstration4 {

    public static void main(String[] args) {
        System.out.println("***Demonstration-4. A simple class with 2
        different constructors ***");
        System.out.println("*** It is also an example of constructor
        overloading ***");
```

```
        ClassEx4 obA = new ClassEx4();
        ClassEx4 obB = new ClassEx4(75);
        System.out.println("obA.i =" + obA.i);
        System.out.println("obB.i =" + obB.i);
    }
}
```

Output:

```
***Demonstration-4. A simple class with 2 different constructors ***
*** It is also an example of constructor overloading ***
obA.i =5
obB.i =75
```

Additional comments:

- Earlier, you saw the same constructor get used to create different objects that were initialized with different values. In this example, a different constructor was used to create different objects that are initialized with different values.

- Constructors' names are same as their class names. Notice that the class classEx4 has multiple constructors. So, it is an example of **constructor overloading**. Later, you will learn the concept of method overloading in detail, and you will become familiar with the fact that in a class you can have multiple methods with the same name but different parameter lists. (In other words, you can simply say that method signatures are different.) For example, aMethod(int,double) is different from aMethod(int) or aMethod(int,int) or aMethod(double,int). That is, the methods may vary, with different numbers of parameters, different types of parameters, or different sequences of parameters.

- In Java, we could use this (5); instead of this.i=5; but other languages may not support this kind of construct.

Demonstration 5

A class can have either variables or methods or both. So, let's consider another simple program in which you have a class with one method only. This method is used to accept two integer inputs, and in turn it will return the sum of those integers.

```java
package java2e.chapter2;

class ClassEx5 {
    public int sum(int x, int y) {
        return x + y;
    }
}

class Demonstration5 {

    public static void main(String[] args) {
        System.out.println("***Demonstration-5. A simple class with a
        method returning an integer ***\n");
        ClassEx5 ob = new ClassEx5();
        int result = ob.sum(57, 63);
        System.out.println("Sum of 57 and 63 is : " + result);
    }
}
```

Output:

***Demonstration-5. A simple class with a method returning an integer ***

Sum of 57 and 63 is : 120

Additional comments:

- It is not necessary to have a class with only methods, instance variables, or constructors. In real-life programming, your classes may have all these elements together. But for ease of understanding, I have demonstrated each case separately.

Passing Variable-Length Arguments to Methods

You can pass a variable number of arguments in your method. This concept was introduced in Java 5. It is often referred to as varargs (short name for variable-length arguments). A method that can accept variable-length arguments is also termed a vararg method (or, variable-arity method).

In Java, you need to put three dots/periods (...) (as shown in sum() method in Demonstration 6) to be able to use a vararg method. Demonstration6 shows such an usage.

Demonstration 6

Consider the following example.

```
package java2e.chapter2;

class ClassEx6 {
    // The following method supports variable-length arguments
    public int sum(int... vararg) {
        System.out.println("You have passed " + vararg.length + "
        arguments now.");
        int total = 0;
        for (int i : vararg) {
            total = total + i;
        }
        return total;
    }
}

class Demonstration6 {
    public static void main(String[] args) {
        System.out.println("***Demonstration-6. Methods with variable-
        length argument demo ***\n");
        ClassEx6 ob = new ClassEx6();
        int resultOfSummation = ob.sum(57, 63);
        System.out.println("Sum of 57 and 63 is : " + resultOfSummation);
        resultOfSummation = ob.sum(57, 63, 50);
        System.out.println("Sum of 57, 63 and 70 is : " +
        resultOfSummation);
```

```
    resultOfSummation = ob.sum(57, 63, 50, 70);
    System.out.println("Sum of 57, 63, 50 and 70 is : " +
    resultOfSummation);

    }

}
```

Output:

***Demonstration-6. Methods with variable-length argument demo ***

You have passed 2 arguments now.
Sum of 57 and 63 is : 120
You have passed 3 arguments now.
Sum of 57, 63 and 70 is : 170
You have passed 4 arguments now.
Sum of 57, 63, 50 and 70 is : 240

Analysis

You can see that you can pass a variable number of integer arguments to the sum method because it is a vararg method. Notice that the three periods are used in the following line of code in the previous demonstration:

```
public int sum(int... vararg) {
```

Q&A Session

2.12 Why do I need vararg methods?

They give you the flexibility to pass some default arguments to a method. As a result, you are not bound to supply a certain number of arguments to invoke a particular method.

2.13 Can you give examples of some vararg methods in the Java library?

The methods printf() and format() are very common in this context. So, in the prior demonstration, you could use the following code snippet:

```
//System.out.println("You have passed " + vararg.length + " arguments now.");
System.out.print(String.format("%s, you have passed %d arguments now.",
"Dear reader",vararg.length));
```

to get an output like the following:

```
*** Methods with variable-length argument demo ***
```

Dear reader, you have passed **2** arguments now.
Sum of 57 and 63 is : 120
Dear reader, you have passed **3** arguments now.
Sum of 57, 63 and 70 is : 170
Dear reader, you have passed **4** arguments now.
Sum of 57, 63, 50 and 70 is : 240

2.14 What are the alternatives to vararg methods?

In earlier days (prior to Java 5), developers had the two choices. Either they could put the arguments inside an array and then pass the array to the methods, or they could use the concept of overloading. The first approach was preferred if the argument list was big or unknown prior to execution. You will learn the concept of overloading in more detail shortly.

2.15 In OOP, I see that code is always bundled inside objects. What are the benefits of this type of design in real-world scenarios?

There are many advantages. Think of a real-world scenario; for example, consider your laptop or your printer. You can reuse the parts of these devices in a similar model of laptop or printer.

If any of the parts in your laptop malfunction, or, let's say, if your print cartridge runs out of ink, you can simply replace those parts. You do not need to replace the entire laptop or the entire printer.

You likely also agree that you may not be interested in knowing the inner details of how those parts actually function. If those parts are working fine and able to serve your needs, you are simply happy.

In object-oriented programming, objects play the same role: they can be reused, and they can be plugged in. At the same time, they can hide the implementation details. For example, in Demonstration 5, when a client invokes the sum() method with two integer arguments (57 and 63), he gets the sum of those integers. As an outside user, he is unaware of the inner mechanisms of the sum() method. So, you can provide a level of security by hiding information from the outside world.

Lastly, consider another point from the coding perspective. Let's assume the following scenario: you need to store employee information in your program. If you start coding like this:

```
string empName= "emp1Name";
string deptName= "Comp.Sc.";
int empSalary= "10000";
```

Then for a second employee, you would write something like this:

```
string empName2= "emp2Name";
string deptName2= "Electrical";
int empSalary2= "20000";
```

And so on.

Can you really continue like this? The answer is no. To make it simple, it is always a better idea to make an Employee class and process the information like this:

```
Employee emp1, emp2;
```

It is much cleaner and more readable, and, obviously, a better approach.

2.16 Does Java support destructors?

No. Java uses *a* garbage-collection mechanism to free memory. You'll learn about this shortly.

Summary

This chapter discussed the following topics:

- The concepts of class, object, and reference

- The difference between an object and a reference

- The difference between a local variable and an instance variable

- The different types of constructors and their usage

- The differences between a user-defined parameterless constructor and a Java-provided default constructor

- The use of this keyword

- How to pass variable-length arguments to a method

- The benefits of the object-oriented approach in real-world programming

CHAPTER 3

Classes and Objects in Depth

In this chapter, I'll discuss some important topics that are closely related to classes and objects. If you are absolutely new to object-oriented programming, to understand each topic, you may need to come back to this chapter once you have finished Chapter 10.

Static Variables and Methods

Up until now, you have seen that a class can have either variables or methods or both. Collectively, these are called class members. These variables and methods are called instance variables and instance methods because each time you instantiate a class, a new copy of each is created. Once you create an object, you can use the dot operator (.) to access these instance variables or methods (you have experienced this in Chapter 2 with different demonstrations).

But sometimes you may want a class member to be common to all of the class's objects. In this case, it makes sense to be able to access them using the class (instead of using an object of the class). When you create such members, they are called class variables or class methods. A class member is also known as a static member because in Java, to create a class variable or a class method, you tag them with the static keyword just like in the following:

```
//static variables
 static double length=25.5, breadth=10.0;
 //static method
 public static double area() {
   return length * breadth;
 }
```

© Vaskaran Sarcar 2020
V. Sarcar, *Interactive Object-Oriented Programming in Java*, https://doi.org/10.1007/978-1-4842-5404-2_3

Demonstration 1

Now, go through Demonstration 1. Notice that, this time, the class members are accessed without creating any objects of the class Rectangle.

```
package java2e.chapter3;
class Rectangle {
      //static variables
      static double length=25.5, breadth=10.0;
      //static method
      public static double area() {
            return length * breadth;
      }
}
class Demonstration1 {
      public static void main(String[] args) {
            System.out.println("***Demonstration-1. Exploring class
            variables and class methods.***\n");
            System.out.println("Length of the Rectangle is :" +
            Rectangle.length + " unit");
            System.out.println("Breadth of the Rectangle is :" +
            Rectangle.breadth + " unit");
            System.out.println("Area of Rectangle is " + Rectangle.area()
            + " sq.unit");
      }
}
```

Output:

```
***Demonstration-1. Exploring class variables and class methods.***

Length of the Rectangle is :25.5 unit
Breadth of the Rectangle is :10.0 unit
Area of Rectangle is 255.0 sq.unit
```

You'll see a detailed discussion of static members with different case studies in Chapter 8.

Q&A Session

3.1 Can I have a static class?

Java does not allow you to create top-level static classes. The class that contains the static class is termed an outer class. A non-static nested class is termed an inner class. You'll learn about them in Chapter 8.

Access Control

You can provide controlled access to your classes, fields, and methods. When you learn interfaces, you can apply the same idea to them. Actually, by using access control, you can provide encapsulation too.

You implement access control using access modifiers in Java. In Chapter 7, you'll see a table that summarizes the access control in packages using these access modifiers. Java defines the following access modifiers:

- `public`

- `private`

- `protected`

- `default` (it simply means you are not using any modifier)

The power of these modifiers will be better understood when you cover inheritance and packages. You will learn inheritance in the next chapter, and you'll learn about packages in Chapter 7. To understand the upcoming discussion, comprehending `private` and `public` will be sufficient.

When you attach a class member with the `public` modifier, you can access the member from outside the code. On the contrary, when you use a `private` modifier, the member can be accessed only by other members of the class.

Note   This is why the `main()` method is always `public`. It is called by the Java runtime system, which is outside the code.

If you do not use any access modifier for a member, it can be accessed only within the package (in simple words, a package is a mechanism by which to group several classes. You'll learn about them in Chapter 7).

To understand the concept, let's consider Demonstration 2. Here, you will see the effect of using the `public` and `private` modifiers on fields and methods.

Demonstration 2

In this demonstration, you have a class called `Sample` that has two instance fields—`pubInt` and `priInt`. The `Sample` class has also two instance methods—`showPublicMethod()` and `showPrivateMethod()`. You can refer to the supported comments in following demonstration where `pubInt` and the `showPublicMethod()` are public members, and the remaining two are private members.

Inside `main()`, you will instantiate a `Sample` class object. Now notice the commented lines in the `main()` method:

```
// Compile-time error
// System.out.println(" The priInt="+ sampleOb.priInt);
// Compile-time error
// sampleOb.showPrivateMethod() ;
```

It says that when using the dot operator with `sampleOb` you cannot access the private members of the `Sample` class inside the `main()` method. But the same approach works for the public members of the `Sample` class:

```java
package java2e.chapter3;

class Sample {
    // Public field
    public int pubInt = 1;

    // Public method
    public void showPublicMethod() {
        System.out.println("The showPublicMethod() is a public method.");
    }

    // Private field
    private int priInt = 2;
    // Private method

    private void showPrivateMethod() {
```

```
            System.out.println("The showPrivateMethod() is a private
            method.");
    }
}

class Demonstration2 {
    public static void main(String[] args) {
        System.out.println("***Demonstration-2. Introducing access
        control using private and public modifiers.***\n");
        Sample sampleOb = new Sample();
        System.out.println("The pubInt=" + sampleOb.pubInt);// 1
        sampleOb.showPublicMethod();
        // Compile-time error
        // System.out.println(" The priInt="+ sampleOb.priInt);
        // Compile-time error
        // sampleOb.showPrivateMethod() ;
    }
}
```

Output:

```
***Demonstration-2. Introducing access control using private and public
modifiers.***

The pubInt=1
The showPublicMethod() is a public method.
```

If you uncomment the commented line, you will receive the compile-time errors shown in Figure 3-1—one for the private field and one for the private method.

Description	Location
✓ ⊗ Errors (2 items)	
🕮 The field Sample.priInt is not visible	line 29
🕮 The method showPrivateMethod() from the type Sample is not visible	line 31

Figure 3-1. *An error snapshot from Eclipse IDE*

Getter-Setter Methods

Experts always suggest you make your instance variables private unless there is a specific reason to use other access modifiers. (Though only for simple demonstration purposes in this book, in many examples you will see the use of public fields and methods only.) Then the obvious question is—how does one access the private members of a class?

The answer is that you can access them using public getter-setter methods.

Demonstration 3

In this demonstration, the Sample3 class has a private field called priInt. Notice the other two public methods in Sample3. You can see that the getPriInt() method is returning the value of priInt and the setPriInt() method can help you to set the value for priInt. Since these two methods are defined in the same class that contains the private variable, they can access the private field priInt in Sample3.

```
package java2e.chapter3;

class Sample3 {
      // Private field
      private int priInt;
      //Getter
      public int getPriInt() {
            return priInt;      }
      //Setter
      public void setPriInt(int priInt) {
            this.priInt = priInt;
      }
}

class Demonstration3 {
      public static void main(String[] args) {
            System.out.println("***Demonstration-3. Introducing Getter-
            Setter method.***\n");
            Sample3 sampleOb=new Sample3();
            //Setting the value for the private field
            sampleOb.setPriInt(2);
```

```
            //Getting the value from the private field.
            System.out.println("The priInt="+ sampleOb.getPriInt());
        }
}
```

Output

```
***Demonstration-3. Introducing Getter-Setter method.***

The priInt=2
```

Using Eclipse, you can easily generate getter-setter methods. For example, in this case, you can right click on the private variable priInt ➤ Source ➤ Generate Getters and Setters… to generate getter-setter methods for the private field.

Q&A Session

3.2 What are the benefits of using a getter-setter method?
Here are some benefits of using getter-setter methods:

- You can provide controlled access to your data. Notice that now the client code cannot access the private field priInt directly.

- You can make your class variable either read-only or write-only. When you provide the getter method only, you can only get the value of the private variable, so it becomes read-only. Similarly, when you provide only the setter method, you make the variable write-only.

- The prior two points promote the security of the data.

Initialization Block

You have already seen the use of constructors. You can get an alternative to constructors when you use initialization blocks. An initialization block can be either static or non-static. In the upcoming section, you'll become familiar with non-static initialization blocks, which are also known as instance initialization blocks (IIBs). Static initialization blocks will be discussed in Chapter 8.

Note   Apart from initialization blocks and constructors, you can also initialize instance variables in final methods. A final method is a method that cannot be overridden in the subclass. You will be familiar with them once you cover the concepts of inheritance.

Demonstration 4

As the name suggests, an instance initialization block is used to initialize the instance variables. When you have both a constructor and an initialization block, you will see that the initialization block is called before the constructor, as follows:

```
package java2e.chapter3;

class Sample4 {
    int a, b, c;
    // Initialization block-1
    {
        System.out.println("Initialization block-1 is executed.
        Setting a=1.");
        a = 1;
    }
    // Initialization block-2
    {
        System.out.println("Initialization block-2 is executed.
        Setting b=2;");
        b = 2;
    }

    // Constructor
    Sample4() {
        System.out.println("User-defined parameterless constructor is
        executed.Setting c=3.");
        c = 3;
    }
}
```

```
class Demonstration4 {

        public static void main(String[] args) {
                System.out.println("***Demonstration-4.Use of instance
                Initialization blocks.***\n");
                Sample4 sample4Object = new Sample4();
                System.out.println("The sample4Object.a=" + sample4Object.a);// 1
                System.out.println("The sample4Object.b=" + sample4Object.b);// 2
                System.out.println("The sample4Object.c=" + sample4Object.c);// 3
        }

}
```

Output:

```
***Demonstration-4.Use of instance Initialization blocks.***

Initialization block-1 is executed.Setting a=1.
Initialization block-2 is executed.Setting b=2;
User-defined Parameterless constructor is executed.Setting c=3.
The sample4Object.a=1
The sample4Object.b=2
The sample4Object.c=3
```

Notice that initialization blocks are executed in the order in which they appear in your class.

Q&A Session

3.3 I have constructors, so why would I want to use an initialization block?

If you have multiple constructors in your class, you can share common code between the constructors.

3.4 Can I have multiple initialization blocks in the same class?

Yes. Demonstration 4 shows that you can place multiple instance initialization blocks inside your class and they execute in the order in which you place them inside your class.

3.5 Can I have static initialization blocks?

Yes. You'll see a detailed discussion on them in Chapter 8.

3.6 Can you predict the output of the following program?

```
package java2e.chapter3;

class Test1 {
    int a;
    // Initialization block-1
    {
        System.out.println("Initialization block-1 is executed.");
        a = 1;
    }

    // Constructor
    Test1() {
        System.out.println("Constructor is executed.");
        a = 2;
    }

    // Initialization block-2
    {
        System.out.println("Initialization block-2 is executed.");
        a = 3;
    }
}

class Quiz1 {
    public static void main(String[] args) {
        System.out.println("***Quiz1.Execution order of
        Initialization block and Constructor***");
        System.out.println("The new Test1().a=" + new Test1().a);
    }
}
```

Answer:

```
***Quiz1.Execution order of Initialization block and Constructor***
Initialization block-1 is executed.
Initialization block-2 is executed.
Constructor is executed.
The new Test1().a=2
```

Initialization blocks will be executed before the constructor regardless of their appearance in the class.

Nested Class

When you place one class inside another class, such a class is called a nested class. Java supports both static nested classes and non-static nested classes. A non-static nested class is often called an ***inner class***. In this chapter, our focus will be on inner classes only. In this context, you need to remember following points:

- The outer class is the one that contains the nested class.

- An inner class can have access to both the static and the non-static members of the outer class.

Note   Initially, nested classes were not supported in Java 1.0, but in Java 1.1 they were added.

Demonstration 5

The following demonstration shows a simple use of a nested class. Here, I show two different ways to invoke an inner class method. In the first case, I call the inner class method through an outer class method. In the second case, it is called directly from main() though an inner class object.

```
package java2e.chapter3;

class OuterClass {
        static int staticInt=1;
        int nonStaticInt=2;
```

```java
        // Inner class
        class InnerClass {
                void showInnerMethod() {
                        System.out.println("Inside InnerClass.");
                        System.out.println("The staticInt ="+staticInt );
                        System.out.println("The nonStaticInt ="+nonStaticInt +"\n");
                }
        }

        // An outer class method that can invoke an inner class method
        void invokeInner() {
                InnerClass innerOb = new InnerClass();
                System.out.println("**Invoking an inner class method from an
                outer class method.**");
                //Calling the inner class method
                innerOb.showInnerMethod();
        }
}

class Demonstration5 {

        public static void main(String[] args) {
                System.out.println("***Demonstration-5.Inner class
                demonstration.***\n");
                OuterClass outer = new OuterClass();// Ok
                //Calling the inner class method through an outer class method
                System.out.println("**Calling the inner class method through
                an outer class object.**");
                outer.invokeInner();
                // InnerClass inner=new InnerClass();//Error
                OuterClass.InnerClass inner = outer.new InnerClass();// Ok
                //Invoking the inner class method through an inner class object.
                System.out.println("Invoking the inner class method through an
                inner class object.");
                inner.showInnerMethod();
        }
}
```

Output:

```
***Demonstration-5.Inner class demonstration.***

**Calling the inner class method through an outer class object.**
**Invoking an inner class method from an outer class method.**
Inside InnerClass.
The staticInt =1
The nonStaticInt =2

Invoking the inner class method through an inner class object.
Inside InnerClass.
The staticInt =1
The nonStaticInt =2
```

Q&A Session

3.7 Why are nested classes useful?

They can promote encapsulation with better security. The logical grouping of the classes is easily maintainable too.

Copying an Object

Sometimes you'll be interested in copying an object. In a real-world application, creating a new instance from scratch is a costly, time-consuming, and boring operation. Sometimes the overall process is also complicated.

You can accomplish the task of copying in various ways. Serialization methods, object cloning, copy constructors, and so forth are used in this context. But to implement these concepts, you need to be familiar with advanced features.

Fortunately, Java supports cloning mechanisms, which you will learn in Chapter 15 when I discuss prototype design patterns.

In the upcoming discussion, I'll discuss copy constructors only.

Using Copy Constructors

The following demonstration shows how you can write your own copy constructor.

Demonstration 6

Look at the following program, which demonstrates such a usage:

```java
package java2e.chapter3;

class Student
{
    int rollNo;
    String name;
    //Instance Constructor
    public Student(int rollNo, String name)
    {
        this.rollNo = rollNo;
        this.name = name;
    }
    //Copy Constructor
    public Student( Student student)
    {
        this.name = student.name;
        this.rollNo = student.rollNo;
    }
    public void displayDetails()
    {
        System.out.println(" Student name: " + name + ",Roll no: "+rollNo);
    }
}

class Demonstration6 {
    public static void main(String[] args) {
        System.out.println("***Demonstration-6.User-defined copy
        constructor example in Java***\n");
        Student student1 = new Student(1, "Bob");
        System.out.println(" The Student1 details is as follows:");
        student1.displayDetails();
        System.out.println("\n Copying student1 to student2 now");
```

```
        //Invoking the user-defined copy constructor
        Student student2 = new Student (student1);
        System.out.println(" The details of Student2 is as follows:");
        student2.displayDetails();
    }
}
```

Output

```
***Demonstration-6.User-defined copy constructor example in Java***

The Student1 details is as follows:
Student name: Bob,Roll no: 1

Copying student1 to student2 now
The details of Student2 is as follows:
Student name: Bob,Roll no: 1
```

Q&A Session

3.8 Does Java support a default copy constructor?

No, you have to write your own copy constructor.

Wrapper Class

In Chapter 12, you'll become familiar with generic programming, which is an advanced concept in Java. There, you'll see the use of wrapper classes. In this section, you will get a quick overview of wrapper classes.

In some special situations, you may need to convert a primitive type into an object. For example, when you simply need to pass an object in a method parameter, this conversion is useful. The same thing applies for generic programming. In this context, you may remember that some collection classes like Vector can store only objects, but not primitive types. Wrapper classes are used in those contexts (because these classes "wrap" the primitives in the corresponding object types). In Java, the wrapper classes are included in the java.lang package. Java provides wrapper classes for each of the primitive types. Table 3-1 shows the wrapper classes corresponding to the primitive types.

Table 3-1. *Wrapper Classes for Primitive Types*

Primitive Type	Wrapper class
boolean	Boolean
int	Integer
double	Double
float	Float
long	Long
char	Char
byte	Byte
short	Short

The following code segment shows a simple use case of the wrapper class. Here, a primitive int myInt is converted to an Integer object intOb, and later on you bring back the int from the Integer object:

```
int myInt1=1;
//Coverting primitive int to Integer object
Integer intOb=new Integer(i);
//Converting back from Integer Object to primitive int
int myInt2=intOb.intValue();
```

A similar conversion can be done from double to Double, long to Long, and so on (and vice versa). But you have to use the appropriate method. For example, you used intOb.intValue() for an int. Similarly, you can use doubleOb.doubleValue() for a double and longOb.longValue() for a long, where doubleOb is a Double object and longOb is a Long object, respectively.

Demonstration 7

This demonstration shows some common use cases of wrapper classes. The program is very simple, but you can refer to the associated comments for a better understanding.

```
package java2e.chapter3;

class Demonstration7 {
```

```java
public static void main(String[] args) {
    System.out.println("***Demonstration7.Exploring Wrapper
    classes.***\n");
    int myInt1 = 1;
    // Coverting primitive int to Integer object
    Integer intOb = new Integer(myInt1);
    // Converting back from Integer Object to primitive int
    int myInt2 = intOb.intValue();
    System.out.println("The myInt2=" + myInt2);

    long myLong1 = 1234567890123L;
    // Coverting primitive long to Long object
    Long longOb = new Long(myLong1);
    // Converting back from Long Object to primitive long
    long myLong2 = longOb.longValue();
    System.out.println("The long2=" + myLong2);

    // Coverting primitive int to String object
    String myString1 = Integer.toString(myInt1);
    System.out.println("The myString=" + myString1);

    String myString2 = "5.7";
    // Converting a String object to primitive type
    Double doubleOb = Double.valueOf(myString2);
    double myDouble = doubleOb.doubleValue();
    System.out.println("The myDouble=" + myDouble);

    //Converting numeric String to primitive int
    int myInt3=Integer.parseInt("125");
    System.out.println("The myInt3=" + myInt3);
    //Following line of code will cause runtime error
    //(NumberFormatException)because you cannot convert "Hello" to
    //an int
    //int myInt4=Integer.parseInt("Hello");
    //System.out.println("The myInt4=" + myInt4);
}
}
```

Output:

Demonstration7.Exploring Wrapper classes.

The myInt2=1
The long2=1234567890123
The myString=1
The myDouble=5.7
The myInt3=125

Note   The process of converting a primitive type into an object of the corresponding wrapper class is termed autoboxing. For example, `int` to `Integer`, `double` to `Double`, `float` to `Float`, etc. The reverse procedure is called unboxing. It is also important to note that the constructors `Interger(int)` and `Long(long)` are deprecated since java9. But to understand some legacy code these are important.

Garbage Collection

Up until now, you have just been instantiating objects. But I have not discussed freeing up memory by deleting those objects. If you are familiar with **C++,** you may know that in C++ programmers need to use the `delete` keyword to free the memory occupied by an object. If you do not free the memory properly, you'll see the impact of a memory leak, which can crash your application.

There is no such keyword in Java. JVM uses a background thread, commonly known as the garbage collector, to detect unused objects and free up the memory occupied by them. This technique is called garbage collection (GC).

Note   Different Java runtime systems can employ different approaches to garbage collection, but, as mentioned before, you do not need to worry about it while writing your application.

The biggest advantage of GC is that normally you do not need to worry about memory leaks, because you can rely on the automatic garbage-collection technique. But in some special cases, you may explicitly need to free up memory to avoid memory leaks, because the garbage collector is for some reason unable to detect those special scenarios.

The basic thing to remember is that when an object is unreachable from a root object (a root object is a root in an object tree), the object is eligible for garbage collection. An object can have multiple references to it. It is also important to understand that when the reference count is zero, only the object will be garbage collected; this is a common misunderstanding. Also, two objects can be garbage collected if there is a connection between them. But if such a connection is further connected to a root object, those two objects will not be garbage collected. Q&A 3.11 will show some highlights of root objects.

Q&A Session

3.9 What is a memory leak?

In general, when a computer program runs over a long period of time but fails to release memory resources that are no longer needed, you can feel the impact of memory leaks (for example, machines become slow over time, or, in the worst case, they can crash). With this information, it is apparent that "how fast it comes to our attention" depends on the leaking rate of our application.

Consider a very simple example. Suppose that you have an online application where users need to fill in some data and then click a 'Submit' button. Now, assume that the developers of the application mistakenly forgot to deallocate some memory that is no longer needed once a user presses the Submit button, and due to this misjudgment, the application is leaking 512 bytes per click. You probably won't notice any performance degradation in some initial clicks. But what happens if thousands of online users are using the application simultaneously? If 100,000 users press the Submit button, you will eventually lose 48.8 MB of memory; 10,000,000 clicks leads to the loss of 4.76 GB; and so on.

In short, even if your application or program is leaking a very small amount of data per execution, you will see some kind of malfunctioning over a period of time; for example, operations in the device might become so slow that you need to restart the application often.

In an unmanaged language like C++, you need to deallocate the memory when the intended job is done; otherwise, over a period of time, the impact of memory leaks will be huge. Java's garbage-collection mechanism rescues us from most of these cases. Still, there are instances that you may need to handle with care; otherwise, you may notice the impact of memory leaks.

There are many tools available on the market to detect memory leaks. Still, many organizations prefer to use their own memory-leak tool to detect and analyze leaks.

3.10 What do you mean by automatic garbage collection?

It is a process that investigates the heap memory and identifies which objects are in use and which are not. Then, it deletes the unused object. In this context, you may notice the following terms:

A *referenced object*: It means that the object is currently in use. In other words, in your program, there is still a pointer to this object.

An *unreferenced object*: This object is no longer referenced by any part of the program, so GC can reclaim the memory occupied by the unused object.

After these deletion operations, to improve performance, the compaction technique can be used. (In very simple words, a compaction technique moves all free blocks of memory to one contiguous location and all occupied block in a different location. As a result, if needed, you can allocate a large block of memory which may not possible when available memories are scattered or the memory pool is fragmented. After the compaction, objects generally stay in the same area, so, accessing them also becomes faster and easier.)

3.11 You used the term "root object" when discussing garbage collection. What does it mean?

This may seem a little bit complicated at this stage. In simple words, you should just know that objects are allocated on a heap area, which is managed by JVM. You can draw/imagine a tree that connects all these objects. In general, you say an object is live if you have a reference to it. Now, the question is—what is the first reference in the tree?

To answer this question, you need to know that an object tree can have one or more roots. When your application can reach these roots, the entire tree is reachable. Consider the following figure (Figure 3-2) to understand it better. From this figure, you can see that reachable objects are those that can be reached only through a root object. Otherwise, even if there is a link between the objects, those objects are treated as unreachable and can be garbage collected.

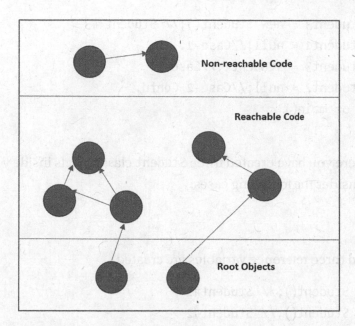

Figure 3-2. Root objects, reachable code, and unreachable code in an object tree

3.12 How can I mark an object as unreachable?

You make sure the object (which you want to mark eligible for garbage collection) does not have any references that are still in the scope of your Java application. Commonly, you set such a reference to null. You can also assign these references to point to some other object, or you can allow them to go out of scope.

Demonstration 8

Consider a simple case with the following program:

```
package java2e.chapter3;
class Student{
//Some code
}

class GarbageCollectionDemo {
    public static void main(String args[]) {
        Student student1, student2, student3;
        student1 = new Student();// Student#1
        student2 = new Student();// Student#2
```

```
        student3 = new Student();// Student #3
        student1 = null;//Case-1.
        student3 = student2;//Case-2
        student2 = null;//Case-2 Contd.
    }// End of main()
}
```

Notice that here you have created three Student class objects inside your main() method. Now consider the following cases:

Stage 1

Three objects and three reference variables are created.

```
student1 = new Student();// Student#1
student2 = new Student();// Student#2
student3 = new Student();// Student #3
```

See Figure 3-3.

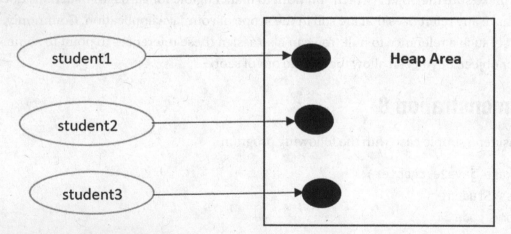

Figure 3-3. *Memory allocation after Stage 1*

Stage 2

When you assign student1=null, the Student#1 object is now eligible for garbage collection. See Figure 3-4.

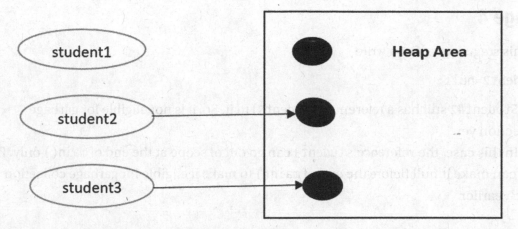

Figure 3-4. *Memory allocation after Stage 2*

Stage 3

When you write

student3=student2;

both student2 and student3 refer to Student#2. And the Student#3 object is now eligible for garbage collection. See Figure 3-5.

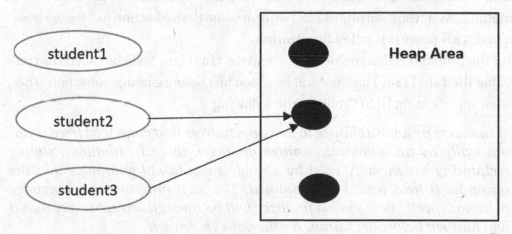

Figure 3-5. *Memory allocation after Stage 3*

Stage 4

In this stage, even if you write

```
student2=null;
```

Student#2 still has a reference (student3) to it. So, it is not eligible for garbage collection yet.

In this case, the reference student3 can go out of scope at the end of main() only. But you can make it null before the end of main() to make it eligible for garbage collection much earlier.

Finalization

Just before destroying an object and reclaiming the memory, the GC calls the finalize() method. It is a protected method defined in the Object class. You'll see this general form of finalize() method:

```
protected void finalize() {
        //Some code
    }
```

It is suggested that you put your cleanup code (for example, closing a file, closing a database connection, releasing any occupied non-Java resources, etc.) inside this method. As a result, an object can perform some desired action just before it is destroyed. This process is called **finalization.**

But the problem is that you never know when finalize() will be called. You only know that the finalize() method will be called just before garbage collection. The language specification (JLS11) tells us the following:

> *"Finalizers provide a chance to free up resources that cannot be freed automatically by an automatic storage manager. In such situations, simply reclaiming the memory used by an object would not guarantee that the resources it held would be reclaimed. The Java programming language does not specify how soon a finalizer will be invoked, except to say that it will happen before the storage for the object is reused."*

So, you cannot always rely on finalize(), and you may implement other ways to release the resources. Still, there is a workaround. You can make a request to the garbage collector when you invoke System.gc(). It simply tells the GC that you want it to start its job.

Note   `System.gc()` is equivalent to the call `Runtime.getRuntime().gc()` because its definition is as follows:

```
public static void gc() {
Runtime.getRuntime().gc();
}
```

Now, go through the modified version of Demonstration 9 to get an idea of how can you use the concept of finalization.

Demonstration 9

You will learn about the protected keyword, the throws keyword, and exceptions later in the book. To give you an idea about the garbage collection technique, the complete implementation is presented here for your reference. The output of this demonstration should be your key area of focus.

```
package java2e.chapter3;

class StudentDemo9 {
//Some code
    protected void finalize() {
        System.out.println("Freeing memory. The object with hashcode "
        + hashCode() + " is collected.");
    }
}

class GarbageCollectionDemo {
    public static void main(String args[]) throws InterruptedException {
        System.out.println("***Demonstration 9.Exploring Garbage
        Collection.***\n");
        //Stage-1
        StudentDemo9 student1, student2, student3;
        student1 = new StudentDemo9();// Student#1
        System.out.println("The student1.hashCode()=" + student1.
        hashCode());
```

```
        student2 = new StudentDemo9();// Student#2
        System.out.println("The student2.hashCode()=" + student2.
        hashCode());
        student3 = new StudentDemo9();// Student #3
        System.out.println("The student3.hashCode()=" + student3.
        hashCode());

        //Stage-2
        student1 = null;
        // Requesting JVM to run Garbage Collector
        System.out.println("Requesting GC-1");
        System.gc();
        Thread.sleep(3000);

        //Stage-3
        student3 = student2;
        // Requesting JVM to run Garbage Collector
        System.out.println("Requesting GC-2");
        System.gc();
        Thread.sleep(3000);

        //Stage-4
        student2 = null;
        // Requesting JVM to run Garbage Collector
        System.out.println("Requesting GC-3");
        System.gc();
        Thread.sleep(3000);

        student3 = null;
        // Requesting JVM to run Garbage Collector
        System.out.println("Requesting GC-4");
        System.gc();
        Thread.sleep(3000);

    }// End of main()
}
```

Here is a possible output from the modified demonstration. This output may vary because you never know whether GC will respond to your request or not.

```
***Demonstration 9.Exploring Garbage Collection.***

The student1.hashCode()=366712642
The student2.hashCode()=1829164700
The student3.hashCode()=2018699554
Requesting GC-1
Freeing memory. The object with hashcode 366712642 is collected.
Requesting GC-2
Freeing memory. The object with hashcode 2018699554 is collected.
Requesting GC-3
Requesting GC-4
Freeing memory. The object with hashcode 1829164700 is collected.
```

You can review the analysis section of Demonstration 9 for a better understanding. The sleep() methods were not necessary in this demonstration but they are added to allow garbage collector some time to finish its job.

Summary

This chapter covered the following topics:

- A brief overview of static variables and methods

- An introductory discussion on access control using different modifiers and getter-setter methods

- Use of initialization blocks

- A discussion on the nested class (with inner class)

- Use of copy constructor

- Shallow copy and deep copy

- Use of wrapper classes

- Garbage collection

- Memory leak

- Root objects in an object tree

- Finalization technique

CHAPTER 4

The Concept of Inheritance

The main objective of inheritance is to promote reusability and eliminate redundancy in code. It also demonstrates how a child class can obtain the features (or characteristics) of its parent class. Since a parent class is placed at a higher level in the class hierarchy, and a child class can derive from it. A child class is often referred to as a **derived class** or **subclass**. A parent class is also referred to as a **super class**.

Types of Inheritance

In general, you will deal with four types of inheritance. In Java, a class can inherit from another class using the extends keyword. For your easy reference, I present you with a summarized description for each type of inheritance.

Single Inheritance

A child class is derived from one parent class. Here is a sample diagram (Figure 4-1) and code for this type of inheritance.

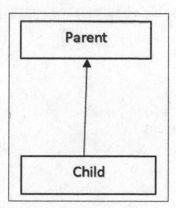

Figure 4-1. *Single inheritance*

© Vaskaran Sarcar 2020
V. Sarcar, *Interactive Object-Oriented Programming in Java*, https://doi.org/10.1007/978-1-4842-5404-2_4

Sample code:

```
class Parent
{
 //Your code...
}
class Child extends Parent
{
 //Your code...
}
```

Hierarchical Inheritance

Multiple child classes can be derived from one parent class. Here is a sample diagram (Figure 4-2) and code for this type of inheritance.

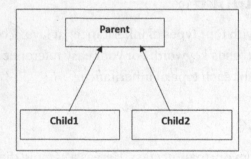

Figure 4-2. *Hierarchical inheritance*

Sample code:

```
class Parent
{
 //Your code...
}
class Child1 extends Parent
{
 //Your code...
}
```

```
class Child2 extends Parent
{
 //Your code...
}
```

Multi-level Inheritance

The parent class can have a grandchild. Here is a sample diagram (Figure 4-3) and code for this type of inheritance.

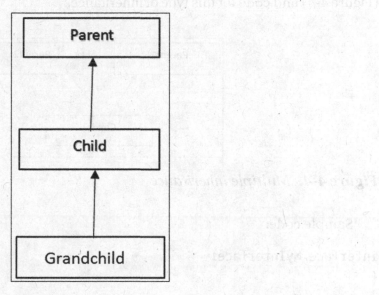

Figure 4-3. *Multi-level inheritance*

Sample code:

```
class Parent
{
 //Your code...
}
class Child extends Parent
{
 // Your code..
}
```

```
class Grandchild extends Child
{
 // Your code...
}
```

Multiple Inheritance

A child can derive from multiple parents. But this type of inheritance is not supported in Java through classes. You would need to learn about interfaces. Here is a sample diagram (Figure 4-4) and code for this type of inheritance.

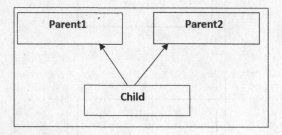

Figure 4-4. *Multiple inheritance*

Sample code:

```
interface MyInterface1
{
        // Your code
}
interface MyInterface2
{
        //Your code
}
class MyClass implements MyInterface1,MyInterface2
{
//Some code
}
```

Note

1. Java does not support multiple inheritance (through classes); that is, a child class cannot derive from more than one parent class. To deal with this type of situation, you need to understand interfaces.

2. There is another type of inheritance known as **hybrid inheritance.** It is a combination of two or more types of inheritances.

Demonstration 1

Let's start with a simple program on inheritance. In the following demonstration, you have two classes—ParentClass and ChildClass. So, as their names suggest, ChildClass is derived from the ParentClass using the extends keyword.

```java
package java2e.chapter4;

class ParentClass {
        public void showParentMethod() {
                System.out.println("I am a Parent Class method.");
        }
}

class ChildClass extends ParentClass {
}

class Demonstration1 {
        public static void main(String[] args) {
                System.out.println("***Demonstration-1.Testing
                Inheritance.***");
                // Creating a ChildClass object
                ChildClass child1 = new ChildClass();
                // Invoking showParentMethod() through ChildClass object
                child1.showParentMethod();
        }
}
```

Output:

```
***Demonstration-1.Testing Inheritance.***
I am a Parent Class method.
```

Notice that you have invoked showParentMethod()through a child class object.

POINTS TO REMEMBER

- In Java, Object (in java.lang package) is the superclass for all classes. All other classes directly or indirectly are an inheritor of that class.

- Apart from constructors (instance and static), all members are inherited. But due to their accessibility restrictions, all the inherited members may not be accessible in the child/derived class.

- The child class can add new members, but it cannot remove the definition of the parent member. (Just as you can choose a new name for yourself but cannot change the surname of your parents).

- The inheritance hierarchy is transitive; that is, if class C inherits from class B, which in turn is derived from class A, then class C contains all the members from class B and class A.

Q&A Session

4.1 This means that private members are also inherited. Is this understanding correct?

Yes.

4.2 How can I examine the fact that private members are also inherited?

You can refer to the program and output shown in Demonstration 2.

Demonstration 2

Consider the following:

```
package java2e.chapter4;

class A {
    private int a;
}
```

```
class B extends A {
}

class Demonstration2 {

        public static void main(String[] args) {
System.out.println("***Demonstration-2.Private members are also inherited***");
            B obB = new B();
            A obA = new A();
            // This is a proof that a is also inherited. See the error
            //message.
            System.out.println(obB.a);// Error:The field A.a is not visible
            System.out.println(obB.b);// Error: b cannot be resolved or
            //is not a field
            System.out.println(obA.a);// Error:The field A.a is not visible
            System.out.println(obA.b);// Error: b cannot be resolved or
            //is not a field
        }
}
```

Figure 4-5 is the output snapshot from the Eclipse editor.

Description	Resource
✔ ⊗ Errors (4 items)	
⊠ b cannot be resolved or is not a field	Demonstration2.java
⊠ b cannot be resolved or is not a field	Demonstration2.java
⊠ The field A.a is not visible	Demonstration2.java
⊠ The field A.a is not visible	Demonstration2.java

Figure 4-5. *An output snapshot from the Eclipse editor*

71

We have encountered two different types of errors:

- ***The field A.a is not visible***. It indicates that the private member a from class A is inherited in the child class B.

- You have done an experiment with a field b, which is not present in this class hierarchy (i.e., the field is not present—neither in A nor in B). When you try to access the field with a class A or class B object, you encounter a different error—***b cannot be resolved or is not a field***. Therefore, if a were absent in class B, you would get a similar error.

Q&A Session

4.3 Why doesn't Java support multiple inheritance through class?

The main reason is to avoid ambiguity. It can cause confusion in typical scenarios; for example, let's suppose that you have a method named show() in your parent class. The parent class has multiple children, Child1 and Child2, which *override* the show() method for their own purposes. The code may look like what's shown in Demonstration 3.

Demonstration 3

Try this out:

```java
class Parent {
    public void show() {
        System.out.println("I am in Parent");
    }
}

class Child1 extends Parent {
    public void show() {
        System.out.println("I am in Child1");
    }
}
```

```
class Child2 extends Parent {
    public void show() {
        System.out.println("I am in Child2");
    }
}
```

Now let's assume that your Grandchild class derives from both Child1 and Child2 but has not overridden the show() method. Figure 4-6 depicts the scenario.

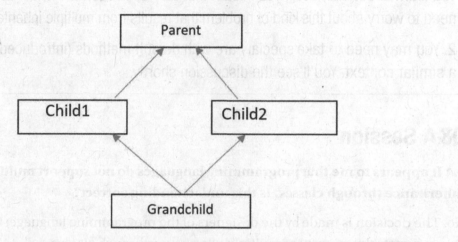

Figure 4-6. *Diamond problem due to multiple inheritance through class in Java*

So, now you have an ambiguity: from which class will GrandChild inherit/call show()—Child1 or Child2? To avoid this type of ambiguity, Java does not support multiple inheritance through classes. This problem has a famous name—the **diamond problem** (the name is given due to the shape of the class inheritance diagram).

So, the Java compiler will always complain about the following code:

```
class GrandChild extends Child1,Child2// Error: Not supported in Java
{
    public void show() {
        System.out.println("I am in Grandchild");
    }
}
```

Note

1. The prior discussion is not limited to methods. When you create an object by instantiating a class, that object inherits fields from the parent class (the super class). Now, suppose your class has multiple super classes. You would encounter the same problem if constructors from different parent classes made an attempt to instantiate the same field, because you would need to decide their order of precedence. When you learn about interfaces, you'll learn that they do not contain fields. So, you do not need to worry about this kind of problem that results from multiple inheritance of state.

2. You may need to take special care with default methods (introduced in Java 8) in a similar context. You'll see the discussion shortly.

Q&A Session

4.4 It appears to me that programming languages do not support multiple inheritance through classes. Is this understanding correct?

No. The decision is made by the designers of the programming language; for example, C++ supports the concept of multiple inheritance through classes.

4.5 Why do C++ designers support the concept of multiple inheritance through classes? It seems that the diamond problem can impact them too.

Here is my point of view: C++ designers probably wanted the feature to be included to make the language rich. They supply you with the features but leave the proper usage to you.

On the other hand, Java designers wanted to avoid any unwanted outcomes resulting from this kind of feature. You will learn that multiple inheritance can make your life difficult in various situations; for example, when you need to maintain constructor chaining, or when you need to involve casting (downcasting is always risky; you will see this discussion in detail in Chapter 5, Q&A 5.14), etc. So, it appears to me that the Java designers simply wanted to make the language simple and less error-prone.

4.6 Is there hybrid inheritance in Java?

Think carefully. Hybrid inheritance is a combination of two or more types of inheritance. So, the answer to this question is "yes" if you are not trying to combine any type of multiple inheritance through classes. But if you try to make a hybrid inheritance with any type of multiple inheritance (through classes), the Java compiler will raise its concern immediately.

4.7 Suppose you have a parent class and a child class. Can you guess in which order constructors of the classes will be called?

You must remember that the constructor's calls follow the path from the parent class to the child class. Let's test this with the following demonstration.

Demonstration 4

Suppose you have a parent class, a child class, and a grandchild class. Let's call them Parent4, Child4, and Grandchild4, respectively. As the names suggest, the Child4 class derives from Parent4, and Grandchild4 derives from the Child4 class. Now, create an object of the Grandchild4 class. From the output of the following demonstration, you can see that constructors are called in the order of their derivation.

```
package java2e.chapter4;

class Parent4 {
    Parent4() {
        System.out.println("Inside Parent Constructor.");
    }
}

class Child4 extends Parent4 {
    Child4() {
        System.out.println("Inside Child Constructor.");
    }
}

class Grandchild4 extends Child4 {
    Grandchild4() {
        System.out.println("Inside GrandChild Constructor.");
    }
}
```

```
class Demonstration4 {
      public static void main(String[] args) {
            System.out.println("***Demonstration-4. Testing constructor
            calling sequence***");
            Grandchild4 grandChild = new Grandchild4();
      }
}
```

Output:

```
***Demonstration-4. Testing constructor calling sequence***
Inside Parent Constructor.
Inside Child Constructor.
Inside GrandChild Constructor.
```

Q&A Session

4.8 Sometimes I am uncertain about which should be the parent class and which should be the child class in an inheritance hierarchy. How can I tackle this kind of situation?

You can try to remember some simple statements like the following: a football player is an athlete, but the reverse is not necessarily true. Or a bus is a vehicle, but the reverse is not necessarily true. This type of "is-a" test can help you to decide which should be the parent; for example, from the prior statement, you can conclude that Vehicle is the parent class and Bus is the child class.

You can also use this "is-a" test to determine in advance whether you can place a class in the same inheritance hierarchy or not. So, when you see that a bus is not a bird, you do not try to place them in the same inheritance hierarchy.

A Special Keyword: super

In Java, there is a special keyword called super. It is used to access the members of a parent class in an efficient way. Whenever a child class wants to refer to its immediate parent, it can use the super keyword.

Let's examine the different uses of the super keyword in the following examples.

Demonstration 5

You can create a child class instance with the following line of code:

```
Child5 obB2 = new Child5(1, 2, 3);
```

The child class constructor can, in turn, call the parent class constructor using the super keyword. Notice the bold line in the following block of code:

```
Child5(int a, int b, int c) {
        //System.out.println("Before setting,c="+ this.c);
        //Error:Constructor call must be the first statement in a
        //constructor
        super(a, b);
        System.out.println("I am in child constructor.");
        System.out.println("Before setting,c="+ this.c);
        this.c = c;
        System.out.println("Now c="+ this.c);
}
```

Other parts of the program are self-explanatory. Now, execute the program and then go through the analysis section for a better understanding.

```
package java2e.chapter4;

class Parent5 {
    private int a;
    private int b;

    Parent5(int a, int b) {
        System.out.println("I am in parent constructor.");
        System.out.println("Before setting,a="+ this.a);
        System.out.println("Before setting, b="+ this.b);
        System.out.println("Setting the values for instance variables
        a and b.");
        this.a = a;
        this.b = b;
        System.out.println("Now a="+ this.a);
        System.out.println("Now b="+ this.b);
    }
}
```

77

```java
        void parent5Method() {
                System.out.println("I am a parent method.");
        }
}

class Child5 extends Parent5 {
        private int c;
        Child5(int a, int b, int c) {
                //System.out.println("Before setting,c="+ this.c);
                //Error:Constructor call must be the first statement in a
                //constructor
                super(a, b);
                System.out.println("I am in child constructor.");
                System.out.println("Before setting,c="+ this.c);
                this.c = c;
                System.out.println("Now c="+ this.c);
        }

        void child5Method() {
                System.out.println("I am a child method.");
                System.out.println("I am calling the parent method.");
                super.parent5Method();
        }

}

public class Demonstration5 {

        public static void main(String[] args) {
                System.out.println("***Demonstration-5. The uses of the
                'super' keyword Demo***");
                Child5 obB2 = new Child5(1, 2, 3);
                //System.out.println("a in ObB2=" + obB2.a);//Error:a is private
                //System.out.println("b in ObB2=" + obB2.b);//Error:b is private
                //System.out.println("c in ObB2=" + obB2.c);//Error:c is private
                obB2.child5Method();
        }
}
```

Output:

```
*** Demonstration-5. The uses of the 'super' keyword Demo***
I am in parent constructor.
Before setting,a=0
Before setting, b=0
Setting the values for instance variables a and b.
Now a=1
Now b=2
I am in child constructor.
Before setting,c=0
Now c=3
I am a child method.
I am calling the parent method.
I am a parent method.
```

You need to understand why it is necessary to use the keyword super. If you did not use it in the preceding example, you may have to write code similar to this:

```
public Child(int a, int b, int c)
        {
                this.a = a;
                this.b = b;
                this.c = c;
        }
```

There are two major issues with this kind of approach. You are trying to write repeated code to initialize the instance variables a and b. Also, in this case, you will receive a compile-time error because both a and b are inaccessible due to their protection level (note that they are private). With the use of the super keyword, you can handle both scenarios efficiently. You may also notice that the parent class constructor is invoked before the child class constructor. Ideally, your goal should be to always maintain the proper *constructor chaining*.

POINTS TO REMEMBER

- Notice the commented line: `//System.out.println("Before setting, c="+ this.c);`*//Error:Constructor call must be the first statement in a constructor.* It is used to remind you that Java design guidelines say that invocation of the super class constructor should be the first statement in the child (or derived) class constructor. You can use either `super()` or `super(parameter list)` to invoke the correct version of your super class constructor.

- The guideline also says: "*If a constructor does not explicitly invoke a super class constructor, the Java compiler automatically inserts a call to the no-argument constructor of the super class. If the super class does not have a no-argument constructor, you will get a compile-time error. Object does have such a constructor, so if Object is the only super class, there is no problem.*"

  `https://docs.oracle.com/javase/tutorial/java/IandI/super.html`

- Notice the last two lines of the output. It demonstrates that you can invoke a super class method from a derived class method using the `super` keyword.

Let's examine another use of `super` in the following example. The keyword `super` can be used in the context of a method, a constructor, or an instance variable. When you consider only methods and instance variables, you can generalize the usage with the following form:

```
super.member;
```

where `member` can be an instance variable or a method.

Sometimes a derived class can hide an instance variable that is originally defined in a super class. In such a situation, `super` can allow you to access the instance variable in the super class using an object of the derived class. So, in the following demonstration, you can see the following line of code:

```
super.myInt = 12;
```

where `myInt` is an instance variable of the parent class.

Demonstration 6

In Demonstration 5, you saw that you can invoke a parent class method in the same way. In Demonstration 6, you have a derived class (Child6) that is derived from the class Parent6. Also, the Parent6 class has a method called parentClassMethod(). So, from the child class, you can refer to the parent class method using the following code:

```
super.parentClassMethod();
```

Both cases are demonstrated in the following example:

```
package java2e.chapter4;

class Parent6 {
    int myInt;

    Parent6() {
        myInt = 25;// some default value
    }
    public void parentClassMethod(){
        System.out.println("I am inside the parentClassMethod().");
    }
}

class Child6 extends Parent6 {
    int myInt;// this will hide myInt in Parent6

    Child6() {
        System.out.println("Initially, the value of myInt in parent
        class=" + super.myInt);
        System.out.println("Setting  the new value( 12) of myInt in
        parent class now.");
        super.myInt = 12;// Setting myInt in parent class
        System.out.println("Setting the value (50) of myInt in child
        class now.");
        myInt = 50;// Setting myInt in child class
    }
```

```java
        void display() {
                System.out.println("The value of myInt in parent class=" +
                super.myInt);
                System.out.println("The value of myInt in child class=" + myInt);
        }
        void invokeParentMethod()
        {
                System.out.println("Invoking the parent class method from the
                child class.");
                super.parentClassMethod();
        }
}

class Demonstration6 {

        public static void main(String[] args) {
                System.out.println("***Demonstration-6:The alternative use of
                'super' keyword***\n");
                Child6 childObject = new Child6();
                childObject.display();
                childObject.invokeParentMethod();
        }
}
```

Output:

```
***Demonstration-6:The alternative use of 'super' keyword***

Initially, the value of myInt in parent class=25
Setting  the new value( 12) of myInt in parent class now.
Setting the value (50) of myInt in child class now.
The value of myInt in parent class=12
The value of myInt in child class=50
Invoking the parent class method from the child class.
I am inside the parentClassMethod().
```

POINTS TO REMEMBER

- As per the language specification (JLS 11): The forms using the keyword `super` are valid only in an instance method, instance initializer, or constructor of a class, or in the initializer of an instance variable of a class. Otherwise, you'll see compile-time errors.

- The `java.lang.Object` class is placed at the top of the class hierarchy. All other classes are either direct or indirect descendants of it. Some useful methods in the `Object` class include `protected native Object clone() {}`, `String toString()`, `public final native void notify(){}`, `public final native void notifyAll(){}`, and `public native int hashCode(){}`.

- You use the `super` keyword to refer *to* the objects of the immediate parent class. But the `Object` class does not have any super class, so you cannot use the `super` keyword in the declaration of an `Object` class.

- The `super` keyword is similar to the `base` keyword in C++ or C#. But you need to remember the restriction that says that the invocation of a super class constructor must be the first line in the subclass constructor.

Q&A Session

4.9 Can you summarize the different uses of the `super` keyword?

In Demonstrations 5 and 6, you have seen that the `super` keyword can be used in any of the following situations:

- To invoke parent class constructors

- To access a parent class member that is a method or a data member.

4.10 Suppose there are methods that have a common name in both the parent class and its child class. If you create a child class object and try to invoke the same-named method, which one will be called?

You are trying to introduce the concept of method overriding here. You will see the discussion shortly in this book (Chapter 5). But you have already learned that you can refer to a parent class method using the keyword `super`. So, to answer your question, consider the following program.

Demonstration 7

Here, both the parent class (Parent7) and child class (Child7) have a method called showMe(). I suggest you go through the program and its corresponding output. Then, go through the analysis section for a better understanding.

```
package java2e.chapter4;

class Parent7 {
    public void showMe() {
        System.out.println("At present, I am inside the parent method.");
    }
}

class Child7 extends Parent7 {

    public void showMe() {
        System.out.println("I am inside the child method.");
        //System.out.println("Invoking the parent method now.");
        //super.showMe();
    }
}

public class Demonstration7 {
    public static void main(String[] args) {
        System.out.println("***Demonstration-7.Testing the use of
        super keyword.****");
        Child7 obChild = new Child7();
        obChild.showMe();
    }
}
```

Output:

```
***Demonstration-7.Testing the use of super keyword.***
I am inside the child method.
```

Here, your derived class (Child7) method hides its parent class (Parent7) method.

If you want to invoke the parent class method, you can create objects and invoke the method like the following:

```
Parent7 obParent = new Parent7();
obParent.showMe();//Now Parent class method will be invoked.
```

Alternatively, you can *uncomment* the following lines (shown in bold) inside the child class method to invoke the parent class method from a child class method:

```
//System.out.println("Invoking the parent method now.");
//super.showMe();
```

Now, if you compile and run the program, you will obtain the following output:

```
***Demonstration-7:Testing the use of super keyword.***
I am inside the child method.
Invoking the parent method now.
At present, I am inside the parent method.
```

Q&A Session

4.11 I know that a subclass method can invoke a super class method. But how can a super class method invoke a subclass method?

You cannot do that. You must remember that a super class is completed before its subclass, so it has no idea about its subclass methods. It only announces something (think about some contract/methods) that can be used by its children. It is only giving, without any expectation of getting anything in return from its children.

If you look carefully, you will find that the "is-a" test is one-way (e.g., a bus is always a vehicle, but the reverse is not necessarily true; so, there is no concept of backward inheritance).

4.12 I realize that inside a subclass method, if I want to invoke a parent class method and put code inside it, I can use the keyword super. Is this correct?

Yes.

4.13 In OOP, the inheritance mechanism helps us to reuse behavior. Is there any other way to achieve this?

Yes. Although the concept of inheritance is used in many places, it is not always the best solution. To understand it better, you need to understand the concept of design patterns. A very common alternative to inheritance is to use composition, which is covered in Chapter 9 in the book.

4.14 It appears to me that if a user already developed a method for an application, other users in the system should always reuse the same method through the concept of inheritance to avoid duplicate efforts. Is this understanding correct?

No. You should not generalize inheritance in this manner. It depends on the particular application and use. Let's assume that someone has already made a `show()` method to describe the details of a `Car` class. Now, let's say that you have also created a class called `Animal` and need to describe the characteristics of an animal with a method. Suppose that you believe that the name `show()` best suits your method. In this case, since you already have a `show()` method in a class called `Car`, and if you think that you should reuse the method for your `Animal` class, you would write something like this:

```
class Animal extends Car{...} .
```

Now, think for a moment. "Is this good design?" You must agree that there is no relationship between a car and an animal. So, you should not relate them in the same inheritance hierarchy.

4.15 How can I inherit a constructor or a destructor in Java?

In Java, constructors are not inherited. You should also remember that destructors are absent in Java (though you can think of the `finalize()` method as a close approximation to it).

Demonstration 8

Consider the following code segment. It works fine. But look at the commented lines closely. You can see that you need to be careful about a common mistake. For example, you cannot replace Line-15 with Line-12 and Line-13 to compile the code. But, it may appear that both approaches are doing the same thing.

```
package java2e.chapter4;

class Demo8A {
        public Demo8A(int x) {
                System.out.print(x);
        }
}

class Demo8B extends Demo8A {
        public Demo8B(int a, int b) {
                //Incorrect coding
                // int c = a + b;//Line-12
                // super(c); //error//Line-13
                // Correct coding
                super(a + b); // Line-15
        }
}
```

From the Java documentation, it appears to me that Java developers did not want to break the constructor chaining. It looks like they felt that if you were allowed to put statements like this before a super call, someone might misuse it; for example, they could perform some invalid operations before the creation of the parent object itself.

Q&A Session

4.16 Some documents say that `this()` should be the first statement. Now, you are telling us `super()` should be the first statement. What will happen if you have both in the same constructor?

Good question. You must notice that both are constructor calls. If you have a constructor call, it must be the first statement. So, you cannot have both in the same constructor.

4.17 If that is the case, then it is a very restrictive design. Isn't it?

The following program and output analysis can remove your doubt.

Demonstration 9

So, let's go through the following program and output.

```
package java2e.chapter4;

class Parent9 {
    int i;
    Parent9() {
        System.out.println("Invoking parameterless constructor of
        Parent class.");
    }
}

class Child9 extends Parent9 {
    int b;
    Child9() {
        // both this() and super() cannot be used together
        // super();
        this(2);
        System.out.println("Invoking parameterless constructor of Child9.");
    }

    Child9(int b) {
        this.b = b;
        System.out.println("Inside Child9 constructor with one
        parameter where b= " + b);
    }
}

class Demonstration9 {
    public static void main(String[] args) {
        System.out.println("***Demonstration-9.A case study with this
        and super keyword.***");
        Child9 obChild9 = new Child9();
    }
}
```

Output:

```
***Demonstration-9.A case study with this and super keyword.***
Invoking parameterless constructor of Parent class.
Inside Child9 constructor with one parameter where b= 2
Invoking parameterless constructor of Child9.
```

Now, enable the super statement and comment out the `this()` constructor like in the following:

```
Child9() {
            // both this() and super() cannot be used together
             super();
            //this(2);
            System.out.println("Invoking parameterless constructor of Child9.");
    }
```

And run the program again. You'll see the following output:

```
***Demonstration-9.A case study with this and super keyword.***
Invoking parameterless constructor of Parent class.
Invoking parameterless constructor of Child9.
```

Have you noticed the interesting thing? In this case, it does not matter whether you make an explicit call to the parent class constructor through `super()` or not, as the parent class constructor is always called. So, you can assume that if Java designers allowed us to put `super()` and `this()` in the same constructor, you would likely end up with multiple super calls in the calls of constructor chaining, which is obviously not a good design.

Q&A Session

4.18 To implement the concept of inheritance, I need to extend the class. Is this understanding correct?

Yes. But you need to remember that you can use the concept by implementing an interface also. Interfaces are discussed in Chapter 6 in this book.

Summary

This chapter covered the following topics:

- The concept of inheritance
- The different types of inheritance
- Why multiple inheritance through class is not supported in Java
- The kind of hybrid inheritance allowed in Java
- The different uses of the super keyword
- The constructor calling sequence in an inheritance hierarchy
- How to call a parent class method if its child class also contains a method with the same name
- How to put classes in an inheritance hierarchy
- The proper uses of the concept of inheritance

CHAPTER 5

Get Familiar with Polymorphism

Let's review what you have already learned about polymorphism. Polymorphism is generally associated with *one name with many forms*; for example, if you have two integer operands with the *addition* operation, you expect to get a sum of the integers, but if the operands are two strings, you expect to get a concatenated string. I also mentioned that polymorphism can be of two types: compile-time polymorphism and runtime polymorphism.

Here, I'll start our discussion with compile-time polymorphism.

In compile-time polymorphism, the compiler can bind the appropriate methods to the respective objects at compile time because it has all the necessary information (for example, method arguments) and knows which method to call much earlier once the program is compiled. This is why it is also known as *static binding* or *early binding*. In Java, compile-time polymorphism can be achieved with method overloading.

Method Overloading

Let's start with the following program and analyze the corresponding output.

Demonstration 1

In this program, you have an Addition class, which contains three methods. Each of these methods has the same name, sum(), but they can accept different arguments. In Java, this kind of coding is allowed.

Now, compile and run the program and then analyze the output.

© Vaskaran Sarcar 2020
V. Sarcar, *Interactive Object-Oriented Programming in Java*, https://doi.org/10.1007/978-1-4842-5404-2_5

```java
package java2e.chapter5;

class Addition {
        int sum(int x, int y) {
                return x + y;
        }

        double sum(double x, double y) {
                return x + y;
        }

        String sum(String s1, String s2) {
                return s1.concat(s2);
        }
}

class Demonstration1 {
        public static void main(String[] args) {
                System.out.println("***Demonstration-1.Method overloading
                example***");
                Addition additionOb = new Addition();
                int sumOfIntergers = additionOb.sum(10, 20);
                System.out.println("10 + 20 is :" + sumOfIntergers);
                double sumOfDoubles = additionOb.sum(10.5, 20.7);
                System.out.println("10.5 + 20.7 is :" + sumOfDoubles);
                String sumOfStrings = additionOb.sum("Smith", "Turner");
                System.out.println("'Smith'+ 'Turner' is :" + sumOfStrings);
        }
}
```

Output:

```
***Demonstration-1.Method overloading example***
10 + 20 is :30
10.5 + 20.7 is :31.2
'Smith'+ 'Turner' is :SmithTurner
```

You can see that the methods have the same name, "sum," but once executed they are capable of doing different things.

When you do this kind of coding, you call it method overloading. In method overloading, the method names are the same, but the method signatures are different. In this context, Java language specification (11) says that "a class cannot have multiple methods with the same signature and different **primitive** return types."

POINTS TO REMEMBER

- In Java, method overloading can help you to achieve compile-time polymorphism.

- In method overloading, the method parameters can vary with number, order, or the types of parameter.

- This kind of coding is also known as static binding, early binding, static method dispatch, or static polymorphism.

- In method overloading, a call to an overloading method is resolved at compile time, rather than at execution time.

Q&A Session

5.1 What is a method signature?

In general, a method name with the number, types, and order of the parameters makes up its signature. Oracle Java documentation confirms the same, saying that two of the components of a method declaration make up the method signature—the method's name and the parameter types. See the following:

```
https://docs.oracle.com/javase/tutorial/java/javaOO/methods.html
```

So, the Java compiler can distinguish among methods with the same name but different parameter lists; for example, for the Java compiler, the method `double add(int x, double y){}` is different from the method `double add(double x, int y) {}` or `double add( int x, int y, int z)`.

5.2 Is the following code segment an example of method overloading?

```
class Addition
{
    public int sum(int x, int y)
    {
        return x + y;
    }
    public double sum(int x, int y, int z)
    {
        return x + y+ z;
    }
}
```

Yes.

5.3 Is the following code segment an example of method overloading?

```
class Addition
{
    int sum(int x, int y)
    {
        return x + y;
    }
    double sum(int x, int y)
    {
        return x + y;
    }
}
```

No. The compiler will not consider the primitive return type to differentiate these methods. In other words, Java will not support primitive return type–based overloading. Eclipse IDE will raise its concern with the error shown in Figure 5-1.

Duplicate method sum(int, int) in type Addition

Figure 5-1. *An output snapshot with error message in the Eclipse editor*

When you learn about the covariant return type in Java, you'll see that JVM (1.5 onward) allows return type–based overloading, where a class can have two or more methods that differ only by return type, but in that case the return type of an overriding method should be a subtype of the overridden method's return type. You'll learn these terms shortly.

5.4 Can we have constructor overloading?

Definitely. You can think of constructors as a special kind of method with no return type.

Demonstration 2

You can write the following program to demonstrate constructor overloading.

```
package java2e.chapter5;

class ConstructorOverloadEx {
    ConstructorOverloadEx() {
        System.out.println("Constructor cannot accept any argument.");
    }

    ConstructorOverloadEx(int a) {
        System.out.println("Constructor can accept one integer
        argument: " + a);
    }

    ConstructorOverloadEx(int a, double b) {
        System.out.println("Constructor can accept one integer
        argument: " + a + " and one double argument: " + b);
    }
}

public class Demonstration2 {

    public static void main(String[] args) {
        System.out.println("***Demonstration-2.Constructor
        Overloading.***");
        ConstructorOverloadEx ob1 = new ConstructorOverloadEx();
        ConstructorOverloadEx ob2 = new ConstructorOverloadEx(2);
        ConstructorOverloadEx ob3 = new ConstructorOverloadEx(2, 3.7);
    }
}
```

Output:

```
***Demonstration-2.Constructor Overloading.***
Constructor cannot accept any argument.
Constructor can accept one integer argument: 2
Constructor can accept one integer argument: 2 and one double argument: 3.7
```

Q&A Session

5.5 It appears to me that Demonstration 2 also describes method overloading. What is the difference between a constructor and a method?

I already talked about constructors in the discussion on classes (see Chapter 2). For your reference, you can consider a constructor as a special kind of method that has the same name as a class and no return type. But there are many other differences. You need to remember the key job of a constructor, which is to initialize objects. You cannot call them directly.

5.6 Can you compile the code in Demonstration 3?

Demonstration 3

Here is the code:

```
class Test {
    public Test() {
        System.out.println("A Constructor with no argument");
    }

    public void Test() {
        System.out.println("This is a method.");
    }
}
```

Java allows this, but in the Eclipse editor you will notice the warning message "This method has a constructor name." This feature may vary in different computer languages. For example, a C# compiler will raise an error in a similar context, as shown in Figure 5-2.

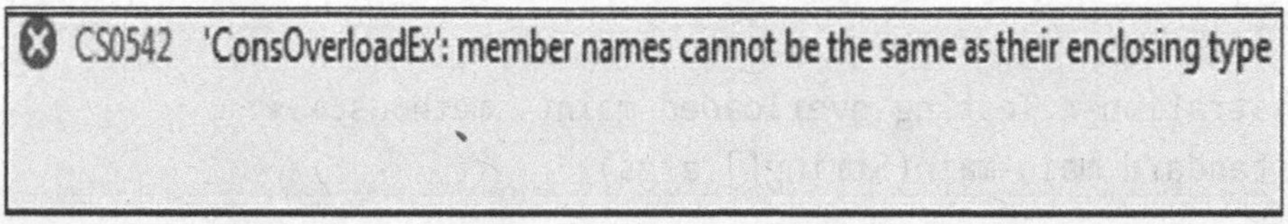

> ⊗ CS0542 'ConsOverloadEx': member names cannot be the same as their enclosing type

Figure 5-2. *An output snapshot from the Visual Studio 2017 IDE*

Q&A Session

5.7 Can you overload the main() method?

Yes. Please review the following program and output, along with the analysis.

Demonstration 4

In the following demonstration, you will notice the presence of three different overloaded versions of the main() method.

```
package java2e.chapter5;

class Demonstration4 {

    public static void main(String[] args) {
        System.out.println("**Demonstration-4.Testing overloaded
        main() methods.***");
        System.out.println("Inside standard main-main(String[] args).");
        // main("hello");
        // main(5,"hello");
    }

    public static void main(String arg1) {
        System.out.println("Overloaded main() with one string
        parameter is called.");
    }

    public static void main(int arg1, String arg2) {
        System.out.println("Overloaded main() with one integer and one
        string parameter is called.");
    }
}
```

Output:

```
***Demonstration-4.Testing overloaded main() methods.***
Inside standard main-main(String[] args).
```

As you can see, the preceding program is compiled successfully. When you run the program, it will invoke the standard main() method. In addition, you can invoke other overloaded methods from this standard main() method. For example, if you uncomment the following two lines in the preceding program,

```
// main("hello");
// main(5,"hello");
```

you'll receive the following output:

```
***Demonstration-4.Testing overloaded main() methods.***
Inside standard main-main(String[] args).
Overloaded main() with one string parameter is called.
Overloaded main() with one integer and one string parameter is called.
```

Q&A Session

5.8 I am confused. Why am I getting a compilation error for the following program?

```
package chapter5.testcodes;

public class Test2 {
    public static void main(String[] args) {
        System.out.println("***Demonstration-4.Testing overloaded
        main() methods.***");
        System.out.println("Inside standard main-main(String[] args).");
        // main("hello");
        // main(5,"hello");
    }

    public static void main(String... args) {
        System.out.println("Inside String... args");
    }
}
```

In this case, there is an ambiguity because the call can be translated by either of these two methods. The Eclipse editor also points this out with error messages that say you are using duplicate methods (see Figure 5-3).

Description	Resource
✔ ⊗ Errors (2 items)	
⊠ Duplicate method main(String...) in type Test2	Test2.java
⊠ Duplicate method main(String[]) in type Test2	Test2.java

Figure 5-3. *The output snapshot of the error messages in the Eclipse editor when you use duplicate methods*

5.9 Does Java support the concept of user-defined operator overloading?

No.

5.10 Will the code in the following demonstration compile?

Demonstration 5

Here is the code:

```
package java2e.chapter5;

class Class5
{
    public void myMethod(int... a){
        System.out.println("Inside myMethod(int... a)");
    }
    public void myMethod(int a, int b){
        System.out.println("Inside myMethod(int a, int b)");
    }
    public void myMethod(boolean... b){
        System.out.println("Inside myMethod(boolean... a)");
    }
}
```

```
class Demonstration5 {

    public static void main(String[] args) {
        System.out.println("***Demonstration-5.Testing Method
        overloading.***");
        Class5 ob5=new Class5();
        ob5.myMethod(1);
        ob5.myMethod(1,2);
        ob5.myMethod();
    }
}
```

No. The compiler is able to resolve both the calls ob5.myMethod(1) and ob5.myMethod(1,2), but it is confused by ob5.myMethod(). This call can be translated by either myMethod(int... a) or myMethod(boolean... a).

Because of this ambiguity, it raises a compile-time error (see Figure 5-4).

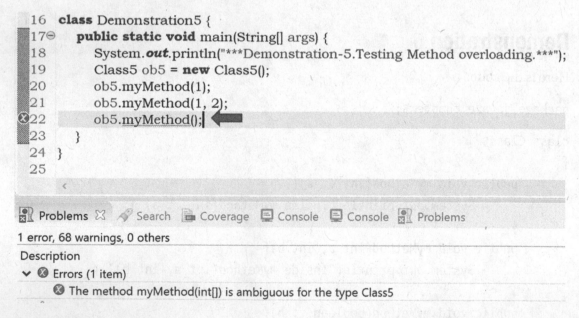

Figure 5-4. A code snapshot with error message in the Eclipse editor resulting from an ambiguous call

If you remove myMethod(boolean... a){} from the preceding code, you'll receive the following output:

```
***Demonstration-5.Testing Method overloading.***
Inside myMethod(int... a)
Inside myMethod(int a, int b)
Inside myMethod(int... a)
```

Note   You may notice the syntactical difference in code segments between Q&A 5.8 and 5.10. In 5.8, you were dealing with Sting[] and String..., but in 5.10, you were dealing with int... and boolean...

TIPS FOR GOOD PROGRAMMING PRACTICE

Try to be consistent with parameter names and their corresponding orders for overloaded methods.
The following is an example of good design:

```
public void showMe(int a) {..}
public void showMe(int a, int b){...}
```

Notice that in the second line, the position of int a is the same as in the first line.
The following is not a recommended design:

```
public void showMe(int a) {..}
public void showMe(int x, int b){...}
```

Notice that in the second line, the code is started with int x instead of int a.

Method Overriding

In some situations, your derived class may want to redefine or modify the behavior of the parent class. Method overriding comes into the picture in such a scenario. Consider the following program and the output. Then, go through each of the points carefully in the analysis section.

Here are the important points about the following program:

- You have two classes—ParentClass and ChildClass. As the name suggests, ChildClass is a derived class that is derived from its parent, ParentClass.

- A method named showMe() with the same signature and return type is defined in both the ParentClass and the ChildClass. It simply means the ChildClass wants to redefine the showMe() method that is already present in the ParentClass, but it is ok with the other method, doNotChangeMe().

- In the main() method, a child class object childOb is created. When you invoke the method doNotChangeMe() through this object, it calls the method that is defined in the ParentClass (following the inheritance property). There is no magic.

- When you invoke the method showMe() through this object, it calls the showMe() version defined in ChildClass; that is, the parent method version is overridden. Hence, the scenario is known as **method overriding.**

- The showMe() in the ParentClass is called the **overridden method,** and the showMe() in the ChildClass is called the **overriding method.**

Demonstration 6

Now, go through Demonstration 6.

```
package java2e.chapter5;

class ParentClass {
    // Overridden method
    public void showMe() {
        System.out.println("Inside ParentClass.showMe()");
    }
```

```
    public void doNotChangeMe() {
        System.out.println("Inside ParentClass.doNotChangeMe().");
    }
}

class ChildClass extends ParentClass {
    // Overriding method
    public void showMe() {
        System.out.println("Inside ChildClass.showMe().");
    }
}

class Demonstration6 {
    public static void main(String[] args) {
        System.out.println("*** Method overriding demonstration.***");
        ChildClass childOb = new ChildClass();
        childOb.doNotChangeMe();
        childOb.showMe();//Will display the overridden method
    }
}
```

Output:

```
*** Method overriding demonstration.***
Inside ParentClass.doNotChangeMe().
Inside ChildClass.showMe().
```

You will notice that in this case the return types, signatures, and access-specifiers of the parent class and child class methods are the same. In the preceding example, if you change the accessibility from public to protected in the child class's showMe(), as follows,

```
//Error
protected void showMe() {
    System.out.println("Inside ChildClass.showMe().");
}
```

you will receive a compilation error that says Cannot reduce the visibility of the inherited method from ParentClass (Figure 5-5).

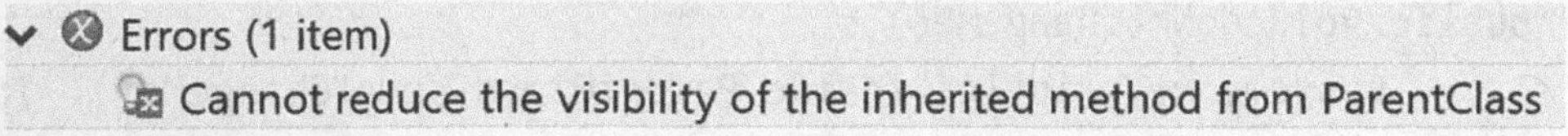

> ∨ ⊗ Errors (1 item)
>   ▣ Cannot reduce the visibility of the inherited method from ParentClass

Figure 5-5. *An error message snapshot in the Eclipse editor when you reduce the visibility of the inherited method*

Note   There is a concept called covariant return type in Java. I'll discuss this topic later. Since it is a relatively advanced concept, it is suggested that you understand the original concept first.

Q&A Session

5.11 What are the key benefits of method overriding?

Method overriding can help you to implement runtime polymorphism. Also, if a parent class has multiple child classes, each of the child classes can decide whether it wants to use the method from the parent class or wants its own specific implementation.

5.12 In method overloading, return types did not matter. But here it matters. Is this correct?

Yes. Here the child class method's return type must be the same (or subclass type, which will be discussed later) as the parent class method's return type (or, simply, both types must be compatible).

5.13 Can I compile the following code snippet?

```java
class ParentClassQ2 {
    public void showMe() {
        System.out.println("I am in Parent class");
    }
}

class ChildClassQ2 extends ParentClassQ2 {
```

```
        public int showMe() {
                System.out.println("I am in Child class");
                return 5;
        }
}
```

No. In this case, you basically tried to implement return type–based overloading, but not overriding. Now `ChildClassQ2` has two methods with the same name and same signature, and only their return types are different. So, you will receive a compilation error that says `The return type is incompatible with ParentClassQ2.showMe()`, as shown in Figure 5-6.

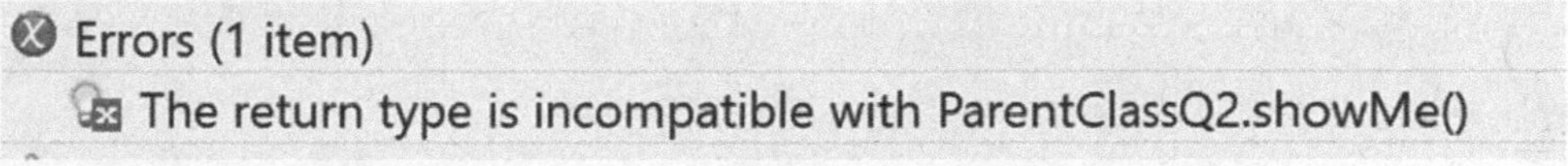

⊗ Errors (1 item)
    📇 The return type is incompatible with ParentClassQ2.showMe()

Figure 5-6. *An error message snapshot in the Eclipse editor resulting from incompatible return types*

To overcome this, you can do some simple changes in the child class's method, like the following. (Here, you pass a dummy argument, which has no effect at all.)

```
//It will work
    public int showMe(int i)
    {
            System.out.println("I am in Child class.");
            return i;
    }
```

Now, you can use the methods from both the parent and the child classes. You can refer to the following program with its output for reference:

```
package java2e.chapter5;

class ParentClassQ2 {
    public void showMe() {
            System.out.println("I am in Parent class.");
    }
}
```

105

```
class ChildClassQ2 extends ParentClassQ2 {
    // Error
    /*
    public int showMe() {
        System.out.println("I am in Child class.");
        return 5;
    }
    */
    // It will work
    public int showMe(int i) {
        System.out.println("I am in Child class.");
        return i;
    }
}

public class Quiz2 {

    public static void main(String[] args) {
        System.out.println("*** Method overriding demonstration.
        Quiz2.***");
        ChildClassQ2 childOb = new ChildClassQ2();
        childOb.showMe();// I am in Parent class.
        childOb.showMe(5);// I am in Child class.
    }
}
```

Output:

```
*** Method overriding demonstration.Quiz2.***
I am in Parent class.
I am in Child class.
```

Demonstration 7

Now, let's test the concept of overloading and overriding in the same program. Consider the following:

```
package java2e.chapter5;

class ParentClass7 {
      public int showMe(int i) {
            System.out.println("I am in Parent class");
            return i;
      }
}

class ChildClass7 extends ParentClass {
      public int showMe(int i) {
            System.out.println("In Child.showMe(int i)");
            System.out.println("I am overriding the parent method and
            adding 5 to the argument.");
            return i + 5;// Must return an int
      }

      public void showMe() {
            System.out.println("In Child.showMe().I am overloaded here.");
      }
}

class Demonstration7 {
      public static void main(String[] args) {
            System.out.println("*** Demonstration-7.Overloading with
            Overriding Demo***\n");
            ChildClass7 childOb = new ChildClass7();
            int value = childOb.showMe(5);
            System.out.println("The value returned is : " + value);// 5+5=10
            childOb.showMe();
      }
}
```

Output:

```
*** Demonstration-7.Overloading with Overriding Demo***

In Child.showMe(int i)
```

```
I am overriding the parent method and adding 5 to the argument.
The value returned is : 10
In Child.showMe().I am overloaded here.
```

The previous output is self-explanatory. From the output messages, you can easily identify which method is overloaded and which one is overridden.

It is said that object-oriented programmers pass through three important stages. In the first stage, they become familiar with non-object-oriented constructs/structures. In this stage, they use decision statements, looping constructs, and so forth. In the second stage, they start creating classes and objects, and use the inheritance mechanism. And finally, in the third stage, they use polymorphism to achieve late binding and to make their programs flexible. Till now, you have gone through the first two stages. Now, let's enter the third stage of expertise and learn how to implement polymorphism in Java programs.

Runtime Polymorphism

You already know that polymorphism is generally associated with one method name that has multiple forms (or constructs). Method overloading is known for compile-time polymorphism. But an important feature of Java is its ability to support the concept of runtime polymorphism. It is also referred to as **dynamic method dispatch.** Here, the call to an overridden method is resolved dynamically at runtime. In other words, you can invoke the appropriate method based on the object to which you are referring.

In dynamic method dispatch, you have a parent class, *which* has at least one child class. The child class contains an overridden method, and you use a parent class reference to point to a child class object. In such a situation, *the* call to an overridden method is determined at runtime.

In the following demonstration, there are two lines of code like the following:

```
Vehicle obVehicle = new Bus();
obVehicle.showMe();
```

where Vehicle is the parent class and Bus is the child class, and the Bus class contains an overridden method, showMe(). So, in this demonstration, following the rule of dynamic method dispatch, you can invoke this overridden method of the Bus class at runtime.

Demonstration 8

Go through the following demonstration and then analyze the output.

```
package java2e.chapter5;

class Vehicle {
    public void showMe() {
        System.out.println("Inside Vehicle.showMe()");
    }
}

class Bus extends Vehicle {
    public void showMe() {
        System.out.println("Inside Bus.showMe()");
    }

    public void busSpecificMethod() {
        System.out.println("Inside Bus.busSpecificMethod()");
    }
}

class Demonstration8 {

    public static void main(String[] args) {
        System.out.println("***Demonstration 8.Experimenting runtime
         polymorphism.***\n");
        //Parent class reference is pointing to a child object.
        Vehicle obVehicle = new Bus();// ok
        // Bus obBus = new Vehicle();//Compilation Error

        obVehicle.showMe();//Inside Bus.showMe()

        // obVehicle.busSpecificMethod();//Error
        //((Bus) obVehicle).busSpecificMethod();// Ok
    }
}
```

Output:

Demonstration 8.Experimenting runtime polymorphism.

Inside Bus.showMe()

In the discussion of method overriding or runtime polymorphism, you may often encounter the concept of casting. Casting can be further categorized into the following two types:

- Upcasting
- Downcasting

Upcasting means casting to a super type (or parent type), and downcasting is the reverse procedure. Let's say, as in the previous demonstration, Vehicle is a parent class and Bus is the class derived from Vehicle. In Java , you can treat a derived class object as a parent class object. So, in this case, if you write the following lines:

```
Vehicle obVehicle ;
obVehicle= new Bus();// Upcasting
```

you are using upcasting. But if you use something like the following:

```
Bus obBus=(Bus)obVehicle;
```

you are using downcasting. Downcasting requires a type check, and it is risky.

Again, notice the two important lines of codes in the preceding program:

```
Vehicle obVehicle = new Bus();
obVehicle.showMe();
```

Here, you are pointing to a derived class object (a Bus object) through a parent class reference (Vehicle reference), and then you are invoking the showMe() method. This way of invoking is allowed, and you will not have any compilation issues; that is, a parent class reference can point to a derived class object.

But you cannot use either of the following lines:

- obVehicle.busSpecificMethod();//Error

    (Since the apparent type in the code is a Vehicle, but not a Bus).
    To remove this error, you need to downcast, as follows:

    ((Bus) obVehicle).busSpecificMethod();// Ok

- Bus obBus = new Vehicle();//Error

As mentioned, to remove this error, you may want to downcast, as follows:

```
Bus obBus=new Bus();
//May encounter with a runtime error:ClassCastException
obBus=(Bus)obVehicle;
```

But downcasting is risky because you may encounter a runtime exception (mentioned with the comment). For example, in this case you will encounter a runtime exception like the following:

```
Exception in thread "main" Inside Bus.showMe()
java.lang.ClassCastException: java2e.chapter5.Vehicle cannot be cast to
java2e.chapter5.Bus at java2e.chapter5.Demonstration8.main(Demonstration8.
java:33)
```

Q&A Session

5.14 "Downcasting is risky." Can you please elaborate?

If not implemented properly, downcasting can cause a ClassCastException. To understand it clearly, let's consider Demonstration 9.

Demonstration 9

Add another class, Train, similar to Bus in the previous demonstration, and then put some test code inside the main() method, like in the following:

```
package chapter5.testcodes;
class Vehicle {
    public void showMe() {
        System.out.println("Inside Vehicle.showMe()");
    }
}

class Bus extends Vehicle {
    public void showMe() {
        System.out.println("Inside Bus.showMe()");
    }
```

```java
        public void specificMethod() {
                System.out.println("Inside Bus.showMe()");
        }
}

class Train extends Vehicle {
        public void showMe() {
                System.out.println("Inside Train.showMe()");
        }

        public void specificMethod() {
                System.out.println("Inside Train.specificMethod()");
        }
}

class Test3 {
        public static void main(String[] args) {
                System.out.println("***Test Demonstration.Demonstration-9.
                Downcasting involves risk.***\n");
                //Upcasting
                Vehicle obVehicle=new Train();//ok
                obVehicle.showMe();//Output: Inside Vehicle.showMe()
                //obVehicle.specificMethod();//error

                //Creating two subtype(one Bus and one Train) object
                Bus obBus=new Bus();
                Train obTrain=new Train();

                //Downcasting example:Casting to a subtype
                //obBus=(Bus)obVehicle;//Run-time error:Train cannot be cast to Bus

                obTrain=(Train)obVehicle;//Ok, this time it is ok.
                obTrain.specificMethod();//also ok
        }
}
```

Output:

```
***Test Demonstration.Demonstration-9.Downcasting involves risk.***
```

```
Inside Train.showMe()
Inside Train.specificMethod()
```

Notice the following segment of code, which is commented:

```
//obBus=(Bus)obVehicle;//Run-time error: Train cannot be cast to Bus
```

If you uncomment this line, you will not receive any compilation errors, but you will encounter a runtime exception, as follows:

```
***Test Demonstration.Demonstration-9.Downcasting involves risk.***
```

```
Inside Train.showMe()
Exception in thread "main" java.lang.ClassCastException: chapter5.
testcodes.Train cannot be cast to chapter5.testcodes.Bus
        at chapter5.testcodes.Test3.main(Test3.java:41)
```

So, you may notice that obVehicle was intended to be used for a Train object, but while downcasting you wanted to convert it into a Bus object, and hence you have received this error. But if you downcast obVehicle to a Train object, there is no error, and your code will work properly.

POINTS TO REMEMBER

- Through a parent class reference, you can refer to a child class object, but the reverse is not true.

- An object reference can implicitly upcast to a super class reference and explicitly downcast to a derived class reference. So, in simple terms, upcasting means casting to a supertype, and downcasting is just the opposite; that is, in downcasting, you try to cast to a derived type.

- Now, let's do a quick check of how the concept is implemented in a similar programming language; for example, C#. If you are familiar with the C# language, you may notice the use of the keywords virtual and override in the examples of method overriding. For example, here is a C# code snippet:

```
class Vehicle
{
        public virtual void ShowMe()
        {
            Console.WriteLine("Inside Vehicle.ShowMe");
        }
    }
    class Bus : Vehicle
    {
        public override void ShowMe()
        {
            Console.WriteLine("Inside Bus.ShowMe");
        }
        public void BusSpecificMethod()
        {
            Console.WriteLine("Inside Bus.ShowMe");
        }
    }
```

- In C#, if you want to override a parent class method in the derived class, mark the parent class method with 'virtual' keyword. But in C#, all methods are by default non-virtual. In the derived class, by tagging a method with the keyword override, you deliberately redefine the corresponding virtual method. So, in C#, you need to tag the keyword override to avoid any unconscious overriding. C# also uses another keyword, new, to mark a method as non-overriding. But, in Java, things are straightforward because all methods are virtual by default.

Q&A Session

5.15 I understand that a parent class reference can point to a child object, but the reverse is not true. Why do we support this kind of design?

You can compare with some basic real-life facts. For example, you can say that all buses are vehicles, but the reverse is not necessarily true, because there are other vehicles like trains and ships that are definitely not buses.

In the same manner, in programming terminology, all derived classes are of type base classes, but the reverse is not true. For example, suppose you have a class called Rectangle that is derived from another class called Shape. You can say that all rectangles are shapes, but the reverse is not true.

You can always do an "is-a" test in an inheritance hierarchy to identify the direction of inheritance, because the "is-a" test is always simple and straightforward.

5.16 You are saying that the call will be resolved at runtime for the following code:

```
Vehicle obVehicle = new Bus();
obVehicle.showMe();
```

But I can clearly see that a Bus object is pointed at by the parent class reference, and the compiler could bind the method showMe() to the Bus object during early binding (or compile-time binding). Why did it delay the process unnecessarily?

If you only consider the preceding code, this question may come to your mind. But let's assume that you have one more child class, Taxi, which is also inherited from the parent class Vehicle. And at runtime, based on some situation, you need to invoke the showMe() method either from Bus or from Taxi. Consider a case like the following: you are generating a random number between 0 and 9. Then, you are checking whether the number is an even number or an odd number. If it is an even number, you need to use a Bus object; otherwise, you use a Taxi object to invoke the corresponding showMe() method.

Demonstration 10

Now, go through the following demonstration. Since it is Demonstration 10, I have marked the Vehicle class as Vehicle10, Bus class as Bus10, and Taxi class as Taxi10.

```
package java2e.chapter5;
import java.util.Random;

class Vehicle10 {
    public void showMe() {
        System.out.println("Inside Vehicle.showMe()");
    }
}
```

115

```java
class Bus10 extends Vehicle10 {
    public void showMe() {
        System.out.println("Inside Bus.showMe()");
    }
}

class Taxi10 extends Vehicle10 {
    public void showMe() {
        System.out.println("Inside Taxi.showMe()");
    }
}

class Demonstration10 {

    public static void main(String[] args) {
        System.out.println("***Demonstration 10.A case study with
        runtime polymorphism ***\n");
        Vehicle10 obVehicle;
        int count = 0;
        Random random = new Random();
        // Considering 5 choices
        while (count < 5) {
            int tick = random.nextInt(10);//0 to 9
            if (tick % 2 == 0) {
                obVehicle = new Bus10();

            } else {
                obVehicle = new Taxi10();
            }
            obVehicle.showMe();// Output will be determined at runtime
            count++;
        }
    }
}
```

Notice that the output may vary.

This is the first run:

```
***Demonstration 10.A case study with runtime polymorphism ***

Inside Bus.showMe()
Inside Taxi.showMe()
Inside Taxi.showMe()
Inside Bus.showMe()
Inside Taxi.showMe()
```

This is the second run:

```
***Demonstration 10.A case study with runtime polymorphism ***

Inside Taxi.showMe()
Inside Bus.showMe()
Inside Bus.showMe()
Inside Taxi.showMe()
Inside Bus.showMe()
```

And so on.

Now you can see why the compiler may need to delay the decision until runtime for this kind of coding, and how you are achieving runtime polymorphism.

Using the final Keyword

In some cases, you may want to prevent the inheritance process. For example, you may want to put in a restriction such that a method in the parent class cannot be overridden by a method of its child class. So, you make the parent class method final to preserve the consistent state of the object. (Similarly, you can also make a "final" class if you want to create an immutable class like the String class in Java.) You must remember that you can prevent overriding in various ways. In the following section, you will see the use of the final keyword only. It is very useful because the compiler itself will prevent the process of overriding.

Consider the following code:

```
final class ParentClassTest4
{
    public void showMe(){
            System.out.println("Inside Parent.showMe()");
    }
}
class ChildClassTest4 extends ParentClassTest4 //Error
{
    //Some code
}
```

You will receive a compilation error: The type ChildClassTest4 cannot subclass the final class ParentClassTest4 (see Figure 5-7).

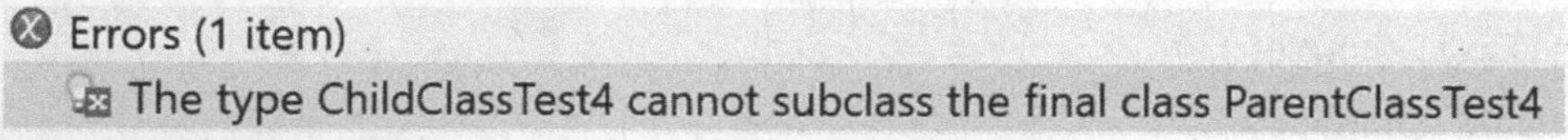

⊗ Errors (1 item)
  The type ChildClassTest4 cannot subclass the final class ParentClassTest4

Figure 5-7. *The final keyword used to prevent inheritance*

You can use it for methods also. For example, consider the following code snippet:

```
class ParentClassTest4 {
        final public void showMe() {
                System.out.println("Inside Parent.showMe()");
        }
}
class ChildClassTest4 extends ParentClassTest4 {
        public void showMe() { // error
                System.out.println("Inside Parent.showMe()");
        }
}
```

You will again receive a compilation error: Cannot override the final method from ParentClassTest4 (see Figure 5-8).

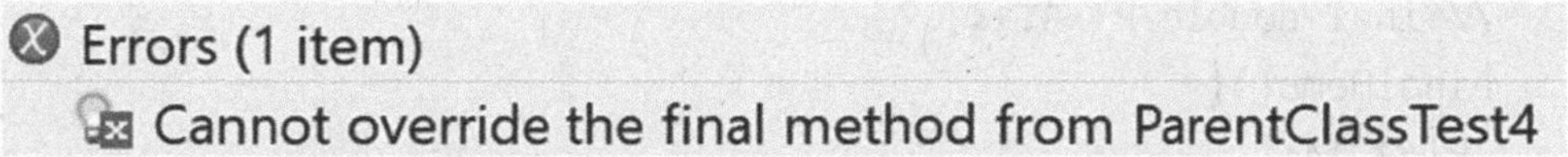

> ⊗ Errors (1 item)
>   ⊠ Cannot override the final method from ParentClassTest4

Figure 5-8. *Final keyword used to prevent method overriding*

Blank final Variables

You can apply `final` keyword to variables like the following:

```
final double PI=3.14;
```

If you do not initialize the `final` variable, you may receive a compilation error. For example, consider the following code snippet:

```
class ParentClassTest4 {
    final int a=10;
    // final double PI=3.14;//ok
    final double PI;//error
}
```

For the preceding code snippet, you will receive a compilation error: `The blank final field PI may not have been initialized` (see Figure 5-9).

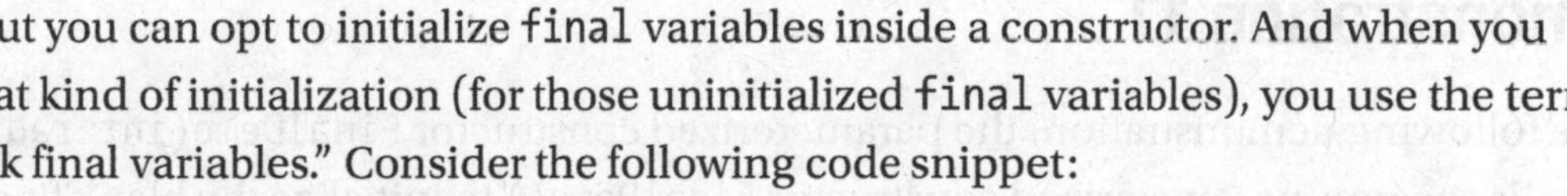

> ⊗ Errors (1 item)
>   ⊗ The blank final field PI may not have been initialized

Figure 5-9. *A compilation error snapshot in Eclipse IDE resulting from an uninitialized blank `final` field*

But you can opt to initialize `final` variables inside a constructor. And when you do that kind of initialization (for those uninitialized `final` variables), you use the term "blank final variables." Consider the following code snippet:

```
class FinalDemo
{
        //Must be initialized inside a constructor
        final double PI;
        double area;
```

```
        //final double PI=3.14;
        FinalDemo(){
         PI=3.14;
        }
}
```

In this case, the compiler will not raise any issues.

It is important to note that there is no keyword like `const` that is a reserved keyword that simply has not been used yet. But you may notice the use of 'const' in other languages like C++ or C#. Instead, in Java, to implement a similar concept, you can use the `final` keyword. In this context, JLS11 says the following:

> *"A constant variable is a final variable of primitive type or type String that is initialized with a constant expression (§15.28). Whether a variable is a constant variable or not may have implications with respect to class initialization (§12.4.1), binary compatibility (§13.1), reachability (§14.21), and definite assignment (§16.1.1)."*

Q&A Session

5.17 If I have multiple constructors, do I need to initialize the final variables in each of them?

Yes. Otherwise, you can call another constructor that can do that initialization for you. The following demonstration can help you to understand the concept better. In this demonstration, there are two constructors—`FinalDemo(int radius)` and `FinalDemo()`. If the parameterized constructor does not call a non-parameterized constructor prior to area calculation, it needs to initialize the value for PI itself.

Demonstration 11

In the following demonstration, the parameterized constructor `FinalDemo(int radius)` first calls the non-parameterized constructor `FinalDemo()` to initialize the blank final variable PI.

```
package java2e.chapter5;

class FinalDemo {
        // Must be initialized inside a constructor
```

```
        final double PI;
        double area;

        FinalDemo() {
            PI = 3.14;
        }

        FinalDemo(int radius) {
            // Invoking the no-argument constructor to initialize the
            // final variable
            this();
            this.area = this.PI * radius * radius;
        }
}

class Demonstration11 {
        public static void main(String[] args) {
            System.out.println("***Demonstration-11. Testing the behavior
            of final keyword.***\n");
            FinalDemo fdemo = new FinalDemo(10);
            System.out.println("Area of a circle with radious 10 unit is "
            + fdemo.area + " square unit.");
        }
}
```

Output:

```
***Demonstration-11. Testing the behavior of final keyword.***
Area of a circle with radious 10 unit is 314.0 square unit.
```

If you comment out the following line in the preceding example

```
FinalDemo(int radius) {
            // Invoking the no-argument constructor to initialize the
                final variable
            //this();
            this.area = this.PI * radius * radius;
        }
```

you'll encounter the same compilation error again: The blank final field PI may not have been initialized (see Figure 5-10).

❌ The blank final field PI may not have been initialized

Figure 5-10. *A compilation error when the statement* this(); *is commented out in Demonstration 11*

Note   You can have both *static blank final variables* and *instance blank variables*. The Java Language Specification(11) says that "a blank final **class** variable must be definitely assigned by a static initializer of the class in which it is declared, or a compile-time error occurs." It also says "a *blank final* **instance** *variable* must be definitely assigned and moreover not definitely unassigned at the end of every constructor of the class in which it is declared, or a compile-time error occurs."

Q&A Session

5.18 Is constructor overriding allowed in Java?

No. Do not forget that overriding allows us to change the object's behavior at runtime, but constructors are used to initialize objects, and they cannot be inherited.

5.19 Why do I need to initialize final variables?

These act like constants throughout your program. If you do not initialize them at the beginning, others can modify them in the future. By declaring final, you are preventing the change at some later stage.

5.20 Suppose I want to have a variable (say, PI) that is accessible from all parts of my code, but at the same time I want to prevent any accidental modification of it. How can I achieve that?

Basically, you are trying to use the concept of global variable, which is not supported in Java. But in such a case, you can declare a variable like the following:

```
public static final double PI=3.14;
```

You'll find out more about `static` in Chapter 8 of this book.

5.21 Will I receive any compilation errors as a result of the following code snippet?

```
class MyClassEx{
        final MyClassEx()//Error
        {
                System.out.println("I am a no argument constructor");
        }
}
```

Yes. Constructors cannot be final. So, in this case, you will receive a compilation error, as in Figure 5-11.

> ⊗ Errors (1 item)
> 🔲 Illegal modifier for the constructor in type MyClassEx; only public, protected & private are permitted

Figure 5-11. *Compile-time error: constructors cannot be final*

5.22 Why am I encountering compile-time errors when I try to use final keywords with constructors?

Let's think from a general point of view: the keyword `final` is used to prevent overriding, but constructors cannot be overridden at all as per the language specification. JLS11 clearly says that "constructor declarations are not members. They are never inherited and therefore are not subject to hiding or overriding."

5.23 Can I override the main() method?

No. Static methods cannot be overridden, and a call to a static method is resolved at compile time only. Also, it is important to note that you can hide a static method, but you cannot override it.

5.24 "You can hide a static method, but you cannot override it"—what is meant by this statement?

The two terms—method hiding and method overriding—are different. The distinction between these two can be summarized as follows:

> *The version of the overridden instance method that gets invoked is the one in the subclass. The version of the hidden static method that gets invoked depends on whether it is invoked from the super class or the subclass.*

Demonstration 12

Consider the following program and go through the output and analysis:

```
package java2e.chapter5;

class Vehicle12 {
    public static void showMe() {
        System.out.println("Vehicle.showMe()-inside the parent class.");
    }

    public void showInstanceMethod() {
        System.out.println("Vehicle.showInstanceMethod()");
    }
}

class Bus12 extends Vehicle12 {
    public static void showMe() { // hides Vehicle.showMe()
        System.out.println("Bus.showMe()-inside the child class.");
    }

    public void showInstanceMethod() {// overrides
        System.out.println("Bus.showInstanceMethod()");
    }
}

public class Demonstration12 {

    public static void main(String[] args) {

        System.out.println("***Demonstration-12. Method hiding vs
        method overriding***\n");
        Vehicle12.showMe();// Vehicle.showMe()-inside the parent class.
        Vehicle12 vehicle = new Bus12();
        // Warning:The following method should be accessed in a static way.
        vehicle.showMe();// Vehicle.showMe()-inside the parent class.
        vehicle.showInstanceMethod();// Bus.showInstanceMethod()
```

```
                System.out.println("----------");
                Bus12.showMe();// Bus.showMe()-inside the child class.
                // Warning:The following method should be accessed in a static way.
                Bus12 bus = new Bus12();
                bus.showMe();// Bus.showMe()-inside the child class.
                bus.showInstanceMethod();// Bus.showInstanceMethod()
        }
}
```

Output:

```
***Demonstration-12. Method hiding vs method overriding***

Vehicle.showMe()-inside the parent class.
Vehicle.showMe()-inside the parent class.
Bus.showInstanceMethod()
----------
Bus.showMe()-inside the child class.
Bus.showMe()-inside the child class.
Bus.showInstanceMethod()
```

The first line and last three lines of the output are obvious. Those were given for your immediate reference. But notice the output for the following code:

```
vehicle.showMe();// Vehicle.showMe()-inside the parent class.
vehicle.showInstanceMethod();// Bus.showInstanceMethod()
```

Have you noticed the interesting behavior of the compiler? In the first case, it picked the parent class method (which is a static method), but in the case of an instance method, it picked the derived class method. This is because in the case of method overriding, the JVM uses the actual class of the instance to pick the method, and the decision is made at runtime.

But for the static method, the compiler considers only the declared type of reference (and you can see vehicle is a parent class reference), and the decision of invoking the particular method is decided at compile time only. So, you can say that method hiding is in no way related to runtime polymorphism.

POINTS TO REMEMBER

- Method hiding is associated with static methods and compile-time polymorphism. Method overriding is associated with non-static methods and runtime polymorphism.

- The hiding of methods and the hiding of fields may have some similarities or dissimilarities, depending on the particular application or usage. You may refer to the language specification for a detailed case-by-case study. For example, the Java language specification says that if the class declares a field with a certain name, then the declaration of that field is said to hide the accessible declarations of fields with the same name in super classes and superinterfaces of the class. In this respect, the hiding of fields differs from the hiding of methods, for there is no distinction drawn between static and non-static fields in field hiding, whereas a distinction is drawn between static and non-static methods in method hiding. A hidden field can be accessed by using a qualified name if it is static, or by using a field-access expression that contains the keyword super or a cast to a super class type. In this respect, the hiding of fields is like the hiding of methods.

Q&A Session

5.25 Can I make the `main()` method final?

In Eclipse 2019-03, Photon (or, in its previous versions, for example, Neon), if you try the following program, you will not find any compile-time or runtime errors. But I do not see any significant benefit to making this change to our conventional `main()`:

```
package chapter5.testcodes;

//Case-1
class Test5 {
    public static final void main(String[] args) {
        System.out.println(" Making main() method final.");
    }
}
```

Output:

```
Making main() method final.
```

But you need to remember the normal behavior of final. For example, the following program will raise a compile-time error:

```
//Case-2
class Test5A {
        public static final void main(String[] args) {
                System.out.println("In Parent-Test5A.Making main() method
                final...");
        }
}
class Test5 extends Test5A {
        public static final void main(String[] args) {
                System.out.println(" In Child-Test5.Making main() method final...");
        }
}
```

The output is shown in Figure 5-12.

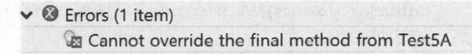

Figure 5-12. *Compile-time error due to improper use of final keyword in program*

5.26 Can I override an overloaded method?

Yes, you can. Consider the following demonstration and corresponding output.

Demonstration 13

Here is the code:

```
package java2e.chapter5;

class ParentOverloadedClass {
        public void showMe() {
                System.out.println("I am in Parent class");
        }
```

```java
    public void showMe(int x) {
        System.out.println("Overloaded method in Parent.Here x= " + x);
    }
}

class ChildOverridingClass extends ParentOverloadedClass {
    public void showMe() {
        System.out.println("Overriding method in Child class.");
    }
}

class Demonstration13 {

    public static void main(String[] args) {
        System.out.println("***Demonstration-13.Method Overriding with
        overloading Demo***\n");
        ChildOverridingClass childObject = new ChildOverridingClass();
        childObject.showMe();//Will call the overriding method from
        //derived class.
        childObject.showMe(25);//Will call the overloaded method from
        //parent class.
    }
}
```

Output:

```
***Demonstration-13.Method Overriding with overloading Demo***

Overriding method in Child class.
Overloaded method in Parent.Here x= 25
```

Q&A Session

5.27 Give me some pointers so that I can easily distinguish between method overloading and method overriding.

The following points can help you to brush up on your knowledge:

- In method overloading, *all methods may reside inside the same class* (you must notice the word *may* here, because you have already seen an example [Demonstration13] where both method overloading and method overriding were implemented and the concept of method overloading spanned two classes—both the parent/super class and its child/derived class). In method overriding, the inheritance hierarchy of a parent class and a child class is involved, which means that at least a parent class and its child class (i.e., minimum of two classes) are involved.

- In method overloading, method signatures are different. In method overriding, method signatures are the same (no need to consider covariant return type at this point).

- You can achieve compile-time (static) polymorphism through method overloading, and you can achieve runtime (dynamic) polymorphism through method overriding.

5.28 Can you predict the output in Demonstration 14? Is there a compilation error?

Demonstration 14

Here is the code:

```
package java2e.chapter5;

class QuizOnFinal {
    public void testMe() {
        System.out.println("I am in parent class");
    }
}

class Q4Child1 extends QuizOnFinal {
    @Override
    final public void testMe() {
        System.out.println("I am in child-1");
    }
}
```

```
class Q4Child2 extends QuizOnFinal {
      @Override
      public void testMe() {
            System.out.println("I am in child-2");
      }
}

class Quiz4 {
      public static void main(String[] args) {
            System.out.println("***Quiz on final keyword usage***\n");
            Q4Child2 obClass2 = new Q4Child2();
            obClass2.testMe();
      }
}
```

The program will compile and run successfully. You will receive the following output:

```
***Quiz on final keyword usage***

I am in child-2
```

You did not encounter any issues here because Q4Child2 is not a child class of Q4Child1. It is also derived from the same parent class, QuizOnFinal, and so it has the freedom to override the non-final method testMe() of the parent class.

Covariant Return Type

Demonstration 15

Consider the following program and output carefully. Then, go through the analysis section for a detailed discussion.

```
package java2e.chapter5;

//Without using covariant return type

class ParentCov {
      int i;
```

```
    int getMultipliedNumber(int x) {
        System.out.println("Inside Parent.");
        this.i = x;
        return i * 10;
    }
}

class ChildCov extends ParentCov {
    int getMultipliedNumber(int x) {
        // error:Return type is incompatible
        // double getMultipliedNumber(int x ){
        System.out.println("Inside Child.");
        this.i - x;
        return i * 50;
    }

}

public class Demonstration15 {
    public static void main(String args[]) {
        System.out.println("***Demonstration-15.Covariant return type
        is NOT used here***\n");
        System.out.println("***Only primitive(int) datetype is used in
        this example.***");
        ParentCov pOb = new ParentCov();
        int result = pOb.getMultipliedNumber(10);
        System.out.println("Multiplied result=" + result);

        pOb = new ChildCov();
        result = pOb.getMultipliedNumber(10);
        System.out.println("Multiplied result=" + result);
    }
}
```

Output:

Demonstration-15.Covariant return type is NOT used here

```
***Only primitive(int) datetype is used in this example.***
Inside Parent.
Multiplied result=100
Inside Child.
Multiplied result=500
```

You must notice the comments in this section:

```
int getMultipliedNumber(int x )
//error:Return type is incompatible
//double getMultipliedNumber(int x )
```

If you change the return type int to double like in the following:

```
// int getMultipliedNumber(int x )
//error:Return type is incompatible
double getMultipliedNumber(int x )
```

you'll get a compilation error saying that the return type is incompatible (Figure 5-13).

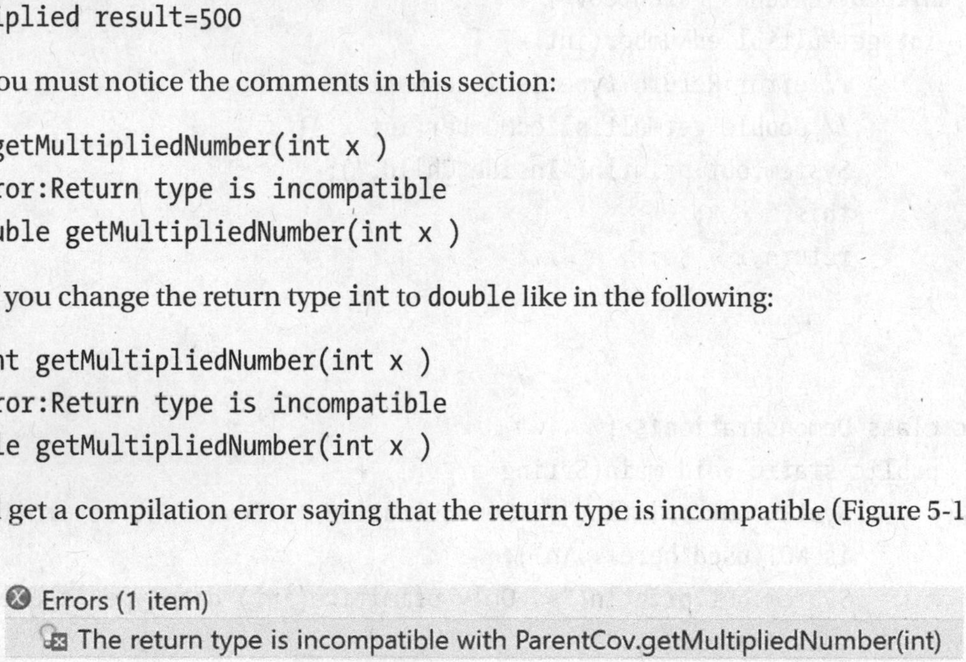

> ❌ Errors (1 item)
>   🔳 The return type is incompatible with ParentCov.getMultipliedNumber(int)

Figure 5-13. *Compile-time error due to incompatible return types*

Now, suppose you are dealing with methods that return "class names" as their return types. In this case, you'll not receive the same kind of error if you vary the return type in the direction of the subclass.

Demonstration 16

Let's go through the modified program.

```
package java2e.chapter5;
//Using covariant return types in this demonstration

class ParentCov2 {
    int i;

    ParentCov2 getMultipliedNumber(int x, int y) {
        System.out.println("Inside Parent class.");
        this.i = x * y;
        return this;
    }
}

class ChildCov2 extends ParentCov2 {
    // No compilation error this time
    ChildCov2 getMultipliedNumber(int x, int y) {
        System.out.println("Inside derived class.");
        this.i = x * y * 25;
        return this;
    }
}

public class Demonstration16 {
    public static void main(String args[]) {
        System.out.println("***Demonstration-16.Testing the behavior
        of the covariant return type***");
        ParentCov2 pOb = new ParentCov2();
        System.out.println("Multiplied result is: " + pOb.
        getMultipliedNumber(10, 2).i);
        pOb = new ChildCov2();
        System.out.println("Now the multiplied result is:" + pOb.
        getMultipliedNumber(10, 2).i);
    }
}
```

Output:

```
***Demonstration-16.Testing the behavior of the covariant return type***
Inside Parent class.
Multiplied result is: 20
Inside derived class.
Now the multiplied result is:500
```

Notice the return type of the method:

ChildCov2 getMultipliedNumber(int x,int y)

You can see that this time, instead of ParentCov2, I have used ChildCov2 as the return type, but the compiler did not complain about this (though it complained about the primitive data types in Demonstration 15).

This is how you use the covariant return type in Java.

Note   The concept of covariant return type is useful when you override the clone() method in Java.

Q&A Session

5.29 Why did Java start supporting this concept?

The Java Oracle documentation says the following:

> *"Note that there may be more than one matching method in a class because while the Java language forbids a class to declare multiple methods with the same signature but different return types, the Java virtual machine does not. This increased flexibility in the virtual machine can be used to implement various language features. For example, covariant returns can be implemented with bridge methods; the bridge method and the method being overridden would have the same signature but different return types."*

See https://docs.oracle.com/javase/8/docs/api/java/lang/Class.
html#getMethod-java.lang.String-java.lang.Class...-

Use of Private Constructors

Now, consider a case study with private constructors. If a class has only private constructors, it cannot be subclassed. This concept can be used to implement a singleton design pattern where you prevent unnecessary objects' creation in the system with the use of the new keyword; for example, the following code snippet will give you a compilation error:

```
class ParentClass {
        private ParentClass() {          }
        public void showMe() {
            System.out.println("Inside Parent.showMe()");
        }
}
class ChildClass extends ParentClass // Error
{
        // Some code
}
```

The output is shown in Figure 5-14.

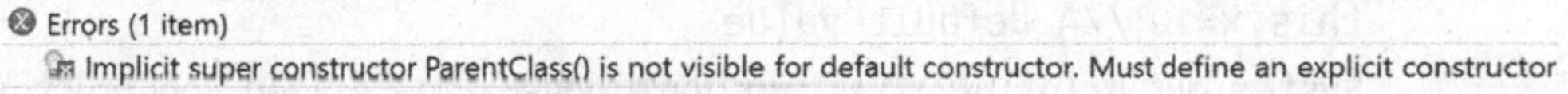

⊗ Errors (1 item)
    Implicit super constructor ParentClass() is not visible for default constructor. Must define an explicit constructor

Figure 5-14. *Preventing inheritance using a private constructor*

Q&A Session

5.30 To prevent inheritance, which process needs to be preferred: case 1 or case 2?

- Case 1:

```
class Demo17
    {
        private Demo17() { }
        }
```

- Case 2:

```
final class Demo17Final
    {
        //some code..
    }
```

First of all, you need to be aware of your requirements. You should not generalize any decision in advance. In Case 1, you can add some additional code, and then you can easily derive a new class from that. But in Case 2, you cannot derive a child class from it.

Demonstration 17

To better understand it, let's add some code to Case 1 and follow the case study.

```
package java2e.chapter5;

class Demo17 {
       int x;

       private Demo17() {
               System.out.println("Called the private constructor.");
               System.out.println("Setting the default the value x=10.");
               this.x=10;//A default value
               System.out.println("\tExit-private non-parameterized constructor.");
       }
       public Demo17(int x) {
               this();
               System.out.println("Updating the default value of x.");
               this.x=x;
               System.out.println("\tExit-parameterized constructor.");
       }
}

final class Demo17Final {
       // some code..
}
```

```
class Child17 extends Demo17 {
      int y;

      public Child17(int x, int y) {
            super(x);
            this.y = y;
      }
}
//class Child2 extends Demo17Final { }//Cannot derive from the final class
//'Demo17Final'

class Demonstration17 {
      public static void main(String[] args) {
            System.out.println("***Demonstration-17.A comparison
            study:Using a final class vs using a private constructor***");
            Demo17 parent = new Demo17(15);
            System.out.println("\tThe parent.x=" + parent.x);
            Child17 child = new Child17(2, 3);
            System.out.println("\tThe child.x=" + child.x);
            System.out.println("\tThe child.y=" + child.y);
      }
}
```

Here is the output. Notice the lines in bold.

***Demonstration-17.A comparison study:Using a final class vs using a
private constructor***
Called the private constructor.
Setting the default the value x=10.
        Exit-private non-parameterized constructor.
Updating the default value of x.
        Exit-parameterized constructor.
        The parent.x=15
Called the private constructor.
Setting the default the value x=10.
        Exit-private non-parameterized constructor.

```
Updating the default value of x.
        Exit-parameterized constructor.
        The child.x=2
        The child.y=3
```

You can see that you can extend the class in Case 1. Now notice the commented line:

```
//class Child2 extends Demo17Final { }
```

If you uncomment this, you'll get the compilation error: `The type Child2 cannot subclass the final class Demo17Final.`

The key thing to remember is that if you use a private constructor only to prevent inheritance, then you may not be following the right path, because the concept can be used in a different context more effectively. The private constructors are commonly used in classes that contain only static members. When you learn about design patterns, you will know that you can use private constructors for a singleton design pattern to stop additional instantiation. And in those cases the intent is different.

Q&A Session

5.31 Why should I prefer writing polymorphic code?

Your code will be flexible, and it can adopt upcoming changes easily. You must agree that if you implement only static binding, you are actually restricting runtime polymorphism.

5.32 How is inheritance related to polymorphism?

To implement polymorphism, you need to use inheritance, because in Java polymorphism is type based, but to create type hierarchy, you need inheritance.

5.33 What is the key difference between inheritance and polymorphism?

Inheritance is used to reuse code, and it supports the parent–child relationship. But if the child wants to redefine the existing parent class behavior, it can do so using the concept of polymorphism.

5.34 Can I override a private method?

To override a method, it should be accessible or visible first. In Chapter 2, you saw that private members are not accessible in the subclass. So, how could you override them?

5.35 Based on the answer to the previous question, can I conclude that private methods can be overridden inside an inner class?

Yes. In this case, since you can access them, overriding is possible. Here is a sample code snippet for you:

```
class OuterClass2 {
        private void showOuter2() {
        System.out.println("Inside OuterClass");
        // showInner2();//Error
    }

    class InnerClass2 {
        void showInner2() {
            System.out.println("Inside InnerClass");
            System.out.println("Calling an outer class method from
            inner class");
            showOuter2();// Ok
        }
        // Overriding
        private void showOuter2() {
            System.out.println("Overiding showOuter2()");
        }
    }
}
```

Summary

This chapter covered the following topics:

- Method overloading

- Method overriding

- How to identify if methods are overloaded or not

- How to overload constructors

- How to overload the main() method

- How to achieve compile-time polymorphism and runtime polymorphism

- Why late binding is necessary

- How to prevent inheritance with different techniques

- A brief comparison between method overloading and method overriding

- A comparison study between using the `final` keyword in our application versus using a private constructor in our application

- How to override a private method inside an inner class

- Seventeen complete program demonstrations and outputs to cover these concepts in detail

CHAPTER 6

Abstract Classes and Interfaces: The True Art in OOP

In the previous chapter, you learned that method overriding can help you to achieve runtime polymorphism. In this chapter, you will further explore the concept with two powerful techniques—abstract classes and interfaces. In addition to this, you will also learn how interfaces can help you to implement the concept of multiple inheritance in Java. Once you master these concepts, you can make your program super flexible. Let's start with abstract classes.

Abstract Classes

Sometimes you start a work, but you may not complete it, and then you expect that someone else will carry out the incomplete work. A real-life example can be seen in the case of property purchases and remodeling a house. For example, you may notice that a grandparent bought a property, and then parents constructed a house on that property, and later a grandchild made the house bigger or redecorated the old house. The basic idea is the same: you may want someone to continue and complete the incomplete work. You give them freedom so that upon completion they can remodel the existing architecture per their needs. The concept of an abstract class best suits in similar scenarios in the programming world.

These are incomplete classes, and you cannot instantiate objects from them. The derived class of an abstract class needs to complete the "incomplete portion" first. It can also redefine the parent class method (by overriding).

141

© Vaskaran Sarcar 2020
V. Sarcar, *Interactive Object-Oriented Programming in Java*, https://doi.org/10.1007/978-1-4842-5404-2_6

In general, if a class contains at least one incomplete method (in programming terms, one abstract method), the class itself is an abstract class. The term *abstract method* tells you that the method has a declaration (or signature) but no implementation. In other words, you can think of abstract members as virtual members without a default implementation.

POINT TO REMEMBER

A class that contains at least one abstract method must be marked as an abstract class.

The subclass must finish the incomplete task; that is, a subclass needs to provide the complete method body for the abstract method, but if it fails to provide that, the subclass itself will be marked as another abstract class.

This kind of coding is very useful when a super class wants to define a generalized form that will be shared by its subclasses. It simply passes the responsibility of filling in the details to its subclasses.

Let's start with a simple demonstration.

Demonstration 1

In the following program, the class MyAbstractClass is an abstract class because it has an abstract method, showMe().

MyConcreteClass is a derived class of MyAbstractClass and gives the complete implementation of the method showMe(). So, MyConcreteClass is not abstract.

```
package java2e.chapter6;

abstract class MyAbstractClass {
    public abstract void showMe();
}

class MyConcreteClass extends MyAbstractClass {
    @Override
    public void showMe() {
        System.out.println("MyConcreteClass.showMe()");
```

```
                System.out.println("I am supplying the method body for showMe()");
        }
}

class Demonstration1 {
        public static void main(String Args[]) {
                System.out.println("***Demonstration-1.Abstract class
                example.***\n");
                // Error:Cannot instantiate from MyAbstractClass
                //MyAbstractClass abstractOb=new MyAbstractClass();
                MyConcreteClass concreteOb = new MyConcreteClass();
                concreteOb.showMe();
        }
}
```

Output:

Demonstration-1.Abstract class example.

MyConcreteClass.showMe()
I am supplying the method body for showMe()

It is important to note that an abstract class can also contain concrete methods. The derived class may or may not override those methods. Let's examine this in Demonstration 2.

Demonstration 2

In this program, the class AbstractClass is an abstract class because it has an abstract method, showMe(). But this class also contains two concrete methods: completeMethod1() and completeMethod2().

ConcreteClass is a derived class of AbstractClass and gives the complete implementation of the method showMe(). So, ConcreteClass is not abstract. Following the inheritance hierarchy, it has access to other parent methods—completeMethod1() and completeMethod2(). But it modified the parent method completeMethod1() and provides its own implementation.

Lastly, you may notice the presence of the integer variable `myInt` in `AbstractClass`. This field is accessed from the method `showMe()` in `ConcreteClass`.

```java
package java2e.chapter6;

abstract class AbstractClass {
    protected int myInt = 25;
    public abstract void showMe();
    public void completeMethod1() {
        System.out.println("I am from completeMethod1 in
        MyAbstractClass and I am complete.");
    }
    public void completeMethod2() {
        System.out.println("I'm the initial version of
        completeMethod2() in MyAbstractClass.I am complete.");
    }
}

class ConcreteClass extends AbstractClass {
    @Override
    public void showMe() {
        System.out.println("ConcreteClass-showMe().I'm complete.");
        System.out.println("The value of myInt is:" + myInt);
    }
    @Override
    // It wants to override completeMethod1() in MyAbstractClass
    public void completeMethod1() {
        System.out.println("ConcreteClass-completeMethod1().");
    }
}

class Demonstration2 {
    public static void main(String Args[]) {
        System.out.println("***Demonstration-2.Abstract classes can
        have concrete methods and fields.***\n");
        ConcreteClass concreteOb = new ConcreteClass();
        concreteOb.showMe();
```

```
        // It will show that completeMethod1 is redefined in ConcreteClass.
        concreteOb.completeMethod1();
        // It will show the details of completeMethod2 defined in
            AbstractClass.
        concreteOb.completeMethod2();

        System.out.println("\n**Invoking methods through parent class
        reference now.**");
        AbstractClass abstractRef = new ConcreteClass();
        abstractRef.showMe();
        abstractRef.completeMethod1();
        abstractRef.completeMethod2();
    }
}
```

Output:

```
***Demonstration-2.Abstract classes can have concrete methods and fields.***
ConcreteClass-showMe().I'm complete.
The value of myInt is:25
ConcreteClass-completeMethod1().
I'm the initial version of completeMethod2() in MyAbstractClass.I am
complete.

**Invoking methods through parent class reference now.**
ConcreteClass-showMe().I'm complete.
The value of myInt is:25
ConcreteClass-completeMethod1().
I'm the initial version of completeMethod2() in MyAbstractClass.I am
complete.
```

In Chapter 5, you learned that a parent class reference can point to a child class object. Following the same rule, you can use the abstract class reference to point to the complete child class objects, and then you can invoke the associated methods. Remember that you can get a significant benefit from this kind of coding.

Q&A Session

6.1 How can you implement the concept of runtime polymorphism here?

You saw it in the previous example. Note the following portion of code:

```
System.out.println("\n*** Invoking methods through parent class
reference now.***");
AbstractClass abstractRef = new ConcreteClass();
abstractRef.showMe();
abstractRef.completeMethod1();
abstractRef.completeMethod2();
```

6.2 Can an abstract class contain fields?

Yes. In the previous example, you saw such a field; that is, myInt.

6.3 In the preceding example, the access modifier is protected. Is this mandatory?

No. You can use other types of modifiers also; for example, you can replace the protected modifier with the public modifier. Later, you will learn that the presence of different access modifiers in abstract classes can give you a better flexibility. It can also make an abstract class different from an interface.

6.4 Suppose, in a class, I have more than ten methods, and out of those only one is an abstract method. Do I need to mark the class with the keyword **abstract**?

Yes. If a class contains at least one abstract method, the class itself is abstract. You can simply recognize the fact that an abstract keyword is used in a sense to represent the incompleteness. So, if your class contains one incomplete method, the class is incomplete, and hence it needs to be marked with the keyword abstract.

So, the simple formula is: whenever your class has at least one abstract method, the class is an abstract class.

6.5 Now consider a reverse scenario. Suppose you have marked your class with the **abstract** keyword but there is no abstract method in it, like the following:

```
abstract class AbstractClassQuiz1 {
    public void completeMethod1() {
        System.out.println("completeMethod-1");
    }
```

```java
public void completeMethod2() {
        System.out.println("completeMethod-2.");
    }
}
```

Can you compile this program segment?

Yes. It will compile, but you must remember that you cannot create an object for this class. So, if you code like this:

```java
AbstractClassQuiz1 absRef = new AbstractClassQuiz1 ();//Error
```

the compiler will raise its concern (see Figure 6-1).

Errors (1 item)

Cannot instantiate the type AbstractClassQuiz1

Figure 6-1. *You cannot create an instance of an abstract class*

Note   It is not necessary for an abstract class to have abstract methods only.

6.6 How can you create an object from an abstract class?

You cannot create objects from an abstract class.

6.7 It appears to me that an abstract class has virtually no use if it is not extended. Is this correct?

Yes.

6.8 If a class extends an abstract class, it has to implement all the abstract methods. Is this correct?

The simple formula is that if you want to create objects in a class, the class needs to be completed; that is, it should not contain any abstract methods. So, if the child class cannot provide implementation (i.e., complete method body) of all the abstract methods, it should mark itself again with the keyword abstract, like in the following example:

```
abstract class AbstractClass
{
        public abstract void inCompleteMethod1();
        public abstract void inCompleteMethod2();
}
abstract class child1 extends AbstractClass
{
//Here our child class is implementing only one of the abstract methods.
//But it does not complete the other one.
//So, the class is abstract again.
        @Override
        public void inCompleteMethod1()
        {
                System.out.println("Implementing the inCompleteMethod1()");

        }
}
```

In this case, if you forget to use the keyword abstract, the compiler will raise an error saying that ChildClass has not implemented InCompleteMethod2(), as shown in Figure 6-2.

⊗ Errors (1 item)
   The type child1 must implement the inherited abstract method AbstractClass.inCompleteMethod2()

Figure 6-2. *A concrete class cannot contain abstract methods*

6.9 I can say that a concrete class is a class that is not abstract. Is this correct?

Yes.

6.10 Sometimes I am confused about the order of keywords; for example, in the preceding case you are using:

   public abstract void inCompleteMethod1();

   Is it following any specific order?

The method must have a return type, and it should be preceded by your method name. So, if you can remember this concept, you will never write something like public void abstract inCompleteMethod1();, which is incorrect in Java. In Eclipse, you will get the error messages shown in Figure 6-3:

148

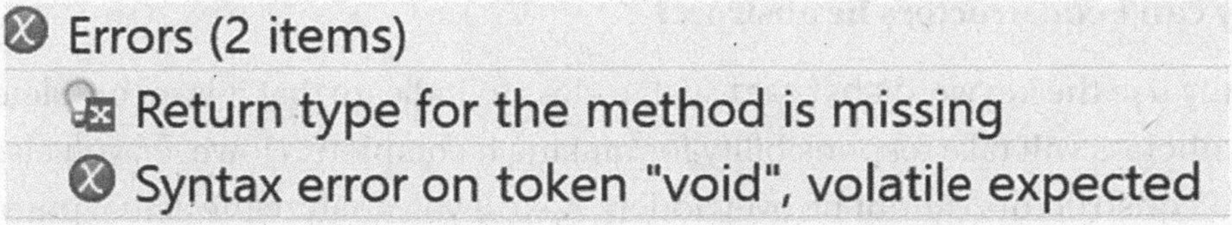

> ⊗ Errors (2 items)
>   ⊠ Return type for the method is missing
>   ⊗ Syntax error on token "void", volatile expected

Figure 6-3. *An output snapshot with error message in the Eclipse editor*

6.11 Can you mark a method with both the keywords **abstract** and **final**?

No. It is like if you say that you want to explore Java but will not go through any reference material. Similarly, by declaring abstract, you want to share some common information across the derived classes, and you agree that overriding is necessary for them; that is, the inheritance chain needs to grow but at the same time, by declaring final, you want to put an end marker to the derivational process, so that the inheritance chain cannot grow. You are trying to implement two opposite concepts simultaneously.

6.12 Can you compile the following code?

```
class Test2 {
    // Constructors cannot be final/abstract/static
    abstract Test2() { //Error
        System.out.println("abstract constructor?Is it possible?");
    }
}
```

Answer:

No. You'll encounter a compile-time error (Figure 6-4).

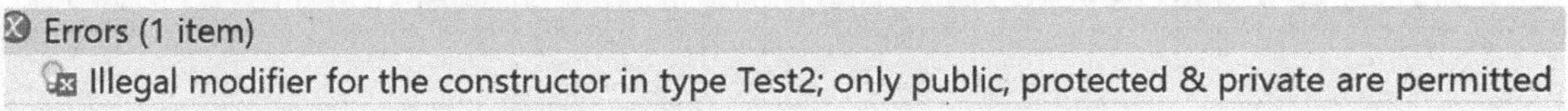

> ⊗ Errors (1 item)
>   ⊠ Illegal modifier for the constructor in type Test2; only public, protected & private are permitted

Figure 6-4. *Constructors cannot be abstract*

6.13 Why can't constructors be abstract?

You usually use the keyword abstract with a class to indicate that it is incomplete, and the subclass will take responsibility for making it complete. However, you also know that constructors cannot be overridden. Also, if you analyze the actual purpose of constructors (i.e., to initialize objects), you must agree that since you cannot create objects from abstract classes, this design suits here perfectly.

6.14 Can you predict the output of the following code segment?

```
package java2e.chapter6;

abstract class IncompleteClass {
      public abstract void showMe();
}

class CompleteClass extends IncompleteClass {
      private void showMe() {
              System.out.println("I am complete.");
              System.out.println("I supplied the method body for showMe().");
      }
}

class Quiz2 {
      public static void main(String[] args) {
              System.out.println("***Quiz2: Experiment with access
              specifiers***\n");
              IncompleteClass myRef = new CompleteClass();
              myRef.showMe();
      }
}
```

The output is a compile-time error, as shown in Figure 6-5.

> ⊗ Errors (1 item)
>   🗐 Cannot reduce the visibility of the inherited method from IncompleteClass

Figure 6-5. *You cannot reduce the visibility of an inherited method*

This error occurs because you cannot reduce the visibility in the derived class method. So, in this case, you need to use the `public` access modifier instead of the `private` access modifier in the `CompleteClass`. Then, you can get the following output:

```
***Quiz2 : Experiment with access specifiers***
```

```
I am complete.
I supplied the method body for showMe().
```

Java language specification (Java SE 11) says the following:

- The access modifier of an overriding or hiding method must provide at least as much access as the overridden or hidden method itself, as follows:

    - *If the overridden or hidden method is public, then the overriding or hiding method must be public; otherwise, a compile-time error occurs.*

    - *If the overridden or hidden method is protected, then the overriding or hiding method must be protected or public; otherwise, a compile-time error occurs.*

    - *If the overridden or hidden method has package access, then the overriding or hiding method must not be private; otherwise, a compile-time error occurs.*

Also, think from another point of view. If you are allowed to compile the previous code snippet, you may try to write something like the following:

```
IncompleteClass myRef = new CompleteClass();
myRef.showMe();
```

In this case, you are trying to invoke a private method from the derived class, which would defeat the actual purpose of the `private` modifier.

Interfaces

An interface is a special type in Java. An interface contains method signatures to define some specifications. The subtypes need to follow those specifications. When you use an interface, you may find many similarities with an abstract class.

With the interface, you declare *what* you are trying to implement, but you are not specifying *how* you are going to achieve that. An interface is similar to a class, with some major differences. For example, all of the methods in an interface are declared without a body (i.e., methods are actually abstract). Also, an interface may contain only final fields. The keyword `interface` is used to declare an interface type; it is followed by the interface name, like the following:

```
interface MyInterface{
//Some code
}
```

POINTS TO REMEMBER

- In simple terms, interfaces help us separate "what parts" from "how parts."

- To declare them, you use the `interface` keyword.

- It is a reference type, where members can be classes, interfaces, constants, and methods.

- Normally, interface methods do not have bodies (in other words, they are abstract methods). You simply replace the body with a semicolon, like in the following:

  ```
  void someMethod();
  ```

- From Java 8 onward, you can prefix the word `default` before your intended method signature and can provide a default implementation. I'll discuss this later.

- A Java class cannot have more than one parent class (or super class), but it can implement more than one interface. This way, it supports the concept of multiple inheritance in Java.

- In general, when you define an interface, you follow syntax similar to that for a class; for example:

  ```
  interface MyInterface{..}
  ```

Note   Basically, you may need to deal with any of these—simple interfaces, nested interfaces, and annotation types. In this chapter, the discussion will start with simple interfaces only.

You can support dynamic method resolution during runtime with the help of interfaces. Once defined, a class can implement any number of interfaces.

Demonstration 3

Let's look at an interface in action:

```
package java2e.chapter6;

interface MyInterface {
        void implementMe();
}

class MyClass implements MyInterface {
        public void implementMe() {
                System.out.println("MyClass is implementing the interface
                method implementMe().");
        }
}

class Demonstration3 {

        public static void main(String[] args) {
                System.out.println("***Demonstration-3.Exploring
                Interfaces.***\n");
                MyClass myClassOb = new MyClass();
                myClassOb.implementMe();
        }
}
```

   Output:

```
***Demonstration-3.Exploring Interfaces.***

MyClass is implementing the interface method implementMe().
```

Q&A Session

6.15 If these methods are incomplete, then the class that is using the interface needs to implement all the methods in the interface. Is this correct?

Exactly. If the class cannot implement all of them, it will announce its incompleteness by marking itself abstract. The following example will help you better understand this.

Here, the interface MyInterface has two methods, show1() and show2(). But the class MyClass is implementing only one. As a result, MyClass itself becomes an abstract class.

```
interface MyInterface{
    void show1();
    void show2();
}
//MyClass becomes abstract. It has not implemented show2() of MyInterface
abstract class MyClass implements MyInterface
{
    @Override
    public void show1() {
        System.out.println("MyClass is implementing the interface method
        show1 ().");
    }
    // public abstract void show2();
}
```

A class needs to implement all the methods defined in the interface; otherwise, it will be an abstract class.

If you forget to implement show2() and you do not mark your class with abstract, keyword as follows:

```
class MyClass implements MyInterface
{
    @Override
    public void show1() {
```

```
        System.out.println("MyClass is implementing the interface method
        show1().");
    }
    // public abstract void show2();
}
```

You will notice the following compilation error in Eclipse (Figure 6-6).

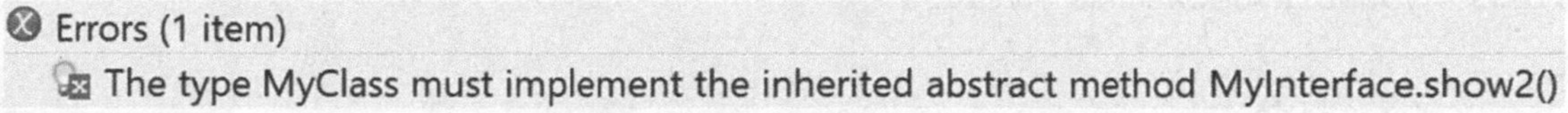

⊗ Errors (1 item)
   ⊡ The type MyClass must implement the inherited abstract method MyInterface.show2()

Figure 6-6. *A class needs to implement all the methods defined in the interface; otherwise, it is an abstract class*

6.16 In the previous scenario, a subclass of MyClass can complete the task by implementing only show2(). Is this correct?

Correct. Demonstration 4 depicts a complete implementation for you.

Demonstration 4

In the following demonstration, the class MyClass implements only the show1() method of MyInterface. Since it does not implement the other method, show2(), it becomes an abstract class.

The class MySubClass is a derived class of MyClass. This class implements the show2() method. As a result, following the inheritance hierarchy, an object of MySubclass can invoke both methods—show1() and show2().

```
package chapter6.testcodes;

interface MyInterface{
    void show1();
    void show2();
}
//MyClass becomes abstract. It has not implemented show2() of MyInterface
//class MyClass implements MyInterface //error
abstract class MyClass implements MyInterface
{
```

```
    @Override
      public void show1() {
          System.out.println("MyClass is implementing the interface method
          show1().");
      }
      // public abstract void show2();
}
class MySubClass extends MyClass
{
      @Override
      public void show2() {
              System.out.println("MySubClass is implementing the interface
              method show2().");
      }
}
class Test4 {
      public static void main(String[] args) {
          System.out.println("***Test4.Exploring Interfaces.***\n");
          //MyClass myClassOb = new MyClass();//Error:MyClass is abstract now
          MyInterface myOb = new MySubClass();
          myOb.show1();
          myOb.show2();
      }
}
```

Output:

```
***Test4.Exploring Interfaces.***

MyClass is implementing the interface method show1().
MySubClass is implementing the interface method show2().
```

Q&A Session

6.17 You said earlier that interfaces can help us implement the concept of multiple inheritance. Can our class implement two or more interfaces?

Yes. The following demonstration shows you how to implement that.

Demonstration 5

In the following demonstration, the class MyClass5 implements the show5A() method of MyInterface5A and show5B() method of MyInterface5B.

```java
package java2e.chapter6;

interface MyInterface5A {
    void show5A();
}

interface MyInterface5B {
    void show5B();
}
```

When your class implements multiple interfaces, the interfaces' names are separated by commas, like in the following:

```java
class MyClass5 implements MyInterface5A, MyInterface5B {
    @Override
    public void show5A() {
        System.out.println("Inside MyClass5,show5A() is completed.");
    }

    @Override
    public void show5B() {
        System.out.println("Inside MyClass5,show5B() is completed.");
    }
}

class Demonstration5 {
    public static void main(String[] args) {
        System.out.println("***Demonstration-5.Implementation of
        multiple interfaces.***\n");
        MyClass5 myClassOb = new MyClass5();
        myClassOb.show5A();
        myClassOb.show5B();
    }
}
```

Output:

Demonstration-5.Implementation of multiple interfaces.

Inside MyClass5,show5A() is completed.
Inside MyClass5,show5B() is completed.

Q&A Session

6.18 In the preceding program, method names are different in the different interfaces. But if both of the interfaces' methods have the same name, how can you implement them?

Good question. The class that is implementing the interfaces can supply a common implementation. Demonstration6 provides you such an implementation.

Demonstration 6

Let's go through the following implementation and refer to the supporting comments to aid in your understanding.

```java
package java2e.chapter6;

//Note: Both of the interfaces have the same method name, "show()".
interface MyInterface6A {
      void show();
}

interface MyInterface6B {
      void show();
}

class MyClass6 implements MyInterface6A, MyInterface6B {
      @Override
      public void show() {
            System.out.println("MyClass6 is completing the show() method.");
      }
}
```

```
class Demonstration6 {

    public static void main(String[] args) {
        System.out.println("***Demonstration-6.Exploring multiple
        interfaces\n");
        // All the following ways of callings are fine.

        // Approach-1
        MyClass6 myClassOb = new MyClass6();
        System.out.print("Approach-1:");
        myClassOb.show();

        // Approach-2
        System.out.print("Approach-2:");
        MyInterface6A inter6A = myClassOb;
        inter6A.show();

        // Approach-3
        System.out.print("Approach-3:");
        MyInterface6B inter6B = myClassOb;
        inter6B.show();

        // Approach-4
        System.out.print("Approach-4:");
        ((MyInterface6A) myClassOb).show();

        // Approach-5
        System.out.print("Approach-5:");
        ((MyInterface6B) myClassOb).show();
    }
}
```

Output:

***Demonstration-6.Exploring multiple interfaces

Approach-1:MyClass6 is completing the show() method.
Approach-2:MyClass6 is completing the show() method.
Approach-3:MyClass6 is completing the show() method.
Approach-4:MyClass6 is completing the show() method.
Approach-5:MyClass6 is completing the show() method.

Note   In C#, there is the concept of explicit interfaces, which can be used in a similar situation. But till now, Java has not directly supported a similar mechanism.

Q&A Session

6.19 Can an interface inherit or implement another interface?

It can inherit but not implement (by definition). Consider the following example.

Demonstration 7

There are three interfaces: `Interface7A`, `Interface7B`, and `Interface7C`. `Interface7A` and `Interface7B` are both the parents of `Interface7C`. Each of these interfaces has its own method. When the class `MyClass7` implements `Interface7C`, it needs to implement all the methods from its immediate parent interface (`Interface7C`) as well as those from its grandparent interfaces (`Interface7A`, `Interface7B`).

```
package java2e.chapter6;

interface Interface7A {
    void showInterface7AMethod();
}

interface Interface7B {
    void showInterface7BMethod();
}

//Interface extending another interface
interface Interface7C extends Interface7A, Interface7B {
    void showInterface7CMethod();
}

class MyClass7 implements Interface7C {
    // Now MyClass7 needs to implement methods from Interface1,
    //Interface2, and Interface3
```

```
        @Override
        public void showInterface7AMethod() {
                System.out.println("MyClass7 has implemented the
                showInterface7AMethod() method.");

        }

        @Override
        public void showInterface7BMethod() {
                System.out.println("The showInterface7BMethod() method is
                implemented by MyClass7.");
        }

        @Override
        public void showInterface7CMethod() {
                System.out.println("MyClass7 has completed the
                showInterface7CMethod() method.");

        }
}
class Demonstration7 {

        public static void main(String[] args) {
                System.out.println("***Demonstration-7.Interface  can extend
                other interfaces\n");

                //Creating a MyClass7 object
                MyClass7 myClassOb = new MyClass7();

                Interface7A inter7A = myClassOb;
                inter7A.showInterface7AMethod();

                Interface7B inter7B = myClassOb;
                inter7B.showInterface7BMethod();

                Interface7C inter7C = myClassOb;
                inter7C.showInterface7CMethod();
```

```
        //Calling directly through myClassOb.
        System.out.println("\n**Now invoking the methods directly
        through a MyClass object.**\n");
        myClassOb.showInterface7AMethod();
        myClassOb.showInterface7BMethod();
        myClassOb.showInterface7CMethod();
    }

}
```

Output:

```
***Demonstration-7.Interface  can extend other interfaces

MyClass7 has implemented the showInterface7AMethod() method.
The showInterface7BMethod() method is implemented by MyClass7.
MyClass7 has completed the showInterface7CMethod() method.

**Now invoking the methods directly through a MyClass object.**

MyClass7 has implemented the showInterface7AMethod() method.
The showInterface7BMethod() method is implemented by MyClass7.
MyClass7 has completed the showInterface7CMethod() method.
```

When a class extends from another class and implements multiple interfaces, you need to follow the following format, which says that extends needs to appear before implements. If you reverse these, you will get a compile-time error.

```
class MyClass7B extends AnotherClass implements Interface7A,Interface7B{

    @Override
    public void showInterface7AMethod() {
        // Some code

    }

    @Override
    public void showInterface7BMethod() {
        // Some code

    }

}
```

POINTS TO REMEMBER

- An interface can extend multiple interfaces.

- A class cannot extend from multiple parent classes, but it can implement multiple interfaces.

Q&A Session

6.20 Can we extend from a class and implement an interface at the same time?

Yes. You can always extend from one class (provided it is not final or there are no other similar constraints). In that case, you need to follow *positional notations* like the following:

```
class ChildClass extends ParentClass implements Interface1,Interface2{...}
```

6.21 Is there any specific reason why the keyword **extends** comes before the keyword **implements** in the previous scenario?

Here, you are just following the recommended Java coding rules. It is always a better idea to point out errors (if any) as early as possible. Following this design, the compiler knows about the parent class first and can point out any compilation errors in the parent class. (Do you remember that parent class constructors are called before the derived class constructors?) But if you are allowed to place the keyword extends in between the implements, the compilation time may go up.

Also, in a case like this, you can extend only one parent class, but you can implement any number of interfaces, so from the compiler's point of view, it may want to be sure about your class's existing methods (or fields) before you implement new ones.

Marker Interface

An empty interface is known as a marker interface or a tagging interface. Here is a sample for you (note there is no method):

```
//Marker interface example
interface MyMarkerInterface{
}
```

Some key utilities of a marker interface are as follows:

- You can create a common parent. (When you have a common parent, you can use a super type reference to point to subtype objects, and it can help you to achieve runtime polymorphism).

- A class can claim membership in the set; for example, if your class implements the `Serializable` interface, it becomes serializable. So, your class actually becomes an interface type through polymorphism. Even a class that implements a tagging interface need not define any new method, because the interface itself does not have any methods.

Note   The `java.lang.Cloneable` and `java.io.Serializable` interfaces are examples of marker interfaces in Java.

A Quick Tour with Annotations

In the context of marker interfaces, you should also know about annotations. A detailed discussion of annotations is out of the scope of this book, but in the following section, you'll get a quick overview that basically covers what an annotation is and how you can use it effectively in your programs.

JDK5 introduced the concept of annotations. JLS 11 says that "an annotation is a marker which associates information with a program construct but has no effect at run time." Annotations are more popular than marker interfaces. They do not have any direct impact on the compiled program. An annotation simply provides some additional information that can be used as an alternative to a marker interface. These annotations can be useful to a compiler or your software tools to detect errors, suppress warning messages, generate XML files, and so on. Some of this information can be used during the program's execution time. Initially, annotations were used for declaration purposes, but JDK8 added more flexibility to annotation type use.

You'll notice that an annotation starts with @. The simplest form of an annotation is @MyAnnotation. For example, you have used the built-in annotation @Override in some of the programs already. Here, the annotation name is `Override`. In its simplest form, an annotation does not contain any elements, and in such cases it is called a **marker annotation.** So, @Override is an example of a marker annotation. @Deprecated, @ SupressWarning, and @Override are pre-built annotations in `java.lang`.

Demonstration 8

To mark a deprecated method, you can use @Deprecated like in the following. To show you the visual behavior in Eclipse, notice the struck-though interface method—oldMethod()—in Figure 6-7.

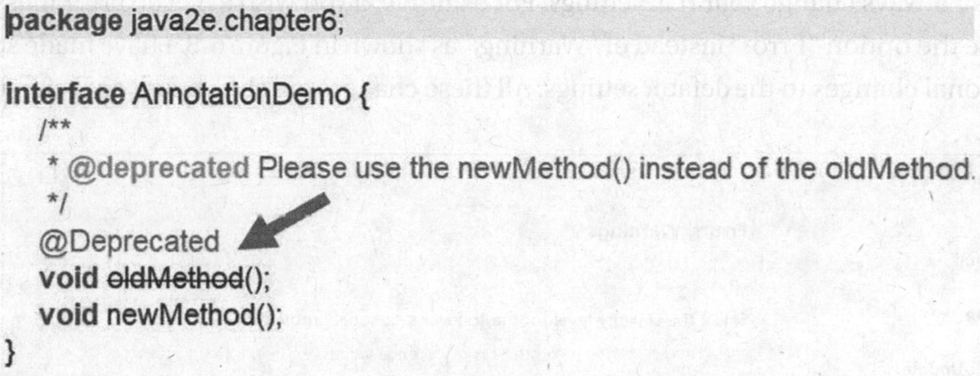

```
package java2e.chapter6;

interface AnnotationDemo {
    /**
     * @deprecated Please use the newMethod() instead of the oldMethod.
     */
    @Deprecated
    void oldMethod();
    void newMethod();
}
```

Figure 6-7. *A snapshot for a deprecated method in the Eclipse IDE*

Now, go through a sample demonstration that uses different annotations.

```
package java2e.chapter6;

interface AnnotationDemo {
    /**
     * @deprecated Please use the newMethod() instead of the oldMethod.
     */
    @Deprecated
    void oldMethod();
    void newMethod();
}

class MyClass8 implements AnnotationDemo {

    @Override
    public void oldMethod() {
            System.out.println("The oldMethod() is in action.");
    }

    @Override
    public void newMethod() {
```

```
        System.out.println(" The recommendation is to use this updated
        method-newMethod().");
    }
}
```

You can see the warning messages that result from the use of a deprecated method. You can always change your IDE settings. For example, if you wish to get an error message, choose the option "Error" instead of "Warning," as shown in Figure 6-8. I have made some additional changes to the default settings. All these changes are shown for your reference.

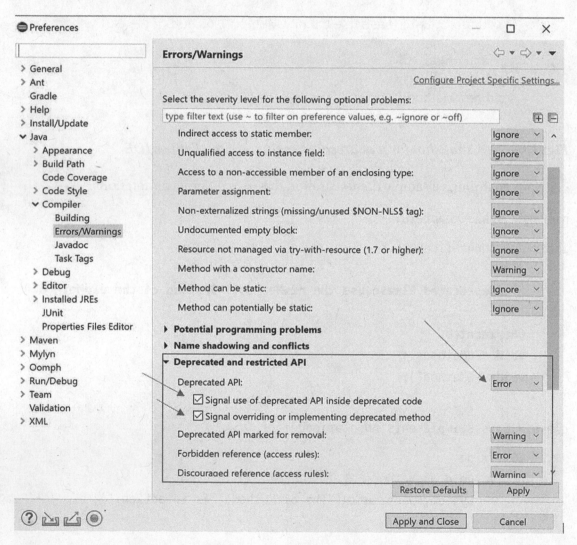

Figure 6-8. *A snapshot from Eclipse IDE to demonstrate the usage of a deprecated method*

Note   You can also use @Deprecated to mark a deprecated element in Javadoc. As per the suggested guideline, this tag should be followed by a newline or a space. You should also explain why you marked it as a deprecated element and what the recommended alternative is.

Annotations can be applied to other annotations, and in that case they are called **meta-annotations**. @Retention, @Documented, @Target, and @Inherited are examples of meta-annotations that are defined in java.lang.Annotation.

In short, by using annotations you can add some metadata information to your source code. To understand the use of an annotation clearly, let's look at an example. Let's say you are a software developer who puts the following comments in every time you write a method or a class:

```
//Author Sarcar V
//Current version: Revision number, say 1
```

But if you are familiar with annotations, you may start with something like the following. In this case, I am supplying some default values, which is optional for you.

```
@interface SoftwareDetails{
      String author() default "Sarcar V";
      int currentVersion() default 1;
}
```

Notice that by default, the author is *Sarcar V* and currentVersion is 1. Once defined, you can use this annotation in a method like the following:

```
@SoftwareDetails(author="Vaskaran", currentVersion=2)
public void myMethod2() {
      System.out.println("Method-2");
}
```

In this case, the author is *Vaskaran* and currentVersion is 2. Similarly, you can apply the annotation to a class.

> **Note**   The application of annotations is not limited to declarations of classes or methods. You can use them in fields or other program elements also. By convention, each annotation appears on its own line.

There is a special case to consider. It is called **single-member annotation**. It has the following characteristics:

- It has only one element.

- Since there is only one member, instead of specifying the name of the member, you can simply name it as value(), like the following:

```
//A single-member annotation
@Documented
@interface MyReviewerDetails{
    //It is single-member annotation. By convention, you use
    //the name value().
    String value();//You need to supply a reviewer name.
}
```

Now you can use it in a method, like the following:

```
@MyReviewerDetails("Joe")
public void myMethod3() {
        System.out.println("A single-member annotation is applied to
        myMethod3()");
}
```

> **Note**   Notice that in this case, you do not need to write @MyReviewerDetails (value="Joe"); instead, you can simply supply the reviewer's name as "Joe." If you choose any other name instead of value() in your single-member annotation, you will not have this flexibility.

Now consider Demonstration 9, where different annotations are used in different methods.

Demonstration 9

A custom annotation is also used in this demonstration. See the following:

```
package java2e.chapter6;
import java.lang.annotation.Documented;

//Marker Annotation
@interface MarkerAnnotation {
}

//User-Defined Annotation
@Documented
@interface MySoftwareDetails{
    String author();//You need to supply an author name.
    int currentVersion() default 1;//You may supply a different version,
    which is optional.
}
//A single-member user-defined annotation
@Documented
@interface MyReviewerDetails{
    //It is single-member annotation. By convention, you use the name value().
    String value();//You need to supply a reviewer name.
}

@MySoftwareDetails(author="Vaskaran Sarcar")
public class Demonstration9 {
    @MarkerAnnotation
    public void myMethod1() {
        System.out.println("A marker annotation is used in this method.");
    }
    @MySoftwareDetails(author="Sarcar V", currentVersion=2)
    public void myMethod2() {
        System.out.println("A custom annotation is used in myMethod2()");
    }

    @MyReviewerDetails(value = "Joe")
    public void myMethod3() {
```

```
        System.out.println("A single-member annotation is applied to
        myMethod3()");
    }
    // A method without annotations
    public void myMethod4() {
        System.out.println(" Method4() is used without annotations.");
    }
}
```

In Eclipse, you can select your project, and then inside the Project tab you get the option "Generate Javadoc…" Using this option, I have generated Javadoc for the Demonstration9 class. A JavaDoc provides API documentation in HTML format from Java source file.

Let's investigate some portions of the generated document to get an idea of how annotations work.

Javadoc Snapshots

Figure 6-9 shows a snapshot from the generated Javadoc.

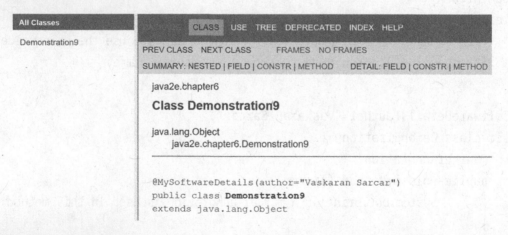

Figure 6-9. *A Javadoc snapshot*

In Figure 6-10, you can see that there is no information associated with myMethod4(), because no annotation is applied to this method. But some additional information is attached to the myMethod2() and myMethod3() methods, as well as to the Demonstration9 class. You may also notice the use of the @Documented annotation. It enables Javadoc to include the annotation type information in the generated document.

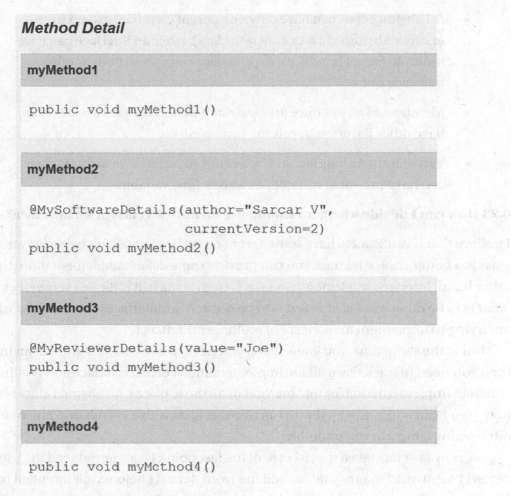

Method Detail

myMethod1

```
public void myMethod1()
```

myMethod2

```
@MySoftwareDetails(author="Sarcar V",
                   currentVersion=2)
public void myMethod2()
```

myMethod3

```
@MyReviewerDetails(value="Joe")
public void myMethod3()
```

myMethod4

```
public void myMcthod4()
```

Figure 6-10. *A Javadoc snapshot*

So, in this section, you have covered all three types of annotations; namely, marker annotation, normal annotation, and single-member annotation.

Q&A Session

6.22 How is an abstract class different from an interface?

- An abstract class can have concrete methods in it, but an interface cannot. I'll come to this point shortly. From Java 8 onward, you can have a keyword called default. You can use this keyword in an interface to provide some default implementation.

- An abstract class can have only one parent class (can extend from another abstract class or concrete class), while an interface can have multiple parent interfaces. An interface can extend from another interface only.

- Members of an interface are by default public. An abstract class can have other flavors; e.g., private, protected, etc.

- Variables in an interface are by default static final. An abstract class can have non-final variables as well as final variables.

6.23 How can I decide whether I should use an abstract class or an interface?

I believe that if you want to have some sort of centralized or default behavior, an abstract class is a better choice because you can provide some default implementation. On the other hand, interface implementation starts from scratch. It indicates some rules about *what* is to be done instead of *how* it is to be done. Also, interfaces are preferred when you are trying to implement the concept of multiple inheritance.

But at the same time, you know that if you need to add a new method in an interface, then you need to track down all the implementations of that interface and put the concrete implementation for that method in all those places. An abstract class is ahead here—you can add a new method in an abstract class with a default implementation and our existing code can run smoothly.

So, now Java has taken special care of the last point: Java 8 introduced the use of the `default` keyword. So, now you can add the word `default` before your intended method signature and it can provide a default implementation. Interface methods are public by default, so you do not need to mark it by the keyword `public`. The Oracle Java online documentation (`https://docs.oracle.com/javase/tutorial/java/IandI/abstract.html`) briefly summarizes the following points:

We should give preference to abstract classes for these scenarios:

- We want our code sharing done among multiple closely related classes.

- We expect that classes that extend our abstract class may have many common methods or fields, or they may require non-public access modifiers inside them.

- We want to use non-static or/and non-final fields, which enables us to define methods that can access and modify the state of the object to which they belong.

On the other hand, we should give preference to interfaces for these scenarios:

- You expect that several unrelated classes are going to implement your interface; e.g., comparable interfaces can be implemented by many unrelated classes.

- We want to specify the behavior of a particular data type, but are not concerned about the implementer.

- We want to use the concept of multiple inheritance of type in the application.

Default Methods in Interfaces

In versions prior to Java 8, an interface can contain only abstract methods; in other words, the interface methods can have only declarations, not any body or implementation. But from Java 8 onward, you can have a method with a body in an interface, but the method must be preceded by the word default.

Demonstration 10

So, in Demonstration 10 you will see that interface10 is an interface that contains two methods—traditionalInterfaceMethod() and defaultMethod(). The first method is a traditional interface method without a body, while the second one has a body but has the method signature preceded by the default keyword.

MyClass10 implements this interface and provides the body for the traditionalInterfaceMethod() method. The overriding method for defaultMethod() in MyClass10 is commented to show you that you can still compile and run this program successfully.

```
package java2e.chapter6;

interface Interface10 {
    // Traditional interface method without a body.
    void traditionalInterfaceMethod();
    // Java 8 onwards:
    // A default method in the interface.
```

```java
        // It can have a body.
        default void defaultMethod() {
                System.out.println("It is a default implementation in the
                interface- Interface10.");
        }
}

class MyClass10 implements Interface10 {
        @Override
        public void traditionalInterfaceMethod() {
                System.out.println("MyClass10 is implementing the interface
                method-traditionalInterfaceMethod()");
        }

        /*
         * @Override
         * public void defaultMethod() {
         * System.out.println("MyClass10 is overriding the default interface
           method.");
         * }
         */
}
class Demonstration10 {
        public static void main(String[] args) {
                System.out.println("***Demonstration-10.Use of default methods
                in Java***\n");
                Interface10 interfaceOb = new MyClass10();
                interfaceOb.traditionalInterfaceMethod();
                interfaceOb.defaultMethod();
        }
}
```

Output:

```
***Demonstration-10.Use of default methods in Java***

MyClass10 is implementing the interface method.
It is a default implementation in the interface- Interface10.
```

You can see that `MyClass10` has implemented only the `traditionalInterfaceMethod()` method, but the program can still run without any compile-time errors.

Q&A Session

6.24 Can we override the default method in an interface?

Yes, you can. Uncomment the following portion of code from Demonstration 10:

```
/*
* @Override
* public void defaultMethod() {
* System.out.println("MyClass10 is overriding the default interface
  method.");
* }
*/
```

Now, if you compile and run the program, you'll receive the following output:

```
***Demonstration-10.Use of default methods in Java***
```

MyClass10 is implementing the interface method-traditionalInterfaceMethod()
MyClass10 is overriding the default interface method.

6.25 With the use of default methods, are we not going back to the diamond problem?

No. Here is the trick: Java puts a restriction in saying that if a class is implementing from multiple interfaces, where each interface has its own default implementation with the same method name, the class needs to implement its own implementation for the same-named method, otherwise you'll receive a compilation error.

Demonstration 11

In this demonstration, each of the interfaces has a default method named myDefaultMethod(). Now, Class11 implements both the interfaces—DefaultInterface11A and DefaultInterface11B. So, to avoid the conflict, it must provide its own implementation for myDefaultMethod(), otherwise you'll receive the following compile-time error:

> "Duplicate default methods named myDefaultMethod with the parameters () and () are inherited from the types DefaultInterface11B and DefaultInterface11A"

```
package java2e.chapter6;

interface DefaultInterface11A {
    void show();

    default void myDefaultMethod() {
        System.out.println("Default implementation for interface3 is
        called.");
    }
}

interface DefaultInterface11B {
    void show();

    default void myDefaultMethod() {
        System.out.println("Default implementation for interface4 is
        called.");
    }
}

class Class11 implements DefaultInterface11A, DefaultInterface11B {
    public void show() {
        System.out.println("Class11 is implementing the Interface
        method-show().");
    }
```

```
        @Override
        public void myDefaultMethod() {
                System.out.println("Class11 needs to implement this method.");
        }
}

class Demonstration11 {
        public static void main(String[] args) {
                System.out.println("***Demonstration-11.Avoiding diamond
                problem when default methods are involved***\n");
                System.out.println("Using DefaultInterface11A reference:");
                DefaultInterface11A interfaceOb11A = new Class11();
                interfaceOb11A.show();
                interfaceOb11A.myDefaultMethod();

                System.out.println("-----------------------");
                System.out.println("Using DefaultInterface11B reference:");
                DefaultInterface11B interfaceOb11B = new Class11();
                interfaceOb11B.show();
                interfaceOb11B.myDefaultMethod();
        }
}
```

Output:

```
***Demonstration-11.Avoiding diamond problem when default methods are
involved***

Using DefaultInterface11A reference:
Class11 is implementing the Interface method-show().
Class11 needs to implement this method.
-----------------------
Using DefaultInterface11B reference:
Class11 is implementing the Interface method-show().
Class11 needs to implement this method.
```

Q&A Session

6.26 It appears to me that the default methods in the interfaces are not used at all in the prior program. Is there any way to call the default interface methods?

Definitely. You can modify the myDefaultMethod() for Class11 as follows:

```
    @Override
public void myDefaultMethod() {
        System.out.println("Class11 needs to implement this method.");
        // Modified for Q&A 6.26
        // Calling default method of DefaultInterface11A
        DefaultInterface11A.super.myDefaultMethod();
        // Calling default method of DefaultInterface11B
        DefaultInterface11B.super.myDefaultMethod();
}
```

If you compile and run the program again, you'll receive this modified output. Notice the bold lines in the following output.

```
***Demonstration-11.Avoiding diamond problem when default methods are
involved***

Using DefaultInterface11A reference:
Class11 is implementing the Interface method-show().
Class11 needs to implement this method.
Default implementation for interface3 is called.
Default implementation for interface4 is called.

----------------------
Using DefaultInterface11B reference:
Class11 is implementing the Interface method-show().
Class11 needs to implement this method.
Default implementation for interface3 is called.
Default implementation for interface4 is called.
```

6.27 Can we make the interface final?

If you make the interface final, then who will implement the incomplete methods of that interface? You must remember that before Java 8, static methods (we'll discuss them later) were not supported in interfaces. So, basically, there was no point to making an interface final.

Demonstration 12

Consider the following declaration:

```
final interface MyInterface

{
        void show();
}
```

Eclipse raises the compile-time error: Illegal modifier for the interface MyInterface; only public & abstract are permitted (Figure 6-11). Here is a snapshot from the Eclipse IDE.

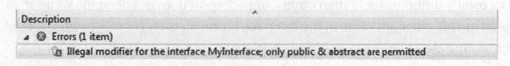

Figure 6-11. *An interface cannot be final*

6.28 Can I use the keyword **abstract** before the **interface** method?

There is no need to do that, because by default they are abstract. But the compiler will not raise any issues here.

```
interface MyInterface
{
        //void show();
        //no need to mention abstract
        abstract void show();
}
```

6.29 Can I use constants inside interfaces?

Yes. They are by default public, static, and final. To test this, you can experiment with the following code segment. Let's save it with the name MyInter.java.

```
interface MyInter{
int myConstant = 10;
void myMethod();
}
```

First, you compile this code using javac. Once compiled, let us decompile it again using javap. Here is the output for your immediate reference:

```
Compiled from "MyInter.java"
interface MyInter {
  public static final int myConstant;
  public abstract void myMethod();
}
```

So, you can omit these modifiers. It is important to note that there is a hot debate on whether one should use constants in an interface or not. Each side has its own pros and cons. Consider a simple case: if you allow a constant in an interface, all implementing classes can have the value to use. But let's consider a case where an implementing class needs a totally different value than others, or perhaps it does not need the value at all. In this case, this constant value in the interface is unnecessary (or misleading) for the implementing class.

6.30 Can I inherit an interface from a class?

No. A class can have some implementations. So, if you allow an interface to inherit from them, the interface may contain the implementations, which is against the core aim of an interface.

6.31 Can you summarize the benefits of using interfaces?

Here are some important use cases of an interface:

- You can implement polymorphism

- You can implement the concept of multiple inheritance

- You can develop loosely coupled systems

- You can support parallel developments

Summary

This chapter answered the following questions:

- What is an abstract class?

- How do you achieve runtime polymorphism with abstract classes?

- Why can't constructors be abstract?

- What is an interface?

- How do you design an interface?

- What are the basic characteristics of an interface?

- How can you implement multiple interfaces?

- How do you deal with interfaces that have a method with the same name?

- What are the different types of interfaces?

- What is a marker interface?

- What can you learn from a quick tour on annotations?

- How do you use default methods in Java and how can you avoid the diamond problem when you use default methods in the context of multiple inheritance?

- What is the difference between an abstract class and an interface?

- How can you decide whether you should use an abstract class or an interface?

- What are the benefits of using an interface?

CHAPTER 7

Packages

Let's consider a simple scenario. Can you use the same name for different classes in a Java file? No. The compiler would raise an issue and would point toward this naming collision. When you define a class, you need to follow unique naming conventions. In real-world programming, class names should be somewhat meaningful, and there is the possibility that different programmers will opt for class names that are not unique. Then the obvious question is: how can you deal with such situations? Packages can rescue us in these instances.

You can bundle your classes or interfaces inside your own packages. This approach helps you to avoid naming conflicts. To simplify, two classes from two different packages can have the same name. A package can also control the visibility of the package elements. So, it is your choice as to whether you want your classes to be exposed to the outside world.

Note You can have two different classes with the same name In two different packages, but in the same package you cannot have two classes with the same name. JLS11 gives a nice example, saying that if there is a package named `mouse` and a member type `Button` in that package (which then might be referred to as `mouse.Button`), then there cannot be any package with the fully qualified name `mouse.Button` or `mouse.Button.Click`.

In Java, directories are the physical representation of packages. Creating a package in Eclipse is quite easy. You do not even have to worry about how the Java runtime will find the proper packages or classes inside it. However, you may need to pay special attention to the PATH and CLASSPATH environment variables. These variables play important role before you write your first Java program in a command-line environment.

© Vaskaran Sarcar 2020
V. Sarcar, *Interactive Object-Oriented Programming in Java*, https://doi.org/10.1007/978-1-4842-5404-2_7

Before you proceed further, remember the following points:

- The `package` statement should be at the top of your source file. If you do not explicitly define this statement, then all the classes/interfaces etc. will be located in the current default package.

- By convention, the name of a package starts with lowercase letters; for example, some of the built-in Java packages are `java.lang`, `java.awt`, `java.util`, `java.io`, etc.

- A package can contain subpackages; for example, if you have a package `p`, and `q` is a subpackage of `p` and contains a class, namely, `MyClass`, then you can refer to `MyClass` with the fully qualified name `p.q.MyClass`. So, the name of the package must follow the directory structure.

- When one class refers to another class inside the same package, the `package` statement need not be included. Otherwise, you may need to use the fully qualified class name, like `packagename.MyClass`, or you may need to use `import` statements.

- A complete package can be imported as follows:

```
import packagename.*;
```

- Or, if you want to import only a particular class—say, `MyClass` from a package called `mypack`—use something like the following:

```
import mypack.MyClass;
```

- Every class in Java resides inside a package. Sometimes you may see Java source files without any package declaration. It means that those classes are inside a default or unnamed package. JLS 11 says the following about unnamed packages: "An ordinary compilation unit that has no package declaration is part of an unnamed package. Unnamed packages are provided by the Java SE Platform principally for convenience when developing small or temporary applications or when just beginning development."

Creating a Package

In this book, I am using Eclipse IDE. Creating a package in Eclipse is easy. Here are the steps on how to create a package in Eclipse IDE.

1. Click File menu ➤ New ➤ Package (consider Figure 7-1).

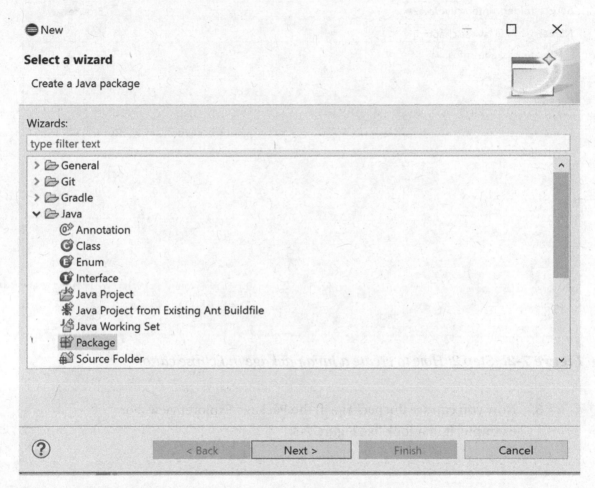

Figure 7-1. *Step 1: How to create a Java package in Eclipse editor*

2. Supply the required information and click Finish (consider Figure 7-2).

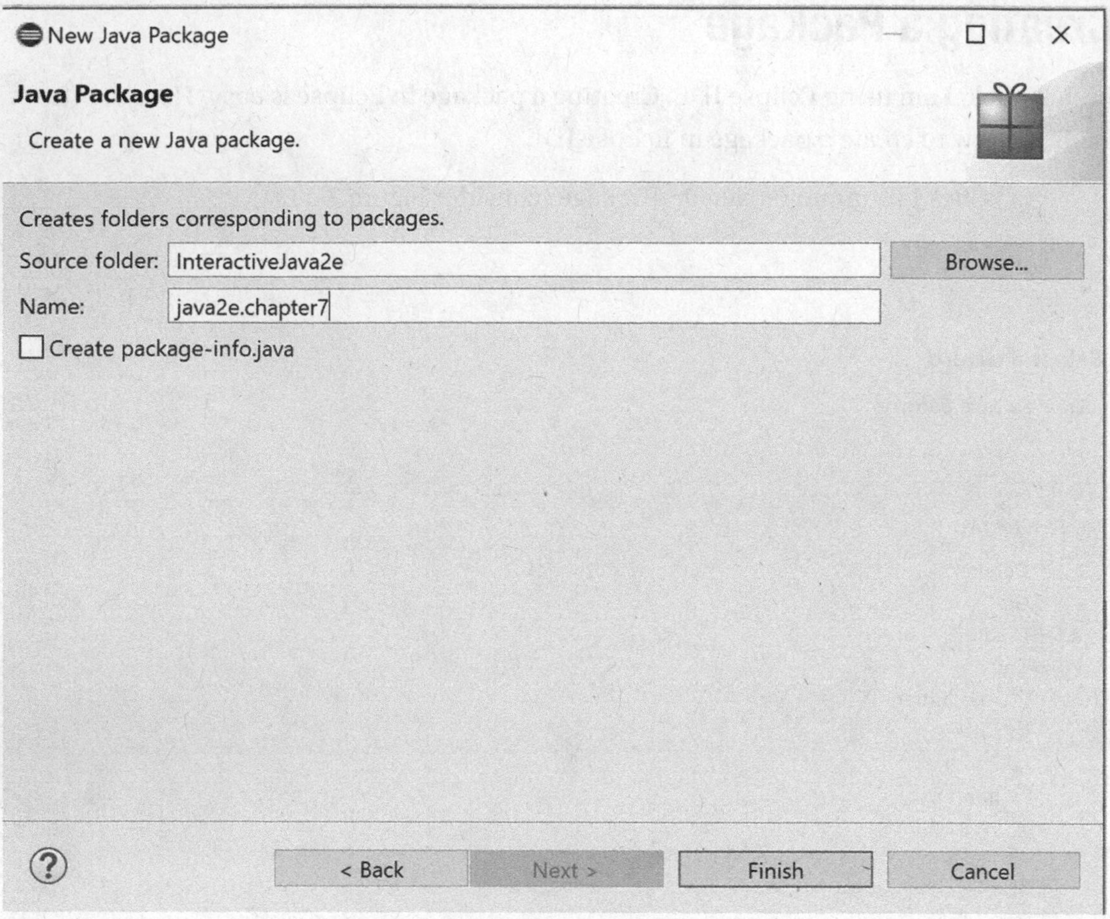

Figure 7-2. *Step 2: How to create a Java package in Eclipse editor*

3. Now you can see the package in the Package Explorer view. For example, it may look like Figure 7-3.

> ✓ 📁 InteractiveJava2e
> > 📚 JRE System Library [jdk1.8.0_172]
> > ⊞ chapter2.codes.testcodes
> > ⊞ chapter4.codes.testcodes
> > ⊞ chapter5.testcodes
> > ⊞ chapter6.testcodes
> > ⊞ java2e.chapter2
> > ⊞ java2e.chapter3
> > ⊞ java2e.chapter4
> > ⊞ java2e.chapter5
> > ⊞ java2e.chapter6
> > ⊞ java2e.chapter7

Figure 7-3. *An empty Java package is created*

Note   The newly created package is empty. But other packages in the snapshot already have some classes inside them. Those packages were created earlier.

---

4. Now right-click on the package name ➤ New ➤ Class/Package to put classes/subpackages/etc. inside the created package. Once you put one or more classes inside the package, it may look similar to the following. For example, in the following diagram, one class, Demonstration1.java, is placed inside the package java2e. chapter7. But the package java2e.chapter7.companya contains two classes—GoaPackage.java and KeralaPackage.java.

```
✔ ⊞ java2e.chapter7
    › 🗊 Demonstration1.java
✔ ⊞ java2e.chapter7.companya
    › 🗊 GoaPackage.java
    › 🗊 KeralaPackage.java
✔ ⊞ java2e.chapter7.companyb
    › 🗊 AndamanPackage.java
    › 🗊 GoaPackage.java
```

Figure 7-4. *Sample Package Explorer view of non-empty Java packages in Eclipse editor*

Demonstration 1

Now, let us go through an example. Consider two travel companies, **A** and **B**. Company A conducts tours for Goa and Kerala. Company B conducts tours for Goa and Andaman. Any tourist can seek information from them for a particular tour package. As per the naming, in the following example, company A is using the package `java2e.chapter7.companya` and company B is using `java2e.chapter7.companyb` package. You can consider Figure 7-4 to understand the overall structure.

Here, I have covered the following scenarios:

- **Less-challenging situation**: Only Company A conducts tours for Kerala, and only Company B conducts tours for Andaman.

- **More-challenging situation**: Notice that both companies conduct a Goa tour, and you need to get tariff information through the respective `GoaPackage.java` class. Notice that both packages use the same class name.

```
// GoaPackage.java [For Company A, in java2e.chapter7.companya package]
package java2e.chapter7.companya;

public class GoaPackage
{
        int basePrice=10000;
```

```
        public void showPrice()
        {
                System.out.println("***Tariff for Goa tour in Company A***" );
                System.out.println("For two person , Goa tour package is
                Rs."+ basePrice*2 );
                System.out.println("For four person , Goa tour package is
                Rs."+ basePrice*4 );
                System.out.println("*************" );
        }
}
```

// KeralaPackage.java [For Company A, in java2e.chapter7.companya package]
```
package java2e.chapter7.companya;

public class KeralaPackage
{
        int basePrice=7000;
        public void showPrice()
        {
                System.out.println("***Tariff for Kerala tour in Company
                A***" );
                System.out.println("For two person , Kerala tour package is
                Rs."+ basePrice*2 );
                System.out.println("For four person, Kerala tour package is
                Rs."+ basePrice*4 );
                System.out.println("*************" );
        }
}
```

// AndamanPackage.java [For Company B, in java2e.chapter7.companyb package]
```
package java2e.chapter7.companyb;

public class AndamanPackage
{
        int basePrice=12000;
        public void showTariff()
        {
```

```
            System.out.println("***Tariff for Andaman tour in Company
            B***" );
            System.out.println("In Company B:For two persons, Andaman
            tour package is Rs."+ basePrice*2 );
            System.out.println("In Company B:For four persons, Andaman
            tour package is Rs."+ basePrice*4 );
            System.out.println("*************" );
        }
}
```

// GoaPackage.java [For Company B, in java2e.chapter7.companyb package]
```
package java2e.chapter7.companyb;

public class GoaPackage {
        int basic_price = 15000;
        int serviceTax = 2000;

        public void showTariff() {
                int forTwoPerson = basic_price * 2 + serviceTax;
                int forFourPerson = basic_price * 4 + serviceTax;
                System.out.println("***Tariff for Goa tour in Company B***");
                System.out.println("In Company B:For two persons , Goa tour
                package is Rs." + forTwoPerson);
                System.out.println("In Company B:For four persosn , Goa tour
                package is Rs." + forFourPerson);
                System.out.println("***************");
        }
}
```

//Demonstration-1
```
package java2e.chapter7;
import java2e.chapter7.companya.*;
import java2e.chapter7.companyb.*;

/*import java2e.chapter7.companya.GoaPackage;
import java2e.chapter7.companya.KeralaPackage;
import java2e.chapter7.companyb.AndamanPackage;*/
```

```
public class Demonstration1 {

        public static void main(String[] args) {
        System.out.println("***Demonstration-1.Exploring packages.***");
        //Only Company-a has KeralaPackage
        KeralaPackage companyAKeralaPackage=new KeralaPackage();
        companyAKeralaPackage.showPrice();
        //Only Company-b has AndamanPackage
        AndamanPackage companyBAndamanPackage=new AndamanPackage();
        companyBAndamanPackage.showTariff();
        //Company-a and company-b both have package tours for Goa.
        java2e.chapter7.companya.GoaPackage companyAGoaPackage=new java2e.
        chapter7.companya.GoaPackage();
        companyAGoaPackage.showPrice();

        java2e.chapter7.companyb.GoaPackage companyBGoaPackage=new java2e.
        chapter7.companyb.GoaPackage();
        companyBGoaPackage.showTariff();
        }
}
```

   Output:

```
***Demonstration-1.Exploring packages.***
***Tariff for Kerala tour in Company A***
For two person , Kerala tour package is Rs.14000
For four person, Kerala tour package is Rs.28000
*************
***Tariff for Andaman tour in Company B***
In Company B:For two persons, Andaman tour package is Rs.24000
In Company B:For four persons, Andaman tour package is Rs.48000
*************
***Tariff for Goa tour in Company A***
For two person , Goa tour package is Rs.20000
For four person , Goa tour package is Rs.40000
*************
```

```
***Tariff for Goa tour in Company B***
In Company B:For two persons , Goa tour package is Rs.32000
In Company B:For four persosn , Goa tour package is Rs.62000
****************
```

Have you noticed an interesting fact? Since the GoaPackage class is available in both Java packages, you needed to use the fully qualified name inside the main() method to refer to the intended class from the particular package. But you did not need to refer to the fully qualified name for the other classes, KeralaPackage or AndamanPackage, since those are classes with unique names.

This example also demonstrates the fact that you will not receive any compile-time errors if you import full packages with star form, where the packages may contain a class with the same name. But while accessing the class, you need to use the fully qualified name of the class. For instance, you must write java2e.chapter7.companya.GoaPackage because the GoaPackage class is available for both companies.

Note   I have kept the dead (commented) code to show you how to import a particular class from a package instead of importing the whole package.

Key Notes About Packages in Java

Here are some important points about packages:

- All classes in the java.lang package are imported by default. (Q&A 7.3 talks about import statements in detail.)

- If you want to rename your package, first rename the directory in which your classes are stored.

- Package naming conventions should be followed carefully; for example, if we use a statement like package a.b.c, we mean to say that directory c is placed inside directory b, which is again placed in inside directory a.

- You can remember the visibility control mechanism by referring to Table 7.1.

Table 7-1. *Access Protection Chart Using Packages*

	public	protected	private	Default/No modifier
Same class	Yes	Yes	Yes	Yes
Subclass in same package	Yes	Yes	No	Yes
Non-subclass in same package	Yes	Yes	No	Yes
Subclass in different package	Yes	Yes	No	No
Non-subclass in different package (outside world)	Yes	No	No	No

Q&A Session

7.1 If every class stays in a package, then how could I use System.out.print() up to now without importing any packages?

In Java, all classes in the java.lang package are imported by default. This is why you were able to use System.out.println()—the System class also resides inside the default java.lang package.

If you import a package, subpackages will not be imported by default. For example, let's say there is a subpackage, namely subpacka, in the package companya, and you have following code:

```
package java2e.chapter7.companya.subpacka;

public class SubGoaPackage {
    int basePrice = 500;

    public void showPrice() {
        System.out.println("**I am in SubGoaPackage.I need to update
        myself**");
    }
}
```

Now, if you do not import this subpackage in Demonstration 1, the bold lines in the following code segment will cause compile-time errors:

```
//Subpackages will not be imported by default.
//Need to import the package explicitly.
//import java2e.chapter7.companya.subpacka.*;
SubGoaPackage companyASubGoaPackage=new SubGoaPackage();
companyASubGoaPackage.showPrice();
```

Note   If you import a package, subpackages will not be imported by default.

7.2 Can you explain about the default access specifier?

You can always refer to Table 7-1 for your reference. From the table, it is obvious that if you do not mention any specific access modifier, like public, private, etc., with regards to a member, it will be considered to have a default modifier, and then your particular member will be visible inside the same package only; in other words, all other classes inside the package can see and use it.

By the same token, you can give visibility to outside classes with a restriction that only those outside classes that are in the same inheritance hierarchy (i.e., subclass) can see the intended member, in which case you can use the modifier protected. And if you do not want to put any restrictions in place at all, simply use the public modifier, and to provide maximum restriction, use the private modifier.

Note   A default or no modifier is also known as a **package-private** modifier because it provides visibility within the containing package only.

7.3 What is the purpose of import statements?

JLS11 says that "an import declaration allows a named type or a static member to be referred to by a simple name that consists of a single identifier." You bring all classes (or packages) from a specified location to your intended location with the use of import statements. Otherwise, you need to use the fully qualified name. For example, suppose you have a class named MyClass with some methods (for simplicity, let's say you have used public modifiers only). This class is placed inside a package (or directory), packageb, which, in turn, is placed inside another directory, packagea. Now, you want to reuse those methods/class from a different location. So, as per the directory structure, you need to refer to the class as packagea.packageb.Myclass. So, you can see that it becomes tedious and looks ugly to type the long dot-separated package name first for the classes you need to use. So, in short, you can save a lot of typing and increase the readability of our program by using import statements. Once imported, you can refer to a class by its name only.

7.4 Then technically I can avoid import statements. Is this understanding correct?

Yes, but you have to pay a lot in terms of typing and readability in a real-life programming situation. So, I do not recommend that practice.

7.5 Suppose I have used the same class name inside two packages. And then in some other program, I have imported both packages. Will I face any compiler issues? Also, how can I access a particular class?

First of all, there is no compiler issue. If you have same-named classes in two or more packages, just use their fully qualified names to avoid the conflict. Refer to the program in Demonstration 1. You can see that both of the packages have the class GoaPackage. java, and I have used their fully qualified names inside the main() method.

7.6 In some examples, I see the import statement is the first statement. But you told me that the package statement should be the first statement. I have both, which one should come first?

You must remember that package statements should be the first statements. Then import statements should be placed. See Demonstration 2.

Demonstration 2

Consider the following program, which demonstrates the incorrect order of package and import statements.

```
import java.util.Date;
package java2e.chapter7;//error

class Demonstration2 {
        public static void main(String[] args) {
                System.out.println("***Demonstration-2.Exploring the order of
                package and import statements.***");
                Date currentTime = new Date();
                System.out.println(currentTime.toString());
        }
}
```

The result is a compilation error (Figure 7-5).

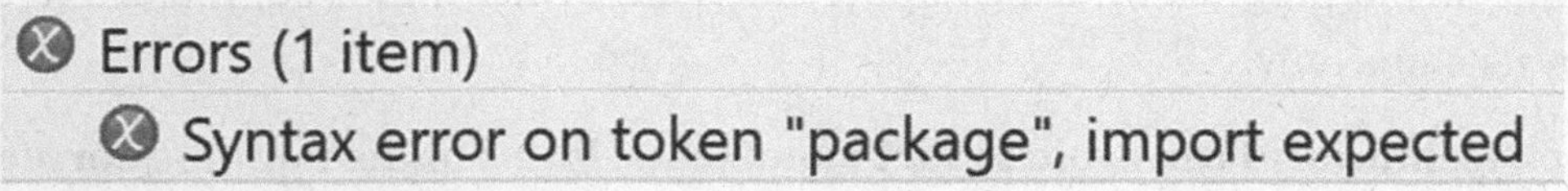

❌ Errors (1 item)
   ❌ Syntax error on token "package", import expected

Figure 7-5. *An output snapshot with error message in the Eclipse editor*

Let's change the order of the package and import statements, like the following:

```
package java2e.chapter7;//package statement should be the first statement
import java.util.Date;// ok
```

Now you will get the expected output:

```
***Demonstration-2.Exploring the order of package and import statements.***
Sat Mar 16 20:53:58 IST 2019
```

Q&A Session

7.7 Why does Java use this kind of design, where package statements must be placed before import statements?

My personal opinion is that you should always fix a location before you start writing the code. For example, you may decide to create classes for your application. If the classes already exist inside the same package (i.e., in same location), you can refer to it immediately and you do not need an import statement. But if this is not the case, you need to bring those classes into the intended location (and import takes its place). So, it's like first fixing a location in order to build a house. You never build a house and then change the location. Likewise, if you look carefully, you will find that package naming conventions follow the directory structure of the corresponding bytecode; i.e., your intention is to fix a location first, and then you proceed.

7.8 How can I deal with multiple package statements in a source file?

You can have only one package statement in a source file.

7.9 Sometimes I do not see any package statement at all in a source file. Will I face any compiler issues for that?

No. It means that you are using the current default package.

7.10 I have some idea about the usage of packages. It'll be helpful if you can summarize the overall usefulness of the packages.

If you look carefully, you can see that packages cover following scenarios:

- They provide an organized structure, which is very useful for understanding and debugging the program.

- You can avoid naming collisions by using package statements when different packages contain classes with the same name.

- With different access modifiers inside packages, you can provide a level of security that is very much required in the real-life software development process.

- You can reuse the classes that are already written and used in a package of other programs.

7.11 Name some built-in Java packages.

java.lang, java.util, java.io, and java.net are commonly used Java packages.

Troubleshooting Common Errors in Command-line Environment

In this book, Java programs are executed in Eclipse. It is a very user-friendly IDE. But sometimes you may want to compile and run a Java program using only Notepad and the command-line environment, but you may encounter some errors. Actually, programming with packages and then compiling and running those programs using the command line can be challenging. For example, suppose you put your class MyClass inside a package, mypack.pkg. Then, you would need to place the source code file in the subdirectory named pkg inside the directory mypack, which is in turn within the main Java working directory. In addition to this, to compile or run the program, you should be in the main directory, not in the subdirectory. I'll show you this use case in detail at the end of this section.

To begin with, let's analyze some fundamental errors in the command-line environment. Suppose you have written the following program and saved it in C:\TestClass\Hello.java:

```
public class Hello {
    public static void main(String[] args) {
        System.out.println("***Hello Vaskaran***");

    }
}
```

When you compile it, you may encounter the following error:

```
C:\TestClass>javac Hello.java
'javac' is not recognized as an internal or external command,
operable program or batch file.
```

This kind of problem occurs when you do not set the environment variables properly. You can set your PATH environment variable to remove this error, as follows:

```
C:\TestClass>set path="C:\Program Files\Java\jdk1.8.0_172\bin";
C:\TestClass>javac Hello.java
C:\TestClass>
```

But instead of setting this environment variable at the command prompt, it is suggested that you edit your environment variables and add this. It will be a one-time activity for you.

Sometimes you can compile the program but cannot run it. For example, during execution, you may encounter a problem saying: Error: Could not find or load main class XXX, where XXX is the class name. Here is a screenshot of such an event:

```
C:\TestClass>javac Hello.java

C:\TestClass>java Hello
Error: Could not find or load main class Hello
```

In my case, a quick fix for this problem was to set the following variables properly (since I installed jdk1.8.0_172 in my system):

```
C:\TestClass>set class="C:\Program Files\Java\jdk1.8.0_172\bin";
C:\TestClass>set classpath="C:\Program Files\Java\jre1.8.0_172\lib\rt.jar";
```

Now I can recompile and run the program again. This time, the program is executed properly.

```
C:\TestClass>javac Hello.java
C:\TestClass>java Hello
***Hello Vaskaran***
```

But in some cases, for a similar error message, you may need to search for other probable causes of failure. For example, let's modify the program using a package statement at the beginning, as follows:

```
package mypack;
public class Hello2 {
        public static void main(String[] args) {
                System.out.println("***Hello Vaskaran***");

        }
}
```

Let's suppose you put this Hello2.java in C:\TestClass\mypack. Now, try to compile and run the program as follows:

```
C:\TestClass\mypack>javac Hello2.java
```

```
C:\TestClass\mypack>java Hello2
Error: Could not find or load main class Hello2
```

You can see that this time the program is not running properly. Notice that you are currently in mypack. As said before, in a case like this, you should be in the *main directory*, not in the *subdirectory*. So, in this case, you need to go one level up and try the following commands:

```
C:\TestClass\mypack>cd ..
```

```
C:\TestClass>java mypack.Hello2
***Hello Vaskaran***
```

In short, if you want to use simple command prompts and Notepad to run your Java program, you need to set your PATH and CLASSPATH environment variables properly. In addition to this, if you use a package statement, you should maintain the directory structure properly, and you should run your program by following the correct directory structure.

Summary

This chapter discussed the following topics:

- What is a package?

- How can you create packages in Eclipse IDE?

- How should import statements be used?

- What restrictions are associated with packages?

- How can you write simple programs to demonstrate packages in Java?

- How can you avoid some command-line environment errors?

CHAPTER 8

Understanding Class Variables and Class Methods

Sometimes developers do not want to operate through instances of a type. Instead, they prefer to work on the type itself. The concept of class variables or class methods appears in these scenarios. They are commonly known as **static variables** or **static methods**.

Let's consider a case where you want a variable to be shared among all objects of a class regardless of how many objects are created from the class. Other times, you may also want to maintain a single copy to handle some specific scenarios; for example, when you maintain a log file. In situations like these, you use the concept of class variables and class methods.

In Java, a nested class itself can be static. When you prefix the keyword `static` to a nested class, it is a nested static class; when it is tagged on a method, it is called a static method; and when you associate it with a variable, it is known as a static variable.

Before you proceed further, you need to remember the following points:

- Java does not allow us to create a top-level static class. The class that contains the static class is termed the outer class. A non-static nested class is termed an inner class. For your easy reference, you should remember the following:

```
class OuterClass//Cannot be static
{
      //some code may present
      class NestedClass // Can be either static or non-static
      {
```

© Vaskaran Sarcar 2020

V. Sarcar, *Interactive Object-Oriented Programming in Java*, https://doi.org/10.1007/978-1-4842-5404-2_8

```
                    //some code may present
            }
        }
```

- Java language specification (11) says that you cannot place an enum type inside the body of an inner class. This is because a nested enum type is implicitly static, and an inner class cannot have static members except for constant variables.

Class Variables and Class Methods

In Chapter 3, you got a very simple overview of static classes and methods. In this chapter, you'll explore it in more detail. To get the flow, let us begin with a simple example that contains both static and non-static members. In this demonstration, notice the supported comments, which simply inform you that static fields should be accessed in a static way.

Demonstration 1

In the following program, you have a class Rectangle, which has an area() method. The method is tagged with the static keyword, so you can invoke the method as Rectangle. area(). In this case, you do not need to create an object from the Rectangle class to invoke the method.

```
package java2e.chapter8;

class Rectangle {
    //static members
    static double length=25.5, breadth=10.0;
    static String myStaticString="I am a static string";
    //Non-static members
    int myNonStaticInt=25;
    public static double area() {
        return length * breadth;
    }
}
```

```
class Demonstration1 {

    public static void main(String[] args) {
        System.out.println("***Demonstration-1.Exploring class
        variables and class methods.***\n");
        System.out.println("Area of Rectangle is " + Rectangle.area()
        + "sq. unit");
        System.out.println("The myStaticString is : " +
        Rectangle.myStaticString);

        Rectangle rectOb=new Rectangle();
        System.out.println("The myNonStaticInt is : " + rectOb.
        myNonStaticInt);
        //Warning: The static field Rectangle.myStaticString should
        //be accessed in a static way
        //System.out.println("The myStaticString is : " + rectOb.
          myStaticString);
    }
}
```

Output:

Demonstration-1.Exploring class variables and class methods.

Area of Rectangle is 255.0sq. unit
The myStaticString is : I am a static string
The myNonStaticInt is : 25

Working with Nested Classes

Now, go through Demonstration 2 and then analyze the important characteristics of a nested static class.

Demonstration 2

This demonstration will also help you to notice the difference between a nested static class and a non-static nested (or inner) class.

203

Here are the important points to note in this demonstration.

- In this program, the top-level class Rectangle2 contains two nested classes—StaticRectangle2 and InnerClass2. As per their names, StaticRectangle2 is a static nested class and InnerClass2 is a non-static nested class (or inner class).

- Notice how an inner class is instantiated. The inner class resides inside the outer class, so you need to instantiate the outer class first. I have instantiated it in a single line of code, but it can be divided into the following two lines, which are shown in comments in the demonstration code.

  ```
  Rectangle2 rect2=new Rectangle2();
  Rectangle2.InnerClass2 innerOb2=rect2.new InnerClass2();
  ```

- Inside staticDisplay(), if you uncomment the following line:

  ```
  //System.out.println("The nonStaticOuterInt is :
  " + nonStaticOuterInt);
  ```

  you'll encounter a compile-time error, as shown in Figure 8-1:
  Cannot make a static reference to the non-static field
  nonStaticOuterInt

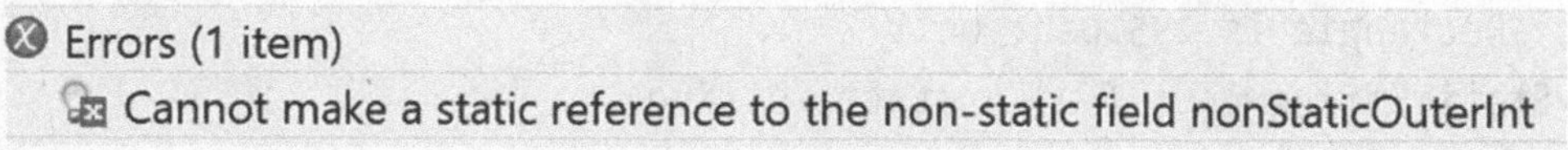

Figure 8-1. *You cannot use a static reference to refer to a non-static field*

So, it is important to note that only the static members of the outer class can be accessed inside the static class. But an inner class can have access to both the static and non-static members of the outer class (notice that the nonStaticDisplay() method does not have any issue accessing the variables of the outer class).

```
package java2e.chapter8;

class Rectangle2 {
    static int staticOuterInt = 25;
    int nonStaticOuterInt = 125;
```

```
    //Static class
    static class StaticRectangle2 {
         void staticDisplay(){
              System.out.println("Inside the static class.");
              System.out.println("The staticOuterInt is : " +
              staticOuterInt);
              //System.out.println("The nonStaticOuterInt is : " +
                nonStaticOuterInt);//error
              }

    }
    //Inner class
    class InnerClass2 {
         void nonStaticDisplay(){
              System.out.println("\nInside the inner class.");
              System.out.println("The staticOuterInt is : " +
              staticOuterInt);
              System.out.println("The nonStaticOuterInt is : " +
              nonStaticOuterInt);//ok
              }

    }

}

class Demonstration2 {

    public static void main(String[] args) {
         System.out.println("***Demonstration-2.Exploring class
         variables and class methods.***\n");

         Rectangle2.StaticRectangle2  nestedStaticOb=new Rectangle2.
         StaticRectangle2();
         nestedStaticOb.staticDisplay();
         //Instantiating an inner class
         //Inner class is contained in an outer class, so you need to
         //instantiate the outer class first.
         Rectangle2.InnerClass2 innerOb=new Rectangle2().new InnerClass2();
         //Or, use these multiple lines of codes to instantiate an
         //inner class as follows:
```

```
        /*Rectangle2 rect2=new Rectangle2();
        Rectangle2.InnerClass2 innerOb2=rect2.new InnerClass2();*/
        innerOb.nonStaticDisplay();
    }
}
```

Output:

Demonstration-2.Exploring class variables and class methods.

Inside the static class.
The staticOuterInt is : 25

Inside the inner class.
The staticOuterInt is : 25
The nonStaticOuterInt is : 125

POINTS TO REMEMBER

- In Java, a top-level static class is not allowed. A static class in Java is nested.

- A non-static nested class is often termed an **inner** class.

- Only the static members of the outer class can be accessed inside the nested static class.

- To instantiate an inner class, you need to instantiate the outer class first.

- The keyword `static` is used to denote "singular thing that can be used something like a global variable." Some developers also believe that static methods are faster than non-static methods. But, the key thing to remember is that they are not part of any instance.

- You may notice that the `main(String[] args)` method is static. So, you call this method without creating any instance of the class.

Q&A Session

8.1 In Demonstration 1, can I create an instance of the **Rectangle** class and then invoke the **area()** method?

That is not a recommended practice. In Eclipse editor, you will encounter a warning message for such an attempt. For example, if you uncomment the following line in that demonstration:

```
//System.out.println("The myStaticString is : " + rectOb.myStaticString);
```

you will get the following warning message (also shown in Figure 8-2): The static field Rectangle.myStaticString should be accessed in a static way.

> ⚠ The static field Rectangle.myStaticString should be accessed in a static way

Figure 8-2. *Warning message: The static field should be accessed in a static way.*

8.2 Can I simulate the top-level static class behavior in Java?

As already said, in Java a top-level static class is not allowed. But you can simulate something close if you follow the example that is already present in Java. For example, notice that by using built-in Math class you can find the smaller of 12 and 15, as follows:

```
System.out.println(" Minimum of (12,15) is "+ java.lang.Math.min(12, 15));
```

In this case, the Math class is behaving like a top-level static class. If you open the java.lang.Math class declaration in Eclipse editor, you will see Figure 8-3.

```
 * @since   JDK1.0
 */

public final class Math {

    /**
     * Don't let anyone instantiate this class.
     */
    private Math() {}

    /**
     * The {@code double} value that is closer than any other to
     * <i>e</i>, the base of the natural logarithms.
     */
    public static final double E = 2.7182818284590452354;
```

Figure 8-3. *A partial snapshot of the java.lang.Math class details in Eclipse editor*

So, you can make your class final, make the constructor private, and make other members of the class static to simulate a behavior that is very close to a top-level static class.

Initialization Blocks Versus Constructors

In Java, constructors cannot be static. Instead, you can use initialization blocks, which can be either static or non-static. Non-static initialization blocks are also called instance blocks. In the upcoming demonstrations, you will experience both static and non-static initialization blocks.

Static blocks have some important characteristics, as follows:

- A static block will be executed exactly once, and it comes into the picture when the class is first loaded.

- A static block can perform some common operations at the beginning of the execution flow. In general, they often initialize the static variables.

- Inside a static block, you can refer only to static variables.

- The following code segment presents a sample illustration of a static block inside a class. This code segment will be used in the upcoming demonstration.

```java
class Parent
{
    int intInstanceParent;
    static int intStaticParent, count;
    static void testMethod() {
        count++;
        System.out.println("Inside static testMethod(), count ="+ count);
    }

    //The static block
    static {
        System.out.println("Inside static block of Parent");
        //intInstanceParent=10;//error
        intStaticParent=10;//ok
```

```
        testMethod();//ok
        //System.out.println("intInstanceParent="+ intInstanceParent);
        //error
        System.out.println("intStaticParent="+ intStaticParent);
    }
}
```

- An instance block can be executed multiple times. It executes prior to
  the constructor each time you instantiate an object. Here is a sample
  illustration of an instance block inside a class. This code segment will
  also be used in the upcoming demonstration.

```
class Parent
{
    int intInstanceParent;
    static int intStaticParent, count;
    static void testMethod() {
        count++;
        System.out.println("Inside static testMethod(), count ="+ count);
    }

    //The instance block
    {
        System.out.println("\nInside instance block of parent");
        intInstanceParent++;
        intStaticParent++;
        System.out.println("intStaticParent changed to :"+ intStaticParent);
        System.out.println("intInstanceParent changed to :"+
        intInstanceParent);
        testMethod();//No compilation error
    }
}
```

- When you have all three—a static block, an instance block, and a
  constructor—the static block will be executed first, then the instance
  block will be executed, and then the constructors will follow.

- In the output of Demonstration 3, you can confirm the execution flow when a program has all of these (both kinds of initialization blocks and the constructor).

Note   To understand Demonstration 3, you may need to revisit the prior points repeatedly.

Demonstration 3

In Demonstration 3, both a parent class and a child class are present. So, as expected, when you instantiate an object, the parent class constructor will be invoked prior to the child class constructor.

```
package java2e.chapter8;

class Parent
{
    int intInstanceParent;
    static int intStaticParent, count;
    static void testMethod() {
        count++;
        System.out.println("Inside static testMethod(), count ="+ count);
    }

    //The static block
    static {
        System.out.println("Inside static block of Parent");
        //intInstanceParent=10;//error
        intStaticParent=10;//ok
        testMethod();//ok
        //System.out.println("intInstanceParent="+ intInstanceParent);//error
        System.out.println("intStaticParent="+ intStaticParent);
    }
```

```
//The instance block
{
        System.out.println("\nInside instance block of parent");
        intInstanceParent++;
        intStaticParent++;
        System.out.println("intStaticParent changed to :"+
        intStaticParent);
        System.out.println("intInstanceParent changed to :"+
        intInstanceParent);
        testMethod();//No compilation error
}
//The constructor
public Parent()
{
        System.out.println("\n Inside Parent() constructor");
        intInstanceParent++;
        intStaticParent++;
        System.out.println("intStaticParent changed to ="+ intStaticParent);
        System.out.println("intInstanceParent changed to="+
        intInstanceParent);

}

//static constructor is not possible, only public, private, and
  protected are allowed
//static Parent(){}//error
}
class Child extends Parent
{
        //The static block
        static {
                System.out.println("\nInside static block of Child");
                //intInstanceParent=10;//error
                intStaticParent++;
                System.out.println("intStaticParent="+ intStaticParent);
        }
```

211

```java
    //The instance block
    {
            System.out.println("\nInside instance block of child");
            intInstanceParent++;
            intStaticParent++;
            System.out.println("intStaticParent changed to :"+
            intStaticParent);
            System.out.println("intInstanceParent changed to :"+
            intInstanceParent);
    }
    //The constructor
    public Child()
    {
            System.out.println("\nInside Child() constructor");
            intInstanceParent++;
            intStaticParent++;
            System.out.println("intStaticParent changed to ="+
            intStaticParent);
            System.out.println("intInstanceParent changed to="+
            intInstanceParent);

    }

}
public class Demonstration3 {

    public static void main(String[] args) {
            System.out.println("***Demonstration-3.Exploring
            initialization blocks***\n");
            Parent parentOb=new Child();

            System.out.println("--------------------");
            //Again instantiating an object.
            Parent parentOb2=new Child();

    }

}
```

Output:

```
***Demonstration-3.Exploring initialization blocks***

Inside static block of Parent
Inside static testMethod(), count =1
intStaticParent =10

Inside static block of Child
intStaticParent =11

Inside instance block of parent
intStaticParent changed to :12
intInstanceParent changed to :1
Inside static testMethod(), count =2

Inside Parent() constructor
intStaticParent changed to =13
intInstanceParent changed to =2

Inside instance block of child
intStaticParent changed to :14
intInstanceParent changed to :3

Inside Child() constructor
intStaticParent changed to =15
intInstanceParent changed to =4
--------------------

Inside instance block of parent
intStaticParent changed to :16
intInstanceParent changed to :1
Inside static testMethod(), count =3

Inside Parent() constructor
intStaticParent changed to =17
intInstanceParent changed to =2

Inside instance block of child
intStaticParent changed to :18
intInstanceParent changed to :3
```

213

```
Inside Child() constructor
intStaticParent changed to =19
intInstanceParent changed to =4
```

From the demonstration, you can see the following points:

- Static blocks will be executed first.

- Prior to the constructor calls, initialization blocks will be executed. This will happen each time you instantiate an object.

- You already know that a parent class constructor will be executed prior to a child class constructor.

- Notice that `intStaticParent` kept its value and kept increasing when you instantiated an object a second time. But the same thing did not happen to `intInstanceParent`. It did not retain its last value when you instantiated another object.

Method Hiding Versus Method Overriding

In Chapter 5, Q&A 5.24, you saw a demonstration that differentiated hiding from overriding. At that time, you were not familiar with the `static` keyword in detail. So, let's revisit the concept.

Method hiding is an important concept in Java. The JLS11 says this:

"If a class C declares or inherits a `static` method m, then m is said to hide any method m', where the signature of m is a subsignature (§8.4.2) of the signature of m', in the superclasses and superinterfaces of C that would otherwise be accessible (§6.6) to code in C. It is a compile-time error if a `static` method hides an instance method."

To explain the concept better, I'll demonstrate another program to compare method hiding with method overriding. To understand this program, you need to remember the following: *When a parent class and the derived class contain `static` methods with the same signature, the parent class's static method is hidden by the derived class's static method.*

For non-static methods, method calls are decided at runtime (which object you are pointing to at that moment), and overriding plays its role. But in the case of static methods, method calls are decided at compile time only, so it is not dependent on which object you are pointing to at runtime. So, in Chapter 5, you noticed the line: "method hiding is in no way related to runtime polymorphism."

Demonstration 4

Now let's analyze the following demonstration and output for better understanding:

```java
package java2e.chapter8;

class Parent4 {
    static void staticMethod() {
        System.out.println("I am a static method in Parent4.");
    }

    void nonStaticMethod() {
        System.out.println("A non-static method in Parent4.");
    }
}

class Child4 extends Parent4 {
    static void staticMethod() {
        System.out.println("Inside Child4 class, I am hiding the
        parent class static method.");
    }

    void nonStaticMethod() {
        System.out.println("Overriding a non-static method in Parent4.");
    }
}

class Demonstration4 {
    public static void main(String[] args) {
        System.out.println("***Demonstration-4.Derived class method
        hides the static method of the parent class***\n");
        Child4.staticMethod();// Hides the parent class method
        // Checking dynamic method dispatch
        Parent4 parent = new Child4();
        Parent4.staticMethod();//Invokes parent class method
        System.out.println("xxx-Doing a bad practice.Invoking a static
        method on instance.-xxx");
        parent.staticMethod();//Bad practice:Invokes parent class method
        parent.nonStaticMethod();// Invokes child class method
```

```
            /* Bad practice:
            Following code can also invoke the child class static method.
            But you'll receive the  warning message saying:
             "staticMethod() from the type Child4 should be accessed in a
             static way"*/
            //new Child4().staticMethod();
    }
}
```

Output:

```
***Demonstration-4.Derived class method hides the static method of the
parent class***

Inside Child4 class,I am hiding the parent class static method.
I am a static method in Parent4.
xxx-Doing a bad practice.Invoking a static method on instance.-xxx
I am a static method in Parent4.
Overriding a non-static method in Parent4.
```

Here, Child4.staticMethod() hides the parent class method. Also, you can see that parent.nonStaticMethod() invokes the child class method, but parent. staticMethod() invokes the parent class method, because, in case of method hiding, the reference variable (which is of Parent type) matters and does not depend on the actual calling object.

POINTS TO REMEMBER

- When a parent class and the derived class contain static methods with the same signature, the subclass static method hides the parent class static method.

- In the case of method hiding, the invoked method version does not depend on the invoking object; instead, it depends on the reference type.

- Invoking static methods with instances is not a recommended practice at all. It is presented here only to demonstrate to you how method hiding differs from method overriding.

Q&A Session

8.3 I understand that I cannot override static methods in Java by design. But what may be the probable causes behind this design?

For static methods, method calls are decided at compile time only; that is, it is not dependent on which object you are pointing to at runtime. But for non-static methods, method calls can be decided at runtime (i.e., the actual object to which you are pointing at that moment).

Method Overloading

The following demonstration shows that you can overload static methods.

Demonstration 5

In this program, the StaticDemo5 class contains a different, overloaded version of the showMe() method.

```java
package java2e.chapter8;

class StaticDemo5 {
    static void showMe() {
        System.out.println("Inside showMe().");
    }
    static void showMe(String s) {
        System.out.println("Hi," + s +".You are inside showMe
        (String s) now.");
    }
    static void showMe(int i) {
        System.out.println("Inside showMe(int i),you have supplied the
        argument " + i +".");
    }
}

class Demonstration5 {
    public static void main(String[] args) {
```

```
        System.out.println("***Demonstration-5.Static methods can be
        overloaded***\n");
        StaticDemo5.showMe();
        StaticDemo5.showMe("John");
        StaticDemo5.showMe(25);
    }
}
```

Output:

```
***Demonstration-5.Static methods can be overloaded***

Inside showMe().
Hi, John.You are inside showMe(String s) now.
Inside showMe(int i),you have supplied the argument 25.
```

8.4 Can you compile the following code?

```
class Quiz1 {
    static void showMe() {
        System.out.println("Static method");
    }

    void showMe() {
        System.out.println("Non-static method");
    }
}
```

No. In this case, the compiler will raise the following error in Eclipse IDE: Duplicate method showMe() in type Quiz1 (Figure 8-4).

⊗ Errors (2 items)
   🔲 Duplicate method showMe() in type Quiz1
   🔲 Duplicate method showMe() in type Quiz1

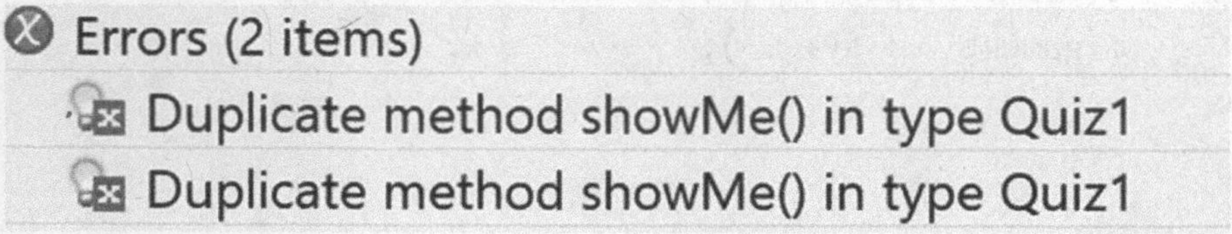

Figure 8-4. *The presence of* static *keyword cannot ensure method overloading*

The concept of method overloading works fine if the method signatures are different. In this case, the inclusion of a static keyword before a method name is not considered a different signature. You can also explain this behavior from a different perspective. For example, you know that Java allows you to call a static method through objects. Now, in a case like this, if you have another non-static method with the same signature, the Java compiler will be confused as to which one to call.

8.5 Can you compile the following code?

```java
class Quiz2 {
    int i;
    static void showMe() {
        this.i = 7;
        System.out.println("Static method");
    }
}
```

No. In this case, the compiler will raise the error shown in Figure 8-5 in Eclipse IDE:

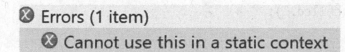

Figure 8-5. *The keyword this cannot be used in a static context*

In this context, you can remember that the this keyword is used in the context of the current object. But static methods can be called with the class name (and this is the true intention of the keyword static). There is no need to create an object to call a class method (or a static method).

219

Q&A Session

8.6 In C#, static constructors are allowed, but in Java they are not allowed. What is the key advantage that a developer can achieve with static constructors?

Each programming language has its own pros and cons. The designers obviously can have different thoughts behind a particular feature. In C#, a top-level static class is also allowed with static constructors. They believe that this feature can be useful for writing log entries. This feature can also be used to create wrapper classes for unmanaged code (which is supported in C#).

Static Methods in Interfaces

From Java 8 onward, you can add static methods to an interface. Here is a sample for you:

```
interface MyInterface {
     // The static interface method (Java 8 onward)
     static void staticMethod() {
          System.out.println("\nStatic interface method in MyInterface
          is called.");
     }
}
```

And similar to static methods in a class, you can invoke a static method in an interface by adding the interface name after the period, like the following:

```
MyInterface.staticMethod();
```

It is important to note that if a class implements MyInterface, the implementing class can have its own version of staticMethod(), but in that case, you cannot use the @Override annotation. Consider the following code segment:

```
class ClassDemo8 implements MyInterface{
     //@Override  <-Will cause Error
     public static void staticMethod() {
          System.out.println("This is the static method of the
          implementing class(ClassDemo8).");
          System.out.println("You cannot override the static method in
          MyInterface");
     }
```

Demonstration 6

You'll finish this chapter with Demonstration 6, in which you will see a comparative study of a traditional interface method, a default interface method, and a static interface method.

```
package java2e.chapter8;

interface MyInterface {
    // The traditional interface method
    void traditionalInterfaceMethod();

    // The default interface method
    default void defaultInterfaceMethod() {
        System.out.println("Default interface method in MyInterface is
        called.");
    }

    // The static interface method (Java 8 onward)
    static void staticMethod() {
        System.out.println("Static interface method in MyInterface is
        called.");
    }
}

class ClassDemo8 implements MyInterface {
    @Override
    public void traditionalInterfaceMethod() {
        System.out.println("Overriding the
        traditionalInterfaceMethod() in ClassDemo8");
    }

    @Override
    public void defaultInterfaceMethod() {
        System.out.println("Overriding the defaultInterfaceMethod() in
        ClassDemo8");
    }
```

221

```java
        // @Override //Will cause Error
        public static void staticMethod() {
                System.out.println("This is the static method of the
                implementing class(ClassDemo8).");
                System.out.println("You cannot override the static method in
                MyInterface.");
        }

}

class Demonstration6 {

        public static void main(String[] args) {
                System.out.println("***Demonstration-6.Exploring static
                methods in an interface.***\n");
                System.out.println("Calling static interface method.");
                MyInterface.staticMethod();
                MyInterface inter = new ClassDemo8();
                System.out.println("\nCalling the default interface method
                from implementing class.");
                inter.defaultInterfaceMethod();
                System.out.println("\nCalling the traditional interface method
                from implementing class.");
                inter.traditionalInterfaceMethod();
                System.out.println("\nCalling the static method from
                implementing class.");
                ClassDemo8.staticMethod();
        // Compile-time error: The static method of interface MyInterface
        //can only be accesed as MyInterface.staticMethod();
                // inter.staticMethod();//error
        }
}
```

Output:

```
***Demonstration-6.Exploring static methods in an interface.***

Calling static interface method.
Static interface method in MyInterface is called.
```

```
Calling the default interface method from implementing class.
Overriding the defaultInterfaceMethod() in ClassDemo8

Calling the traditional interface method from implementing class.
Overriding the traditionalInterfaceMethod() in ClassDemo8

Calling the static method from implementing class.
This is the static method of the implementing class(ClassDemo8).
You cannot override the static method in MyInterface.
```

The output is self-explanatory. Still, I want to draw your attention to the following points:

- You can apply @Override annotation to the default method in the implementing class, but if you apply it to the static method, you will receive a compile-time error.

- Notice that the following line

  ```
  // inter.staticMethod();//error
  ```

  will cause a compile-time error. (In this context, can you remember that static methods in Java cannot be overridden?) So, you need to invoke the static methods of an interface with interface name like the following:

  ```
  MyInterface.staticMethod();//ok
  ```

Summary

This chapter covered the following:

- The concepts of static classes, methods, and variables

- Different types of initialization blocks and their usage

- Method hiding versus method overriding in Java revisited

- Static methods in an interface and how they are different from traditional interface methods or default methods

- How these concepts can be implemented in Java and the restrictions associated with them

CHAPTER 9

Quick Recap of OOP Principles

Welcome to the final chapter of Part I. So far, you have learned the fundamentals of object-oriented programming with the basic building blocks in Java. Before you proceed to Part II, let's review the core principles that you have already covered in this book.

- **Class and objects**. Throughout the book, in almost every example, I have used different types of classes and objects. The use of the static keyword was little bit different, and you accessed the static fields through the class names.

- **Polymorphism**. Both types of polymorphism were covered. Compile-time polymorphism was covered through method overloading, and runtime polymorphism was covered through method overriding techniques. You have seen that dynamic method dispatch is an important concept in Java.

- **Abstraction**. This feature was tested through abstract classes and interfaces.

- **Encapsulation**. Each class with different access modifiers can be considered in this category. But a better example can be a class with a private member and a getter-setter. As per experts' suggestions, you should make your instance variables private and access them through public getter-setter methods.

- **Inheritance**. You explored different types of inheritance in multiple chapters.

© Vaskaran Sarcar 2020
V. Sarcar, *Interactive Object-Oriented Programming in Java*, https://doi.org/10.1007/978-1-4842-5404-2_9

- **Message passing**. Normally, a message for an object is to request to invoke a method in the receiving object. In simple words, message passing is just communication among different objects. This feature is very common in a multi-threaded environment. But you experimented with runtime polymorphisms, in which a super class reference pointed to a subclass object, and this can also be considered in this category. Multi-threading is discussed in Chapter 11 in the book.

- **Dynamic binding**. Runtime polymorphism through method overriding examples can fall into this category.

Q&A Session

9.1 Can you summarize the difference between abstraction and encapsulation?

The process of wrapping up the data and methods into a single entity is known as **encapsulation**. Using this technique, you can prevent arbitrary and unsecured access to your data. You can use different access modifiers to restrict direct access to your data. But the use of getter and setter methods is a better example in this category. In case of encapsulation, your entire code works like a capsule, so it is termed as an encapsulation.

In abstraction, you show the essential features but hide the detailed implementation (or background details) from the user; for example, when you use a remote control to switch on a television, the internal circuits of the device are not your concern. You are OK with the device as long as your preferred channel appears properly on your television once the button is pressed.

Note   Encapsulation focuses on the true implementation, that is, *how* you can make an implementation, but abstraction focuses on *what* the implementation can do for you. But these concepts are interrelated. So, for a nice abstraction, your implementation should be properly encapsulated.

Grady Booch, in his famous book *Object-Oriented Analysis and Design with Applications* (Third Edition, Addison-Wesley), says the following: "Abstraction focuses on the observable behavior of an object, whereas encapsulation focuses on the implementation that gives rise to this behavior. Encapsulation is most often achieved through information hiding (not just data hiding), which is the process of hiding all the secrets of an object that do not contribute to its essential characteristics."

You can revisit the Chapter 1 for these definitions.

9.2 Which one is faster between these—compile-time polymorphism or runtime polymorphism?

In general, if you resolve a call (for example, invocation of a method) early, it is faster. This is why you can conclude that compile-time binding is faster than runtime binding or polymorphism—because it is known in advance which method to call.

9.3 You told us earlier that inheritance might not always provide the best solution. Can you please elaborate?

In some cases, composition can provide a better solution. But to understand composition, you may need to know these concepts:

- Association

- Aggregation

Association can be one way or both ways. When you see this kind of UML diagram, it means ClassA knows about ClassB, but the reverse is not true.

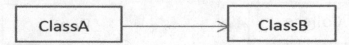

The following diagram indicates a two-way association because both classes know each other.

227

Consider an example. In a college, a student can learn from multiple teachers, and a teacher can teach multiple students. There is no *ownership* in this kind of relationship. So, when you represent them with classes and objects in programming, you can say that both kinds of objects can be created and deleted independently.

Aggregation is a stronger type of association. The aggregation between a professor and department can be represented as follows.

Let's go deeper. Suppose that Professor X submits his resignation letter to his existing organization to join a new organization. Although both Professor X and his former institution can survive without each other, Professor X needs to associate himself with a department in an institution. In this situation, you'd say that the department is the owner of this relationship and the department has professors.

Similarly, you can say that a human body has hands, a car has seats, a bike has tires, and so forth.

Note   In general, you say that a department has a professor. This is why an association relationship is also known as **"has-a"** relationship. (You can note down the key difference with inheritance here. Inheritance is associated with the **"is-a"** relationship.

Composition is a stronger form of aggregation, and this time you have a filled diamond in place.

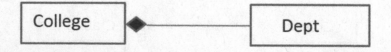

A department in a college cannot exist without the college. The college only creates or closes its departments. (You can argue that if there is no department at all, a college cannot exist, but you do not need to complicate things by considering this type of corner case.) In other words, the lifetime of a department entirely depends on its college.

This is also known as a **death relationship** because if you destroy the college, all of its departments are destroyed automatically. Similarly, you can say the hands (or legs, etc.) of a human being cannot exist without the body.

Revisiting the Diamond Problem

To show the power of aggregation/composition, let's revisit the diamond problem that was discussed in Chapter 4, and then analyze the following program. Let's start with the following code.

```
class Parent {
      public void show() {
            System.out.println("I am in Parent");
      }
}

class Child1 extends Parent {
      public void show() {
            System.out.println("I am in Child1");
      }
}

class Child2 extends Parent {
      public void show() {
            System.out.println("I am in Child2");
      }
}
```

Java does not allow you to write something like the following:

```
class GrandChild extends Child1,Child2// Error: Not supported in Java
{
      public void show() {
            System.out.println("I am in Grandchild");
      }
}
```

Demonstration 1

Now, let's see how to handle this situation with aggregation (a lighter form of composition). Consider the following code:

```java
package java2e.chapter9;

class Parent {
    public void show() {
        System.out.println("I am in Parent");
    }
}

class Child1 extends Parent {
    @Override
    public void show() {
        System.out.println("I am in Child1");
    }
}

class Child2 extends Parent {
    @Override
    public void show() {
        System.out.println("I am in Child2");
    }
}

//Not supported in Java
/*
 * class GrandChild extends Child1,Child2// Error: Not supported in Java {
 * public void show() { System.out.println("I am in Grandchild"); } }
 */
class GrandChild {
    Child1 ch1 ;
    Child2 ch2 ;
    GrandChild() {
        ch1 = new Child1();
        ch2 = new Child2();
    }
```

```
    public void showFromChild1() {
        ch1.show();
    }

    public void showFromChild2() {
        ch2.show();
    }
}
```

And here is code for Demonstration1.java which contains the main() method:

```
class Demonstration1 {
    public static void main(String[] args) {
        System.out.println("***Demonstration-1.The concept of aggregation/
        composition to handle the diamond Problem***\n");
        GrandChild gChild = new GrandChild();
        gChild.showFromChild1();
        gChild.showFromChild2();
    }
}
```

Output:

```
***Demonstration-1.The concept of aggregation/composition to handle the
diamond Problem***

I am in Child1
I am in Child2
```

You can see that both Class1 and Class2 have overridden their parent's show() method. And the Grandchild class doesn't have its own show() method. Still, you can invoke those class-specific methods through the Grandchild object.

The Grandchild class allows you to create the objects from both Class1 and Class2 inside its constructor body. In the prior example, though the Child1 and Child2 objects can survive without the Grandchild objects, there are no individual objects from either Class1 or Class2. So, in this implementation, if Grandchild objects are not present in your application (let's say, have been garbage collected), there will be no Class1 or Class2 object that can reside inside the system. You can also place some restrictions on users so that they are not able to create objects of Class1 and Class2 directly inside the application; for simplicity, I have ignored that part.

231

Note   You are aware of generalization, specialization, and realization. You have used these concepts in your applications. When your class extends another class (i.e., inheritance), you use the concepts of **generalization** and **specialization**; for example, a footballer (a.k.a. a soccer player) is a special kind (specialization) of athlete. Or, you can say that both a footballer and a basketball player are athletes (generalization). And when your class implements an interface, you use the concept of **realization**.

Q&A Session

9.4 In Demonstration 1, inside the client code, I can instantiate a `Child1` or `Child2` object. For example, I can use the following line of code:

```
Child1 child1=new Child1();
```

And in such a case, a `Child1` object can persist in my system without a `GrandChild` object. Is this understanding correct?

Yes. You can say that this is an example of aggregation, or a lighter form of composition. But you can always restrict the user to directly instantiating objects from the `Parent`, `Child1`, or `Child2` classes. For example, you can place these classes inside a package and let your `Grandchild` class be the only public class inside that. Inside the client code, one can create `GrandChild` objects only.

Consider the structure in Figure 9-1, which is the Package Explorer view for the upcoming demonstration.

- ✓ ⊞ java2e.chapter9
  - › Demonstration1.java
- ✓ ⊞ java2e.chapter9.mypackage
  - › Child1.java
  - › Child2.java
  - › GrandChild.java
  - › Parent.java

Figure 9-1. *Using composition to solve the diamond problem*

And the classes inside the package (java2e.chapter9.mypackage) are as follows (key changes are shown in bold):

//Parent.java

package java2e.chapter9.mypackage;

```java
class Parent {
    public void show() {
        System.out.println("I am in Parent");
    }
}
```

//Child1.java
package java2e.chapter9.mypackage;

```java
class Child1 extends Parent {
    @Override
    public void show() {
        System.out.println("I am in Child1");
    }
}
```

//Child2.java
package java2e.chapter9.mypackage;

```java
class Child2 extends Parent {
    @Override
    public void show() {
        System.out.println("I am in Child2");
    }
}
```

//GrandChild.java
package java2e.chapter9.mypackage;

```java
public class GrandChild { //This class is public here
    Child1 ch1 ;
    Child2 ch2 ;
```

```
    public GrandChild() {
        ch1 = new Child1();
        ch2 = new Child2();
    }

    public void showFromChild1() {
        ch1.show();
    }

    public void showFromChild2() {
        ch2.show();
    }
}
```

The client code may look like the following:

//Demonstration1.java
```
package java2e.chapter9;

import java2e.chapter9.mypackage.GrandChild;

class Demonstration1 {

    public static void main(String[] args) {
        System.out.println("***Demonstration-1.The concept of
        aggregation/composition to handle the diamond Problem***\n");
        //Child1 child1=new Child1();//Error: not visible to client
        //Child2 child1=new Child2();//Error: not visible to client
        GrandChild gChild = new GrandChild();
        gChild.showFromChild1();
        gChild.showFromChild2();
    }
}
```

Now, if you execute the program, you'll receive the same output, but in this structure you allow an outsider to create only a Grandchild object. So, in such a case, you provide more restriction, and your application will not hold any object from Child1 or Child2 if there is no GrandChild object.

9.5 What are the challenges and drawbacks of OOP?

Many experts believe that, in general, the size of object-oriented programs is larger. Due to the larger size, you may need more storage (but nowadays, these issues hardly matter).

Some developers find difficulties in the object-oriented programming style. They may still prefer other approaches, such as structured programming, logic programming, and so forth, so if they are forced to work in an OOP environment, life becomes tough for them.

It is also true that you cannot efficiently solve every real-world problem in the object-oriented style. There are always some problems that can be solved better with a different approach; for example, a particular sudoku puzzle can be solved much more easily with Prolog (a logic programming language) than with Java (an object-oriented programming language).

Also, a common problem with the object-oriented style may arise when you need to find bugs in an execution flow, particularly if, in your codebase, there are many small methods (or functions) that call each other for a simple event. However, I personally like object-oriented programming because I believe that its merits are greater than its demerits.

Summary

This chapter included the following:

- A quick review of the core OOP principles in this book

- How to differentiate abstraction from encapsulation

- How to implement the concept of composition/aggregation in your application

- The challenges and drawbacks associated with OOP

PART II

Get Familiar with Advanced Programming

CHAPTER 10

Managing Exceptions

When you write code for your application, you expect that it will execute without any problems. So, it is important to manage and detect all possible errors in your program. Even so, sometimes you may encounter surprises during program execution. These surprises may occur for various reasons, such as some careless mistake in the program, implementation of incorrect logic, loopholes in the code paths of the program, and so on. However, it is also true that many of the failures are beyond the control of a programmer. Programmers often term these unwanted situations as *exceptions*. Handling these exceptions is essential when you write any application.

Types of Mistakes

Normally, you can broadly classify the mistakes (or errors) in a program into two categories, as follows:

- Compile-time error

- Runtime error

Compile-time errors are detected by the Java compiler and are easy to detect. The Java compiler acts as your friend to figure out the error details. For example, it may point out a line number (where the error is encountered) and display a brief description of the error. Once you correct it, you need to recompile it to check whether the updated program is ready for execution. Sometimes, you may need to fix multiple errors, and, as a result, multiple recompilations may be needed. The Java compiler will not generate the class file if it finds these kinds of errors in your program.

© Vaskaran Sarcar 2020
V. Sarcar, *Interactive Object-Oriented Programming in Java*, https://doi.org/10.1007/978-1-4842-5404-2_10

Let's consider some typographical errors in the following program:

```
package java2e.chapter10;

class IncorrectClass //{
        void SampleMethod() {
                System.out.println("Semicolon missing") //error
        }
}
```

Here, the Java compiler will display error messages. In Eclipse, you can see the error description and the corresponding line numbers, as shown in Figure 10-1.

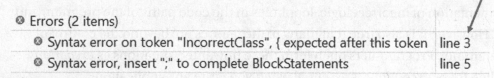

Figure 10-1. *Two typographical errors in Eclipse IDE*

So, you can see that you missed the bracket { after the class definition and you forgot to put a semicolon at the end of line number 5.

This type of error is common but sometimes hard to find with human eyes at the very beginning. So, the Java compiler will rescue you in these situations.

On the other hand, runtime errors are challenging. In this case, you get a green signal from the compiler, and on successful compilation you get the .class file, but your program still produces wrong results and may terminate prematurely. Here are some examples of runtime errors that can be caused by the following operations:

- Dividing an integer by 0

- Trying to access an array element that is out of bounds of an array

- Using a null object to invoke a method

- Trying to do invalid conversions, such as trying to convert an invalid string to an integer

Intentionally in some places, I am using the term *mistake* instead of *error*. The reason will be revealed to you shortly.

Definition of Exception

You can define an exception as an event that breaks the normal execution or the instruction flow of the program.

When exceptional situations arise, an exception object is created and thrown into the method that created the exception. That method may or may not handle the exception. If it cannot handle the exception, it will pass the responsibility to another method. (Similar to our daily life, when a situation goes beyond our control, we seek advice from others.) If there is no method to take responsibility for handling a particular exception, an error dialog box appears (indicating an unhandled exception), and the execution of the program stops.

POINTS TO REMEMBER

An exception-handling mechanism deals with runtime errors, and if they are not handled properly, an application will produce unwanted output, and it may die prematurely. Therefore, you should try to write applications that can detect and handle surprises in a graceful manner and prevent the premature death of the application.

Demonstration 1

Let's begin with a simple example. The following program compiles successfully, but it will raise an exception during runtime because in this program, the divisor (b) becomes 0 prior to the division operation. The application produces a runtime error because, in this case, you are trying to divide 100 by 0.

```
package java2e.chapter10;

class Demonstration1 {

    public static void main(String[] args) {
        System.out.println("***Demonstration-1.Exploring
        Exceptions.***");
        int a = 100, b = 2, result;
        b -= 2;//b beomes 0
```

```
        result = a / b;
        System.out.println("The result of a/b is :" + result);
    }
}
```

Output:

```
***Demonstration-1.Exploring Exceptions.***
Exception in thread "main" java.lang.ArithmeticException: / by zero
at java2e.chapter10.Demonstration1.main(Demonstration1.java:9)
```

Key Points of the Exception-handling Mechanism

Before you proceed further, I'll highlight some key points of the exception-handling mechanism. You may need to come back to these points repeatedly. It is suggested that once you finish this chapter, you come back here to review your understanding of exception handling in Java.

- An exceptional object is created when a runtime error occurs. So, a Java exception is basically an object to describe an erroneous situation.

- Any method in an application can raise surprises during the application's runtime. If such a situation occurs, in programming terminology, you say that the method has thrown an exception.

- You use the following keywords to deal with Java exceptions: try, catch, throw, throws, and finally.

- You try to guard against an exception with a try-catch block. The code that may throw an exception is placed inside a try block, and this exceptional situation is handled inside a catch block. But if there is no exception raised in the try block, the catch blocks are bypassed completely.

- You can associate multiple catch blocks with a try block. When a particular catch block handles the sudden surprise (the exception), you say that the catch block has caught the exception.

- The code in the finally block must execute. A finally block is generally placed after a try block or a try-catch block. This block is used to perform some housekeeping so that the application can be gracefully closed. For example, if a file is already opened, you should close it here, or if you already allocated some resources, those should be released inside this block.

- When an exception is raised inside a try block, the control jumps to the respective catch or finally block. The remaining part of the try block will not execute.

- Exceptions follow the inheritance hierarchy. So, it is important to remember the hierarchy, shown in Figure 10-2.

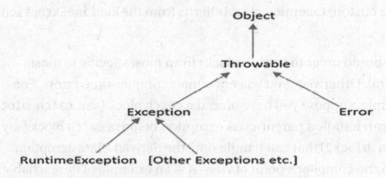

Figure 10-2. Exception hierarchy

- You can see that both the Exception class and the Error class are subclasses of the Throwable class, which in turn derives from Object (in the java.lang package). By other exceptions, I mean classes like IOException (already defined in Java), our own custom exception classes (not defined in Java), and so on. So, you can simply say that in Java, the Throwable class is the ultimate super class of all errors and exceptions.

- Exceptions are broadly categorized into two types: **checked** and **unchecked**. The runtime exception classes (RuntimeException class and its subclasses) and error classes (Error class and its subclasses) fall into the category of unchecked exceptions, and the others remaining are called checked exceptions. You'll see a detailed discussion of each category shortly, and Q&A 10.8 will summarize the details.

- This chapter primarily focuses on runtime exceptions. Errors, in general, are caused by some catastrophic failures, like JVM being out of memory, stack overflow, and so on. You can hardly do anything with them. The Java runtime environment itself needs to take care of these severe situations.

- When you create your custom exception classes, in general, you'll subclass from the Exception class. But it is not a rule. So, in Demonstration 7, you'll see that a custom exception class extends from the Throwable class, and in Demonstration 8, you will notice that a custom exception class inherits from the RuntimeException class.

- You should order the catch blocks from most specific to most general. Otherwise, you will encounter compile-time errors. For example, suppose you have placed a catch block (say, catch block1) that can handle a parent-class exception before a catch block (say catch block2) that can handle only the derived-class exception. From the compiler's point of view, it is an example of unreachable code, because in this case catch block1 is always capable of handling the exceptions that catch block2 can handle. Therefore, control does not need to reach catch block2 at all. You will examine this scenario in an upcoming example.

- You can use any of these combinations: try-catch, try-catch-finally, or try-finally.

- The Java runtime system can generate exceptions. At the same time, you can also create your own exception class and throw your own exception.

- If you do not handle exceptions, a default handler of the Java runtime system will handle it on your behalf, and the program may die prematurely.

POINTS TO REMEMBER

- In Java, the Throwable class is the ultimate super class of all errors and exceptions.

- In an exception-handling mechanism, there is a key difference between Java and C#. There is no concept of the throws keyword in C#. This is a hot topic of debate.

Demonstration 2

Now, let's see how you can handle the exception that was encountered in the previous example.

```
package java2e.chapter10;

public class Demonstration2 {

    public static void main(String[] args) {
        System.out.println("***Demonstration-2.Exploring Exceptions-
        Demonstration1 is modified.***");
        int a = 100, b = 2, result;
        b -= 2;// b beomes 0
        try {
            result = a / b;
            System.out.println(" So, the result of a/b is : " +
            result);
        } catch (Exception ex) {
            System.out.println("Encountered an exception " +
            ex.getMessage());
            System.out.print("Here is the stack trace:");
            ex.printStackTrace();
        } finally {
            System.out.println("I am in finally. You cannot skip me!");
        }
    }
}
```

245

Output:

```
***Demonstration-2.Exploring Exceptions-Demonstration1 is modified.***
Encountered an exception / by zero
Here is the stack trace:java.lang.ArithmeticException: / by zero
I am in finally. You cannot skip me!
at java2e.chapter10.Demonstration2.main(Demonstration2.java:10)
```

You can confirm the following points from the output of the program:

- When an exception was raised inside a try block, the control jumped to the respective catch block. The remaining part of the try block did not execute. (Notice that you are not seeing the line "So, the result of a/b is :" in the output.)

- The code in the finally block executed even though the program encountered an exception. (Notice the line "I am in finally. You cannot skip me!" in the output).

- To get the details of the exception, some built-in methods are already defined in the java.lang.Throwable class. The getMessage(), printStackTrace(), getCause(), etc. are some common examples in this category. I have used two of them—getMessage() and printStackTrace()—in this demonstration. For your immediate reference, I am just picking a sample source code snapshot to get details of the getMessage() method from Eclipse IDE, which is shown in Figure 10-3.

```
/**
 * Returns the detail message string of this throwable.
 *
 * @return  the detail message string of this {@code Throwable} instance
 *          (which may be {@code null}).
 */
public String getMessage() {
    return detailMessage;
}
```

Figure 10-3. *A sample source code snapshot from Eclipse IDE*

Q&A Session

10.1 I could easily put an if block like if(b==0) before the division operation to avoid a 0 divisor, and in that case I could easily exclude the use of the try-catch block. Is this understanding correct?

You are considering only this simple example, which is why it appears to you this way. Yes, in this case, you can guard your code using your proposed method. However, think of a case where the value of b is also computed at runtime (for example, you may pick a random value from a specified range, and you cannot predict the value earlier). Also, if you need to put guards like this in all probable cases, your code may look clumsy and difficult to read. But if you like a defensive programming style, you may keep asking for a valid input. So, at the end, it's your choice as to how you want to design your software.

Demonstration 3

Now, consider the following example, which examines how to handle multiple type exceptions with multiple catch blocks. In the following program, the value of the integer b can be 0, 1, or 2. This value is generated at random. So, you cannot predict the value. Based on the generated value, you may encounter different types of exceptions. To understand it better, you may need to visit the output and analysis section multiple times.

```
package java2e.chapter10;

import java.util.Random;

public class Demonstration3 {
    public static void main(String[] args) {
        System.out.println("***Demonstration-3.Handling multiple
        Exceptions***");
        int a = 5;
        Random randomGenerator = new Random();
        // Will generate 0 to 2.
        int b = randomGenerator.nextInt(3);
        System.out.println("Current value of b is : " + b);
        int c = 0;
```

```
        try {
                / Case-1:if b=0,it will raise ArithmeticException*/
                c = a / b;
                System.out.println("c=" + c);
                int[] arr = new int[2];
                arr[0] = 0;
                arr[1] = c + 1;
                if (b % 2 == 0) {
                        /* Case-2: (b is not zero here) it will raise
                        ArrayIndexOutOfBoundsException*/
                        arr[2] = c + 2;
                } else {
                        Object myObject = null;
                        // case-3: It raises NullPointerException
                        int hashcode = myObject.hashCode();
                }
        } catch (ArithmeticException ex) {
                System.out.println("Caught the ArithmeticException :" +
                ex.getMessage());
                ex.printStackTrace();
        } catch (ArrayIndexOutOfBoundsException ex) {
                System.out.println("Caught the
                ArrayIndexOutOfBoundsException :" + ex.getMessage());
                ex.printStackTrace();
        } catch (Exception ex) {
                System.out.println("Caught the Exception :" +
                ex.getMessage());
                ex.printStackTrace();
        } finally {
                System.out.println("I am finally here");
        }
    }
}
```

Output:

When you compile and run the program, you may notice any of the following outputs. I have shown all possible outputs in different runs. You may get a different order because the value of b is generated at random.

Case 1:

```
***Demonstration-3.Handling multiple Exceptions***
Current value of b is : 1
c=5
Caught the Exception :null
I am finally here
java.lang.NullPointerException          at java2e.chapter10.Demonstration3.
main(Demonstration3.java:27)
```

Case 2:

```
***Demonstration-3.Handling multiple Exceptions***
Current value of b is : 2
c=2
Caught the ArrayIndexOutOfBoundsException :2
I am finally herejava.lang.ArrayIndexOutOfBoundsException: 2
at java2e.chapter10.Demonstration3.main(Demonstration3.java:23)
```

Case 3:

```
***Demonstration-3.Handling multiple Exceptions***
Current value of b is : 0
Caught the ArithmeticException :/ by zero
I am finally here
java.lang.ArithmeticException: / by zero at java2e.chapter10.
Demonstration3.main(Demonstration3.java:16)
```

You can observe the following points from the output of the program:

- When an exception is raised, only one catch block is executed. For example, if the block catch (ArithmeticException ex){..} can handle the exception, the block catch (Exception ex){..} does not need to handle the exception again.

- In the preceding program, all types of exceptions can be caught inside the catch (Exception ex) block, and so this block must be placed as the last catch block. For example, in this case:

    - The ArithmeticException class derives from the RuntimeException class, which in turn derives from the Exception class.

    - The ArrayIndexOutOfBoundsException class derives from the IndexOutOfBoundsException class, which in turn derives from the RuntimeException class, which in turn derives from the Exception class.

Note   In Eclipse, you can hover your mouse pointer on the exception name and then choose the option "Open Declaration" to reveal the inheritance hierarchy.

Multiple catch Clauses

From Java 7 onward, you can use a different variation of the catch clause. Now a single catch block can be used to catch multiple exception types. The following code snippet shows how to use multiple catch clauses in a common block:

```
//Java 7 onward, you can write multiple catch clauses like the following
catch (ArithmeticException | ArrayIndexOutOfBoundsException ex)
{  System.out.println("Caught either ArithmeticException or
ArrayIndexOutOfBoundsException :" + ex.getMessage());
                ex.printStackTrace();
        }
```

10.2 Can you predict the output of the following?

```
package java2e.chapter10;

import java.util.Random;
```

```java
public class Quiz1 {

    public static void main(String[] args) {
        System.out.println("***Quiz1.It is about how to place the
        catch clauses in the program.***");
        int a = 5;
        Random randomGenerator = new Random();
        // Will generate 0 to 2.
        int b = randomGenerator.nextInt(3);
        System.out.println("Current value of b is : " + b);
        int c = 0;
        try {
                //Here b=0,it will raise an ArithmeticException
                c = a / b;
                System.out.println("c=" + c);
        }
        //Incorrect placement of following catch clause
        catch (Exception ex) {
                System.out.println("Caught the Exception :" +
                ex.getMessage());
                ex.printStackTrace();
        }
    //Java 7 onward, you can write multiple catch clauses like the
    //following
        catch (ArithmeticException | ArrayIndexOutOfBoundsException  ex) {
                System.out.println("Caught either ArithmeticException or
                ArrayIndexOutOfBoundsException  :" + ex.getMessage());
                ex.printStackTrace();
        }

    //Correct placement of the catch clause
        /*catch (Exception ex) {
                System.out.println("Caught the Exception :" +
                ex.getMessage());
                ex.printStackTrace();
```

```
        }*/finally {
            System.out.println("I am finally here");
        }
    }
}
```

You'll encounter a compile-time error: Unreachable catch block for ArithmeticException. It is already handled in the catch block for Exception, as shown in Figure 10-4.

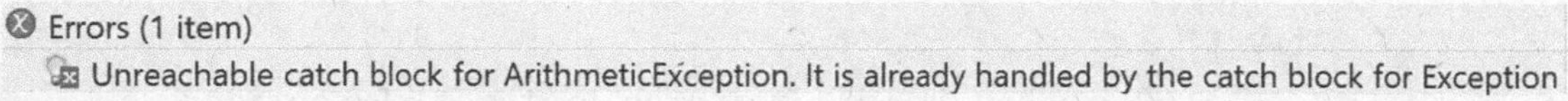

⊗ Errors (1 item)
   🖼 Unreachable catch block for ArithmeticException. It is already handled by the catch block for Exception

Figure 10-4. *Unreachable catch block*

Exceptions follow the inheritance hierarchy. Therefore, you need to place catch blocks properly. It has already been mentioned that the ArithmeticException class derives from the RuntimeException class, which in turn derives from the Exception class. For your easy understanding, follow the associated comments in the program.

POINT TO REMEMBER

When you deal with multiple catch blocks, you need to place the more-specific exception clause first. In other words, you should place the catch blocks from most specific to most general.

It will be good to note that if you are familiar with C#, you may notice that it supports some additional variations of catch clauses. For example, in C#, you may notice the following variations of catch blocks:

```
catch ()
{
    Console.WriteLine("Encountered an Exception");
}
```

Or:

```
catch (WebException ex) when (ex.Status == WebExceptionStatus.Timeout)
 {
 //some code
 }
```

Q&A Session

10.3 Can I use try and finally only as follows?

```
try{
   //Some code
}
finally{
   //Some code
}
```

Yes.

10.4 Then why do you need a catch block at all?

The catch block is used to handle the exception in some specified manner. At the same time, you must note that the actual use of finally is different. It has been previously mentioned that inside finally you should do housekeeping so that the application can be gracefully closed. For example, if a file is already opened, you should close it, or, if you already allocated some resources, those should be released inside this block (to prevent memory leaks). In Chapter 14, you will learn to use a try-with-resource statement, where by using the term "resource" we mean an object that must be closed after the program finishes execution.

10.5 What will happen if I encounter an exception inside a finally block?

You should not forget the purpose of finally, which basically is to close files, release occupied resources, etc. But if you put your erroneous logic in the finally block, you may encounter an exception again. (The solution is the same—you can guard against a probable exception in the finally block with a try-catch, try-finally, or try-catch-finally block. In fact, prior to Java 6, you may notice such usage to close a resource.)

Demonstration 4

Here is such an example for your ready reference. You can see that once you receive the exception (when b becomes 0 in finally block), as usual, the subsequent lines inside the `finally` block will not execute. For example, in the following case the line "I am at the end of finally block" is not appearing in the output.

```
package java2e.chapter10;

import java.util.Random;

public class Demonstration4 {

    public static void main(String[] args) {
        System.out.println("***Demonstration-4.Incorrect way of
        writing code inside the finally block***");
        try {
         System.out.println("I am inside the try block.");
        }
        finally {
            System.out.println("I am at the beginning of finally
            block.");
            int a = 5;
            Random randomGenerator = new Random();
            // Will generate 0 to 2.
            int b = randomGenerator.nextInt(3);//Can produce 0
            System.out.println("Current value of b is : " + b);
            int c = a / b;
            System.out.println("c=" + c);
            System.out.println("I am at the end of finally block.");
        }
    }
}
```

Here is the output when the value of b is 0:

```
***Demonstration-4.Incorrect way of writing code inside the finally
block***
I am inside the try block.
```

```
I am at the beginning of finally block.
Current value of b is : 0
Exception in thread "main" java.lang.ArithmeticException: / by zero
at java2e.chapter10.Demonstration4.main(Demonstration4.java:19)
```

It is also useful to note that if you kill or interrupt a thread, the `finally` block may not execute, even though other threads can run and make the application as a whole alive. You will learn about threads in Chapter 11.

Q&A Session

10.6 Up until now, you have given examples like ArrayIndexOutOfBoundsException, ArithmeticException, etc. How can I remember these names?

These are built-in exceptions in Java. All of these are already defined in the `java.lang` package. Since this package is the default package, you'll get all these exceptions imported by default. Upon practice, you can remember their names. I personally take help from Eclipse. Similar IDEs can help you with this as well.

In this context, you can notice what the exception is that your default handler is throwing. From that report, you can get the name of the exception. For example, notice the output of our Demonstration 1, which is as follows:

```
***Demonstration-1.Exploring Exceptions.***
Exception in thread "main" java.lang.ArithmeticException: / by zero
at java2e.chapter10.Demonstration1.main(Demonstration1.java:9)
```

From this output, you know that an `ArithmeticException` is raised.

Throwing an Exception

Up until now, you have seen examples of handling exceptions thrown by the Java runtime system. When you process Java statements, you may encounter such exceptions due to the wrong logic, loopholes, and so forth. But there is an alternative way to raise an exception—you also have the freedom to throw an exception explicitly by using the throw keyword. This method is useful when you make your own application and want to control the exceptional situation.

When you use the throw keyword, you need to follow the basic format, which is as follows:

throw anObjectOfThrowable;

where anObjectOfThrowable must be an instance of the Throwable class or its subclass.

Demonstration 5

Consider the following program and corresponding output:

```
package java2e.chapter10;

class DemoClass {
        void thowingException() {
                System.out.println("I always throw a NullPointerException");
                throw new NullPointerException("Forcefully throwing a
                NullPointerException");
                // System.out.println("I'll never print this line");
        }
}

class Demonstration5 {

        public static void main(String[] args) {
                System.out.println("***Demonstration5.The use of 'throw'
                keyword***\n");
                DemoClass demo = new DemoClass();
                try {
                        demo.thowingException();
                } catch (Exception e) {
                    System.out.println(e.getMessage());
                        e.printStackTrace();
                }
        }
}
```

Output:

```
***Demonstration5.The use of 'throw' keyword***

I always throw a NullPointerException
Forcefully throwing a NullPointerException
java.lang.NullPointerException: Forcefully throwing a
NullPointerException        at java2e.chapter10.DemoClass.thowingException(D
emonstration5.java:6)
at java2e.chapter10.Demonstration5.main(Demonstration5.java:17)
```

Rethrowing an Exception

Sometimes you need to rethrow an exception; for example, when you want to write a log entry or when you want to send a new higher-level exception. When you rethrow an exception from a `catch` block, it is rethrown to the next enclosing `try` block. Demonstration 6 shows such an example.

Here is a sample format that you can use to rethrow an exception:

```
try{
  //some code
 }
catch(Exception ex){
 //some code, for example, you log the exception
 //Now rethrow it
 throw ex;
}
```

Demonstration 6

Consider the following:

```
package java2e.chapter10;

class Demonstration6 {
      static int c;
```

```java
    static void divide(int a, int b) {
        try {
            b--;
            c = a / b;
            // some code
        } catch (ArithmeticException ex) {
            //Log it now
            System.out.println("a= " + a + " b= " + b);//a=100,b=0
            System.out.println("Caught an exception: " +
            ex.getMessage());
            // Now rethrow it
            throw ex;// rethrowing the exception
        }
    }

    public static void main(String[] args) {
        System.out.println("***Demonstration-6.Rethrowing an
        exception.***");
        int a = 100, b = 1;
        try {
        divide(a,b);
        }
        catch (Exception ex) {
            System.out.println("Recaught the exception inside main()
            method.");
            System.out.println("a= " + a + " b= " + b);//a=100,b=1
            System.out.println("Here is the stackTrace :");
            ex.printStackTrace();
        }
    }
}
```

Output:

```
***Demonstration-6.Rethrowing an exception.***
a= 100 b= 0
Message: / by zero
Recaught the exception inside main() method.
a= 100 b= 1
Here is the stackTrace :
java.lang.ArithmeticException: / by zero
        at java2e.chapter10.Demonstration6.divide(Demonstration6.java:10)
        at java2e.chapter10.Demonstration6.main(Demonstration6.java:25)
```

You can see why logging some additional details before you rethrow an exception is important. As soon as you encountered the exception, you logged it, and from that log you discovered that the divisor (b) became 0 in the divide() method. If you do not use the try-catch block inside the divide() method and you do not log the values of a and b immediately, then you are dependent on the catch block inside the main() method only. In a case like this, when you see the final log statements, you may wonder why you see this exception even if the value of b is 1.

Note   You'll learn to create and use your own exception shortly, and you may combine the original exception with your custom exception message and then rethrow it for better readability.

10.7 Can you compile the following code fragment?

```
package java2e.chapter10;

class TestClass {
        // some code
}

class Quiz2 {
        void raiseException() {
                System.out.println("I love to throw an exception");

                try {
                        throw new TestClass();
```

```
        } catch (TestClass e) {
            //some code
        }
    }
}
```

You will get a compiler error—No exception of type TestClass can be thrown; an exception type must be a subclass of Throwable—as shown in Figure 10-5.

> ⊗ Errors (2 items)
>   ⊗ No exception of type TestClass can be thrown; an exception type must be a subclass of Throwable
>   ⊗ No exception of type TestClass can be thrown; an exception type must be a subclass of Throwable

Figure 10-5. *An exception type must be a subclass of Throwable*

To remove the errors in the previous program, you can follow the compiler's suggestion. For example, in this case, if you just make the following change in the previous code, the compiler will not complain:

```
class TestClass extends Throwable{
//remaining code as it is
```

Use of throws Keyword

Java supports both the keywords throw and throws. You have already seen the use of the throw keyword in Demonstrations 5 and 6. Before you use the throws keyword, you need to remember the following points:

- A throws keyword will be needed to indicate all the exceptions that a method can throw. Otherwise, you'll encounter compile-time errors (except for the next point).

- The previous rule is not applicable for Error or RuntimeException or any of their subclasses.

- You must remember that checked exceptions must be included in a method's throws list.

The upcoming demonstrations will illustrate these points in detail.

Note   Q&A 10.8 can help you to differentiate the checked exceptions from the unchecked exceptions. I suggest you go through Demonstration 7 and Demonstration 8 before you enter into that discussion.

Demonstration 7

Consider the following:

```
package java2e.chapter10;

class TestClassException extends Throwable {
    String str;

    TestClassException(String str) {
        this.str = str;
    }

    public String getMessage() {
        return str;
    }
}

class DemoClass7 {
    void raiseException() throws TestClassException {
        throw new TestClassException("A TestClassException is raised");
    }
}

class Demonstration7 {
    public static void main(String[] args) {
        System.out.println("***Demonstration-7.The use of throws
        keyword***\n");
        DemoClass7 demo = new DemoClass7();
        try {
            demo.raiseException();
        } catch (TestClassException e) {
```

261

```
                    System.out.println(e.getMessage());
                    // A TestClassException is //raised
                    System.out.println("Here is the stacktrace:");
                    e.printStackTrace();
                }
        }
}
```

Output:

```
***Demonstration-7.The use of throws keyword***

A TestClassException is raised
Here is the stacktrace:
java2e.chapter10.TestClassException: A TestClassException is raised at
java2e.chapter10.DemoClass7.raiseException(Demonstration7.java:17)at
java2e.chapter10.Demonstration7.main(Demonstration7.java:27)
```

Now, go through the following points:

- You can see that inside DemoClass7, the method raiseException()
  is throwing an exception, but I have not used a try-catch block
  around this code. Instead, I have added throws statements after the
  method names, as follows:

  void raiseException() **throws** TestClassException {

- It is used to confirm that this method has the capability of throwing
  the exception of type TestClassException. The class has a
  constructor to accept a String message, so you can provide a
  meaningful message when you intend to throw such exceptions.

- If you ignore the throws clause and just use the following code in
  Demonstration 7:

  void raiseException(){

your program will not compile. It will raise the errors shown in Figure 10-6.

Errors (2 items)
  Unhandled exception type TestClassException
  Unreachable catch block for TestClassException. This exception is never thrown from the try statement body

Figure 10-6. *Compile-time error because TestClassException is not included in raiseException()'s throws list*

You may have to do the same for the `main()` method if you do not surround the line of code `demo.raiseException();` with a try-catch block. So, in that case, your `main()` method also could be like the following:

```
public static void main(String[] args) throws TestClassException {
//rest of the code
```

Demonstration 8

Now, consider the following demonstration. In this program, notice that `TestClass8Exception` derives from `RuntimeException`, and in this case I have not included the custom exception in the `raiseException()` method's `throws` list. But the program still compiles.

```
package java2e.chapter10;

//The class derives from RuntimeException
class TestClass8Exception extends RuntimeException {
    String str;

    TestClass8Exception(String str) {
        this.str = str;
    }

    public String getMessage() {
        return str;
    }
}
```

```
class DemoClass8 {
        // This time it will NOT raise compilation error
        void raiseException() {
        throw new TestClass8Exception("A TestClass8Exception is raised");
        }
}

class Demonstration8 {
        public static void main(String[] args) {
                System.out.println("***Demonstration-8.The use of  an
                unchecked exception***\n");
                DemoClass8 demo = new DemoClass8();
                try {
                        demo.raiseException();
                } catch (TestClass8Exception e) {
                        System.out.println(e.getMessage());
                        // A TestClassException is raised
                        System.out.println("Here is the stacktrace:");
                        e.printStackTrace();
                }
        }
}
```

Output:

Demonstration-8.The use of an unchecked exception

A TestClass8Exception is raised
Here is the stacktrace:
java2e.chapter10.TestClass8Exception: A TestClass8Exception is raised
at java2e.chapter10.DemoClass8.raiseException(Demonstration8.java:19)at
java2e.chapter10.Demonstration8.main(Demonstration8.java:28)

You can see that TestClass8Exception is derived from RuntimeException. So, it is not a checked exception. This is why the compiler will not raise any errors when you do not include this exception in the method's throws list.

Checked Versus Unchecked Exceptions

Now you understand the difference between checked and unchecked exceptions. I have already mentioned that there are some kinds of exceptions where either a throws clause needs to list all of the exceptions that a method can throw or you need to handle the scenario with a try-catch block. Otherwise, you'll encounter compile-time errors. This is why these are called **checked exceptions** or compile-time exceptions. The remaining exceptions are termed **unchecked exceptions**.

Note   As I mentioned before, to understand the difference between checked exceptions and unchecked exceptions, you may need to visit Demonstration 7 and Demonstration 8 again.

The following list includes some of the checked exceptions:

- ClassNotFoundException

- NoSuchMethodException

- NoSuchFieldException

- InstantiationException

- CloneNotSupportedException

- IllegalAccessException

- InterruptedException

Here are some unchecked exceptions:

- ArithmeticException

- ArrayIndexOutOfBoundsException

- IndexOutOfBoundsException

- SecurityException

- NullPointerException

> ### POINT TO REMEMBER
>
> If a method can throw a checked exception, then either the method should specify the exception using the `throws` keyword or it needs to handle the exception itself using `try-catch` block. Otherwise, you'll encounter compile-time errors.

Q&A Session

10.8 I understand that checked exceptions are subclasses of Exception. You are also saying that unchecked exceptions are subclasses of RuntimeException. But from the hierarchy, I am seeing that RuntimeException is also a direct subclass of Exception. Then how they become unchecked exceptions?

Let's see what JLS11 says about this. Under section 11.1.1, it says the following:

> *"The checked exception classes are all exception classes other than the unchecked exception classes. That is, the checked exception classes are* Throwable *and all its subclasses other than* RuntimeException *and its subclasses and* Error *and its subclasses."*

At the same time, it also says that "the *unchecked exception classes* are the run-time exception classes and the error classes."

Following these rules, the Java compiler can detect the `RuntimeException` clearly. So, following the language specification, you can safely say that any exception that is a subclass of the `RuntimeException` or `Error` class is not a checked exception.

Discussion on Chained Exceptions

Sometimes you can receive an exception that may be caused by some other exception. So, you may be interested to know the original cause. The concept of chained exceptions comes into the picture in such a scenario.

Consider a very simple scenario of `ArithmeticException`, which you may receive when you divide an integer by 0. Sometimes your application can compute or update the divisor using various logic. So, when you receive this exception, the original cause may be the result of an I/O that can ultimately make the divisor zero.

Chained exceptions can help us to know about such exceptional scenarios, and at the same time they can point to the layer in which the actual error exists.

To allow chained exceptions, you have the following methods:

```
Throwable getCause() and
Throwable initCause(Throwable cause)
```

And the following constructors:

```
Throwable(Throwable cause)
Throwable(String msg, Throwable cause)
```

Demonstration 9

Consider the following demonstration and output. Do not worry about some commented portions. To make the program short and simple, these portions are ignored. You'll learn shortly that you can extend the chain once you uncomment these portions of code.

```java
package java2e.chapter10;

class OuterException extends RuntimeException {
    String str = null;

    OuterException(String str) {
        this.str - str;
    }

    public String toString() {
        return str;
    }

}

class InnerException extends RuntimeException {
    String str = null;

    InnerException(String str) {
        this.str = str;
    }
```

```
        public String toString() {
                return str;
        }

}

//Indtroducing this class to increase the depth
/*
 class SubInnerException extends RuntimeException {
    String str = null; *
 SubInnerException(String str) {
this.str = str;
 }
   public String toString() {
return str;
}
}
 */

class Demo9Class {
        void raiseException() // throws clause not necessary now
        {
                OuterException outer = new OuterException("An OuterException
                is raised.");
                InnerException inner = new InnerException("It is caused by an
                InnerException.");
                /*SubInnerException subInner = new SubInnerException("It is
                again caused by an SubInnerException.");*/
                outer.initCause(inner);
                // inner.initCause(subInner);
                throw outer;
        }
}

class Demonstration9 {
        public static void main(String args[]) {
                System.out.println("***Demonstration-9.A chained exception
                demo***\n");
```

```
            Demo9Class demo = new Demo9Class();
            try {
                    demo.raiseException();
            } catch (OuterException e) {
                    System.out.println(e);
                    System.out.println("Here is the details:" + e.getCause());
                    System.out.println("Here is the stack trace :");
                    e.printStackTrace();
            }
        }
}
```

Output:

An <u>OuterException</u> is raised.
Here is the details:It is caused by an InnerException.
Here is the stack trace :
An <u>OuterException</u> is raised.at java2e.chapter10.Demo9Class.
raiseException(<u>Demonstration9.java:41</u>)at java2e.chapter10.Demonstration9.
main(<u>Demonstration9.java:55</u>)
Caused by: It is caused by an InnerException.   at java2e.chapter10.
Demo9Class.raiseException(<u>Demonstration9.java:42</u>)
        ... 1 more

You can carry on to the depth you want. It is recommended that you do not make a very long chain, because that can lead to a poor design. For simple demonstration purposes, as said before, if you uncomment the commented portions of the code, you will notice the following output:

Demonstration-9.A chained exception demo

An <u>OuterException</u> is raised.
Here is the details:It is caused by an InnerException.
Here is the stack trace :
An <u>OuterException</u> is raised.
        at java2e.chapter10.Demo9Class.raiseException(<u>Demonstration9.java:46</u>)
        at java2e.chapter10.Demonstration9.main(<u>Demonstration9.java:60</u>)
Caused by: It is caused by an InnerException.

```
        at java2e.chapter10.Demo9Class.raiseException(Demonstration9.java:47)
        ... 1 more
Caused by: It is again caused by an        SubInnerException.
        at java2e.chapter10.Demo9Class.raiseException(Demonstration9.java:48)
        ... 1 more
```

10.9 Can you compile the following program?

```java
package java2e.chapter10;

import java.util.Random;

class OuterQuiz3Exception extends Exception {
    String str = null;

    OuterQuiz3Exception(String str) {
        this.str = str;
    }

    public String toString() {
        return str;
    }

}

class InnerQuiz3Exception extends OuterQuiz3Exception {
    InnerQuiz3Exception(String str) {
        super(str);
    }

    public String toString() {
        return str;
    }

}
```

```java
class Quiz3Class {
        // InnerQuiz3Exception is not needed to include in the throws list
        //because it is a subclass of OuterQuiz3Exception
        void raiseException() throws OuterQuiz3Exception {
        //throws clause is necessary now
                OuterQuiz3Exception outer = new OuterQuiz3Exception("An
                OuterQuiz3Exception is raised.");
                InnerQuiz3Exception inner = new InnerQuiz3Exception("An
                InnerQuiz3Exception is raised.");
                Random randomGenerator = new Random();
                // Will generate 0 to 1.
                int b = randomGenerator.nextInt(2);
                System.out.println("In this case, b="+ b);
                if (b == 0) {
                        throw outer;
                } else
                        throw inner;
        }
}

class Quiz3 {

        public static void main(String[] args) throws OuterQuiz3Exception {
                System.out.println("***Quiz3***\n");
                Quiz3Class demo = new Quiz3Class();
                try {
                        demo.raiseException();
                } catch (OuterQuiz3Exception e) {
                        System.out.println(e);
                        System.out.println("Here is the stack trace :");
                        e.printStackTrace();
                }
        }
}
```

Yes, the program will compile, and here is one **possible** output. (When b = 0).

```
***Quiz3***

In this case, b=0
An OuterQuiz3Exception is raised.
Here is the stack trace :
An OuterQuiz3Exception is raised.
at java2e.chapter10.Quiz3Class.raiseException(Quiz3.java:33)
at java2e.chapter10.Quiz3.main(Quiz3.java:52)
```

Here are some important points to note:

- The OuterQuiz3Exception class inherits from the Exception class. So, it is a checked exception. Since you have not used a try-catch block in the raiseException() method, the throws clause is necessary for the raiseException() method now.

- You needed to list all the exceptions in the throws list that the method can throw. But InnerQuiz3Exception is a subclass of OuterQuiz3Exception. So, only the inclusion of OuterQuiz3Exception in the throws list of the raiseException() method was sufficient for you. But if you include InnerQuiz3Exception also, there will be no compiler issue.

- I am generating a random number between 0 (inclusive) and 2 (exclusive), so output may vary when an InnerQuiz3Exception is thrown (i.e., when b = 1).

Creating a Custom Exception

You have already seen some common uses of Java's built-in exceptions. These are very handy, and, in most cases, they can serve your needs. But sometimes you may want to define your own exception class to get messages that are more meaningful to you. So, you may want to create your own exceptions to handle some specific situations in your application.

Creating a custom exception is easy. But before you proceed further, you should remember the following points:

- A common practice to create a user-defined exception class is to extend from the Exception class. You have learned that Exception is a subclass of the Throwable class. So, you can override or use the methods defined in the Throwable classes.

- The Exception class does not have any method specific to it. But here you'll see different overloaded version of constructors; for example, you will notice the presence of the following constructors. In the discussion of chained exceptions, you got to know about two of them. In the upcoming demonstration, you will see the use of another two:

```
public Exception() {}
public Exception(String message) {}
public Exception(String message, Throwable cause) {}
public Exception(Throwable cause) {}
protected Exception(String message, Throwable cause, boolean
enableSuppression, boolean writableStackTrace) {}
```

Following convention, it is suggested that when you create your own exception, the class name should end with the word Exception.

Demonstration 10

Let's start. For simplicity, assume that you need to consider two integer inputs only. You will display the sum of the integers if and only if the aggregate is less than or equal to 100. If it is not less than 100, you'll throw your custom exception.

```
package java2e.chapter10;

class SumGreaterThan100Exception extends Exception {
    SumGreaterThan100Exception() {
        System.out.println("Greater than 100.");
    }
```

```java
        SumGreaterThan100Exception(String msg) {
            super(msg);
        }
}

interface DemoInterface {
    int sum(int x, int y) throws SumGreaterThan100Exception;
}

class Demo10Class implements DemoInterface {
    public int sum(int x, int y) throws SumGreaterThan100Exception {
        int sumofIntegers = x + y;

        if (sumofIntegers <= 100) {
            System.out.println(" Here first number="+ x + " and
            second Number="+y);
            return sumofIntegers;
        } else {
            System.out.println(" Now first number="+ x + " and
            second Number="+y);
            throw new SumGreaterThan100Exception("Sum is greater
            than 100.");
            //throw new SumGreaterThan100Exception();
        }
    }
}

class Demonstration10 {
    public static void main(String args[]) {
        System.out.println("***Demonstration-10.Creating a custom
        exception***\n");
        Demo10Class demo = new Demo10Class();
        try {
            int result = demo.sum(10, 50);// ok
            System.out.println("Sum of 10 and 50 is : " + result);
            // Now the sum is greater than 100, so, it will raise
            //the  custom exception.
```

```
            result = demo.sum(50, 70);
            System.out.println("Sum of 50 and 70 is :  " + result);
        } catch (SumGreaterThan100Exception e) {
            System.out.println("Caught the custom exception : " + e);
            e.printStackTrace();
        }
    }
}
```

Output:

Demonstration-10.Creating a custom exception

Here first number=10 and second Number=50
Sum of 10 and 50 is : 60
Now first number=50 and second Number=70
Caught the custom exception : java2e.chapter10.SumGreaterThan100Exception:
Sum is greater than 100.
java2e.chapter10.SumGreaterThan100Exception: Sum is greater than 100.
        at java2e.chapter10.Demo10Class.sum(Demonstration10.java:25)
        at java2e.chapter10.Demonstration10.main(Demonstration10.java:39)

You have used the parameterized constructor. If you want to use the default constructor (which is commented here), there is a slightly different message.

Demonstration-10.Creating a custom exception

Here first number=10 and second Number=50
Sum of 10 and 50 is : 60
Now first number=50 and second Number=70
Greater than 100.
Caught the custom exception : java2e.chapter10.SumGreaterThan100Exception
java2e.chapter10.SumGreaterThan100Exception
        at java2e.chapter10.Demo10Class.sum(Demonstration10.java:26)
        at java2e.chapter10.Demonstration10.main(Demonstration10.java:39)

Q&A Session

10.10 I understand that Java does not support pointers. But I am seeing that it supports `NullPointerException`. I am confused.

You need to understand the scenario. When you perform some illegal operations (for example, when you invoke a method incorrectly or try to access some fields incorrectly) through a null object, you encounter this exception. This exception generally indicates that you are treating a null object as an actual object, so your intended operation is illegal. Yes, some developers believe that something like `NullReferenceException` could be a better name for this type of exception.

At the same time, you also remember that Java designers believe that the use of pointers is one of the primary sources of injecting bugs into the application. So, they do not support any pointer datatypes.

10.11 It appears to me that I can suppress errors with exceptions. Am I right?

Yes. But it is never intended. Consider the following demonstration.

Demonstration 11

In this example, when you get the value of b as 0 (which is randomly generated), instead of reporting the true issue, you suppress the error by printing c=7, which is a total misuse of this feature.

```
package java2e.chapter10;

import java.util.Random;

public class Demonstration11 {

        public static void main(String[] args) {
                System.out.println("***Demonstration-11.Incorrect use of try-
                catch block***\n");
                int a = 10;
                Random randomGenerator = new Random();
                // Will generate 0 to 2.
                int b = randomGenerator.nextInt(3);
                System.out.println("b=" + b);
                int c = 0;
```

```
        try {
            c = a / b;
            System.out.println("c=" + c);
        } catch (ArithmeticException ex) {
            // printing c=7, after catching the exception
            System.out.println("c=" + 7);
        }
    }
}
```

Here is one **possible** output. You will get this output when you encounter an ArithmeticException and are using a try-catch block to suppress the true message, which is incorrect.

Demonstration-11.Incorrect use of try-catch block

b=0
c=7

Q&A Session

10.12 Should I make my custom exceptions checked (or unchecked)?

If you can do something to recover from an exception, make it a checked exception; otherwise, make it unchecked. Based on your requirements, you can follow the approach of Demonstration 7 or Demonstration 8 to make your custom exception checked or unchecked.

10.13 You said earlier, "You may combine the original exception with your custom exception message and then rethrow it for better readability." Can you show me a demonstration?

In the Java programming world, it's very common to catch a built-in exception and rethrow the same exception via a custom exception for better readability and understanding. I discussed this regarding Demonstration 6.

Demonstration 12

Let's modify Demonstration 6 so that you can experience the same:

```
package java2e.chapter10;

//A custom exception
class InvalidIntegerInputException extends Exception {
        InvalidIntegerInputException(String msg,Throwable causeEx) {
            super(msg, causeEx);
        }
}

class Demonstration12 {
        static int c;

        static void divide(int a, int b) throws  InvalidIntegerInputException{
            try {
                    b--;
                    c = a / b;
                    // some code
            } catch (ArithmeticException ex) {
                    //Log it now
                    System.out.println("a= " + a + " b= " + b);//a=100,b=0
                    System.out.println("Message: " + ex.getMessage());
                    // Now rethrow it
                    throw new InvalidIntegerInputException(" The divisor
                    becomes zero", ex);
            }
        }

        public static void main(String[] args) {
            System.out.println("***Demonstration-12.Rethrowing an
            exception which is wrapped in a custom exception.***");
            System.out.println("Actually, we are modifying the
            demonstration-6.");
            int a = 100, b = 1;
```

```
try {
divide(a,b);
}
catch (Exception ex) {
        System.out.println("Recaught the exception inside main()
        method.");
        System.out.println("a= " + a + " b= " + b);//a=100,b=1
        System.out.println("Here is the stackTrace :");
        ex.printStackTrace();
    }
  }
}
```

Output:

Demonstration-12.Rethrowing an exception which is wrapped in a custom exception.
Actually, we are modifying the demonstration-6.
a= 100 b= 0
Message: / by zero
Recaught the exception inside main() method.
a= 100 b= 1
Here is the stackTrace :
java2e.chapter10.InvalidIntegerInputException: **The divisor becomes zero**
        at java2e.chapter10.Demonstration12.divide(Demonstration12.java:23)
        at java2e.chapter10.Demonstration12.main(Demonstration12.java:32)
Caused by: java.lang.ArithmeticException: / by zero
        at java2e.chapter10.Demonstration12.divide(Demonstration12.java:16)
        ... 1 more

Notice the message "The divisor becomes zero" appeared in your output, which is the actual cause of the ArithmeticException in this program.

Summary

This chapter answered the following questions:

- What is an exception?

- How can you handle errors in our program?

- What are the common keywords used when we deal with exceptions in Java?

- How should you place `try`, `catch`, and `finally` blocks in your program, and what is their purpose?

- What are the different variations of the `catch` clause?

- How can you throw an exception?

- How can you rethrow an exception?

- How is `throw` different from `throws`?

- How can you classify exceptions? How are checked exceptions different from unchecked exceptions?

- How can you make chained exceptions?

- How do you make a custom exception?

- How can you catch a built-in exception and combine it with a custom exception?

CHAPTER 11

Thread Programming

The Java programs that you have seen so far have had a single sequential flow of control; in other words, once the program starts executing, it goes through all statements sequentially until the end. So, in a particular moment, there is only one statement under execution.

A thread is similar to a program. It has a single flow of control. It also has a body between the starting point and end point, and it executes the commands sequentially. Each program has at least one thread.

Java supports the concept of multi-threading; that is, in Java you can have multiple flows of control in a program. In those cases, each flow of control is called a thread, and these threads can run in parallel. In a multi-threaded environment, each thread has a unique flow of execution.

It's a programming paradigm where a program is divided into multiple subprograms (or parts) that can be implemented in parallel. But if the computer has only one processor, how can it perform multiple things in parallel? In actuality, the processor switches among these subprograms/parts very fast, so it appears to human eyes that all of them are executing simultaneously.

Multi-threading can be considered a special case of multi-tasking. It is important to note the difference between process-based multi-threading and thread-based multi-threading. Let's investigate what is stated in a theoretical operating system book. Table 11-1 shows the key distinctions between a process and a thread.

© Vaskaran Sarcar 2020

V. Sarcar, *Interactive Object-Oriented Programming in Java*, https://doi.org/10.1007/978-1-4842-5404-2_11

Table 11-1. *Comparison Between a Process and a Thread*

Process	Thread
1. Unit of allocation	1. Unit of execution
2. Architectural construct	2. Coding construct—does not affect architecture
3. Each process has one or more threads.	3. Each thread belongs to one process.
4. Inter-Process Communication (commonly stated as IPC)—expensive due to context switching	4. Inter-Thread Communication—cheap, can use process memory, and may not need context switch
5. Secure—one process cannot corrupt another process	5. Not secure—a thread can write in the memory used by another thread

So, a thread is simply a lightweight process, and context switching between threads is inexpensive. Process-based multi-tasking is not under Java's control, but Java can manage thread-based multi-tasking. So, in this chapter, we'll focus on thread-based multi-tasking, and *from* this *point* onward, I'll simply refer *to* it as multi-threading.

Managing a multi-thread environment can be challenging, but it's a boon for you because you can complete the task much faster and reduce the overall idle time significantly. Consider some typical scenarios: in general, in an automated environment, a computer's inputs are much faster than a user's keyboard inputs. Or, consider the case when you transfer data over a network—the network transmission rate can be slower than the receiving computer's consumption rate. If you need to wait for each task to finish before you start the next one, the overall idle time will be higher. So, a multi-threading environment is always a better choice in cases like these. Java helps you to model a multi-threaded environment efficiently.

Figure 11-1 demonstrates a multi-threaded program, where the main thread creates two more threads—Thread A and Thread B—that run concurrently.

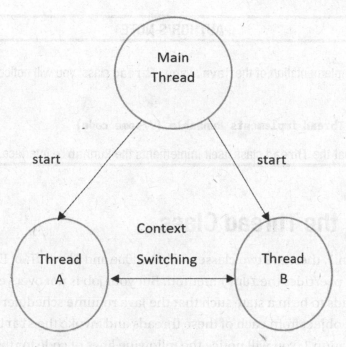

Figure 11-1. *In a multi-threaded program, a main thread creates two more threads, and all of them run in parallel*

Creating Threads

Threads can be created in the following ways:

- **Extend the Thread class** and override the run() method.

- **Implement the Runnable interface**. The Runnable interface has only one method, called run(). So, when a concrete class implements this Runnable interface, it must override the run() method.

So, you can guess that every thread must have a run() method. This method is the heart of a thread, and you can implement the behavior of the thread in the run() method's body.

AUTHOR'S NOTE

If you see the implementation of the `java.lang.Thread` class, you will notice the following line:

```
public class Thread implements Runnable {//some code}
```

which means that the `Thread` class itself implements the `Runnable` interface.

Extending the Thread Class

In Demonstration 1, there are two classes—ThreadOne and ThreadTwo. Each extends the Thread class and overrides the run() method. But your job is not over yet. You need to prepare the threads to be in a state such that the Java runtime scheduler can run them. So, you create an object from each of these threads and invoke the start() method.

In Demonstration 1, you will notice the following lines of code for the ThreadOne **class** and its **object** threadOne (notice the associated comments for your better understanding):

```
//ThreadOne extends from a Thread class here
class ThreadOne extends Thread{

//An instance of ThreadOne
ThreadOne threadOne=new ThreadOne();
```

You'll notice the similar lines of code for the ThreadTwo **class** and its **object** threadTwo. Lastly, the following lines will invoke the run() method of the corresponding threads:

```
threadOne.start();
threadTwo.start();
```

Demonstration 1

Now, let's go through Demonstration 1.

```
package java2e.chapter11;

//ThreadOne extends from the Thread class
class ThreadOne extends Thread {
    @Override
    public void run() {
        for (int i = 0; i < 10; i++) {
            System.out.println("ThreadOne prints ->" + i);
        }
        System.out.println("Exit-ThreadOne");
    }
}
//ThreadTwo extends from the Thread class
class ThreadTwo extends Thread {
    @Override
    public void run() {
        for (int i = 0; i < 10; i++) {
            System.out.println("ThreadTwo prints ->" + i);
        }
        System.out.println("Exit-ThreadTwo");
    }
}

class Demonstration1 {
    public static void main(String[] args) {
        System.out.println("***Demonstration-1.Exploring multi-
        threading by extending Thread class.***");
        //An instance of ThreadOne
        ThreadOne threadOne=new ThreadOne();
        //An instance of Threadtwo
        ThreadTwo threadTwo=new ThreadTwo();
```

```
        //The following lines of code will invoke the run()
        //method of the corrending threads.
        threadOne.start();
        threadTwo.start();
    }
}
```

This is the output from first run:

```
***Demonstration-1.Exploring multi-threading by extending Thread class.***
ThreadOne prints ->0
ThreadTwo prints ->0
ThreadOne prints ->1
ThreadTwo prints ->1
ThreadOne prints ->2
ThreadTwo prints ->2
ThreadOne prints ->3
ThreadTwo prints ->3
ThreadOne prints ->4
ThreadTwo prints ->4
ThreadOne prints ->5
ThreadTwo prints ->5
ThreadTwo prints ->6
ThreadTwo prints ->7
ThreadTwo prints ->8
ThreadTwo prints ->9
Exit-ThreadTwo
ThreadOne prints ->6
ThreadOne prints ->7
ThreadOne prints ->8
ThreadOne prints ->9
Exit-ThreadOne
```

This is the output from the second run:

```
***Demonstration-1.Exploring multi-threading by extending Thread class.***
ThreadOne prints ->0
ThreadTwo prints ->0
ThreadOne prints ->1
ThreadOne prints ->2
ThreadOne prints ->3
ThreadOne prints ->4
ThreadOne prints ->5
ThreadOne prints ->6
ThreadOne prints ->7
ThreadOne prints ->8
ThreadTwo prints ->1
ThreadTwo prints ->2
ThreadTwo prints ->3
ThreadOne prints ->9
ThreadTwo prints ->4
Exit-ThreadOne
ThreadTwo prints ->5
ThreadTwo prints ->6
ThreadTwo prints ->7
ThreadTwo prints ->8
ThreadTwo prints ->9
Exit-ThreadTwo
```

Notice that the output from the first run is different from that of the second run. Once these threads start running concurrently, you cannot predict the order of their execution. Each of them can run whenever it gets the processor. In this case, all of them have the same priority, and so the Java scheduler allows them to share the processor on a FCFS (first come first served) basis. Later, you will see that, if you wish, you can opt to prioritize their order of execution by setting the priority.

Note   When you execute a Java program, one thread starts automatically. This thread is called the **main thread**. So, the main() method in Demonstration 1 creates the main thread, which dies at the end of the main() method.

Implementing the Runnable Interface

Let's examine an alternative way to create threads. This time, I'll implement the Runnable interface to create threads. In this case, you need to go through the following steps:

1. Declare a class that implements the Runnable interface. For example:

   ```
   class Thread2A implements Runnable{//some other code
   ```

2. Implement the run() method. See the following lines in Demonstration 2:

   ```
   class Thread2A implements Runnable {
       @Override
       public void run() {//some other code}
   }
   ```

3. Create a Thread class object using the following Thread class constructor:

   ```
   public Thread(Runnable target) {}.
   ```

   So, in Demonstration 2, you can see the following line inside main:

   ```
   //Thread2A implements Runnable interface
   Thread thread2A=new Thread(new Thread2A());
   ```

4. Call the start method of the thread, like the following:

   ```
   thread2A.start();
   ```

Demonstration 2

Here is the example:

```
package java2e.chapter11;

class Thread2A implements Runnable {
    @Override
    public void run() {
```

```
        for (int i = 0; i < 10; i++) {
                System.out.println("Thread2A prints ->" + i);
        }
        System.out.println("Exit-Thread2A");
    }
}

class Demonstration2 {
    public static void main(String[] args) {
        System.out.println("***Demonstration-2.Exploring multi-
        threading by implementing Runnable Interface.***");
        //Thread2A implements Runnable interface
        Thread thread2A = new Thread(new Thread2A());
        thread2A.start();
        System.out.println("Exit from main thread");
    }
}
```

Here is one possible output:

```
***Demonstration-2.Exploring multi-threading by implementing Runnable
Interface.***
Exit from main thread
Thread2A prints ->0
Thread2A prints ->1
Thread2A prints ->2
Thread2A prints ->3
Thread2A prints ->4
Thread2A prints ->5
Thread2A prints ->6
Thread2A prints ->7
Thread2A prints ->8
Thread2A prints ->9
Exit-Thread2A
```

In Demonstration 2, the Thread2A class implements the Runnable interface, so objects of Thread2A become the Runnable type. But the objects of Thread2A are NOT threads.

289

So, modify your main() method as follows (notice the bold lines/words for your reference):

```
class Demonstration2Modified {
    public static void main(String[] args) {
        System.out.println("***Demonstration-2.Exploring multi-
        threading by implementing Runnable Interface.***");
        Thread thread2A = new Thread(new Thread2A());// //Thread2A
        implements Runnable interface
        thread2A.start();

        /* Thread2A class implements the Runnable interface, so
         * objects of Thread2A become Runnable type.
         * But the objects of Thread2A are NOT threads.
         */
        System.out.println("Creating another object of Thread2A");
        Thread2A anotherObject=new Thread2A();
        anotherObject.run();
        System.out.println("Exit from main thread");
    }
}
```

You may notice a surprising output, like the following:

```
***Demonstration-2.Exploring multi-threading by implementing Runnable
Interface.***
Creating another object of Thread2A
Thread2A prints ->0
Thread2A prints ->0
Thread2A prints ->1
Thread2A prints ->1
Thread2A prints ->2
Thread2A prints ->3
Thread2A prints ->4
Thread2A prints ->5
Thread2A prints ->6
Thread2A prints ->7
```

```
Thread2A prints ->8
Thread2A prints ->2
Thread2A prints ->3
Thread2A prints ->4
Thread2A prints ->5
Thread2A prints ->6
Thread2A prints ->7
Thread2A prints ->8
Thread2A prints ->9
Exit-Thread2A
Exit from main thread
Thread2A prints ->9
Exit-Thread2A
```

In this case, though you have invoked the run() method, it is invoked in the same thread. To run it in a new thread, you need to instantiate and start a new Thread object.

Note   When a class implements a Runnable interface, it deals with two objects—one is the Runnable object, and the other is the Thread object. The Runnable object contains the code that executes when the thread starts running. So, during the execution of a Thread object, you can see the execution of the run() method of the Runnable object.

Q&A Session

11.1 What is the key advantage of using a multi-threaded environment over a single-threaded environment?

In single-threaded environment, if the thread gets blocked, the entire program stops executing, which is not the case in a multi-threaded environment. In addition to this, you can reduce overall idle time via the efficient use of CPU. And later you'll learn that you can avoid polling in multi-threaded environments.

11.2 I have a dual-core (or multi-core) system. Can multi-threading still help me?

In earlier days, most computers had a single core, and in those systems concurrent threads actually shared the CPU cycle; i.e., they could not run in parallel. But, by using the concept of multi-threading, you could reduce the overall idle time by the efficient use of CPU. And if you have multiple processors, you can run multiple threads concurrently. As a result, you can further enhance the speed of your program.

11.3 What is context switching?

It enables you to store the state of the current thread (or process) so that you can resume the execution from this point later.

11.4 Which approach should I use when I create threads? Should I extend the Thread class, or should I implement the Runnable interface?

It depends on your choice and many other constraints. If your class extends the Thread class, you cannot extend from any other class, because Java does not allow multiple inheritance through class. When you implement the Runnable interface, you can extend from another parent class.

On the other hand, the Runnable interface has only one method, run(), which is also an abstract method (by interface definition). So, there is no fully built-in method available for your immediate use. But the Thread class has many built-in methods, like yield(), sleep(), getName(), setName(), etc. These methods can be used if your class extends from the Thread class. Also, you can have different types of constructors when you instantiate a Thread class.

Demonstration 3

Now consider Demonstration 3. Before you proceed, here are some important points to consider:

- This time I have created the thread using one of the overloaded versions of the Thread class constructor. In this version, I can supply the name of the thread during thread instantiation.

- I have also used some of the available methods from the Thread class; for example, currentThread(), getName(), setName(), getPriority(), and setPriority(). As said before, if you choose to create the thread by implementing the Runnable interface, these methods will not be available to you.

- The method setPriority(int newPriority) is used to set a priority of the thread. Java defines following priorities:

```
//The minimum priority of a thread
    public final static int MIN_PRIORITY = 1;
//The default priority of a thread
    public final static int NORM_PRIORITY = 5;
//The maximum priority of a thread
    public final static int MAX_PRIORITY = 10;
```

Here is the full implementation:

```
package java2e.chapter11;

class Thread3A extends Thread {
    public Thread3A(String name) {
        super(name);
    }

    public void run() {
        for (int i = 0; i < 10; i++) {
            System.out.println(this.getName() + " is executing and
            prints : "+ i);
        }
        System.out.println("Exit-"+ this.getName());
    }
}

class Thread3B extends Thread {
    public Thread3B(String name) {
        super(name);
    }

    public void run() {
        for (int i = 0; i < 10; i++) {
            System.out.println(this.getName() + " is executing.It is
            printing : "+i);
        }
```

```
            System.out.println("Exit-"+ this.getName());
      }
}

class Demonstration3 {
      public static void main(String[] args) throws InterruptedException {
            System.out.println("***Demonstration-3.Exploring
            multithreading by extending Thread class.***");
            // Get reference to Main thread
            Thread mainThread = Thread.currentThread();
            // Get the details of the Main thread
            System.out.println("Current thread: " + mainThread.getName() +
            " and priority: " +mainThread.getPriority());
            Thread3A thread3A = new Thread3A("Thread3A");
            thread3A.setPriority(Thread.MIN_PRIORITY);//1
            Thread3B thread3B = new Thread3B("Thread3B");
            // Updating the name of the thread-ThreadDemo4
            thread3B.setName("ThreadDemonstration3B");
            thread3B.setPriority(Thread.MAX_PRIORITY);//10
            System.out.println("Thread3A priority is " + thread3A.
            getPriority());
            System.out.println("ThreadDemonstration3B priority is " +
            thread3B.getPriority());
            thread3A.start();
            thread3B.start();
            for (int i = 0; i <10; i++) {
                  System.out.println( mainThread.getName() + " is
                  executing and prints : "+ i);
            }
            System.out.println("Exit main()");
      }
}
```

Here is one possible output.

```
***Demonstration-3.Exploring multi-threading by extending Thread class.***
Current thread: main and priority: 5
Thread3A priority is 1
ThreadDemonstration3B priority is 10
main is executing and prints : 0
ThreadDemonstration3B is executing.It is printing : 0
main is executing and prints : 1
ThreadDemonstration3B is executing.It is printing : 1
main is executing and prints : 2
ThreadDemonstration3B is executing.It is printing : 2
Thread3A is executing and prints : 0
ThreadDemonstration3B is executing.It is printing : 3
main is executing and prints : 3
main is executing and prints : 4
main is executing and prints : 5
Thread3A is executing and prints : 1
ThreadDemonstration3B is executing.It is printing : 4
Thread3A is executing and prints : 2
main is executing and prints : 6
main is executing and prints : 7
main is executing and prints : 8
main is executing and prints : 9
Thread3A is executing and prints : 3
ThreadDemonstration3B is executing.It is printing : 5
Thread3A is executing and prints : 4
Exit main()
Thread3A is executing and prints : 5
ThreadDemonstration3B is executing.It is printing : 6
ThreadDemonstration3B is executing.It is printing : 7
ThreadDemonstration3B is executing.It is printing : 8
ThreadDemonstration3B is executing.It is printing : 9
Thread3A is executing and prints : 6
```

```
Exit-ThreadDemonstration3B
Thread3A is executing and prints : 7
Thread3A is executing and prints : 8
Thread3A is executing and prints : 9
Exit-Thread3A
```

Here is another possible output (executed in a different machine with a different configuration).

```
***Demonstration-3.Exploring multi-threading by extending Thread class.***
Current thread: main and priority: 5
Thread3A priority is 1
ThreadDemonstration3B priority is 10
main is executing and prints : 0
ThreadDemonstration3B is executing.It is printing : 0
ThreadDemonstration3B is executing.It is printing : 1
ThreadDemonstration3B is executing.It is printing : 2
ThreadDemonstration3B is executing.It is printing : 3
ThreadDemonstration3B is executing.It is printing : 4
ThreadDemonstration3B is executing.It is printing : 5
ThreadDemonstration3B is executing.It is printing : 6
ThreadDemonstration3B is executing.It is printing : 7
ThreadDemonstration3B is executing.It is printing : 8
ThreadDemonstration3B is executing.It is printing : 9
Exit-ThreadDemonstration3B
main is executing and prints : 1
main is executing and prints : 2
main is executing and prints : 3
main is executing and prints : 4
main is executing and prints : 5
main is executing and prints : 6
main is executing and prints : 7
main is executing and prints : 8
main is executing and prints : 9
```

```
Exit main()
Thread3A is executing and prints : 0
Thread3A is executing and prints : 1
Thread3A is executing and prints : 2
Thread3A is executing and prints : 3
Thread3A is executing and prints : 4
Thread3A is executing and prints : 5
Thread3A is executing and prints : 6
Thread3A is executing and prints : 7
Thread3A is executing and prints : 8
Thread3A is executing and prints : 9
Exit-Thread3A
```

It may appear to you that the output from the second run is expected, but the output from the first run is unexpected (because the main thread exited before the higher-priority thread). But, again, this output may vary in this demonstration. In theory, the higher-priority threads get more CPU time than the lower-priority threads, and they can preempt the lower-priority threads. But in real life, it may depend on many other factors; for example, the configuration of your system, how the operating system implements the concept of multi-tasking, etc. Apart from these factors, the output can vary based on what the thread is doing, how big the job is (for example, a small task can finish before it is preempted by a higher-priority thread), and so on. So, you should not explicitly rely on priorities. If a CPU is available, the lower-priority thread can also get a chance to run and can finish early if it does a very little job. In general, threads run asynchronously; hence, you see the random outputs.

The output in Figure 11-2 was generated when the previous program ran in a system with a configuration as shown (notice that it's a dual-core system; it has a sixth-generation Intel® Core™ i5-6300 processor).

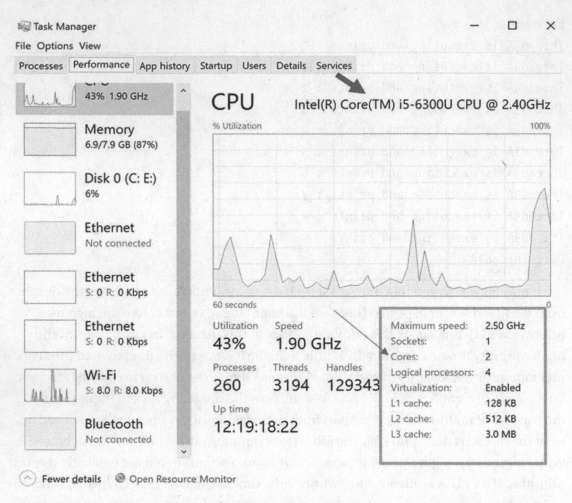

Figure 11-2. *Configuration details snapshot from a dual-core system with sixth-generation Intel® Core™ i5-6300 processor*

But the output varies when the program runs on a different machine, which is also a dual-core system, but with a different configuration, like that in Figure 11-3 (notice that it's a dual-core system with eighth-generation Intel® Core™ i3 processor).

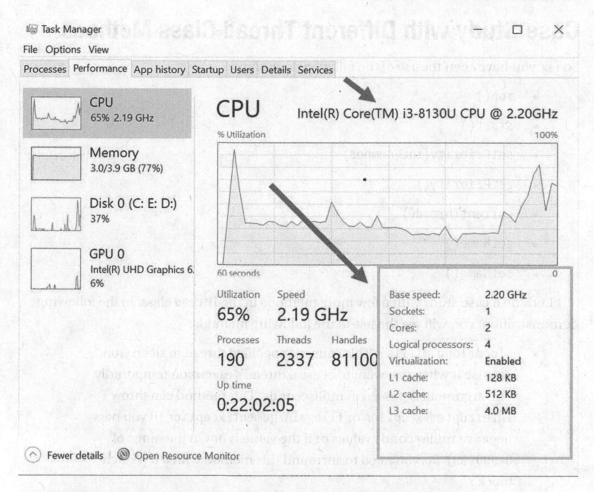

Figure 11-3. *Configuration details snapshot from a different dual-core system with eighth-generation Intel® Core™ i3 processor*

Note In a multi-threaded Java program, you may notice the use of preemptive scheduling where a higher-priority thread preempts a lower-priority thread. But you have seen that the behavior is not always certain. The behavior also depends on the underlying platform. In theory, two same-priority threads cannot preempt each other, which can create issues in a non-preemptive environment. So, for equal priority threads, it's a good idea to release control based on some conditions (for example, waiting for I/O operations, etc.) so that each thread can run and complete its job.

Case Study with Different Thread Class Methods

So far, you have seen the use of the following methods:

- `run()`
- `start()`
- `setPriority(int number)`
- `getPriority()`
- `currentThread()`
- `getName()`
- `setName()`

Let's do a case study with a few more methods in the `Thread` class. In the following demonstration, you will see the use of the following methods:

- `sleep(long millis)`: This causes a specified thread to sleep. You can use it when you want to cease a thread's execution temporarily. The argument is passed in milliseconds. This method can throw `InterruptedException` or `IllegalArgumentException` (if you pass negative milliseconds values or if the value is not in the range of 0–999999). So, you need to surround this method with a try/catch block.

- `yield()`: This can be used when you want a thread (which is currently using the processor) to give up its control to a different thread (though the scheduler can ignore this request). This method can be used for debugging purposes or for designing concurrency control constructs. It is also helpful to reproduce a bug in the race conditions.

- `interrupt()`: This method can be used to send an interrupt signal to a thread.

Demonstration 4

Consider the following demonstration and output, which is self-explanatory if you follow the prior theories:

```java
package java2e.chapter11;

class Thread4A extends Thread {
    public void run() {
        for (int i = 0; i < 5; i++) {
            System.out.println("Thread4A prints ->" + i);
            if (i == 2) {
                System.out.println("Going to interrupt the
                thread.");
                interrupt();// Interrupts this thread
                System.out.println("Is Thread4A interrupted?"+thi
                s.interrupted());
            }
        }
        System.out.println("Exit-Thread4A");
    }
}

class Thread4B extends Thread {
    public void run(){
        for (int j = 0; j < 5; j++) {
            System.out.println("Thread4B prints ->" + j);
            if (j == 3) {
                try {
                    sleep(5000);//sleeps for 5000
                    milliseconds
                } catch (InterruptedException e) {
                    e.printStackTrace();
                }
            }
        }
```

```java
            System.out.println("Exit-Thread4B");
        }
    }

    class Thread4C extends Thread {
        public void run() {
            for (int k = 0; k < 5; k++) {
                System.out.println("Thread4C prints ->" + k);
                if(k==4) {
                    yield();
                }
            }
            System.out.println("Exit-Thread4C");
        }
    }

class Demonstration4 {
    public static void main(String[] args) throws InterruptedException {
        System.out.println("***Demonstration-4.Exploring multi-
        threading with yield(),sleep(), and interrupt() methods of the
        Thread class.***");
        Thread4A thread4A=new Thread4A();
        Thread4B thread4B=new Thread4B();
        Thread4C thread4C=new Thread4C();
        thread4A.start();
        thread4B.start();
        thread4C.start();
        System.out.println("Is Thread4A interrupted now?"+thread4A.int
        errupted());
        Thread.sleep(1000);
        System.out.println("Exit-main()");
    }
}
```

Here is a possible output:

```
***Demonstration-4.Exploring multi-threading with yield(), sleep(), and
interrupt() methods of the Thread class.***
Is Thread4A interrupted now?false
Thread4C prints ->0
Thread4B prints ->0
Thread4B prints ->1
Thread4A prints ->0
Thread4B prints ->2
Thread4B prints ->3
Thread4C prints ->1
Thread4A prints ->1
Thread4C prints ->2
Thread4A prints ->2
Going to interrupt the thread.
Thread4C prints ->3
Is Thread4A interrupted?true
Thread4C prints ->4
Thread4A prints ->3
Exit-Thread4C
Thread4A prints ->4
Exit-Thread4A
Exit-main()
Thread4B prints ->4
Exit-Thread4B
```

Q&A Session

11.5 In previous demonstrations, I saw that the main thread finishes before the child threads. But in many cases, I want to avoid this. In such a case, how should I proceed?

The sleep() method can help you, but it is not an ideal solution. The much better solution is to use the join() method (which has different overloaded versions). Here, I present an updated version of the main() method for Demonstration 4 (notice the bold lines). Once you execute this, you will notice that main always finishes at the end.

```
class Demonstration4 {
    public static void main(String[] args) throws InterruptedException {
        System.out.println("***Demonstration-4.Exploring multi-
        threading with yield(),sleep(), and interrupt() methods of the
        Thread class.***");
        Thread4A thread4A = new Thread4A();
        Thread4B thread4B = new Thread4B();
        Thread4C thread4C = new Thread4C();
        thread4A.start();
        thread4B.start();
        thread4C.start();
        System.out.println("Is Thread4A interrupted now?" +
        thread4A.interrupted());
        Thread.currentThread().sleep(1000);
        //Modified program to show the use of join()
        //Waiting for the threads to complete before main //thread.
        thread4A.join();
        thread4B.join();
        thread4C.join();
        System.out.println("Exit-main()");
    }
}
```

Here is the modified output. Notice that Exit-main() comes at the end.

```
***Demonstration-4.Exploring multi-threading with yield(),sleep(), and
interrupt() methods of the Thread class.***
Thread4B prints ->0
Thread4C prints ->0
Thread4C prints ->1
Thread4C prints ->2
Thread4A prints ->0
Thread4A prints ->1
Is Thread4A interrupted now?false
Thread4A prints ->2
```

```
Going to interrupt the thread
Thread4C prints ->3
Thread4B prints ->1
Thread4B prints ->2
Thread4B prints ->3
Thread4C prints ->4
Is Thread4A interrupted?true
Thread4A prints ->3
Thread4A prints ->4
Exit-Thread4A
Exit-Thread4C
Thread4B prints ->4
Exit-Thread4B
Exit-main()
```

POINTS TO REMEMBER

There is another method called isAlive() that can be used to check whether the thread is alive or dead. For example, the following code can be used inside main() to verify whether the Thread4B object is alive or not:

```
//Testing whether Thread4B object is alive or not.
System.out.println(" Thread 4B is alive? "+ thread4B.isAlive());
```

Synchronization

Sometimes multiple threads need to access some shared resources. Controlling such situations is tricky; for example, consider a situation where one thread is trying to read the data from a file and another thread is still writing or updating in the same file. If you cannot control the situation efficiently, you may get surprising results. The concept of synchronization is useful in similar situations. Java can help you to control the situation with synchronization methods and statements.

Use of Synchronized Methods

Let's begin with synchronized methods. To understand the power of a synchronized method, let's start with a program where the concept is not implemented. In the following demonstration, MyClass5A is a simple class with a method, display(). You can prefix the keyword synchronized to a method as follows to make it a synchronized method:

```
synchronized void display(){
      //some code
}
```

Because we're starting with the non-synchronized version, I have commented the synchronized portion of the code in the upcoming demonstration.

Let's assume that inside display() there are some shared resources. For simplicity, I have put in some simple statements to indicate the entry and exit of a thread. To see the effect precisely, I have also put a simple sleep statement inside the method body. It can help you switch the execution to another thread.

There is a thread class Thread5B that has following constructor:

```
public Thread5B(MyClass5A myObject, String name) {
      super(name);
      this.myClass5AObject = myObject;
}
```

So, to instantiate from the Thread5B class, you can pass a MyClass5A object and a string as arguments. In the following program, I have created two instances from this class, and to identify them clearly, I have passed the string arguments as Thread5B-1 and Thread-5B-2.

Once you run the non-synchronized version of the program, you may notice the following lines:

```
Thread5B-1 has entered and working in the shared location.
Thread5B-2 has entered and working in the shared location.
Thread5B-1 exits.
Thread5B-2 exits.
```

The output indicates that Thread5B-1 has entered the shared location first. But before it finishes its execution, Thread5B-2 also enters into the shared location.

But if a thread is working in the shared location, you may want to restrict any other thread from entering that location. So, this time, you uncomment the synchronized version of display() and comment out the non-synchronized version of it. Now, if you run the program, you will see that you have achieved your goal through the synchronized method.

Demonstration 5

Here is the code in full:

```
package java2e.chapter11;

class MyClass5A {
        //Synchronized version
        //synchronized void display() {
        //Non-synchronized version
        void display() {

                System.out.print(Thread.currentThread().getName() + " has
                entered and working in the shared location. \n");
                try {
                        Thread.sleep(1000);
                } catch (InterruptedException e) {
                        e.printStackTrace();
                }
                System.out.print(Thread.currentThread().getName() + " exits.\n");
        }
}

class Thread5B extends Thread {
        MyClass5A myClass5AObject;

        public Thread5B(MyClass5A myObject, String name) {
                super(name);
                this.myClass5AObject = myObject;
        }
```

```
    @Override
    public void run() {
        myClass5AObject.display();
    }
}

class Demonstration5 {
    public static void main(String[] args) throws InterruptedException {
        System.out.println("***Demonstration-5.Exploring multi-
        threading with synchronized method.***");
        MyClass5A myObject = new MyClass5A();
        Thread5B ob1 = new Thread5B(myObject, "Thread5B-1");
        Thread5B ob2 = new Thread5B(myObject, "Thread5B-2");
        ob1.start();
        ob2.start();
    }
}
```

Output without synchronized method:

```
***Demonstration-5.Exploring multi-threading with( and without)
synchronized method.***
Thread5B-1 has entered and working in the shared location.
Thread5B-2 has entered and working in the shared location.
Thread5B-1 exits.
Thread5B-2 exits.
```

With synchronized method:

```
***Demonstration-5.Exploring multi-threading with( and without)
synchronized method.***
Thread5B-1 has entered and working in the shared location.
Thread5B-1 exits.
Thread5B-2 has entered and working in the shared location.
Thread5B-2 exits.
```

Use of Synchronized Block

In some situations, you won't have synchronized methods that serve your purpose; for example, suppose there is a class that uses third-party code, and you do not have direct access to the codebase. You notice that in your multi-thread environment, there is a method (which is not synchronized) in the class that can be used by multiple threads simultaneously.

To deal with such scenarios, Java provides synchronized blocks. If you want synchronized access to objects of a class you can use it.

Here is the general format of a synchronized block:

```
synchronized (theObjectReference) {
//Some code
}
```

Demonstration 6

The following is an example of a synchronized block:

```
package java2e.chapter11;

class MyClass6A {
    //synchronized void display() {
    void display() {

        System.out.print(Thread.currentThread().getName() + " has
        entered and working in the shared location. \n");
        try {
            Thread.sleep(1000);
        } catch (InterruptedException e) {
            e.printStackTrace();
        }
        System.out.print(Thread.currentThread().getName() + " exits.\n");
    }
}
```

```java
class Thread6B extends Thread {
      MyClass6A myClass6AObject;

      public Thread6B(MyClass6A myObject, String name) {
            super(name);
            this.myClass6AObject = myObject;
      }

      @Override
      public void run() {
            synchronized (myClass6AObject) {
                  myClass6AObject.display();
            }
      }
}

class Demonstration6 {
      public static void main(String[] args) throws InterruptedException {
            System.out.println("***Demonstration-6.Exploring multi-
            threading with synchronized statements.***");
            MyClass6A myObject = new MyClass6A();
            Thread6B thread1 = new Thread6B(myObject, "Thread6B-1");
            Thread6B thread2 = new Thread6B(myObject, "Thread6B-2");
            thread1.start();
            thread2.start();
      }
}
```

Output:

```
***Demonstration-6.Exploring multi-threading with synchronized
statements.***
Thread6B-1 has entered and working in the shared location.
Thread6B-1 exits.
Thread6B-2 has entered and working in the shared location.
Thread6B-2 exits.
```

This time, the display() method is not synchronized, but I have used the synchronized block in Thread6B's run() method, and this thread invokes the display() method of MyClass6A. You will notice that multiple threads cannot enter the shared location simultaneously. Instead, each thread waits for the prior thread to finish its job in the shared location.

Deadlock

Deadlock is a situation or condition where at least two processes (or threads) are waiting for each other to complete (or release control) so that each one can finish its job. This may result in neither of them starting (and both going into a hanging state). You may often hear about these real-life examples:

> You can't get a job without experience; you can't get experience without a job.

Or,

> After a fight between two close friends, each of them expects the other to apologize first.

Note   Without synchronization, you may notice unexpected outcomes (for example, corrupted data), but with improper use of synchronization, you can encounter a deadlock.

Types of Deadlock

Let us quickly revisit the theoretical operating system. There are different types of deadlock, for example:

- **Resource deadlock**: Suppose two processes, P1 and P2, are holding resources R1 and R2, respectively. P1 is asking for the resource R2, and P2 is asking for the resource R1, to complete their jobs. OS generally has concerns about this type of deadlock.

- **Synchronization deadlock**: Suppose process P1 is waiting to perform an action a1, but only after P2 completes the specific action a2, and P2 is waiting to complete action a2 until after P1 completes a1.

- **Communication deadlock**: Similar to preceding scenarios. You can replace the concept of actions/resources with messages; i.e., two processes are waiting to receive messages from each other to proceed further.

Demonstration 7

In this chapter, you are focusing on the multi-threaded environment. So, I'll discuss the deadlock that can be caused by having multiple threads in your Java application.

```
package java2e.chapter11;

class SharedResource1 {
    static synchronized void startingPart() throws InterruptedException {
        System.out.println(Thread.currentThread().getName() + ":
        enters starting part-SharedResource1.");
        Thread.sleep(100);
        System.out.println(Thread.currentThread().getName() + ":
        Waiting to get endPart of SharedResource2.");
        SharedResource2.endPart();
        System.out.println(Thread.currentThread().getName() + ": Exits
        starting part-SharedResource1");
    }

    static synchronized void endPart() throws InterruptedException {
        System.out.println(Thread.currentThread().getName() + ": Exits
        SharedResource1.endingPart .");
    }
}

class SharedResource2 {
    static synchronized void startingPart() throws InterruptedException {
        System.out.println(Thread.currentThread().getName() + ":
        enters starting part of SharedResource2.");
        Thread.sleep(100);
```

```
            System.out.println(Thread.currentThread().getName() + ":
            Waiting to get endPart-SharedResource1.");
            SharedResource1.endPart();
            System.out.println(Thread.currentThread().getName() + ": Exits
            starting part of SharedResource2.");
        }

        static synchronized void endPart() throws InterruptedException {
            System.out.println(Thread.currentThread().getName() + ": Exits
            end part of SharedResource2.");
        }
}

class First extends Thread {
        public First(String name) {
            super(name);
        }
        public void run() {
            try {
                SharedResource1.startingPart();
            } catch (InterruptedException e) {
                e.printStackTrace();
            }
        }
}
class Second extends Thread {
        public Second(String name) {
            super(name);
        }
        public void run() {
            try {
                SharedResource2.startingPart();
            } catch (InterruptedException e) {
                e.printStackTrace();
            }
        }
}
```

```
class Deadlock {
        public static void main(String[] args) {
                System.out.println("***Demonstration- Incorrect design leads
                to deadlock.***\n");
                // An instance of ThreadOne
                First first = new First("FirstThread");
                // An instance of Threadtwo
                Second second = new Second("SecondThread");
                first.start();
                second.start();
        }
}
```

Output:

Demonstration- Incorrect design leads to deadlock.

FirstThread: enters starting part-SharedResource1.
SecondThread: enters starting part of SharedResource2.
SecondThread: Waiting to get endPart-SharedResource1.
FirstThread: Waiting to get endPart of SharedResource2.

Detecting Deadlocks in the System

The examples of the book were tested in a Windows 10 system. Here, you can find the process ID of the application and use the jstack command to investigate long-running processes or deadlocks. For example, when you see that the program is NOT terminating (as expected), you can find the process ID of the application and use the jstack command to investigate. The steps are summarized here.

1. Open Task Manager using Ctrl+Alt+Delete.

2. Select **Details** tab to see the PID, like in Figure 11-4.

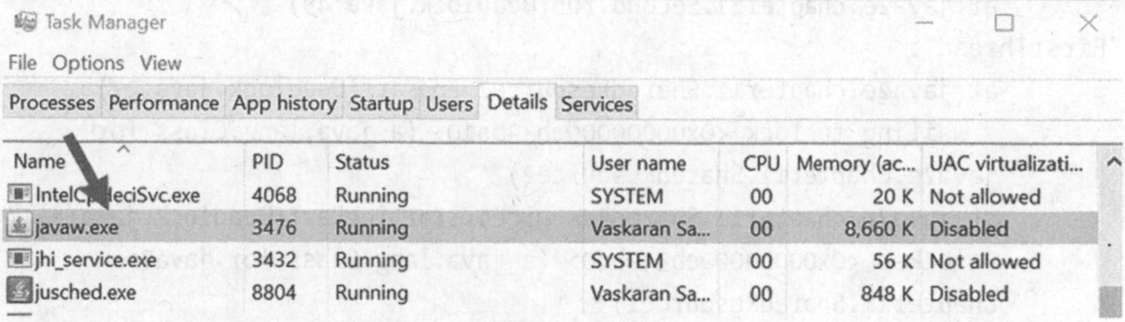

Figure 11-4. Retrieving the details of the process javaw.exe in a Windows 10 system. Use `jstack` command with the process ID like in the following

```
C:\Users\Vaskaran Sarcar>jstack 3476
```

Now you can get the deadlock details:

```
//Some additional information skipped here
```

Found one Java-level deadlock:
```
=============================
"SecondThread":
  waiting to lock monitor 0x000000000288ac38 (object 0x00000000eb349b40, a
  java.lang.Class),
  which is held by "FirstThread"
"FirstThread":
  waiting to lock monitor 0x0000000002888198 (object 0x00000000eb39ba10, a
  java.lang.Class),
  which is held by "SecondThread"

Java stack information for the threads just listed:
===================================================
"SecondThread":
        at java2e.chapter11.SharedResource1.endPart(Deadlock.java:13)
        - waiting to lock <0x00000000eb349b40> (a java.lang.Class for
        java2e.chapter11.SharedResource1)
        at java2e.chapter11.SharedResource2.startingPart(Deadlock.java:22)
        - locked <0x00000000eb39ba10> (a java.lang.Class for java2e.
        chapter11.SharedResource2)
```

```
        at java2e.chapter11.Second.run(Deadlock.java:49)
"FirstThread":
        at java2e.chapter11.SharedResource2.endPart(Deadlock.java:27)
        - waiting to lock <0x00000000eb39ba10> (a java.lang.Class for
        java2e.chapter11.SharedResource2)
        at java2e.chapter11.SharedResource1.startingPart(Deadlock.java:8)
        - locked <0x00000000eb349b40> (a java.lang.Class for java2e.
        chapter11.SharedResource1)
        at java2e.chapter11.First.run(Deadlock.java:37)

Found 1 deadlock.
```

Alternatively, you can use the Java Virtual Machine Process Status (JPS) tool to identify the process ID you need to investigate further. Oracle Java documentation says the following:

> "The jps command lists the instrumented Java HotSpot VMs
> on the target system. The command is limited to reporting
> information on JVMs for which it has access permission."

From the command line, if you type jps -help, you will see the following information:

```
C:\Users\sarcarv>jps -help
usage: jps [-help]
        jps [-q] [-mlvV] [<hostid>]
Definitions:
    <hostid>:       <hostname>[:<port>]
```

So, you can use the following command:

```
jps -l -m
```

As per the documentation,

- -m displays the arguments passed to the main() method. The output may be null for embedded JVMs.

- -l displays the full package name for the application's main class or the full path name to the application's JAR file.

If you want to explore other details, you can refer to the JDK11 documentation or you can directly go to the following link:

https://docs.oracle.com/en/java/javase/11/tools/jps.html#GUID-6EB65B96-F9DD-4356-B825-6146E9EEC81E

Here is a sample of using the jps command:

```
C:\Users\sarcarv>jps -l -m
19520 sun.tools.jps.Jps -l -m
22504
17420 java2e.chapter11.Demonstration7
```

Now you can use the jstack command with the process ID to investigate further, as in the following:

```
C:\Users\sarcarv>jstack 17420
```

Note   The jps and jstack commands are experimental and unsupported by Oracle.

Interthread Communication

Polling is a mechanism that repeatedly checks some condition. Consider a classical producer–consumer problem, where a producer can produce at a higher rate than the consumer can consume (or vice versa). If the producer needs to check on the consumer's consumption status repeatedly, it will waste CPU cycles.

To avoid such problems in a multi-threaded environment, Java defines the following methods in the Object class:

- wait(): It will cause the current thread to wait until another thread calls the notify() or notifyAll() methods. There are overloaded versions available for this method in which you can specify the time to wait.

- `notify()`: It wakes up a single thread. The language documentation says the following: "Wakes up a single thread that is waiting on this object's monitor. If any threads are waiting on this object, one of them is chosen to be awakened. The choice is arbitrary and occurs at the discretion of the implementation." It also suggests that the thread that is the actual owner of the object's monitor should call this method.

- `notifyAll()`: This method wakes up all threads that called `wait()` on the same object. The language documentation further says, "The awakened threads will not be able to proceed until the current thread relinquishes the lock on this object. The awakened threads will compete in the usual manner with any other threads that might be actively competing to synchronize on this object; for example, the awakened threads enjoy no reliable privilege or disadvantage in being the next thread to lock this object." Like the `notify()` call, it also suggests that the thread that is the actual owner of the object's monitor should call this method.

Note   There is a term called *spurious wakeup* that indicates that a thread can wake up without being notified, interrupted, or timing out. Though it is a rare situation, Oracle recommends you guard the situation with a check that will verify the condition that caused the thread to be woken. The thread should continue waiting if the condition is not satisfied.

Implementing interthread communication is tough, and you may need to consider many complicated scenarios. But for an easy understanding, let's go through the following demonstration, which has the following characteristics:

- In this example, there is a singleton class called `SharedResource`. In simple words, a singleton class is a class from which you cannot create multiple objects. Once an object is created from a singleton class, you need to reuse that object instead of instantiating a new object. There are different ways to create a `Singleton` class. In the upcoming demonstration, I show a way to make such a construct. So, you can guess that I am using a singleton class to restrict the number of objects created from this class. At the same time, it will help me to easily get a lock on the same object.

- Two synchronized methods—allowJob() and performJob()—are
  placed in this singleton class. The performJob() will perform a
  simple job that simply prints 0 to 9, and the allowJob() will wait
  for the completion of the performJob(). For simplicity, I have set
  a Boolean flag jobDone, which is by default set as false. Once any
  thread completes the performJob(), it will set the flag to true.

- There are two threads—FirstThread and SecondThread.
  FirstThread starts early and starts working in allowJob(), but since
  it sees that the jobDone flag value is false, it releases control and
  starts waiting for SecondThread to complete performJob().

Demonstration 8

Here is the code:

```
package java2e.chapter11;

//A singleton class
class SharedResource {
    static boolean jobDone = false;
    // We make the constructor private to prevent the use of "new"
    private SharedResource() {
    }
    private static SharedResource sharedInstance;

    public static synchronized SharedResource getInstance() {
        if (sharedInstance == null) {
            System.out.println("Creating the singleton Instance");
            sharedInstance = new SharedResource();
        } else {
            System.out.println("I already created a SharedResource
            instance.I'm using that.");
        }
        return sharedInstance;
    }
```

```java
    synchronized void allowJob() {
        System.out.println(Thread.currentThread().getName() + " enters
        into allowJob().");
        System.out.println("Checking whether a new job is allowed to
        perform or not.");
        if (jobDone != true) {
            System.out.println("Waiting for any existing/pending job
            to complete (i.e.jobDone flag to be true).");
            try {
                System.out.println("Releasing control in
                allowJob().");
                wait();
                System.out.println("wait() performed.");
            } catch (Exception e) {
            }
        }
        System.out.println("Ready to allow new Job.");
    }

    synchronized void performJob() throws InterruptedException {
        System.out.println(Thread.currentThread().getName() + " enters
        into performJob()");
        System.out.println("A job is already in progress.");
        for (int i = 0; i < 10; i++) {
            // Any arbitrary job can be performed.Here we are just
            printing 0 to 9.
            System.out.print("\t" + i);
            Thread.sleep(100);
        }
        System.out.println(" ");
        System.out.println("Job completed. ");
        jobDone = true;
        notify();
        //notifyAll();
    }
}
```

```java
//FirstThread class
class FirstThread extends Thread {
      public FirstThread(String name) {
            super(name);
      }

      @Override
      public void run() {
            SharedResource.getInstance().allowJob();
            // new SharedResource().allowJob();//error
            System.out.println("Exit-FirstThread.");
      }
}
//SecondThread class
class SecondThread extends Thread {
      public SecondThread(String name) {
            super(name);
      }
      @Override
      public void run() {
            try {
                  SharedResource.getInstance().performJob();
            } catch (InterruptedException e) {
                  e.printStackTrace();
            }
            // new SharedResource().performJob();//error
            System.out.println("Exit-SecondThread.");
      }
}

class InterThreadCommunication {
      public static void main(String args[]) throws InterruptedException {
            System.out.println("***Demonstration 8. A simple demo on
            Interthread Communication.***");
            FirstThread first = new FirstThread("FirstThread");
            first.start();
```

```
                // We want FirstThread to start executing first
                Thread.sleep(1000);
                SecondThread second = new SecondThread("SecondThread");
                second.start();
        }
}
```

Here is a possible output:

```
***Demonstration 8. A simple demo on Interthread Communication.***
Creating the singleton Instance
FirstThread enters into allowJob().
Checking whether a new job is allowed to perform or not.
Waiting for any existing/pending job to complete (i.e., jobDone flag to be
true).
Releasing control in allowJob().
I already created a SharedResource instance.I'm using that.
SecondThread enters into performJob()
A job is already in progress.
      0     1     2     3     4     5     6     7    8     9
Job completed.
Exit-SecondThread.
wait() performed.
Ready to allow new Job.
Exit-FirstThread.
```

You can see that I deliberately wanted to start FirstThread to execute early so that you can see the working mechanisms of wait() and notify(). I draw your attention to the singleton instance on which wait() was called. It is important to note that you should always wake up the particular thread that called wait() on the same object.

If you want do not want to use the concept of singleton classes, just comment out the private constructor, and inside main() you can use the following code:

```
final SharedResource c = new SharedResource();
            new Thread() {
                    public void run() {
                            c.allowJob();
                    }
```

```
        }.start();
        new Thread() {
                public void run() {
                        try {
                                c.performJob();
                        } catch (InterruptedException e) {
                                e.printStackTrace();
                        }
                }
        }.start();
```

In this case, you do not need to create classes like FirstThread or SecondThread, and the overall code size is reduced. Though you can create as many instances as you want from the SharedResource class, you'll probably agree with me that this code is not easily readable, so I have used the same approach I used in previous demonstrations.

POINTS TO REMEMBER

You should use wait(), notify(), and notifyAll() from a synchronized context. Otherwise, you may encounter java.lang.IllegalMonitorStateException. If these methods are allowed *for* use in a non-synchronized context, there is a possibility that the waiting thread *will* miss the notification from the notifying thread and wait forever.

Lifecycle of a Thread

You have seen that a thread can be in various states, but at any particular moment, it can be in just one particular state:

- In the **Born** state, it is just created, but the start() method is not yet called.

- Once you invoke the start() method, it is in a **Runnable** state, but the scheduler has yet to allow it to run.

- In the **Running** state, the scheduler allows it to execute.

- The thread can enter into a **Non-Runnable** or **Blocked** state when methods like `suspend()`, `wait()`, `sleep()`, etc. are called. But it can again go back to the Runnable state once `resume()` is called or `sleep()` is over or methods like `notify()` and `notifyAll()` are called.

- Finally, a thread is in **Dead** state once it finishes the execution of the `run()` method.

Note   In Java 11, Oracle removed the deprecated `stop()` and `destroy()` methods from the `java.lang.Thread` class. One of the key reasons to remove the `stop()` method is if you call `stop()` externally, all monitors that were held by the thread will be available immediately, which could raise an unsafe situation.

Let's review the various states with Figure 11-5.

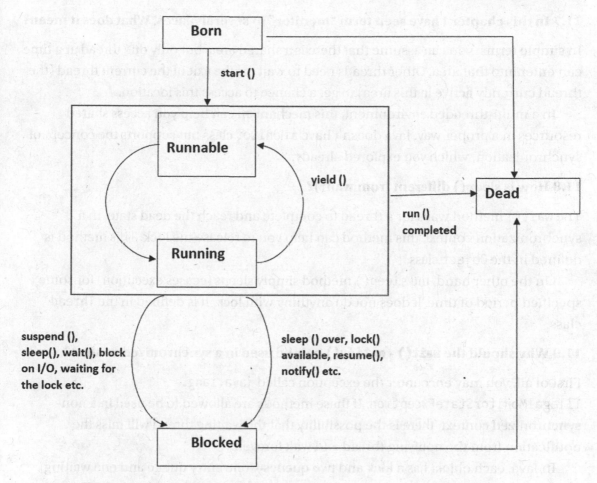

Figure 11-5. *Lifecycle of a thread*

Q&A Session

11.6 What is a thread pool?

A thread pool is another big topic that is not discussed in this chapter. But it is useful to know that these are preinitialized threads that are contained in a collection. You can decide the size of your thread pool. When you want to limit the number of thread creations in your application, you may use this concept. It is helpful because in general, a thread creation is a costly operation and the overall performance of your application can be degraded if you create threads frequently.

11.7 In this chapter I have seen term "monitor" in several places. What does it mean?

In simple terms, you can assume that there is a shared area, but only one thread at a time can enter into that area. Other threads need to wait for the exit of the current thread (the thread currently active in this area) to get a chance to access this location.

In a multi-threaded environment, this mechanism can help you access shared resources in a proper way. Java doesn't have a `Monitor` class but supports the concept of synchronization, which you explored already.

11.8 How is sleep() different from wait()?

The `wait()` method waits for a thread to complete and reach the dead state. In a synchronization context, this method can help you to release the lock. This method is defined in the `Object` class.

On the other hand, the `sleep()` method simply sleeps (ceases execution) for some specified period of time. It does not do anything with lock. It is defined in the `Thread` class.

11.9 Why should the **wait()** - **notify()** pair be used in a synchronized context?

First of all, you may encounter the exception called `java.lang.IllegalMonitorStateException`. If these methods are allowed to be used in a non-synchronized context, there is the possibility that the waiting thread will miss the notification from the notifying thread and wait forever.

In Java, each object has a lock and two queues—one entry queue and one waiting queue. If a thread calls an object's method but the object lock is held with a different thread, the calling thread will enter into the entry queue.

And when you call a `wait()` method, you force the thread to release control and move into a blocked state. It is now placed in the waiting queue.

Now, consider the case where the notification comes from the notifying thread and at the same time the blocking thread is moving to the waiting queue. In this case, the waiting thread can miss the notification and wait forever.

11.10 What will happen if a thread invokes **notify()** (or **notifyAll()**) when there is no thread in the waiting queue?

In this case, there is no impact for the call.

Summary

This chapter discussed the following:

- What is a thread and how is it different from a process?

- How can you create threads?

- What is the lifecycle of a thread?

- What are the different approaches to creating threads in Java?

- What are different Thread class methods and their usage?

- What is the usage of wait(), notify(), and notifyAll() from the Object class?

- What is synchronization and how can you implement the concept in Java?

- What is a deadlock and how can you detect the deadlock in your system?

- How do you experiment with a simple interthread communication technique?

CHAPTER 12

Generic Programming

Generic programming is an important concept in Java. It was introduced in JDK 5, and since then it has become an integral part of Java programming. The power of generic programming is enormous. It will make your program type-safe and flexible. Generics are often used with collections frameworks. So, once you are familiar with Java collections, you will be better able to use generics. This chapter provides a brief overview of generics.

To help you understand the power of generics, I'll start with a non-generic program and then write a generic program. Later, we'll do a comparative analysis to discover the advantages of generic programming.

Compare Generic Programs with Non-Generic Programs

Let's start with a non-generic program to start the analysis.

Demonstration 1

Consider the following non-generic program and the output.

```java
package java2e.chapter12;

class MyNonGenericClass {
    public int showInteger(int i) {
        return i;
    }

    public String showString(String s1) {
        return s1;
    }
}
```

© Vaskaran Sarcar 2020
V. Sarcar, *Interactive Object-Oriented Programming in Java*, https://doi.org/10.1007/978-1-4842-5404-2_12

```
class Demonstration1 {
    public static void main(String[] args) {
        System.out.println("***Demonstration-1.A non-generic program
        example***");
        MyNonGenericClass nonGenericOb = new MyNonGenericClass();
        System.out.println("showInteger returns : " + nonGenericOb.
        showInteger(25));
        System.out.println("showString returns : " + nonGenericOb.
        showString("A non-generic method is called."));
    }
}
```

Output:

```
***Demonstration-1.A non-generic program example***
showInteger returns : 25
showString returns : A non-generic method is called.
```

Now, consider a generic program. Before you start, go through the following points about generic programming in Java:

- In generic programming, you are actually dealing with parameterized types. You will often notice the use of generic classes, generic interfaces, or generic methods in a generic program.

- Angle brackets <> are used to create generic types.

- In your generic program, you can define a class with placeholders for the type of its methods, fields, parameters, etc. At a later stage, these placeholders are replaced with the particular type.

- Prior to JDK5, there was no concept of generic programming in Java. So, in earlier days, to make a generalized class, interface, or method, programmers needed to consider the Object class. Since the Object class is the ultimate super class, an object reference can refer to any subtype object. So, casting was often required to get back the actual type. As a result, type-safety was a big concern prior to the generics era.

- JLS11 says that "it is a compile-time error if a generic class is a direct or indirect subclass of Throwable." This restriction is important because JVM's catch mechanism is compatible only with non-generic classes.

- Experts often suggest the use of generic programming instead of its non-generic counterpart.

Let's start with the following program.

Demonstration 2

Go through the associated comments for a better understanding of the code.

```
package java2e.chapter12;

//A generic class
//T is a type parameter.It will be replaced by the real type when you
//initialize the actual object.
class MyGenericClass<T> {
// A generic method
// The following method's return type is T. It also accepts
// a T type argument.
    public T show(T value) {
            return value;
    }
}

public class Demonstration2 {

        public static void main(String[] args) {
                System.out.println("***Demonstration-2.A generic program
                example***");
                // Creating a MyGenericClass<Integer> type object.
                MyGenericClass<Integer> myGenericClassIntOb = new
                MyGenericClass<Integer>();
                System.out.println("The method show returns the integer
                value : " + myGenericClassIntOb.show(100));
                // Creating a MyGenericClass<String> type object.
```

```
            MyGenericClass<String> myGenericClassStringOb = new
            MyGenericClass<String>();
            System.out.println("The method show returns the string value :
                    "+ myGenericClassStringOb.show("A generic method
                    is called."));
            // Creating a MyGenericClass<Double> type object.
            MyGenericClass<Double> myGenericClassDoubleOb = new
            MyGenericClass<Double>();
            System.out.println("The method show returns the double value :
            " + myGenericClassDoubleOb.show(100.5));
    }
}
```

Output:

```
 ***Demonstration-2.A generic program example***
The method show returns the integer value : 100
The method show returns the string value : A generic method is called.
The method show returns the double value : 100.5
```

Let's now do a comparative analysis of Demonstration 1 and Demonstration 2. You have seen the following characteristics:

- For non-generic methods, you need to specify methods like showInteger() and showString() to handle the particular data type. But in the generic version, the method show() is sufficient. In general, there are fewer lines of code in generic versions (i.e., code size is smaller).

- Inside main() in Demonstration 1, you encounter a compile-time error if you add the following line of code (also shown in Figure 12-1):

```
System.out.println("showDouble returns : " + nonGenericOb.
showDouble(15.9));
```

❌ Errors (1 item)

   🔳 The method showDouble(double) is undefined for the type MyNonGenericClass

Figure 12-1. *A compile-time error in a non-generic program*

The error message is self-explanatory. You know that you did not define something like the showDouble(double d) method for the type MyNonGenericClass. To avoid this error, you may need to include an additional method in the class MyNonGenericClass, as follows (notice the method showDouble() in bold):

```
class MyNonGenericClass {
    public int showInteger(int i) {
        return i;
    }

    public String showString(String s1) {
        return s1;
    }

    public double showDouble(double d) {
        return d;
    }
}
```

The code size of MyNonGenericClass is increased with this addition. You needed to increase the code size because you needed to process a different data type, double.

Now, turn your attention to Demonstration 2, where you get the double data type without modifying MyGenericClass. As a result, you can conclude that the generic version is more flexible and may require fewer lines of code.

Apart from this, consider another useful scenario. Suppose, in Demonstration 2, in the side main() method, you add one more line of code, like the following:

```
myGenericClassIntOb.show(125.7);//Error
```

You will receive a compile-time error now. This is because myGenericIntOb is of type MyGenericClass<Integer>, so the compiler can check whether you are properly passing an Integer argument in the show() method. In this way, you can promote type-safety in your code through generic programming.

You may also wonder why I am not writing something like the following:

```
System.out.println(myGenericClassIntOb.show(new Integer(100)));
// Also ok but no additional benefit
```

instead of

```
System.out.println(myGenericClassIntOb.show(100));
```

It is because Java can perform the autoboxing to encapsulate from an int to the corresponding wrapper class Integer.

Note   Remember, the process of converting a primitive type into an object of the corresponding wrapper class is termed autoboxing. For example, int to Integer, double to Double, float to Float etc. You learned about wrapper classes in Chapter 3.

For a quick review, once again notice the following line of code in Demonstration 2:

MyGenericClass<Integer> myGenericClassIntOb = new MyGenericClass<Integer>();

You need to use similar syntax when you write generic programs in corresponding places. You can observe that the type Integer is specified within the angle brackets after MyGenericClass, and Integer is the type argument that you are passing to the type MyGenericClass. In a similar way, you use MyGenericClass with different types. In this context, you must go through the upcoming statements carefully.

It is also important to note that you are passing the class type; i.e., an Integer argument. But if you pass any primitive datatype, for example, an int, you'll receive a compile-time error. The following declaration is NOT legal in generic programming in Java:

```
// Primitive types are NOT allowed here.
// It must be a reference type.
MyGenericClass<int> myGenericClassIntOb2 = new MyGenericClass<int>();
```

In Eclipse, you will notice an error for this code (as shown in Figure 12-2): Syntax error, insert "Dimensions" to complete ReferenceType. Here is a snapshot from Eclipse IDE.

Errors (2 items)
- ⊗ Syntax error, insert "Dimensions" to complete ReferenceType
- ⊗ Syntax error, insert "Dimensions" to complete ReferenceType

Figure 12-2. Syntax errors when you pass a primitive datatype instead of a reference type

A wrapper class can hold primitive datatypes as objects. So, when you need to pass a primitive datatype in a case like this, you first wrap it in the equivalent wrapper type and proceed (as shown in Demonstration 2).

POINTS TO REMEMBER

It may appear that different versions of MyGenericClass truly exist. But the Java compiler actually removes all this generic type information and performs the necessary cast to make the code behave like this. This removal process is termed *erasure*. In actuality, there is only one version of MyGenericClass that exists for Demonstration 2. You'll learn about erasures shortly.

Demonstration 3

Consider the following program. This demonstration is presented to show how a generic program can perform better than a non-generic program. It should be noted that in this demonstration, I have used the legacy ArrayList (or you can say the non-generic version of ArrayList), which is bad practice and is not recommended. It is presented only for the purpose of comparison with a generic program.

```
package java2e.chapter12;
import java.util.ArrayList;
import java.util.List;

public class Demonstration3 {

    public static void main(String[] args) {
        System.out.println("***Demonstration-3.A bad practice.Using a
        lagacy ArrayList and encountering a runtime error.***");
```

```
            // BAD practice.Following line of code is using a legacy
            //ArrayList
            List myList = new ArrayList();
            myList.add(10);
            myList.add(20);
            myList.add("Invalid");// No compile-time error when you use
            //legacy ArrayList
            // Printing the contents of the ArrayList
            System.out.println("Here is the contents of the ArrayList:");
            for (int i = 0; i < myList.size(); i++) {
                    System.out.println(myList.get(i));
            }
            // Picking last element in the ArrayList
            int lastElement = (int) myList.get(myList.size() - 1);
            System.out.println("Adding 1 to last element and printing");
            System.out.println(++lastElement);// Run-time error
     }
}
```

The program will not raise any compile-time errors, but you will receive a runtime error that says the following:

```
***Demonstration-3.A bad practice.Using a lagacy ArrayList and encountering
a runtime error.***
Here is the contents of the ArrayList:
10
20
Invalid
Exception in thread "main" java.lang.ClassCastException: java.lang.String
cannot be cast to java.lang.Integer
        at java2e.chapter12.Demonstration3.main(Demonstration3.java:21)
```

This is because the third element (i.e., myList [2] in the ArrayList) is not an integer (it is a string). During compile time, you did not encounter any issues, because it was stored as an object. So, you can see that type-safety is a major concern with a non-generic program.

Demonstration 4

One of the notable characteristics of this example is that you can see the use of lambda expressions, which were introduced in Java 8. Since they are not mandatory for this program, I have placed one in the commented block. I have included this because in similar examples, you may notice the use of lambda expressions in different places.

Let's quickly review what a lambda expression is and why it is important. One of the main goals of using a lambda expression is that you can treat it as a function that need not be a part of a class. Here is a sample code for a lambda expression:

```
(int a, int b) -> {return (a + b);}
```

It is a lambda expression that has two parameters and a return statement. It is possible to use lambda expressions without a parameter. A lambda expression can exist without a return statement too. For example, here is a lambda expression that does not accept any parameters and doesn't have any return statements:

```
() -> System.out.println("Lambda expression without a  return statement");
```

Using a lambda expression, you can make your code compact and easily readable. Java lambda expression is treated as a function, so the compiler does not create a .class file for it.

Now, consider the updated program in Demonstration 4, where you use generic programming. The key changes are shown in bold.

```
package java2e.chapter12;

import java.util.ArrayList;
import java.util.List;

public class Demonstration4 {

    public static void main(String[] args) {
        System.out.println("***Demonstration-4.Use Generics to promote
        type-safety and avoid runtime error***");
        ArrayList<Integer> myList = new ArrayList<Integer>();
        myList.add(10);
        myList.add(20);
        // Compile time error when you use ArrayList<Integer>
        //myList.add("Invalid");
```

```
            //Printing the contents of the ArrayList
            System.out.println("Here is the contents of the ArrayList:");
                for (int i = 0; i < myList.size(); i++) {
                System.out.println(myList.get(i));
            }
                /*
                 for (int myInt : myList) { System.out.println(myInt); }
                 System.out.print("Printing the elements using lambda
                 expression:\n");
                 //Or, use the enhanced for loop with lambda expression
                 myList.forEach((myInt) -> System.out.println(myInt));
                 */
                //Picking last element in the ArrayList.
                //No casting is required now.
                int lastElement=myList.get( myList.size()-1);
                System.out.println("Adding 1 to last element and
                printing");
                System.out.println(++lastElement);//No runtime error
        }
}
```

This time, you'll catch the bug much earlier because it is caught at compile time (Figure 12-3). You can see the compile-time error message, which clearly says that you are using a String instead of an Integer.

❌ Errors (1 item)

🔳 The method add(Integer) in the type ArrayList<Integer> is not applicable for the arguments (String)

Figure 12-3. *You can catch an error early in a generic program*

In this case, since the error is caught during compile time, you do not need to wait until runtime to get this error, which is always better. Once you comment out the following line:

```
myList.add("Invalid");
```

you can receive the intended output, as follows:

```
***Demonstration-4.Use Generics to promote type-safety and avoid runtime
error***
Here is the contents of the ArrayList:
10
20
```
Adding 1 to last element and printing
```
21
```

By comparing Demonstration 3 and Demonstration 4, you can say the following:

- To avoid runtime errors, you should prefer the generic version of code to the non-generic version.

- No casting is required now. Notice the following line of code:

  ```
  int lastElement=myList.get( myList.size()-1);
  ```

- Lastly, you can see a commented block of code, which is presented for reference purposes only. In different programs, you may notice one of these variations of a for loop:

  ```
  /*
  for (int myInt : myList) { System.out.println(myInt); }
  System.out.print("Printing the elements using lambda
  expression:\n");
  // Or, use the enhanced for loop with lambda expression
  myList.forEach((myInt) -> System.out.println(myInt));
  */
  ```

- Since you are using the concept of generics, you can print the elements of the ArrayList in a better way. In general, you'll see these versions of code when you traverse and print elements in an ArrayList (or other collection objects).

So, you can surely conclude that the generic version of ArrayList is more flexible and usable than the non-generic version of ArrayList. The same concept is applicable for other collection objects and similar kinds of programming.

Wildcard Types in Generic Programming

In upcoming discussions you'll notice that sometimes you may need to put restrictions on a particular type in generic programming. There are two common ways to implement such constraints—one approach is to use wildcards, and another approach is to use bounded type parameters. Here, I'll start with wildcards.

In generic programming, a wildcard is represented with the question mark (?). It denotes an unknown type. It can be used when you have partial knowledge about the type parameter.

Wildcards can be bounded or unbounded. Bounded wildcards can be used to set either an upper bound or a lower bound for a type argument. Let's start the discussion with an upper-bound wildcard

Upper-bound Wildcard

To begin with, consider the following code segment. In this segment, Vehicle is the super class, and it has two subclasses: Bus and Rocket. Each of these classes has a constructBody() method to construct the particular instances. All of these classes also maintain a counter to track how many instances of these types are created. Here is the code segment:.

```
class Vehicle {
    static int basicVehicleCount;
    // Construct some basic structure of an individual vehicle
    public void constructBody() {
        basicVehicleCount++;
        System.out.println("One basic structure is formed.No of basic
        structure ="+ basicVehicleCount);
    }
}
```

```java
class Bus extends Vehicle {
    static int busCount;

    @Override
    public void constructBody() {
        busCount++;
        System.out.println("Bus completed.It can move on road now. The
        bus count=" + busCount);
    }
}

class Rocket extends Vehicle {
    static int rocketCount;

    @Override
    public void constructBody() {
        rocketCount++;
        System.out.println("Rocket constructed.It can move into space
        now. The rocket count=" + rocketCount);
    }
}
```

Suppose you have stored these vehicles (Vehicle, Bus, or Rocket) in a collection—
say, in an ArrayList. Now you want to invoke the constructBody() method for each
instance in the ArrayList. So, you may start with code like the following:

```java
//May NOT work in this case
    public static void constructBody(List<Vehicle> vehicleList) {
        System.out.println("\nHere is the vehicle list for you : ");
        vehicleList.forEach((vehicle) -> vehicle.constructBody());
    }
```

This segment of code can work when you have an ArrayList<Vehicle> type.
But interestingly, it will not work when you apply it to either the ArrayList<Bus> or
ArrayList<Rocket> types. From the compiler's point of view, ArrayList<Bus> or
ArrayList<Rocket> are different from ArrayList<Vehicle>, though Vehicle is the

supertype of Bus and Rocket (you can refer to the "One Final Suggestion" section at the end of the chapter). In this case, the compiler will suggest you introduce methods like

```
static void constructAllVehicles(ArrayList<Rocket> rockets){//some code}
```

or

```
static void constructAllVehicles(ArrayList<Bus> buses) {//some code}.
```

If you follow those suggestions, the compiler will further complain with different errors, like those in Figure 12-4.

> ⊗ Errors (4 items)
> ⊗ Erasure of method constructAllVehicles(ArrayList<Bus>) is the same as another method in type Demonstration6
> ⊗ Erasure of method constructAllVehicles(ArrayList<Rocket>) is the same as another method in type Demonstration6
> ⊠ The method constructAllVehicles(ArrayList<Bus>) in the type Demonstration6 is not applicable for the arguments (ArrayList<Rocket>)
> ⊠ The method constructAllVehicles(ArrayList<Bus>) in the type Demonstration6 is not applicable for the arguments (ArrayList<Vehicle>)

Figure 12-4. *Eclipse IDE snapshot of some compile-time errors in a generic program*

So, in short, you need to do something special to handle this situation. One possible solution is to use the wildcard type, like the following (shown in bold).

```
// Construct all vehicles in the list
//public static void constructBody(List<Vehicle> vehicleList) {
public static void constructAllVehicles(List<? extends Vehicle>
vehicleList) {
        System.out.println("\nHere is the vehicle list for you : ");
        vehicleList.forEach((vehicle) -> vehicle.constructBody());
    }
```

Here is the full demonstration for you.

Demonstration 5

In this demonstration, some portions are in bold to highlight important lines of code in the program.

```
package java2e.chapter12;

import java.util.ArrayList;
import java.util.List;

class Vehicle {
      static int basicVehicleCount;
      // Construct some basic structure of an individual vehicle
      public void constructBody() {
            basicVehicleCount++;
            System.out.println("One basic structure is formed.No of basic
            structure ="+ basicVehicleCount);
      }
}

class Bus extends Vehicle {
      static int busCount;

      @Override
      public void constructBody() {
            busCount++;
            System.out.println("Bus completed.It can move on road now. The
            bus count=" + busCount);
      }
}

class Rocket extends Vehicle {
      static int rocketCount;

      @Override
      public void constructBody() {
            rocketCount++;
            System.out.println("Rocket constructed.It can move into space
            now. The rocket count=" + rocketCount);
      }
}
```

```java
class Demonstration5 {

    public static void main(String[] args) {
        System.out.println("***Demonstration-5.Use of Wildcard types
        in generic programming.***");
        //One Vehicle object
        Vehicle vehicle1=new Vehicle();
        // Three Bus objects
        Bus bus1 = new Bus();
        Bus bus2 = new Bus();
        Bus bus3 = new Bus();
        // Two Rocket objects
        Rocket rocket1 = new Rocket();
        Rocket rocket2 = new Rocket();

        // List of anytype of vehicles.Vehicle type or its subtypes
        //can be added.
        ArrayList<Vehicle> vehicles = new ArrayList<Vehicle>();
        // Adding one vehicle,one bus and one rocket in the list
        vehicles.add(vehicle1);
        vehicles.add(bus1);//ok
        vehicles.add(rocket1);//ok
        constructAllVehicles(vehicles);// ok

        // List of specific vehicles(buses) only
        ArrayList<Bus> buses = new ArrayList<Bus>();
        // Adding three buses in the list
        buses.add(bus1);
        //error: cannot add a rocket to a bus list
        // buses.add(rocket1);
        buses.add(bus2);
        buses.add(bus3);
        // error if you do not use wildcard in the method
        constructAllVehicles(buses);

        // List of specific vehicles(rockets) only
        ArrayList<Rocket> rockets = new ArrayList<Rocket>();
```

```
            // Adding two rockets in the list
            rockets.add(rocket1);
            rockets.add(rocket2);
            // error if you do not use wildcard in the method
            constructAllVehicles(rockets);
    }

    // Construct all vehicles in the list
    // public static void constructBody(List<Vehicle> vehicleList) {
    public static void constructAllVehicles(List<? extends Vehicle>
    vehicleList) {
            System.out.println("\nHere is the vehicle list for you : ");
            vehicleList.forEach((vehicle) -> vehicle.constructBody());
    }
}
```

Output:

```
***Demonstration-5.Use of Wildcard types in generic programming.***

Here is the vehicle list for you :
One basic structure is formed.No of basic structure =1
Bus completed.It can move on road now. The bus count=1
Rocket constructed.It can move into space now. The rocket count-1

Here is the vehicle list for you :
Bus completed.It can move on road now. The bus count=2
Bus completed.It can move on road now. The bus count=3
Bus completed.It can move on road now. The bus count=4

Here is the vehicle list for you :
Rocket constructed.It can move into space now. The rocket count=2
Rocket constructed.It can move into space now. The rocket count=3
```

You can see that List<Vehicle> is more restrictive than List<? extends Vehicle>. Here, you are relaxing the restriction by using wildcards. As a result, the constructAllVehicles(**List<? extends Vehicle>** vehicleList) can be applied with both the ArrayList<Vehicle> and ArrayList<any subtype of Vehicle> (i.e., with ArrayList<Bus> and ArrayList<Rocket> in this example). So, the ? extends Vehicle syntax simply helps the compiler to match the type Vehicle or any subtype of Vehicle. This is why we say that the extends clause sets an upper bound when you use it with a wildcard.

POINTS TO REMEMBER

It should be noted that extends in this context is used in a general sense, which can mean either extends in classes or implements in interfaces.

Lower-bound Wildcard

You have just learned that when you use the expression <? extends Vehicle> in the argument of a method, you can invoke the method for the Vehicle class or any of its subclasses. So, the Vehicle class here acts as the upper bound. Similarly, you can set the lower bound of a wildcard when you use the expression <? super Vehicle>. In this case, the acceptable arguments are Vehicle and its super class. So, you can roughly interpret the expression <? super T> as "either the class T or any super class of T."

Demonstration 6

Let's consider the following example:

```
package chapter12.testcodes;
import java.util.ArrayList;
import java.util.List;

class Vehicle {
    // Construct some basic structure of an individual vehicle
    public void constructBody() {
        System.out.println("One basic structure is formed.");
    }
}
```

```java
class Bus extends Vehicle {
    static int busCount;

    @Override
    public void constructBody() {
        busCount++;
        System.out.println("Bus completed.It can move on road now. The
        bus count=" + busCount);
    }
}

class Rocket extends Vehicle {
    static int rocketCount;

    @Override
    public void constructBody() {
        rocketCount++;
        System.out.println("Rocket constructed.It can move into space
        now. The rocket count=" + rocketCount);
    }
}

public class TestCodeDemonstration6 {
    public static void main(String[] args) {
        System.out.println("***Demonstration-6.Use of lower-bound
        wildcard types in generic programming.***");
        //Two Vehicle objects
        Vehicle vehicle1=new Vehicle();
        Vehicle vehicle2=new Vehicle();
        // Two Bus objects
        Bus bus1 = new Bus();
        Bus bus2 = new Bus();
        // Two Rocket objects
        Rocket rocket1 = new Rocket();
        Rocket rocket2 = new Rocket();
```

```java
        // List of vehicles
        ArrayList<Vehicle> vehicles = new ArrayList<Vehicle>();
        // Adding two vehicles in the list
        vehicles.add(vehicle1);
        vehicles.add(vehicle2);
        // Adding two buses in the list
        vehicles.add(bus1);
        vehicles.add(bus2);
        constructAllVehicles(vehicles);//ok

        // List of rockets
        ArrayList<Rocket> rockets = new ArrayList<Rocket>();
        // Adding two rockets in the list
        rockets.add(rocket1);
        rockets.add(rocket2);
        //constructAllVehicles(rockets);// Error: Not applicable for
        //ArrayList<Rocket> when you use the lower bound wildcard
    }

    // Construct all vehicles in the list
    public static void constructAllVehicles(List<? super Bus>
    vehicleList) {
        System.out.println("\nHere is the vehicle list for you : ");
        //Compile-time error:Add cast to vehicle
        //vehicleList.forEach((vehicle) ->  vehicle.constructBody());

        /*
        //Runtime error:Vehicle cannot be cast to Bus
        //vehicleList.forEach((vehicle) -> ((Bus) vehicle).
        constructBody());
        */
        vehicleList.forEach((bus) -> ((Vehicle) bus).
        constructBody());//Ok

    }
}
```

```
***Demonstration-6.Use of lower-bound wildcard types in generic
programming.***

Here is the vehicle list for you :
One basic structure is formed.
One basic structure is formed.
Bus completed.It can move on road now. The bus count=1
Bus completed.It can move on road now. The bus count=2
```

You can see that `<? super Bus>` in the method argument helps you to call the method with `ArrayList<Bus>` and `ArrayList<Vehicle>` because `Vehicle` is the supertype of Bus. But you cannot use the method when you use `ArrayList<Rocket>`, because `Rocket` is not a supertype of Bus.

Unbounded Wildcard

Wildcards can be unbounded. You can use the concept of unbounded wildcards when you use just the wildcard character (?). Let's modify the method `constructAllVehicles()` in Demonstration 6 as follows:

```
//The use of an unbounded wildcard
public static void constructAllVehicles(List<?> vehicleList) {
        System.out.println("\nHere is the vehicle list for you : ");
        vehicleList.forEach((anyVehicle) -> ((Vehicle) anyVehicle).
        constructBody());//Ok
}
```

Here, `List<?>` is used to denote a list of unknown types. You can also uncomment the following code in Demonstration 6, as follows:

```
constructAllVehicles(rockets);// Error: Not applicable for
//ArrayList<Rocket> when you use the lower-bound wildcard
```

349

This time there is no compile-time error, and you will receive the following output:

```
***Demonstration-6.Use of lower-bound wildcard types in generic
programming.***

Here is the vehicle list for you :
One basic structure is formed.
One basic structure is formed.
Bus completed.It can move on road now. The bus count=1
Bus completed.It can move on road now. The bus count=2
```

Here is the vehicle list for you :

Rocket constructed.It can move into space now. The rocket count=1
Rocket constructed.It can move into space now. The rocket count=2

Notice the bold lines of the output. You can see that now Rocket objects can also invoke the `constructAllVehicles(List<?> vehicleList)` method.

POINTS TO REMEMBER

You can use generic types, which can contain wildcards as parameter types, fields, or local variables, but not as a type argument for generic methods' invocation. They should not be used for generic class instance creation or supertypes. You can refer to Demonstration 6A for a better understanding.

Q&A Session

12.1 Are `List<?>` and `List<? extends Object>` the same?

No. Let's examine a case. Consider the following code segment:

```java
class Vehicle1Test {
    @Override
    public String toString() {
        return "Vehicle1Test type.";
    }
}
```

```
class Sub1VehicleTest extends Vehicle1Test {
      @Override
      public String toString() {
            return "Sub1VehicleTest type.";
      }
}
```

Now, you can write a method that is something like the following:

```
public static void addElementsVersion2(List<Object> mylist) {
            mylist.add(new Vehicle1Test());// ok
            mylist.add(new Sub1VehicleTest());// ok
            mylist.add(null);// ok
      }
```

But notice the commented code in the following method:

```
public static void addElementsVersion1(List<?> mylist) {
            // mylist.add(new Vehicle1Test());// error
            // mylist.add(new Sub1VehicleTest());// error
            mylist.add(null);// ok
      }
```

In this example, you can add any object type or a subtype into List<Object>, but in case of List<?>, you can only add null. Java language specification (Jls 11 @ section 4.7) further tells us that List<?> is a reifiable type but List<? extends Object> is not.

12.2 What do you mean by reifiable types?

The type whose information is completely available during runtime is called a reifiable type. (You will later learn that some type information is erased during compile time, so it is possible that the complete type information is not available during runtime.)

According to the language specification, a type is reifiable if and only if one of the following holds:

- It refers to a non-generic class or interface type declaration.
- It is a parameterized type in which all type arguments are unbounded wildcards.
- It is a raw type.

351

- It is a primitive type.

- It is an array type whose element type is reifiable.

- It is a nested type where, for each type T separated by a ".", T itself is reifiable.

12.3 Then what is the use of `List<?>`?

Sometimes you may just want to iterate through your collection. For example, consider the following program and output:

```
package chapter12.testcodes;

import java.util.ArrayList;
import java.util.List;

class Vehicle1Test {
    @Override
    public String toString() {
        return "Vehicle1Test type.";
    }
}

class Sub1VehicleTest extends Vehicle1Test {
    @Override
    public String toString() {
        return "Sub1VehicleTest type.";
    }
}

class Test1 {
    public static void main(String[] args) {
        System.out.println("***A sample test.An use of List<?>***");
        Vehicle1Test vehicle1 = new Vehicle1Test();
        Vehicle1Test vehicle2 = new Sub1VehicleTest();
        List<Object> vehicles = new ArrayList<Object>();
        vehicles.add(vehicle1);// ok
```

```
        vehicles.add(vehicle2);// ok
        printElements(vehicles);// ok.An example of use //List<?> in a
        //method argument
    }

    public static void addElementsVersion1(List<?> mylist) {
        // mylist.add(new Vehicle1Test());// error
        // mylist.add(new Sub1VehicleTest());// error
        mylist.add(null);// ok
    }

    public static void addElementsVersion2(List<Object> mylist) {
        mylist.add(new Vehicle1Test());// ok
        mylist.add(new Sub1VehicleTest());// ok
        mylist.add(null);// ok
    }

    public static void printElements(List<?> mylist) {
        mylist.forEach(element -> System.out.println(element));
    }
}
```

Output:

```
***A sample test.An use of List<?>***
Vehicle1Test type.
Sub1VehicleTest type.
```

12.4 What is a raw type?

You will see a discussion of raw types in Demonstration 10.

12.5 Can you present some valid and invalid statements showing when you use wildcards in your program?

Demonstration 6A can help you. Here, you can analyze different case studies.

Demonstration 6A

Review the program and the supporting comments for your understanding.

```java
package chapter12.testcodes;

import java.util.Arrays;
import java.util.Collections;
import java.util.List;

class Sample {
    //Case Study-1:Wildcards in fields
    List<?> myList;  //valid
    //? aField;  //Invalid

    //Case Study-2:Wildcards in method parameter
    //Syntax error for ?
    //Invalid
     //public void invalidMethodWithWildCardParameter(? methodParameter) {
            //Some code
    // }
    //The following method is valid.

    public void validMethodWithWildCardParameter(List<?> myParameter) {
            System.out.println("The validMethodWithWildCardParameter
            (List<?> myParameter) is a valid method.");
            }
    //Case Study-3:Wildcards in return type

    //Error: Return type for the method is missing
    // private ? methodWithWildCardReturnType() {//Invalid
            //return null;
    //    }
}
//Case Study-4:Wildcards in supertype
//Error: A supertype may not specify any wild card
//public class SubList implements List<?>{ //Invalid
    //Some code
//}
```

```
class Test2 {
    public static void main(String[] args) {
      System.out.println("***Demonstration 6A.Some case study with
      wildcards***");
    Sample sample=new Sample();
    //Case Study-5:Wildcards in local variable
    List<?> myList = Arrays.asList(12,27,39);//Valid
    System.out.println("Original list :" + myList);
    Collections.reverse(myList);
    System.out.println("Reversed List:"+myList);
    sample.validMethodWithWildCardParameter(myList);
    }
}
```

Here is the output from Demonstration 6A.

```
***Demonstration 6A.Some case study with wildcards***
Original list :[12, 27, 39]
Reversed List:[39, 27, 12]
The validMethodWithWildCardParameter(List<?> myParameter) is a valid
method.
```

Bounded Type Parameter

You'll learn shortly that wildcards cannot solve all your problems efficiently. There is another option, called bounded type parameters. They help you to restrict the types that you can use as the type arguments in parameterized types.

Let's begin with a very simple use case. Assume that you are dealing with some integers and doubles, and you want to make a generic class that should have a method to calculate the sum of these values. You understand the following:

- You can create a method with the return type double to serve your purpose.

- You are using generics, so you need to consider a wrapper class for int and double. Integer is the wrapper for int, and Double is the wrapper for double.

- Integer and Double are subclasses of the Number class, which
  has methods like intValue(), longValue(), floatValue(),
  doubleValue(), and byteValue(). Let's see from Eclipse IDE what the
  method doubleValue() does. Figure 12-5 is a snapshot from Eclipse.

```
/**
 * Returns the value of the specified number as a {@code double},
 * which may involve rounding.
 *
 * @return  the numeric value represented by this object after conversion
 *          to type {@code double}.
 */
public abstract double doubleValue();
```

Figure 12-5. *A snapshot of the doubleValue() method details from*
Eclipse IDE

- Since doubleValue() is an abstract method, its concrete subclasses
  must implement this method. Now, let's check how the Integer class
  implements the doubleValue() method. Here it is:

```
/**
 * Returns the value of this {@code Integer} as a {@code double}
 * after a widening primitive conversion.
 * @jls 5.1.2 Widening Primitive Conversions
 */
public double doubleValue() {
        return (double)value;
}
```

- Now, let's also check how the Double class implements the
  doubleValue() in the Number class:

```
/**
 * Returns the {@code double} value of this {@code Double} object.
 * @return the {@code double} value represented by this object
 */
public double doubleValue() {
        return value;
}
```

From these definitions, it is obvious that in your case, you can use the `doubleValue()` method. Now you can write the following program.

Demonstration 7

Let's compile and run the program and then analyze the output.

```
package java2e.chapter12;

//A generic class
//T is a type parameter.It will be replaced by the real type when you
//initialize the actual object.
class GenericDemo7Class<T extends Number> {
    T firstNumber, secondNumber;

    GenericDemo7Class(T firstNumber, T secondNumber) {
        this.firstNumber = firstNumber;
        this.secondNumber = secondNumber;
    }

    // Always returning a double value
    public double displaySum() {
        //using the library method doubleValue()
        return firstNumber.doubleValue() + secondNumber.doubleValue();
    }
}

class Demonstration7 {
    public static void main(String[] args) {
        System.out.println("***Demonstration-7.A typical use of
        bounded type parameter.***\n");
        GenericDemo7Class<Double> doubleOb = new
        GenericDemo7Class<Double>(2.5, 5.7);
        System.out.println("2.5+5.7=" + doubleOb.displaySum());

        GenericDemo7Class<Integer> intOb = new
        GenericDemo7Class<Integer>(2, 7);
        System.out.println("2+7=" + intOb.displaySum());
```

```
//GenericDemo7Class<String> stringOb=new GenericDemo7Class<Str
ing>("hello","world!");
// Bound mismatch error if you use class GenericDemo7Class<T
extends Number>
//System.out.println( "2+7=" +stringOb.displaySum());
    }
    }
```

Output:

```
***Demonstration-7.A typical use of bounded type parameter.***

2.5+5.7=8.2
2+7=9.0
```

You can see that the program is compiled and run successfully. Now, consider the following points:

- Let's see what happens when you use <T> instead of <T extends Number> in the prior demonstration, as follows:

```
//class GenericDemo7Class<T extends Number> {
class GenericDemo7Class<T> {
```

This time, you'll encounter the compile-time error as follows (shown in Figure 12-6): The method doubleValue() is undefined for the type T.

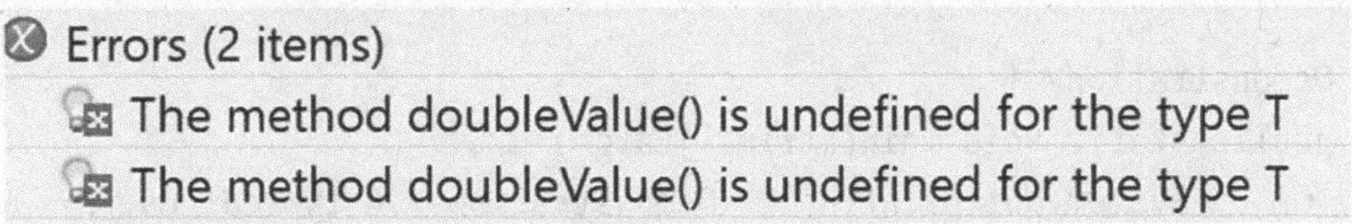

Figure 12-6. *The compile-time error says doubleValue() is undefined for the type T*

The compiler is raising this concern because in this case, it is not sure whether you will use a true number or not. But when you use `<T extends Number>`, you are telling the compiler that you will always pass a `Number` type, not any other types.

- You can see some commented lines in Demonstration 7. If you uncomment the following line

```
GenericDemo7Class<String> stringOb = new GenericDemo7Class
<String>("hello","world!");
```

you'll receive compile-time errors for bound mismatches. Figure 12-7 is the Eclipse IDE snapshot for that.

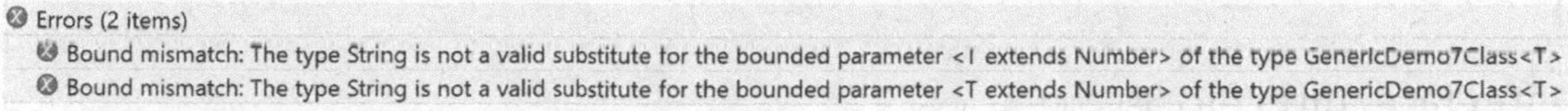

❌ Errors (2 items)
  ❌ Bound mismatch: The type String is not a valid substitute for the bounded parameter <T extends Number> of the type GenericDemo7Class<T>
  ❌ Bound mismatch: The type String is not a valid substitute for the bounded parameter <T extends Number> of the type GenericDemo7Class<T>

Figure 12-7. *Bound mismatch errors*

So, you can see that when you use `<T extends Number>` instead of `<T>`, you cannot pass anything other than the `Number` type.

POINTS TO REMEMBER

In generic programming, `<T extends YourSuperClass>` says that T can be replaced by either `YourSuperClass` or *any subclass of* `YourSuperClass`. This approach helps you to provide an inclusive upper bound. Using this approach, you are promoting type safety in your program.

It should be noted that, like wildcards, `extends` in this context is used in a general sense, which means it either extends the class or implements the interface.

You can use both the class type and the interface type as bounds. But there is an important restriction. You may remember that in Java programming, your class can extend from another class, and it can implement multiple interfaces. The same rule applies here. At the same time, you also need to mention class type before the interface type(s). When you create a bound with a class type and the interface type(s), you use the & operator, as follows:

```
<T extends ClassName & FirstInterfaceName & SecondInterfaceName>
```

Let's assume you have the following code segment:

```
class Demo8AClass {
    //Some code
}

class Demo8BClass {
    //Some code
}

interface Interface8ADemo {
    //Some code
}

interface Interface8BDemo {
    //Some code
}

class ImplementorInterface8ADemo implements Interface8ADemo{
    //Some code
}
```

Demonstration 8

For the prior code segment, Demonstration 8 presents some samples of valid and invalid statements for your reference. *Here invalid statements are marked with the comment //* Error *and valid statements are marked with //*Ok.

```
//class GenericDemo8Class<T extends Demo8AClass & Demo8BClass> {//Error

//class GenericDemo8Class<T extends  Interface8ADemo & Demo8AClass &
Interface8BDemo> {//Error

//class GenericDemo8Class<T extends  ImplementorInterface8ADemo &
Interface8ADemo & Interface8BDemo> {//Ok
```

```
class GenericDemo8Class<T extends Demo8AClass & Interface8ADemo &
Interface8BDemo> {//Ok
}
```

Q&A Session

12.6 How do wildcards differ from bounded type parameters?

It depends on your implementation. In certain situations, bounded type parameters can promote better readability and safety. It'll be helpful to remember the syntax for them. Any wildcard can have only one bound.

- For upper bound, you use: `? extends SuperType`

- For lower bound, you use: `? super SubType`

On the other hand, you can associate multiple bounds with a type parameter. So, you have seen the following statements before.

When you create a bound with a class type and the interface type(s), you use the & operator, as follows:

```
<T extends ClassName & FirstInterfaceName & SecondInterfaceName>
```

Demonstration 8 shows some of the usage of this.

Erasures

Prior to Demonstration 3, I stated that it may appear that different versions of `MyGenericClass` exist. But the Java compiler actually removes all this generic type information and performs the necessary cast to make the code behave like this. This removal process is termed erasure. So, in actuality, only one version of `MyGenericClass` exists for Demonstration 2. You'll go through a detailed discussion of this topic now.

In short, for a parameterized class, there is only one compiled class file. For example, suppose you use `ArrayList<Double>`, `ArrayList<Integer>`, or `ArrayList<String>` in your program. In this case, the type parameters help you to raise compile-time errors if you try to store any unwanted type of object in your container. So, you promote type safety at compile time. But though you use different type parameters in your generic data structures, all these parameterized types use the same compiled class. It is because all the type information is erased at runtime. The process is a little bit complex, but most of the time you do not need to deal with them directly.

As per the Oracle Java documentation, type erasures can work in the following ways:

- All type parameters in generic types will be replaced with their bounds. For an unbounded type, it will be replaced by Object. As a result, the generated bytecode will contain the ordinary classes, interfaces, and methods.

- To preserve type safety, type casts will be inserted.

- It can generate bridge methods to preserve polymorphism in extended generic types.

So, here is the bottom line: **Type erasure ensures that you will not create different classes for different parameterized types in the compiled code**.

Demonstration 9

Let's start with a simple case study. Here, I'll compile the code and then decompile it. To make it simple and straightforward, I am using the javac and javap commands, respectively. I have decompiled this code in a different place in my machine, and this is why I have intentionally removed the package statement in the following demonstration.

```
import java.util.List;
import java.util.ArrayList;

class Demonstration9 {

    public static void main(String[] args) {
        System.out.println("***Demonstration-9.Examine the type
        erasures.***");
        List<Integer> myIntList = new ArrayList<Integer>();
        myIntList.add(10);
        myIntList.add(20);
        //myIntList.add("Invalid");//error

        int firstNumber=myIntList.get(0);
        System.out.println("First number is :"+ firstNumber);
```

```java
        int secondNumber=myIntList.get(1);
        System.out.println("Second number is :"+ secondNumber);

        List<String> myStrList = new ArrayList<String>();
        myStrList.add("Hello");
        myStrList.add(" world !");
        //myStrList.add(30);//error

        String firstString=myStrList.get(0);
        System.out.println("First String is :"+ firstString);
        String secondString=myStrList.get(1);
        System.out.println("Second String is :"+ secondString);
    }
}
```

Output:

```
***Demonstration-9.Examine the type erasures.***
First number is :10
Second number is :20
First String is :Hello
Second String is : world !
```

The output is straightforward and is not important in the upcoming analysis. Let's decompile the class file (that you got after the compilation process). Here are the snapshots for your reference. It's a big snap, so I am presenting it in three parts: Figure 12-8, Figure 12-9, and Figure 12-10.

```
C:\TestGenericCode>javac Demonstration9.java

C:\TestGenericCode>javap -c Demonstration9.class
Compiled from "Demonstration9.java"
class Demonstration9 {
  Demonstration9();
    Code:
       0: aload_0
       1: invokespecial #1                  // Method java/lang/Object."<init>":()V
       4: return

  public static void main(java.lang.String[]);
    Code:
       0: getstatic      #2                  // Field java/lang/System.out:Ljava/io/PrintStream;
       3: ldc            #3                  // String ***Demonstration-9.Examine the type erasures.***
       5: invokevirtual  #4                  // Method java/io/PrintStream.println:(Ljava/lang/String;)V
       8: new            #5                  // class java/util/ArrayList
      11: dup
      12: invokespecial #6                  // Method java/util/ArrayList."<init>":()V
      15: astore_1
      16: aload_1
      17: bipush        10
      19: invokestatic  #7                  // Method java/lang/Integer.valueOf:(I)Ljava/lang/Integer;
      22: invokeinterface #8,  2            // InterfaceMethod java/util/List.add:(Ljava/lang/Object;)Z
      27: pop
      28: aload_1
      29: bipush        20
      31: invokestatic  #7                  // Method java/lang/Integer.valueOf:(I)Ljava/lang/Integer;
      34: invokeinterface #8,  2            // InterfaceMethod java/util/List.add:(Ljava/lang/Object;)Z
      39: pop
      40: aload_1
      41: iconst_0
      42: invokeinterface #9,  2            // InterfaceMethod java/util/List.get:(I)Ljava/lang/Object;
      47: checkcast      #10                 // class java/lang/Integer
      50: invokevirtual #11                 // Method java/lang/Integer.intValue:()I
      53: istore_2
      54: getstatic      #2                  // Field java/lang/System.out:Ljava/io/PrintStream;
      57: new            #12                 // class java/lang/StringBuilder
      60: dup
      61: invokespecial #13                 // Method java/lang/StringBuilder."<init>":()V
```

Figure 12-8. *Partial snapshot of the decompiled Demonstration9.class (Part I)*

```
61: invokespecial #13                     // Method java/lang/StringBuilder."<init>":()V
64: ldc          #14                       // String First number is :
66: invokevirtual #15                      // Method java/lang/StringBuilder.append:(Ljava/lang/String;)Ljava/lang/StringBuilder;
69: iload_2
70: invokevirtual #16                      // Method java/lang/StringBuilder.append:(I)Ljava/lang/StringBuilder;
73: invokevirtual #17                      // Method java/lang/StringBuilder.toString:()Ljava/lang/String;
76: invokevirtual #4                       // Method java/io/PrintStream.println:(Ljava/lang/String;)V
79: aload_1
80: iconst_1
81: invokeinterface #9, 2                  // InterfaceMethod java/util/List.get:(I)Ljava/lang/Object;
86: checkcast     #10                      // class java/lang/Integer
89: invokevirtual #11                      // Method java/lang/Integer.intValue:()I
92: istore_3
93: getstatic     #2                       // Field java/lang/System.out:Ljava/io/PrintStream;
96: new           #12                      // class java/lang/StringBuilder
99: dup
100: invokespecial #13                     // Method java/lang/StringBuilder."<init>":()V
103: ldc          #18                      // String Second number is :
105: invokevirtual #15                     // Method java/lang/StringBuilder.append:(Ljava/lang/String;)Ljava/lang/StringBuilder;
108: iload_3
109: invokevirtual #16                     // Method java/lang/StringBuilder.append:(I)Ljava/lang/StringBuilder;
112: invokevirtual #17                     // Method java/lang/StringBuilder.toString:()Ljava/lang/String;
115: invokevirtual #4                      // Method java/io/PrintStream.println:(Ljava/lang/String;)V
118: new          #5                       // class java/util/ArrayList
121: dup
122: invokespecial #6                      // Method java/util/ArrayList."<init>":()V
125: astore       4
127: aload        4
129: ldc          #19                      // String Hello
131: invokeinterface #8, 2                 // InterfaceMethod java/util/List.add:(Ljava/lang/Object;)Z
136: pop
137: aload        4
139: ldc          #20                      // String world !
141: invokeinterface #8, 2                 // InterfaceMethod java/util/List.add:(Ljava/lang/Object;)Z
146: pop
147: aload        4
149: iconst_0
150: invokeinterface #9, 2                 // InterfaceMethod java/util/List.get:(I)Ljava/lang/Object;
```

Figure 12-9. *Partial snapshot of the decompiled Demonstration9.class (Part II)*

```
155: checkcast     #21                     // class java/lang/String
158: astore       5
160: getstatic     #2                      // Field java/lang/System.out:Ljava/io/PrintStream;
163: new           #12                     // class java/lang/StringBuilder
166: dup
167: invokespecial #13                     // Method java/lang/StringBuilder."<init>":()V
170: ldc          #22                      // String First String is :
172: invokevirtual #15                     // Method java/lang/StringBuilder.append:(Ljava/lang/String;)Ljava/lang/StringBuilder;
175: aload        5
177: invokevirtual #15                     // Method java/lang/StringBuilder.append:(Ljava/lang/String;)Ljava/lang/StringBuilder;
180: invokevirtual #17                     // Method java/lang/StringBuilder.toString:()Ljava/lang/String;
183: invokevirtual #4                      // Method java/io/PrintStream.println:(Ljava/lang/String;)V
186: aload        4
188: iconst_1
189: invokeinterface #9, 2                 // InterfaceMethod java/util/List.get:(I)Ljava/lang/Object;
194: checkcast     #21                     // class java/lang/String
197: astore       6
199: getstatic     #2                      // Field java/lang/System.out:Ljava/io/PrintStream;
202: new          #12                      // class java/lang/StringBuilder
205: dup
206: invokespecial #13                     // Method java/lang/StringBuilder."<init>":()V
209: ldc          #23                      // String Second String is :
211: invokevirtual #15                     // Method java/lang/StringBuilder.append:(Ljava/lang/String;)Ljava/lang/StringBuilder;
214: aload        6
216: invokevirtual #15                     // Method java/lang/StringBuilder.append:(Ljava/lang/String;)Ljava/lang/StringBuilder;
219: invokevirtual #17                     // Method java/lang/StringBuilder.toString:()Ljava/lang/String;
222: invokevirtual #4                      // Method java/io/PrintStream.println:(Ljava/lang/String;)V
225: return
}
```

Figure 12-10. *Partial snapshot of the decompiled Demonstration9.class (Part III)*

Here are the important points in these snapshots that I want to highlight:

- Both line number 8 and line number 118 ensure that, once compiled, you get a non-parameterized version of ArrayList. So, when you run your program, those types' info will not be available.

- Notice how the type casts are added in line numbers 47, 86, 155, and 194. In lines 47 and 86, you can see the presence of Integer, and in lines 155 and 194, you can see the presence of String.

Raw Types

When you refer to a generic type without specifying the type parameter, you create a raw type. For example, in Demonstration 2, we used the following line of code:

```
MyGenericClass<Double> myGenericClassDoubleOb = new
MyGenericClass<Double>();
```

But instead of this, if we write something like the following, we create a raw type of MyGenericClass<T>:

```
// Creating a raw type of MyGenericClass<T>
MyGenericClass rawOb = new MyGenericClass();
```

So, MyGenericClass is a raw type of MyGenericClass<T>.

The raw types were used to support the legacy code in the pre-generic era. To support backward compatibility, you can assign a parameterized type to a raw type, but when you do the reverse, you will get a warning message like the following:

```
Type safety: The expression of type MyGenericClass needs unchecked
conversion to conform to MyGenericClass<Double>
```

This is because the compiler does not have sufficient information to ensure the type-safety. Here are some code segments with supporting comments for your reference:

```
// Creating a MyGenericClass<Double> type object.
MyGenericClass<Double> doubleOb = new MyGenericClass<Double>();
// Creating a raw type of MyGenericClass<T>
MyGenericClass rawOb = new MyGenericClass();
```

```
// To support backward compatibility, you can assign a parameterized type
//to a raw type
rawOb = doubleOb;// Ok
// But if you assign a raw type to a parameterized type, there is a
//warning message.
doubleOb = rawOb;// Warning message
```

It is also important to note that when you use raw types with parameterized types, you need to concentrate on casting, and you may compromise type safety. For example, in the following code segment, notice that no casting is necessary for d1, but before you use d2, you need to type-cast properly:

```
// Creating a MyGenericClass<Double> type object.
MyGenericClass<Double> doubleOb = new MyGenericClass<Double>();
double d1 = doubleOb.show(100.5);
// Creating a raw type of MyGenericClass<T>
MyGenericClass rawOb = new MyGenericClass();
doubleOb = rawOb;// Warning message
double d2 = (double) rawOb.show(200.5);// type casting is required
```

In general, you should try to avoid the use of raw types. Raw types can also create runtime errors.

Demonstration 10

Demonstration 10 is presented here to summarize the prior discussions:

```
package java2e.chapter12;

//class MyGenericClass<T>  is defined in Demonstration2
class Demonstration10 {

        public static void main(String[] args) {
                System.out.println("***Demonstration-10.Case study with raw
                types.***");
                // Creating a MyGenericClass<Double> type object.
                MyGenericClass<Double> doubleOb = new
                MyGenericClass<Double>();
```

```
                double d1 = doubleOb.show(100.5);
                System.out.println("The method show returns the double value :
                " + d1);

                // Creating a raw type of MyGenericClass<T>
                MyGenericClass rawOb = new MyGenericClass();
                // To support backward compatibility, you can assign a
                parameterized type //to a  raw type
                //rawOb = doubleOb;// Ok
                // But if you assign a raw type to a parameterized type, there
                //is a warning message
                doubleOb = rawOb;// Warning message
                double d2 = (double) rawOb.show(200.5);// type casting is
                //required
                System.out.println("The value in d2 is: " + d2);
                // No compile-time error but it'll cause runtime error
                //int i3 = (int) rawOb.show(200.5);
                //System.out.println("The value in i3 is: " + i3);
        }
}
```

Output:

```
***Demonstration-10.Case study with raw types.***
The method show returns the double value : 100.5
The value in d2 is: 200.5
```

Q&A Session

12.7 Are interfaces raw types?

No. JLS11 confirms that a non-generic class or an interface is not a raw type.

12.8 "Raw types can also create runtime errors"—can you please elaborate?

Notice the following few lines in Demonstration 10. You will get runtime errors.

```
                // No compile-time error but it'll cause runtime error
                // int i3 = (int) rawOb.show(200.5);
                // System.out.println("The value in i3 is: " + i3);
```

If you uncomment the last two lines and compile the program, there is no error. But when you run the program, you will get the following error messages:

```
***Demonstration-10.Case study with raw types.***
The method show returns the double value : 100.5
The value in d2 is: 200.5
Exception in thread "main" java.lang.ClassCastException: java.lang.Double
cannot be cast to java.lang.Integer
        at java2e.chapter12.Demonstration10.main(Demonstration10.java:23)
```

Note   JLS 11 says the following: "The use of raw types is allowed only as a concession to compatibility of legacy code. The use of raw types in code written after the introduction of generics into the Java programming language is strongly discouraged. It is possible that future versions of the Java programming language will disallow the use of raw types."

Type Inference Using Diamond Operator

You can make use of a pair of angle brackets (called the diamond operator) to replace the type arguments that are required to invoke the generic class constructor as long as the compiler can infer it properly. For example, if you append the following lines of code to the prior demonstration, there is no warning message for you:

```
//JDK7 onwards, you can use a short syntax using diamond operator
MyGenericClass<Double> doubleOb2 = new MyGenericClass<>();
doubleOb=doubleOb2;//No warning message
```

But you can remember that, in demonstration 10, when you used the following line:

```
doubleOb = rawOb;
```

there was a warning message for you. So, you can use the diamond operator to type less (i.e., you can shorten long declaration statements), and you can also ensure that you are NOT creating a raw type. Since JDK7, this functionality has been available in Java. Lastly, though you can use this concept in method calls, Oracle suggests you primarily use the diamond operator for variable declarations. Personally, I like full-syntax declarations for better readability and understanding, and it allows me to execute my code properly prior to JDK7.

Applying Inheritance

You can apply the concept of inheritance in your generic program; i.e., you can subtype a generic class by extending it, or you can subtype an interface by implementing it. The only restriction is that you should not vary the argument.

Demonstration 11

For example, consider Demonstration 11 with output.

```
package java2e.chapter12;
//class MyGenericClass<T>  is defined in Demonstration2

//Compile-time error
//class SubClass<V> extends MyGenericClass<T> {
//The following declaration is fine
class SubClass<T> extends MyGenericClass<T> {
    //Some code
}
class Demonstration11 {

    public static void main(String[] args) {
        System.out.println("***Demonstration-11.Inheritance in Generic
        Programming.***");
        SubClass<Integer>  subInt = new SubClass<Integer>();
        System.out.println("The method show returns the interger
        value : " + subInt.show(200));
    }
}
```

Output:

```
***Demonstration-11.Inheritance in Generic Programming.***
The method show returns the interger value : 200
```

The previous output is obvious. But notice the commented line:

```
//class SubClass<V> extends MyGenericClass<T> {
```

If you use this line of code, you will receive a compile-time error. This is because, as per the language construct, you should not vary the argument. Your subclass must pass the type argument that is needed in its super class.

When you create a subtype, you can also add a subclass-specific method. For example, in this modified example, SubClass introduces a new type parameter and a subclass-specific method. Let's go through the following program and its modified output.

```
package java2e.chapter12;
//class MyGenericClass<T>  is defined in Demonstration2

//For modified program
class SubClass<T,V> extends MyGenericClass<T> {
    //Subclass-specific method
    public V subMethod(V value) {
        return value;
    }
}

class Demonstration11 {

    public static void main(String[] args) {
        //System.out.println("***Demonstration-11.Inheritance in
        Generic Programming.***");
        System.out.println("***Demonstration-11 Modified.Inheritance
        in Generic Programming.***");
        //For modified program
        SubClass<Integer, String>  subInt = new
        SubClass<Integer,String>();
        System.out.println("The method show returns the integer
        value : " + subInt.show(200));
        System.out.println("The subMethod returns : " + subInt.
        subMethod("It is ok!"));
    }
}
```

Modified output:

```
***Demonstration-11 Modified.Inheritance in Generic Programming.***
The method show returns the integer value : 200
The subMethod returns : It is ok!
```

Bridge Method

An interesting situation may occur where the complier needs to add a method to a class. This method is called a bridge method. In general, you do not need to deal with this case directly.

To understand the scenario, let's go through the following code segment:

```java
class GenericClass12<T> {
    public void show(T value) {
        System.out.println("Inside parent class.The value is:"+value);
    }
}

class SubClass12 extends GenericClass12<Integer> {
    @Override
    public void show(Integer value) {
        System.out.println("Inside Child Class.The value is:"+value);
    }
}
```

Have you noticed the important characteristics? Let's analyze.

- The derived class Subclass12 extends from the Integer specific version of GenericClass12; i.e., GenericClass12<Integer>.

- The derived class SubClass12 also overrides the parent method show().

Though this type of coding is allowed, a problem may arise when type erasure comes into play. Once type erasure performs its job, the expected form of the show( ) method in GenericClass12 is as follows:

public void show(Object value){//other code..}

And the expected form of the show( ) method in SubClass12 is:

public void show()(Integer value){//other code}

So, after the type erasure's action, the method signatures do not match. To handle the situation and preserve polymorphism, the compiler generates a bridge method in Subclass12, with the preceding signature that can call the Integer-specific version. So, the new method show( ) will appear in the derived class (i.e., in SubClass12) as follows:

```
public void show(Object value) {
        show((Integer) value);
}
```

Demonstration 12

Now, consider Demonstration 12 and its corresponding output. Then go through the analysis (after the output section) to experience the presence of the generated bridge method.

```
package java2e.chapter12;

class GenericClass12<T> {
      public void show(T value) {
            System.out.println("Inside parent class.The value is:"+value);
      }
}

class SubClass12 extends GenericClass12<Integer> {
      @Override
      public void show(Integer value) {
            System.out.println("Inside Child Class.The value is:"+value);
      }
}
```

```
class Demonstration12 {
    public static void main(String[] args) {
        System.out.println("***Demonstration-12.Bridge Method in
        Generic Programming.***");
        // Creating a MyGenericClass<Integer> type object.
        GenericClass12<Integer> parentOb = new
        GenericClass12<Integer>();
        parentOb.show(100);
        // A SubClass12 object
        SubClass12 childOb = new SubClass12();
        childOb.show(300);
        //Object ob=(int)400;
        //childOb.show(ob);//Error

        //Using Polymorphism
        System.out.println("Using Ploymorphism :" );
        parentOb=childOb;
        parentOb.show(500);
    }
}
```

Output:

```
***Demonstration-12.Bridge Method in Generic Programming.***
Inside parent class.The value is:100
Inside Child Class.The value is:300
Using Ploymorphism :
Inside Child Class.The value is:500
```

When I used the javap command, I could see that both methods were present in SubClass12 like in Figure 12-11. (The precise output may vary based on your Java version.)

```
C:\Feluda_June12,2017Onwards\MyPrograms\EclipseJavaPrograms\InteractiveJava2e\java2e\chapter12>javap -c SubClass12.class
Compiled from "Demonstration12.java"
class java2e.chapter12.SubClass12 extends java2e.chapter12.GenericClass12<java.lang.Integer> {
  java2e.chapter12.SubClass12();
    Code:
       0: aload_0
       1: invokespecial #8          // Method java2e/chapter12/GenericClass12."<init>":()V
       4: return

  public void show(java.lang.Integer);
    Code:
       0: getstatic     #16         // Field java/lang/System.out:Ljava/io/PrintStream;
       3: new           #22         // class java/lang/StringBuilder
       6: dup
       7: ldc           #24         // String Inside Child Class.The value is:
       9: invokespecial #26         // Method java/lang/StringBuilder."<init>":(Ljava/lang/String;)V
      12: aload_1
      13: invokevirtual #29         // Method java/lang/StringBuilder.append:(Ljava/lang/Object;)Ljava/lang/StringBuilder;
      16: invokevirtual #33         // Method java/lang/StringBuilder.toString:()Ljava/lang/String;
      19: invokevirtual #37         // Method java/io/PrintStream.println:(Ljava/lang/String;)V
      22: return

  public void show(java.lang.Object);
    Code:
       0: aload_0
       1: aload_1
       2: checkcast     #45         // class java/lang/Integer
       5: invokevirtual #47         // Method show:(Ljava/lang/Integer;)V
       8: return
}
```

Figure 12-11. *Snapshot of the decompiled SubClass12.class*

12.9 Why is the bridge method needed?

You have already seen that after type erasure's action, the method signatures in the parent class and its child class did not match, and so it affects the concept of polymorphism. To address these issues, the bridge method is useful.

In this context, notice the last few lines of code in Demonstration 12. This portion of code demonstrates how the concept of polymorphism is preserved.

Important Restrictions in Generic Programming

There are many restrictions associated with generic programming. You'll become familiar with them only upon practice. Let's finish the chapter with a discussion of some common restrictions.

Don't Instantiate Generic Types with Primitive Types

In Demonstration 2, you saw that the following declaration is NOT legal in generic programming in Java. So, the following code segment

//Erroneous code segment-1
```
//Primitive types are NOT allowed here.It must be a reference type.
MyGenericClass<int> myGenericClassIntOb2 = new MyGenericClass<int>();
```

```
will raise a compile-time error: Syntax error, insert "Dimensions" to
complete ReferenceType.
```

Your Generic Class Cannot Subclass Directly or Indirectly from Throwable

JLS11 confirms that JVM's catch mechanism is compatible with the non-generic classes only. So, the following code segment

//Erroneous code segment-2
```
class CustomException<T> extends Throwable{  }
```

```
    will raise a compile-time error: The generic class CustomException<T> may not
subclass java.lang.Throwable.
```

You Cannot Overload a Method Where the Formal Parameter Types of Each Overload Are Erased to the Same Raw Type

The following code segments

//Erroneous code segment-3
```
class OverloadRestriction {
public void printMe(List<Integer> intList) {//Some code }
public void printMe(List<String> strList) {//Some code }
}
```

will raise two compile-time errors:

```
Erasure of method printMe(List<Integer>) is the same as another method in
type OverloadRestriction
```

and

```
Erasure of method printMe(List<String>) is the same as another method in
type OverloadRestriction
```

Static Field Type Parameter Is Not Allowed in Your Generic Class

The following code segments

```
//Erroneous code segment-4
class MyDevice<T> {
        private static T operatingSystem;// 4.1 Compile-time error
        // 4.2 Compile-time error
        /* public static T getOperatingSystem() {
                // some code
        }*/
}
```

will raise a compile-time error: Cannot make a static reference to the non-static type T.

You get the same error if you try to use a static method, which is shown in commented lines.

You Cannot Instantiate the Type Parameters In Your Generic Class

The following code segments

```
//Erroneous code segment-5
class GenericClass<T> {
      T genericObject;
      GenericClass() {
```

```
        //5.Compile-time error
        genericObject = new T();
    }
}
```

will raise a compile-time error: `Cannot instantiate the type T`.

One Final Suggestion

In this chapter, you have gone through the fundamentals of generic programming. But ultimate mastery will come upon repeated practice. Before I finish this chapter, I suggest you take note that when you write your code you should pay special attention to the subtype in generic programming.

Consider an example. Suppose there are two concrete types—TypeA and TypeB. GenericClass<TypeA> is in no way related to GenericClass<TypeB> regardless of whether TypeA and TypeB are related. Object is the common parent for both GenericClass<TypeA> and GenericClass<TypeB>.

For example, you have used the Integer class several times in various examples. But if you go through its original definition, you'll see this:

```
public final class Integer extends Number implements Comparable<Integer> {
//some code
}
```

This basically says that the Integer class extends from the Number class. But following the prior suggestion, you can conclude that there is no relationship between GenericClass<Number> and GenericClass<Integer>.

Summary

This chapter discussed the following:

- What is a generic program?

- Why are generics important in Java?

- What are the advantages of generic programming over non-generic programming?

- How can you use wildcards in generic programming?

- What are the different types of wildcards and how do you use them?

- What is a bounded type parameter? How is it different from wildcards?

- How can you use bounded type parameters in your generic program?

- What is an erasure and how does it work?

- What is a bridge method? How does it work?

- Why are bridge methods helpful?

- What is a raw type?

- How can you use the diamond operator and make the syntax short?

CHAPTER 13

Database Programming

Your Java application can talk to a database using JDBC, which is a Java standard API. It provides you with the necessary interface to connect a relational database. In the context of connecting a database with a Java application, expert programmers might prefer alternatives like JPA, Hibernate, and so on. But this chapter is dedicated to JDBC because it maintains its own significance and usefulness. To do exercises in JDBC programming, you need to be familiar with the following concepts:

- What is a database, and how can it help you to store or organize the data?

- How can a database be connected?

- How can your Java application talk to the database? (Or, how can you establish a connection to the database and then how can you insert, update, or delete a record in the database?)

You will shortly learn that your Java program will use the JDBC API, which supports some JDBC drivers, to connect to a database. Figure 13-1 presents a simplified view of the overall process whereby the application (your Java program) and the database are connected through a JDBC driver.

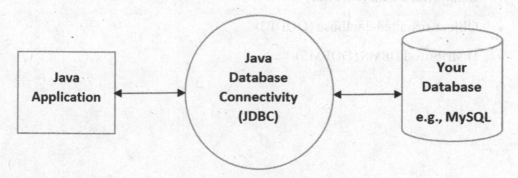

Figure 13-1. *JDBC can connect a Java application and a database (for example, MySQL)*

© Vaskaran Sarcar 2020
V. Sarcar, *Interactive Object-Oriented Programming in Java*, https://doi.org/10.1007/978-1-4842-5404-2_13

So, let's examine each of these parts in this chapter.

Note   If you are absolutely new to database programming, you may need to know some key terms that are mentioned briefly in this chapter. So, it is recommended that you visit these terms and definitions repeatedly for a better understanding. Gradually, these terms will be clear to you, and you will be able to perform complex database programming.

Database and DBMS

A **database** is a collection of related files, usually called tables. A **table** is a collection of related records. A **record** is a collection of related fields, and the smallest piece of meaningful information in a file is called a **field** (or data item).

A **database management system** (DBMS) is a software package to manage these data effectively. Oracle Database, SQL Server, MySQL, MS-Access, and so forth are some commonly used DBMS packages.

Types of DBMS

There are various types of DBMS; for example:)

- Hierarchical DBMS (HDBMS)

- Network DBMS (NDBMS)

- Relational DBMS (RDBMS)

- Object-oriented database (OODB)

- Distributed DBMS (DDBMS)

Each of these has its own pros and cons. Selecting a database depends on your own needs. Based upon your needs, instead of choosing an SQL data structure (which is suitable for an RDBMS), you may prefer NoSQL (it is a non-relational structure and can be suitable for a DDBMS).

In this chapter, you'll see the usage of an RDBMS and simple SQL statements only.

RDBMS

In RDBMS, data are stored in rows and columns, which is similar to tables. These tables are termed **relations**. Rows of a table are referred to as **tuples**, and columns are referred to as **attributes**.

Each row of a table contains a record. Each column contains fields. Consider the table in Figure 13-2.

For your reference, I have marked all the records and attributes in Figure 13-2.

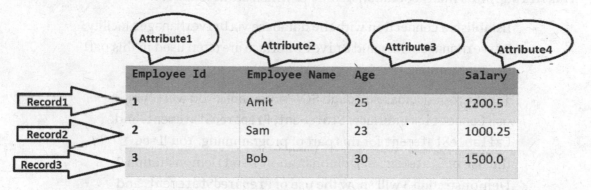

Figure 13-2. *A sample table in an RDBMS.*

You can process different records of a relation based on some mathematical formulation, which is termed **relational algebra.** Since the entire database can be processed using these mathematical formulae, relational algebra is the theoretical foundation for relational databases and SQL.

Oracle Database, MySQL, Microsoft SQL Server, IBM DB2, and so on are common examples of RDBMS. In this chapter, I have used MySQL to demonstrate the examples.

Note   In Appendix C, I have shown the installation steps of MySQL on a Win10 machine.

SQL

The full name of SQL is Structured Query Language. It is a very popular and widely used RDBMS language. It is an English-like language and is considered a fourth-generation language. Create data, update data, read data, and delete data are the most common operations with SQL. In Java, you will see the use of the `java.sql` package, which contains the API to support database programming (usually with a relational database). This API supports many operations, some of which are as follows:

- Establish a connection with the database via `DriverManager` facility. `DriverManager` class and `Driver` interface are often used in this part of programming.

- Talk to your database through SQL statements. You will often use `Connection` interface, `Statement`, `PreparedStatement`, and `CallableStatement` for this part of programming. You'll see the use of `Statement` in Demonstration 1 and Demonstration 2. Demonstration 3 will show the use of `PreparedStatement`, and Demonstration 4 will show the use of `CallableStatement`.

- Process the results obtained through different queries through the `ResultSet` interface.

In this chapter, you will see the use of these basic operations when the Java program interacts with the MySQL database.

POINTS TO REMEMBER

- Java, C++, C, etc. are third-generation languages (3GL). In 3GLs, the focus is on "How to solve a problem?", but in 4GLs, the focus is on "What do you want?" But some advanced 3GLs can combine some of the important aspects of 4GLs.

- It is important to note that SQL does not differentiate between uppercase and lowercase character sets.

- JDBC is an SQL-level API. It allows you to construct and combine SQL statements inside Java API calls.

Note   The simple SQL statements are used to demonstrate various programs in this chapter. If you are absolutely new to SQL, it is recommended that you do exercises with simple SQL statements in your preferred database to get a better idea before you proceed further.

Connecting to a Database

You can connect to a database through different drivers. These drivers are supported in the JDBC API. A JDBC driver is a software component that stays on client machines to help Java programs talk to the DBMS; i.e., it acts like an adapter. There are four different types of JDBC drivers, as follows:

- **Type-1 (or JDBC-ODBC bridge) driver**: It converts JDBC method calls into ODBC function calls. The ODBC bridge driver must be installed on the client machine. Here, the JDBC driver can talk to a third-party API that may not be written in Java. Also, Type-1 drivers are not written in Java, so these are not portable. These drivers are suitable only for local connections. Oracle stopped supporting these drivers from Java 8 onward. They now recommend you use the JDBC drivers that are available from specific vendors of the database.

- **Type-2 (or Native-API) driver**: These drivers use client-side libraries of the database so that they can convert JDBC method calls into native calls of database API. It is a partially Java driver. Since both the native driver and the client libraries stay on the local machine, these drivers are not used for remote network connections. But they can provide a better performance than type-1 drivers.

- **Type-3 (or Network Protocol) driver**: These are fully written in Java. Here, the clients first communicate with a middleware application server, which converts the JDBC calls into vendor-specific DBMS calls, and then those calls are forwarded to the database server. For these drivers, no client-side library needs to be installed on the local machine, because the application server is capable of doing the required jobs. A single type-3 driver can also be used to connect multiple databases. But network support is essential for the client machine, and the overall maintenance is costly because you may need to provide database-specific coding in the middle tier.

- **Type-4 (or, Thin) driver**: These are also fully written in Java, but they can provide the highest performance because they are provided by the vendor itself. Here, no special software needs to be installed either on the client machine or on the server machine. The only major drawback is that, since it is provided by a specific vendor, it is dependent on the particular database where the vendor can use different protocols.

Note   In Demonstration 5, you will also see the use of a `javax.sql.DataSource` object to establish a connection between your Java application and the database. From JDBC2.0 onward, this is the recommended approach to connect a datasource. Still I am discussing all of these to help you understand the legacy codes. Also, I believe the learning of "Database Programming in Java" is incomplete without these discussions.

Figure 13-3 demonstrates how three different types of databases can be connected through the JDBC driver.

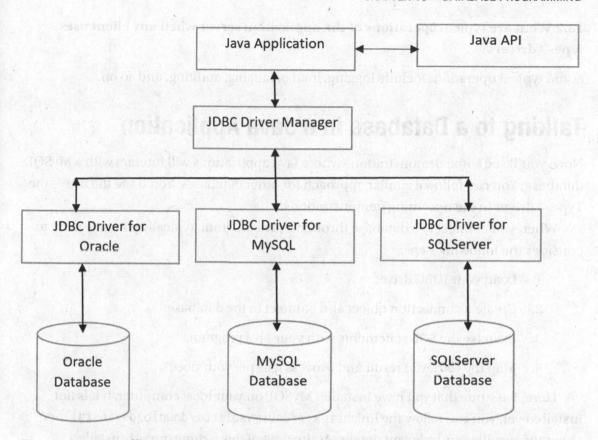

Figure 13-3. *Different types of databases can be connected through the JDBC driver*

You may have different JDBC drivers to connect to different databases. But as an end user, you don't need to worry about their implementation. At this moment, it is sufficient for you to know that you need a JDBC driver to connect to a database.

Q&A Session

13.1 How can I decide which driver is suitable for my application?

If you know that you need only one specific database, pick Type-4. If you need to access multiple databases, choose Type-3. When you do not have either Type-3 or Type-4, you can consider Type-2 drivers. Type-1 is in general not recommended to use, but you can limit its use to testing purposes.

13.2 What are typical operations of the application server when any client uses type-3 drivers?

Some typical operations include logging, load balancing, auditing, and so on.

Talking to a Database in a Java Application

Now, you'll see some demonstrations where Java applications will interact with a MySQL database. You can follow a similar approach for other databases. You'll see the use of the Type-4 driver in the upcoming demonstrations.

When you connect to a database through a Java program, typically you may need to consider the following steps:

1. Load your JDBC driver.

2. Create a connection object and connect to the database.

3. Exercise the SQL statements with your Java program.

4. Map the retrieved result and process it as per your needs.

Here, I assume that you have installed MySQL on your local computer. If it is not installed yet, you can follow the link `https://dev.mysql.com/downloads/installer/` to get the installer and relevant details. At the time of this writing, mysql-installer-community-8.0.16.0 is the latest version. You can also refer to Appendix C, where I have shown the installation steps of MySQL on a Win10 machine.

But installing the database is only the first step. To connect to the database using a Java application you need a vendor-specific connector. I am using MySQL and JDBC. So, I searched for the connector that is used for the JDBC driver in MySQL. At the time of this writing, `mysql-connector-java-8.0.16.zip` is available at the following link `https://dev.mysql.com/downloads/connector/j/`. I have chosen the platform-independent version (Figure 13-4) and downloaded it in the local system.

Connector/J 8.0.16

Select Operating System:

Platform Independent ▾

Looking for previous GA versions?

Recommended Windows Download:

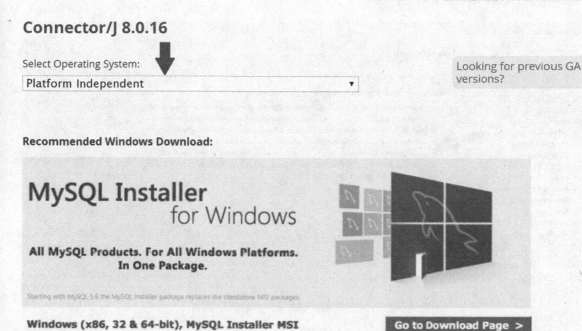

MySQL Installer for Windows

All MySQL Products. For All Windows Platforms. In One Package.

Starting with MySQL 5.6 the MySQL Installer package replaces the standalone MSI packages

Windows (x86, 32 & 64-bit), MySQL Installer MSI

Go to Download Page >

Figure 13-4. *Download MySql Connector/J 8.0.16 Platform Independent version from* https://dev.mysql.com/downloads/connector/j/

Once you download and extract the zip file, you will get the `mysql-connector-java-8.0.16.jar` file (the latest version at the time of this writing), which you need to add in your Java build path in Eclipse (**Project ➤ Properties ➤ Java Build Path ➤ Add External JARs...**). Once you add this external jar in Eclipse, you may get a screen similar to that shown in Figure 13-5.

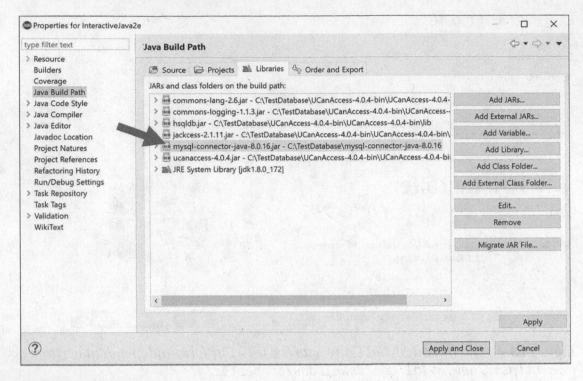

Figure 13-5. *The mysql-connector-java-8.0.16.jar is added in Eclipse*

Important Terms

Now, let's go through some demonstrations. To understand the upcoming demonstrations, you need to be familiar with the following classes, interfaces, and methods:

DriverManager: This *class* manages a set of JDBC drivers. It matches the connection request from a Java application with the proper databse driver. (It is important to note that JDBC 2.0 provides an alternate way to connect to a datasource. The use of a `DataSource` object is a recommended way to connect to a datasource.)

Driver: This is an *interface* to handle the communication with the database server. Each driver must provide a class that will implement this interface. Each `Driver` class should be small and standalone so that it can be loaded without vast supporting codes. When a `Driver` class is loaded, you should create an instance of it and register it with `DriverManager`. So, in Demonstration 1, you may notice the following line of code:

```
// for MySql database
Class.forName("com.mysql.cj.jdbc.Driver").newInstance();
```

POINTS TO REMEMBER

- Similar to connecting with an Oracle database, you may notice the use of the following code:

  ```
  Class.forName("oracle.jdbc.driver.OracleDriver").newInstance();
  ```

- To connect with a MS SQL Server, you may notice the use of *the following code:*

  ```
  Class.forName("com.microsoft.jdbc.sqlserver.SQLServerDriver").
  newInstance();
  ```

Connection: This *interface* provides the methods with which to connect a database. Your SQL statements execute, and results are returned within the context of a connection. You can simply say that all the communication with the database passes through the connection object.

getConnection(): This method attempts to make a connection to the given database URL. Multiple overloaded versions are avaiable for this method. In Demonstration 1, you will notice the following line of code:

```
DriverManager.getConnection("jdbc:mysql://localhost:3306/test", "root",
"admin");
```

That is, I'm using following overloaded version:

```
public static Connection getConnection(String url, String user, String
password) throws SQLException
```

where the user string indicates the database user name and the password string is that user's password.

Note The string `localhost` is used because I have installed the MySQL database in my local system and `test` is my local database name.

Statement: It is an *interface*. A `Statement` object is used to execute the static SQL statement and returns the results for that. By default, only one `ResultSet` object per `Statement` object can be opened in a particular moment.

createStatement(): This method creates a Statement object to send SQL statements to the database.

executeQuery(): This method is used to execute an SQL statement that returns a single ResultSet object.

executeUpdate(): This method is used to execute an SQL statement that can be any of the insert, update, or delete statements. You can also use DDL statements, which return nothing. (You can refer to Q&A 13.10 in this context.)

Note   The executeQuery() or the executeUpdate() methods cannot be called on a PreparedStatement or on a CallableStatement.

ResultSet: This is an *interface* that represents the result set of a database query. The SQL statements that read data (using a database query) return the data in a result set. The select statement is a standard way to select rows and view them in the result set.

In Demonstration 1, you will notice that you retrieve the query result once an SQL statement is executed using a Statement object. It acts like an iterator so that you can easily move through its data. In this context, it is useful to know that a ResultSet object maintains a cursor to point at the current row in the result set.

SQLException: This *class* is used to describe various database access errors (or any other errors that may occur in a database application).

Creating a Database and Inserting Records

Demonstration 1 shows how you can connect to a MySQL database and how you can retrieve the records from a table in the database.

Before that, you can familiar yourself with MySQL Workbench which is a graphical tool and can be used when you work with MySQL servers and databases. Once installed, you can get it in your startup menu, like in Figure 13-6.

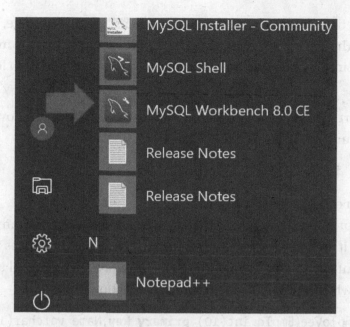

Figure 13-6. *Once installed, MySQL Workbench 8.0 is available in the startup menu*

Before I start, I create a database `test,` and then I create a table `employee` in that database. In the `employee` table, I insert three records only. Creating a database and creating a table inside the database is very easy. You can skip the following section contained in square brackets [ ] if you know these commands.

[For example, once you log in to your database server:

- To create the database called `test`, you can use the following command:

  ```
  create database test;
  ```

- To create the table called `employee`, you can use the following command:

  ```
  create table employee(EmpId int(10),Name varchar(10),Age
  int(10), Salary double);
  ```

It simply says the employee table has four columns: EmpId, Name, Age, and Salary. The datatypes with sizes are also described here. The varchar datatype may seem new to you. For now, simply know that it is used for those who can hold both letters and numbers.

- To insert a record in your employee table, you can use the following command:

```
insert into employee values (1,'Amit',25,1200.5);
```

Similarly, you can insert other records.

Another important point to note is that if you want to make a column unique and not null, you can use it as a primary key. For example, if I want no duplicates in the EmpId column and I want each record to include the information for EmpId, I'll use the concept of a primary key while creating the table, which is as follows:

```
create table employee(EmpId int(10) primary key,Name varchar(10),Age
int(10), Salary double);
```

Now, when you insert a record into the employee table, you need to supply the information for EmpId. In short, by using a primary key, you can uniquely identify a record.]

Figure 13-7 represents the MySQL Workbench view for that. From the figure, you can see that the test database currently contains one table, employee, with three records. The figure also presents the table schema for the employee table.

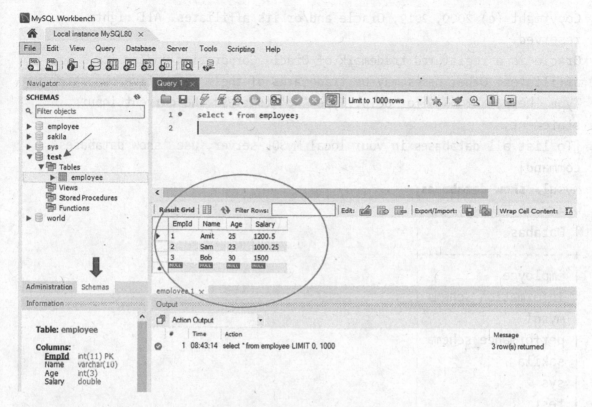

Figure 13-7. *The MySQL Workbench view for the employee table in the test database*

But to understand the upcoming demonstrations, you need not be familiar with MySQL Workbench in detail. Here, I have used this graphical tool to show you the current database and the tables in it before you start programming with JDBC.

MySQL Command Prompt View

Alternatively, you can use the MySQL command prompt. You can exercise the following commands (shown in bold) from this command prompt. For your easy reference, I am putting my comments or command details inside the square brackets [ ].

```
Enter password: *****
Welcome to the MySQL monitor.  Commands end with ; or \g.
Your MySQL connection id is 19
Server version: 8.0.16 MySQL Community Server - GPL
```

Type 'help;' or '\h' for help. Type '\c' to clear the current input statement.
[To list all databases in your local MySQL server, use 'show databases' command]
mysql> **show databases;**

```
+--------------------+
| Database           |
+--------------------+
| employee           |
| information_schema |
| mysql              |
| performance_schema |
| sakila             |
| sys                |
| test               |
| world              |
+--------------------+
```

8 rows in set (0.00 sec)
[To switch to a particular database, use the following command]
mysql> **use test;**
Database changed
[To display all the tables in your database, use the following command]
mysql> **show tables;**

```
+----------------+
| Tables_in_test |
+----------------+
| employee       |
+----------------+
```

1 row in set (0.00 sec)
[To display all records in a table (in this case, 'employee'), use the following command]

```
mysql> select * from employee;
+-------+------+------+---------+
| EmpId | Name | Age  | Salary  |
+-------+------+------+---------+
|     1 | Amit |   25 |  1200.5 |
|     2 | Sam  |   23 | 1000.25 |
|     3 | Bob  |   30 |    1500 |
+-------+------+------+---------+
3 rows in set (0.00 sec)
mysql> desc employee;
+--------+-------------+------+-----+---------+-------+
| Field  | Type        | Null | Key | Default | Extra |
+--------+-------------+------+-----+---------+-------+
| EmpId  | int(11)     | NO   | PRI | NULL    |       |
| Name   | varchar(10) | YES  |     | NULL    |       |
| Age    | int(3)      | YES  |     | NULL    |       |
| Salary | double      | YES  |     | NULL    |       |
+--------+-------------+------+-----+---------+-------+
4 rows in set (0.00 sec)
mysql>
```

Demonstration 1

I already said that Demonstration 1 shows how you can connect to a MySQL database and how can you retrieve records from a table in the database. As noted earlier, I created a database called test and then I created a table employee in that database. Currently, the employee table contains three records, which were also shown prior to this demonstration. To understand this example, you may need to revisit the descriptions of important classes, interfaces, and methods that were covered earlier.

```
package java2e.chapter13;

import java.sql.*;

class Demonstration1 {

public static void main(String[] args) throws SQLException {
```

```java
System.out.println("***Demonstration-1.Connecting to the MySql
server.***");
Connection connectionOb = null;
try {
        // for MySql database
        Class.forName("com.mysql.cj.jdbc.Driver").
        newInstance();
        connectionOb = DriverManager.getConnection("jdbc:mys
        ql://localhost:3306/test", "root", "admin");
        Statement statementOb = connectionOb.createStatement();
        ResultSet queryResult = statementOb.
        executeQuery("select * from Employee");
        System.out.println(" EmployeeId\t" + "EmployeeName\t" +
        "Age\t" + "Salary");
        System.out.print
        ln("-------------------------------------------");
        while (queryResult.next()) {
                System.out.print(queryResult.getString("EmpId")
                + "\t\t" + queryResult.getString("Name") +
                "\t\t"+ queryResult.getInt("Age") + "\t" +
                queryResult.getDouble("Salary"));
                System.out.println();
        }
} catch (SQLException ex) {
        System.out.println(ex.getMessage());
}
// To catch any other exception
catch (Exception ex) {
        System.out.println(ex.getMessage());
        ex.printStackTrace();
} finally {
        // Close the connection
        if (connectionOb != null) {
                connectionOb.close();
        }
```

```
        }
    }
}
```

Output:

```
***Demonstration-1. Connecting to the MySql server. ***
 EmployeeId        EmployeeName          Age         Salary
--------------------------------------------------
1             Amit            25          1200.5
2             Sam             23          1000.25
3             Bob             30          1500.0
```

Demonstration 2

In Demonstration 2, I'll update some records, then I'll delete a record. Finally, I'll update the records in such a way that I can obtain the initial state of the table. For example, you'll see that though Amit's age was updated from 25 to 35, at the end I have reset it back to 25. Also, I have deleted the newly added record for John. Similarly, though I made a change to Bob's salary, at the end I have reset the value.

Another notable change in this demonstration is that, in this example, I have used executeUpdate() to update a record. In Demonstration 1, you saw the use of the executeQuery() method.

```
package java2e.chapter13;

import java.sql.*;

class Demonstration2 {

    public static void main(String[] args) throws SQLException {
        System.out.println("***Demonstration-2.Connecting to the MySql
        server.***");
        Connection connectionOb = null;
        try {
```

```java
// for MySql database
Class.forName("com.mysql.cj.jdbc.Driver").
newInstance();
connectionOb = DriverManager.getConnection("jdbc:mys
ql://localhost:3306/test", "root", "admin");
Statement statementOb = connectionOb.createStatement();
System.out.println("Here is the initial table");
ResultSet queryResult = statementOb.
executeQuery("select * from Employee");
System.out.println(" EmployeeId\t" + "EmployeeName\t" +
"Age\t" + "Salary");
System.out.print
ln("-------------------------------------------");
while (queryResult.next()) {
        System.out.print(queryResult.getString("EmpId")
        + "\t\t" + queryResult.getString("Name") +
        "\t\t"
                        + queryResult.getInt("Age") + "\t"
                        + queryResult.getDouble("Salary"));
        System.out.println();
}
//Updating 2 records and inserting a new record.
System.out.println("Updating Amit's age as 35.");
statementOb.executeUpdate("update Employee set Age=35
where name='Amit' ");

System.out.println("Updating Bob's salary to 2000.25");
statementOb.executeUpdate("update Employee set
Salary=2000.25 where name='Bob' ");
System.out.println("Inserting a new record into the
Employee table\n");
statementOb.executeUpdate("insert into Employee
values(4,'John',27,975)");

System.out.println("**Here is the updated table.**");
queryResult = statementOb.executeQuery("select * from
Employee");
```

```java
System.out.println(" EmployeeId\t" + "EmployeeName\t" +
"Age\t" + "Salary");
System.out.print
ln("-------------------------------------------");
while (queryResult.next()) {
        System.out.print(queryResult.getString("EmpId")
        + "\t\t" + queryResult.getString("Name") +
        "\t\t"
                        + queryResult.getInt("Age") + "\t"
                        + queryResult.getDouble("Salary"));
        System.out.println();
}
//Deleting a record from the Employee table and setting
the initial values again in the Employee table.
System.out.println("\nDeleting the record of John from
the Employee table.");
statementOb.executeUpdate("delete from employee where
name='John' ");
System.out.println("Updating Amit's age as 25 again.");
statementOb.executeUpdate("update Employee set Age=25
where name='Amit' ");
System.out.println("Updating Bob's salary to 1500.0
again.");
statementOb.executeUpdate("update Employee set
Salary=1500.0 where name='Bob' ");

System.out.println("\n**Here is the updated table.**");
queryResult = statementOb.executeQuery("select * from
Employee");
System.out.println(" EmployeeId\t" + "EmployeeName\t" +
"Age\t" + "Salary");
System.out.print
ln("-------------------------------------------");
while (queryResult.next()) {
        System.out.print(queryResult.getString("EmpId")
        + "\t\t" + queryResult.getString("Name") + "\t\t"
```

```
                                      + queryResult.getInt("Age") + "\t"
                                      + queryResult.getDouble("Salary"));
                  System.out.println();
             }

        } catch (SQLException ex) {
             System.out.println(ex.getMessage());
        }
        // To catch any other exception
        catch (Exception ex) {
             System.out.println(ex.getMessage());
             ex.printStackTrace();
        } finally {
             // Close the connection
             if (connectionOb != null) {
                  connectionOb.close();
             }
        }
    }
}
```

Here is the output. The key changes are shown in bold letters.

```
***Demonstration-2.Connecting to the MySql server.***
Here is the initial table
 EmployeeId    EmployeeName    Age    Salary
---------------------------------------------
1             Amit            25     1200.5
2             Sam             23     1000.25
3             Bob             30     1500.0
Updating Amit's age as 35.
Updating Bob's salary to 2000.25
Inserting a new record into the Employee table
```

Here is the updated table.

EmployeeId	EmployeeName	Age	Salary
1	Amit	**35**	1200.5
2	Sam	23	1000.25
3	Bob	30	**2000.25**
4	**John**	**27**	**975.0**

Deleting the record of John from the Employee table.
Updating Amit's age as 25 again.
Updating Bob's salary to 1500.0 again.

Here is the updated table.

EmployeeId	EmployeeName	Age	Salary
1	Amit	**25**	1200.5
2	Sam	23	1000.25
3	Bob	30	**1500.0**

Note   This program can be further improved if you use separate methods for display records and update (or, insert) records and call those methods from your `main()` method. You can follow the same for other demonstrations in this chapter. I just focused on updating and inserting the records in this example and kept it aligned with demonstration 1.

Demonstration 3

This demonstration shows the use of the `PreparedStatement` object. `PreparedStatement` is an interface that extends the `Statement` interface. The use of `PreparedStatement` can provide you the following facilities:

- You can use parameterized SQL statements.

- You can reuse the statement with new values.

- You can provide batch processing and faster execution.

In the following example, you will notice the use of the following lines:

```
PreparedStatement preparedStatementOb=null;
preparedStatementOb=connectionOb.prepareStatement("insert into Employee
values(?,?,?,?)");
```

You can see that a PreparedStatement object is created with four input parameters. Notice the four question marks (?). These are the placeholders for your inputs. You provide values to replace these question marks before you execute a PreparedStatement object. You can supply values using the setter methods defined in the PreparedStatement class. In the upcoming demonstration, you will supply a new record (where employee name is "Ivan") using the following statements:

```
preparedStatementOb.setInt(1,4);
preparedStatementOb.setString(2,"Ivan");
preparedStatementOb.setInt(3,27);
preparedStatementOb.setDouble(4,975.6);
```

It is important to note that the first argument of these setter methods specifies the question mark placeholder. For example, the two setInt() calls specify the first and third placeholders, respectively; setString() specifies the second placeholder; and setDouble() specifies the fourth placeholder.

Finally, you will invoke the executeUpdate() method on the PreparedStatement object as follows:

```
preparedStatementOb.executeUpdate();
```

Now, go through the following demonstration and its corresponding output:

```
package java2e.chapter13;

import java.sql.*;

public class Demonstration3 {

        public static void main(String[] args) throws SQLException {
                System.out.println("***Demonstration-3.Use of
                PreparedStatement.***");
                Connection connectionOb = null;
```

```java
try {
        // for MySql database
        Class.forName("com.mysql.cj.jdbc.Driver").
        newInstance();
        connectionOb = DriverManager.getConnection("jdbc:mys
        ql://localhost:3306/test", "root", "admin");
        Statement statementOb = connectionOb.createStatement();
        System.out.println("Here is the initial table.");
        ResultSet queryResult = statementOb.
        executeQuery("select * from Employee");
        System.out.println(" EmployeeId\t" + "EmployeeName\t" +
        "Age\t" + "Salary");
        System.out.print
        ln("--------------------------------------------");
        while (queryResult.next()) {
                System.out.print(queryResult.getString("EmpId")
                + "\t\t" + queryResult.getString("Name") +
                "\t\t"
                                + queryResult.getInt("Age") + "\t"
                                + queryResult.getDouble("Salary"));
                System.out.println();
        }

        //Inserting a new record in the table
        System.out.println("\nInserting a new record into the
        Employee table.");
        PreparedStatement preparedStatementOb=null;
        preparedStatementOb=connectionOb.
        prepareStatement("insert into Employee
        values(?,?,?,?)");
        preparedStatementOb.setInt(1,4);
        preparedStatementOb.setString(2,"Ivan");
        preparedStatementOb.setInt(3,27);
        preparedStatementOb.setDouble(4,975.6);
        preparedStatementOb.executeUpdate();
        System.out.println("**Here is the updated table.**");
```

```
queryResult = statementOb.executeQuery("select * from
Employee");
System.out.println(" EmployeeId\t" + "EmployeeName\t" +
"Age\t" + "Salary");
System.out.print
ln("-------------------------------------------");
while (queryResult.next()) {
        System.out.print(queryResult.getString("EmpId")
        + "\t\t" + queryResult.getString("Name") + "\t\t"
                    + queryResult.getInt("Age") + "\t"
                    + queryResult.getDouble("Salary"));
        System.out.println();
}
//Deleting a record from the Employee table and setting
the initial values again in the Employee table.
System.out.println("\nDeleting the record of Ivan from
the Employee table.");
statementOb.executeUpdate("delete from employee where
name='Ivan' ");

System.out.println("After the deletion of Ivan's
record, here is the updated table.**");
queryResult = statementOb.executeQuery("select * from
Employee");
System.out.println(" EmployeeId\t" + "EmployeeName\t" +
"Age\t" + "Salary");
System.out.print
ln("-------------------------------------------");
while (queryResult.next()) {
        System.out.print(queryResult.getString("EmpId")
        + "\t\t" + queryResult.getString("Name") + "\t\t"
                    + queryResult.getInt("Age") + "\t"
                    + queryResult.getDouble("Salary"));
        System.out.println();
}
```

```
        } catch (SQLException ex) {
                System.out.println(ex.getMessage());
        }
        // To catch any other exception
        catch (Exception ex) {
                System.out.println(ex.getMessage());
                ex.printStackTrace();
        } finally {
                // Close the connection
                if (connectionOb != null) {
                        connectionOb.close();
                }
        }
    }
}
```

Output:

```
***Demonstration-3.Use of PreparedStatement.***
Here is the initial table.
 EmployeeId   EmployeeName   Age   Salary
-------------------------------------------
1            Amit           25    1200.5
2            Sam            23    1000.25
3            Bob            30    1500.0
```

Inserting a new record into the Employee table.
Here is the updated table.

```
EmployeeId   EmployeeName   Age   Salary
-------------------------------------------
1            Amit           25    1200.5
2            Sam            23    1000.25
3            Bob            30    1500.0
4            Ivan           27    975.6
```

Deleting the record of Ivan from the Employee table.
After the deletion of Ivan's record, here is the updated table.**

EmployeeId	EmployeeName	Age	Salary
1	Amit	25	1200.5
2	Sam	23	1000.25
3	Bob	30	1500.0

Q&A Session

13.3 Why is the use of PreparedStatement objects considered faster than using Statement objects?

PreparedStatement objects can contain precompiled SQL statements. So, if you pass the same query (with the same or different data) multiple times, DBMS can run the query much faster. But, in the case of a Statement object, SQL needs to validate the query each time you use it.

13.4 Is passing the parameters mandatory for PreparedStatement objects?

No. In Demonstration 3, you could simply use the following lines of code to get the same result:

```
//Parameters are not mandatory for PreparedStatement .
preparedStatementOb = connectionOb.preparedStatement("insert into Employee
values(4,'IvanS',27,975.6)");
```

Normally, you use PreparedStatement when your SQL query takes parameters. The SQL statement that takes parameters can help you to execute the statement with different values, which is very common in real-world scenarios. For simplicity and to make the program shorter, I have not used command-line arguments or user-defined inputs. But in practice, you can always pass the arguments using the command line, which in turn will replace the question marks before your query is processed.

13.5 How is the executeQuery() method different from executeUpdate()?

The executeUpdate() method is associated with insert, update, or delete operations or SQL statements that return nothing, such as DDL statements. This method does not return any ResultSet object.

On the other hand, executeQuery() executes an SQL statement that returns a single ResultSet object. This method cannot be called on PreparedStatement or CallableStatement (this will be discussed in the next demonstration).

13.6 What are the key advantages of using **PreparedStatement**?

Here are the key advantages of using PreparedStatement:

- You can pass parameterized SQL statements.

- You can reuse the statement with different values.

- You can provide batch processing.

- Since it supports precompiled SQL statements, you may enhance the execution time.

13.7 What is batch processing? Can you give an example?

By "batch processing," I mean that you can execute a bunch (or group or set) of queries. The addBatch() and executeBatch() methods in the Statement interface can help you in this area.

Let's add the following lines to Demonstration 1:

```
statementOb.addBatch("insert into Employee values(4,'Ivan',27,975.6)");
statementOb.addBatch("insert into Employee values(5,'Jacklin',29,575.5)");
//Batch execution
statementOb.executeBatch();
```

Now, you can see that the records are inserted properly. Similarly, you can delete the records as follows:

```
//Now deleting the records  from the Employee table
//and resetting the original state of Employee table.
System.out.println("\nDeleting the record of Ivan and Jacklin from the
Employee table.");
statementOb.addBatch("delete from employee where name='Ivan' ");
statementOb.addBatch("delete from employee where name='Jacklin' ");
//Batch execution
statementOb.executeBatch();
```

Demonstration 4

This demonstration shows the use of the `CallableStatement` object. `CallableStatement` is an interface that extends `PreparedStatement`, which in turn extends the `Statement` interface. `CallableInterface` is used to execute stored procedures and functions in SQL.

Note   There are some significant differences between stored procedures and functions. For example, in MySQL, a stored procedure can be used to return one or multiple values or no value, whereas a function always returns single value. Also, you can call a function directly with a SQL statement while you cannot do the same for a procedure. A stored procedure can have IN, OUT, INOUT parameters but a stored function can have only IN parameters by default. To make the example short and simple, in Demonstration 4 you'll see the use of a small function only.

Before you start, create a table called `numbertable` (in your test database) as in Table 13-1.

Table 13-1. *The numbertable Table Created in the Database*

FirstNumber	SecondNumber
12.3	15.7
32.5	25.3
25.0	75.0

You can see that the table has two attributes, `FirstNumber` and `SecondNumber`, and each row of the table contains various double type values. Let's say you want to calculate the aggregate of the two double values of each row in the table; you can accomplish this task using a function called `total()`.

So, before you execute Demonstration 4, you may wish to complete the following steps:

1. Create `NumberTable` and fill the table with necessary data.

2. You create a function `total()` that accepts two double type values as parameters and returns the aggregate.

You can complete Step 1 and Step 2 in various ways and in your preferred order. In the following section, I give you the commands (with corresponding outputs) that I used once I connected my database to complete these steps. The SQL statements are shown in bold for a better readability. I am also putting the supporting comments inside brackets [ ].

Step 1

[Creating the NumberTable]

```
mysql> create table NumberTable(FirstNo Double, SecondNo Double);
Query OK, 0 rows affected (2.77 sec)
```

[Check the tables in the test database. This is optional for you.]

```
mysql> show tables;
+-----------------+
| Tables_in_test  |
+-----------------+
| employee        |
| numbertable     |
+-----------------+
2 rows in set (0.08 sec)
```

[Insert the data in the first row in the table.]

```
mysql> insert into numbertable values(12.3,15.7);
Query OK, 1 row affected (2.12 sec)
```

[Insert the data in the second row in the table.]

```
mysql> insert into numbertable values(32.3,25.3);
Query OK, 1 row affected (0.13 sec)
```

[Insert the data in the third row in the table.]

```
mysql> insert into numbertable values(25,75);
Query OK, 1 row affected (0.08 sec)
```

[Check the current status of the table.]

```
mysql> select * from numbertable;
+----------+----------+
| FirstNo  | SecondNo |
+----------+----------+
|     12.3 |     15.7 |
|     32.3 |     25.3 |
|       25 |       75 |
+----------+----------+
3 rows in set (0.08 sec)
```

Step 2

Create the function called total: [A function is a stored program in which you can pass parameters, and, in turn, it will return a value.]

```
mysql> create function total(firstNumber double, secondNumber double)
returns double deterministic return firstNumber + secondNumber;
Query OK, 0 rows affected (1.03 sec)
```

Note As per the MySQL 8.0 reference manual: "A routine is considered 'deterministic' if it always produces the same result for the same input parameters, and "'not deterministic' otherwise. If neither DETERMINISTIC nor NOT DETERMINISTIC is given in the routine definition, the default is NOT DETERMINISTIC."

So, if you miss the word deterministic in the previous query, you may encounter following error:

```
ERROR 1064 (42000): You have an error in your SQL syntax; check the manual
that corresponds to your MySQL server version for the right syntax to use
near 'sum(firstNumber double,secondNumber double)
returns double
return firstNumber+se' at line 1
```

[Now I display the function details. This is optional for you.]

```
mysql> Select Routine_name as "Function Name", routine_Definition as
"Definition", Routine_Schema "Schema", Data_Type as "Types", Created
From  Information_Schema.Routines Where Routine_Name='total' and Routine_
Type= 'FUNCTION';
```

Here is a snapshot from the MySQL 8.0 command-line client for better readability:

```
+---------------+------------------------------+--------+--------+---------------------+
| Function Name | Definition                   | Schema | Types  | CREATED             |
+---------------+------------------------------+--------+--------+---------------------+
| total         | return firstNumber+secondNumber | test | double | 2019-09-02 19:41:28 |
+---------------+------------------------------+--------+--------+---------------------+
1 row in set (0.00 sec)
```

Now, let's analyze the upcoming program. In the following example, you will notice the following line of code:

```
CallableStatement callableStmt=connectionOb.prepareCall("{?= call
total(?,?)}");
```

You can see that a `CallableStatement` object is created by invoking the `prepareCall()` method, and that the `prepareCall()` method accepts a `String` parameter.

Note   Like many other methods, there are various overloaded versions of the `prepareCall()` method. I have used the simplest one in this example.

Notice the three question marks. You know that these are used for method parameters. These parameters are sequential in nature, and the first parameter starts with 1.

The following lines will show the usage of these parameters:

```
callableStmt.setDouble(2,queryResult.getDouble("FirstNo"));
callableStmt.setDouble(3,queryResult.getDouble("SecondNo"));
```

```
/*
```
Here, we have used the registerOutParameter() method of the CallableStatement interface, which registers the OUT parameter in the ordinal position in parameterIndex(first argument) to the JDBC type sqlType(second argument). All OUT parameters must be registered before a stored procedure is executed.
```
*/
callableStmt.registerOutParameter (1,Types.DOUBLE);
callableStmt.execute();
```

It indicates that there are two double type values, in positions 2 and 3. The question mark in position 1 will be replaced with the function (the function name is total() in this case) call, which accepts these double type values as parameters and returns the aggregate (which is also a double type value). Now, go through the full implementation and the corresponding output.

```java
package java2e.chapter13;
import java.sql.*;

class Demonstration4 {
    public static void main(String[] args) throws SQLException {
        System.out.println("***Demonstration-4.Using a Callable
        Statement.***");
        Connection connectionOb = null;
        try {
            // for MySQL database
            Class.forName("com.mysql.cj.jdbc.Driver").
            newInstance();
            connectionOb = DriverManager.getConnection("jdbc:mys
            ql://localhost:3306/test", "root", "admin");
            Statement statementOb = connectionOb.createStatement();
            System.out.println("This is the original table.");
            ResultSet queryResult = statementOb.
            executeQuery("select * from NumberTable");
            System.out.println("FirstNumber \t" + "SecondNumber");
            System.out.println("-------------------------");
```

```
while (queryResult.next()) {
        System.out.print(queryResult.
        getDouble("FirstNo") + "\t\t" + queryResult.
        getString("SecondNo"));
        System.out.println();
}
System.out.println("\nCalling the total() function on
each record of the NumberTable.");
//Using the Callable statement
CallableStatement callableStmt=connectionOb.
prepareCall("{?= call total(?,?)}");
queryResult = statementOb.executeQuery("select * from
NumberTable");
System.out.println("FirstNumber \t" + "SecondNumber\
t"+"Total");
System.out.print
ln("-------------------------------------");
while (queryResult.next()) {
        System.out.print(queryResult.
        getDouble("FirstNo") + "\t\t" + queryResult.
        getDouble("SecondNo")+ "\t\t");
        callableStmt.setDouble(2,queryResult.
        getDouble("FirstNo"));
        callableStmt.setDouble(3,queryResult.
        getDouble("SecondNo"));
        /*Here, we have used the registerOutParameter
        method of the CallableStatement interface, which
        registers the OUT parameter in the ordinal
        position in parameterIndex(first argument) to
        the JDBC type sqlType(second argument). All OUT
        parameters must be registered before a stored
        procedure is executed.*/
        callableStmt.registerOutParameter
        (1,Types.DOUBLE);
        callableStmt.execute();
```

415

```
                    System.out.print(callableStmt.getDouble(1));
                    System.out.println();
                }

        } catch (SQLException ex) {
                System.out.println(ex.getMessage());
        }
        // To catch any other exception
        catch (Exception ex) {
                System.out.println(ex.getMessage());
                ex.printStackTrace();
        } finally {
                // Close the connection
                if (connectionOb != null) {
                        connectionOb.close();
                }
        }
    }
}
```

Output:

```
***Demonstration-4.Using a Callable Statement.***
This is the original table.
FirstNumber       SecondNumber
-----------------------------
12.3              15.7
32.5              25.3
25.0              75.0
```

Calling the total() function on each record of the NumberTable:

```
FirstNumber       SecondNumber      Total
-----------------------------------------
12.3              15.7                 28.0
32.5              25.3                 57.8
25.0              75.0                100.0
```

Q&A Session

13.8 When should I prefer a `Statement` object over a `PreparedStatement` or a `CallableStatement`?

You can remember the following points:

- If you want to execute simple SQL statements (for example, `select * from Table_name;`), use a `Statement` object.

- If you want to use precompiled statements, use `PreparedStatement`.

- If you want to use stored procedures (or functions), use `CallableStatement`.

13.9 What is a stored procedure?

In simple words, if you want to repeat a sequence of tasks, you create a stored procedure. A stored procedure is much like writing a method in Java. The steps to create a stored procedure can vary across the databases.

In this chapter, I have used a simple function, `total()`, in Demonstration 4 to serve our needs.

13.10 You have used the term DDL in the context of SQL in some places. What does it mean?

SQL commands are commonly classified among the following:

- **DDL (Data Definition Language)** statements are used to create or modify a database object's structure. You use `create`, `alter`, `drop`, and `truncate` statements in this context.

- **DML (Data Manipulation Language)** statements are used to retrieve, insert, update, and delete records in a database. For example, you use `insert`, `update`, `delete`, and `select` statements in this context. Some engineers prefer to put `select` statements in a separate category called DQL (Data Query Language).

- **DCL (Data Control Language)** statements can be used to create various roles and permissions to control access to a database. For example, you may use `grant` and `revoke` statements in this context.

417

- **TCL (*Transaction Control Language*)** statements are used to manage different transactions that occur in a database. For example, you may use commit, rollback, etc. statements in this context.

Note   As said before, to understand each of these terms in detail, you may need to exercise SQL statements on your own. In this chapter, our focus was not on detailed coverage of SQL; the focus was on Java applications that can simply talk to a database and perform some basic operations.

Demonstration 5

This demonstration shows the use of a javax.sql.DataSource interface object to connect to a datasource. It is a new addition to the JDBC 2.0 API and a preferred way to connect to a datasource. Using a DataSource object can provide connection pooling and distributed transactions. But since you are just starting your journey, we'll focus on the the connection part only.

In Demonstration 5, the getMySqlDataSource() method is used. In this method, you create a MySqlDataSource object, set the database URL, and pass the user ID and password to connect to the database. Once this information is set, you can use this MySqlDataSource object to connect to the database.

You will understand the changes better if you compare Demonstration 5 with Demonstration 1. To make things simple, only a small portion of code in Demonstration 1 has been changed, and there is no significant change in the output. But you must take note of this new way of connecting to the database.

Before you proceed, I suggest you go through the following points.

POINTS TO REMEMBER

- A DataSource object is used for a particular DBMS (or some other datasource, such as a file). If you need to use multiple datasources, you need to deploy a separate DataSource object for each of them.

- The MysqlDataSource name has recently been changed from com.mysql. jdbc.jdbc2.optional.MysqlDataSource to com.mysql.cj.jdbc. MysqlDataSource.

- The DataSource interface is available in the javax.sql package. It has two overloaded methods: Connection getConnection() throws SQLException and Connection getConnection(String username, String password) throws SQLException. You can use either of them.

- The DataSource interface implementation may vary from vendor to vendor. This is why, to connect to a MySQL database, I imported the com.mysql.cj.jdbc. MysqlDataSource class to get the basic implementation of the DataSource interface. If you wish to connect to a different database, say, Oracle, you may need to import the oracle.jdbc.pool.OracleDataSource class.

So, when you compare with Demonstration 1, you see that this time you are NOT using the static getConnection() method of the DriverManager class to connect to the database called test. Instead, you are using the getConnection() method of a MysqlDataSource object. I have kept the old code in commented lines so that you can notice the key changes easily.

```
package java2e.chapter13;
import java.sql.*;
import javax.sql.DataSource;
/*
The name of the class that implements java.sql.Driver in MySQL Connector/J
has changed from com.mysql.jdbc.Driver to com.mysql.cj.jdbc.Driver. The old
class name has been deprecated. The names of these commonly used classes
and interfaces have also been changed. For example, com.mysql.jdbc.jdbc2.
optional is changed to com.mysql.cj.jdbc.MysqlDataSource
 */
import com.mysql.cj.jdbc.MysqlDataSource;

class Demonstration5 {
static DataSource getMysqlDataSource() throws SQLException {
        MysqlDataSource mysqlDataSourceOb = null;
        mysqlDataSourceOb = new MysqlDataSource();
        mysqlDataSourceOb.setUrl("jdbc:mysql://localhost:3306/test");
        mysqlDataSourceOb.setUser("root");// Set user id.
```

```java
            mysqlDataSourceOb.setPassword("admin");// Set //password
            return mysqlDataSourceOb;
        }

public static void main(String[] args) throws SQLException {
        System.out.println("***Demonstration-5.Connecting to the MySql
        server using a DataSource object.***");
        Connection connectionOb = null;
        try {
                // for MySql database
                //Class.forName("com.mysql.cj.jdbc.Driver").
                newInstance();
                // connectionOb =
                // DriverManager.getConnection("jdbc:mysql://
                localhost:3306/test", "root", "admin");
                connectionOb = getMysqlDataSource().getConnection();
                /*
                The following will also work if you do not supply
                username , password in getMysqlDataSource()
                //connectionOb=getMysqlDataSource().getConnection(
                "root", "admin");
                */
                Statement statementOb = connectionOb.createStatement();
                ResultSet queryResult = statementOb.
                executeQuery("select * from Employee");
                System.out.println(" EmployeeId\t" + "EmployeeName\t" +
                "Age\t" + "Salary");
                System.out.println("--------------------------------");
                while (queryResult.next()) {
                        System.out.print(queryResult.getString("EmpId")
                        + "\t\t" + queryResult.getString("Name") + "\t\t"
                                        + queryResult.getInt("Age") + "\t"
                                        + queryResult.getDouble("Salary"));
                        System.out.println();
                }
```

```
    } catch (SQLException ex) {
            System.out.println(ex.getMessage());
    }
    // To catch any other exception
    catch (Exception ex) {
            System.out.println(ex.getMessage());
            ex.printStackTrace();
    } finally {
            // Close the connection
            if (connectionOb != null) {
                    connectionOb.close();
            }
    }
  }
}
```

Here is the output:

```
***Demonstration-5.Connecting to the MySql server using a DataSource
object.***
EmployeeId  EmployeeName  Age  Salary
---------------------------------------------
1           Amit          25   1200.5
2           Sam           23   1000.25
3           Bob           30   1500.0
```

Summary

This chapter discussed the following topics:

- What is JDBC?

- What is a database?

- What is a DBMS? What are different types of DBMS?

- What is RDBMS?

- What is SQL?

- How can a Java application talk to a database?

- How can you connect to MySQL?

- How do you use `Statement`, `PreparedStatement`, and `CallableStatement` in your program?

- How can you invoke a small function using a `Connection` object?

- As per the new recommendation, how can you use a `javax.sql.DataSource` interface object to connect to a datasource?

CHAPTER 14

Important Features in Java's Enhancement Path

Welcome to Chapter 14. In this book, my focus has been on the fundamental concepts of object-oriented programming in Java only. All programs were compiled in Java 8, which was the baseline in this book. Like other popular languages, Java is continuously growing, with new features added regularly. Though detailed coverage of these features was out of the scope of this book, in this chapter, you will examine some features or enhancements from various versions of Java. You get the most value out of a new enhancement if you are familiar with the existing features. So, for this chapter, I have picked only topics with which you are already familiar.

As a student, I first saw a Java book, which was based on Java 2, in my professor's hand a long time ago. But at the time of this writing, Java 13 has been released, and in the upcoming days Java's release train will be very fast. At present, Java is releasing new versions every six months. As a result, you can expect to see a lot more changes in the near future. But, as was said before, if you are familiar with the fundamental features and architecture, you can adapt to changes easily. All you have learned from this book can help you.

One final comment: for the latest features, I have compiled and executed the programs in the command-line environment. This is because my Eclipse environment was not ready to accept the latest features. So, if your preferred IDE is not ready to accommodate a latest feature, you can do the same thing I did. Now, let's start.

Try-with-resource from Java 7

The `try-with-resource` statement is a `try` statement in which you can declare one or multiple resources. A resource is an object that should be closed when your program finishes execution. But to use this feature, you have to choose an object that implements the `AutoCloseable` interface in the `java.lang` package.

© Vaskaran Sarcar 2020
V. Sarcar, *Interactive Object-Oriented Programming in Java*, https://doi.org/10.1007/978-1-4842-5404-2_14

This is because the close() method of an AutoCloseable object is called automatically once the control exits a try-with-resource block.

Here, I present a simple demonstration for you. In this demonstration, Resource1 is a class that implements the AutoCloseable interface.

So, if you use this concept using the following block:

```
try(Resource1 resource1 = new Resource1())  {
        resource1.useResource();
    }
```

in the output you will notice that the close() method of Resource1 is called automatically.

Demonstration 1

Consider the following code:

```
package java2e.chapter14;

//Resource-1
class Resource1 implements AutoCloseable {
    public void useResource() {
        System.out.println("Using a Resource1 type.");
    }
    @Override
    public void close() throws Exception {
        System.out.println("Close Resource1 type now.");
    }
}

class TryWithResourceDemo {
    public static void main(String[] args) throws Exception {
        System.out.println("***Demonstration 1.Try with Resource
        demo.***\n");
        try(Resource1 resource1 = new Resource1())  {
        resource1.useResource();
        }
```

```
        catch(Exception e) {
            System.out.println(e);
        }
    }
  }
}
```

Output

```
***Demonstration-1.Try with Resource demo.***

Using a Resource1 type.
Close Resource1 type now.
```

Q&A Session

14.1 What is a resource?

A resource is an object. Once your program uses a resource, you should close it before your program finishes execution.

14.2 Can I close multiple resources using this feature?

Yes. Here is a sample syntax for you, where two resources are used:

```
try(Resource1 resource1 = new Resource1();Resource2 resource2 = new
Resource2()) {
    //Some code
}
```

Implementing Functional Interface Methods Using Lambda Expressions from Java 8

In Java, a functional interface is an interface that has only one method. You can use a lambda expression to provide an implementation for the interface method.

Note   In Chapter 12, prior to Demonstration 4, you got a quick overview of the lambda expression and its usage. If needed, you can review it there.

But the notable change is that in this case, you do not need to define the method again before you provide an implementation for it. So, you can save lots of typing.

Demonstration 2

To help you understand this concept, I have provided a usual implementation before using a lambda expression. Here, you will see how to use a lambda expression that can have a return statement. Refer to the supporting comment lines for a better understanding.

```
package java2e.chapter14;

@FunctionalInterface
interface MyFunctionalInterface {
        int addNumbers(int firstNumber, int secondNumber);
//error:You cannot declare multiple methods in a functional interface.
        //int addNumbers2(int firstNumber, int secondNumber);
}
//Usual implementation of an interface method
class Implementor implements MyFunctionalInterface{
        public int addNumbers(int firstNumber, int secondNumber) {
                System.out.println("Implementing the interface method
                'addNumbers' inside the Implementor class.");
                System.out.println("Sum of "+ firstNumber + " and "
                +secondNumber + " is : ");
                return firstNumber+ secondNumber;
        }
}

class LambdaExpressionDemo {
        public static void main(String[] args) {
                System.out.println("***Demonstration 2. Lambda
                expression.***\n");
                //Common way to use an interface method.
                MyFunctionalInterface impl1= new Implementor();
                System.out.println(impl1.addNumbers(1, 2));
```

```
    // Using lambda expression with a return statement.
    System.out.println("Using Lambda expression with the return
    statement now.");
    MyFunctionalInterface impl3 = (int a, int b) -> {
            return (a + b);
    };
    System.out.println("Sum of 50 and 100 is :");
    System.out.print(impl3.addNumbers(50,100));

    }
}
```

Output:

```
***Demonstration 2. Lambda expression.***

Implementing the interface method 'addNumbers' inside the Implementor class.
Sum of 1 and 2 is :
3
Using Lambda expression with the return statement now.
Sum of 50 and 100 is :
150
```

Q&A Session

14.3 Is @FunctionalInterface mandatory in this program to show that it is a functional interface?

No. But using the annotation in a case like this is a good practice that enhances readability. Also, if you use this annotation, in the future, if anyone tries to add another abstract method in the interface by mistake, the compiler can immediately raise an error.

Java Language Specification(11) says the following:

- A *functional interface* is an interface that has just one abstract method (aside from the methods of Object) and thus represents a single function contract. This "single" method may take the form of multiple abstract methods, with override equivalent signatures inherited from superinterfaces; in this case, the inherited methods logically represent a single method.

- It facilitates early detection of inappropriate method declarations appearing in or inherited by an interface that is meant to be functional.

- "[I]nstances of functional interfaces can be created with method reference expressions and lambda expressions."

Private Interface Method from Java 9

Private interface methods were a new addition in Java 9. Prior to Java 7, interface methods were straightforward—those were public abstract methods. Java 8 allows you to add public static methods and public default methods. In Java 9 onward you can use private static methods and private default methods in the interface.

Demonstration 3

Let's consider the following demonstration. Here, you have an interface called MyInterface with four methods:

- The first one is a common interface method; it does not have a body, and it is by default public and abstract.

- Then you have two default methods.

- Finally, you have the private non-static interface method, called privateInterfaceMethod(). Notice that since the method is private, you cannot call the method directly from main().

In this example, I am calling the private method through the default methods:

```
interface MyInterface{
    void commonInterfaceMethod();
    default void defaultInterfaceMethod1() {
        System.out.println("**Default non-static method1()**");
        //Doing the common task using the private interface method
        privateInterfaceMethod();
    }
```

```java
    default void defaultInterfaceMethod2() {
        System.out.println("**Default non-static method2()**");
        //Doing the common task using the private interface method
        privateInterfaceMethod();
    }
    private void privateInterfaceMethod() {
        System.out.println("**Private non-static method in
        MyInterface**");
            System.out.println("**I can do the common tasks of multiple
            default methods.**");
    }
}
class MyInterfaceImplementor implements MyInterface{
    @Override
    public void commonInterfaceMethod() {
        System.out.println("**Implementing the
        commonInterfaceMethod().**");
    }
}
class PrivateInterfaceMethodFromJava9 {
    public static void main(String[] args) {
        System.out.println("***Demonstration 3.Private Interface Method
        From Java 9.***\n");
        MyInterface interOb=new MyInterfaceImplementor();
        interOb.commonInterfaceMethod();
        interOb.defaultInterfaceMethod1();
        interOb.defaultInterfaceMethod2();
    }
}
```

Output:

Demonstration 3.Private Interface Method From Java 9.

Implementing the commonInterfaceMethod().
Default non-static method1()

```
**Private non-static method in MyInterface**
**I can do the common tasks of multiple default methods.**
**Default non-static method2()**
**Private non-static method in MyInterface**
**I can do the common tasks of multiple default methods.**
```

Q&A Session

14.4 What is the use of a private interface method?

If you have multiple default methods in the interface and those interfaces are performing a common task, you can place the common code in the private helper method. Consider Demonstration 4 again. It shows how two default methods— `defaultInterfaceMethod1()` and `defaultInterfaceMethod2()`—can accomplish a common task using a private interface method.

14.5 If the sharing of code is the concern, I can make another default method and share the common code in that method. Is this understanding correct?

You can do that, but that approach cannot be considered a better design than this. It is better to use a private helper method than a public helper method. This approach can promote better encapsulation and security.

14.6 Can a default method be private?

No. You will get a compile-time error if you use the following line of code:

```
default private void defaultPrivateInterfaceMethod() {
 //some code
}
```

The error will be as follows:

```
PrivateInterfaceMethodFromJava9.java:14: error: illegal combination of
modifiers: private and default
        default private void defaultPrivateInterfaceMethod() {//some code
                ^
1 error
```

14.7 Can I make a private interface method static?

Yes. For example, if you add the following two methods in the interface MyInterface:

```
public static void publicStaticInterfaceMethod() {
        System.out.println("**Public static method in MyInterface**");
        System.out.println("**Invoking the private static method in
        MyInterface now.**");
}

private static void privateStaticInterfaceMethod() {
        System.out.println("**Private static method in MyInterface**");
}
```

and then invoke the publicStaticInterfaceMethod() method from main() like the following:

```
MyInterface.publicStaticInterfaceMethod();
```

you will see the following lines in your output:

```
**Public static method in MyInterface**
**Invoking the private static method in MyInterface now.**
```

POINTS TO REMEMBER

- Private methods cannot be abstract.

- You cannot call a private non-static method from a private static method. If you do, you will receive a compile-time error for the following segment of code:

  ```
  private static void privateStaticInterfaceMethod2() {
  System.out.println("**Private static method2 in MyInterface**");
  //Compile-time error
  //privateInterfaceMethod();
  }
  ```

But the reverse is allowed; i.e., you can call a private static method from a non-static private method in the interface. So, there is *no* compile-time error for this segment of code:

```
private void privateInterfaceMethod2() {
System.out.println("**Private Non-static method2 in MyInterface**");
//NO Compile-time error
publicStaticInterfaceMethod();
}
```

Local Variable Type Inference from Java 10

From Java 10 onward, you can declare a local variable without specifying its type.

. Even if you do not declare the variable type, it can assume its type from what it is being set to. For example, from Java 10 onward, you can write something like the following:

```
var myInt=10;
```

Demonstration 4

The upcoming demonstration can show you a simple usage of var:

```
class LocalVariableTypeInterpretation {
 public static void main(String[] args) {
     System.out.println("***Demonstration 4.Local Variable Type
     Interpretation.***\n");
     int myInt1=1;//ok
     var myInt2=2;//Java10 onwards ok
     System.out.println("The value in myInt1 is :"+ myInt2);
     System.out.println("The myInt1 is of type:");
     //It will print java.lang.Integer
     System.out.println(((Object)myInt1).getClass().getName());
     System.out.println("The myInt2 is of type:");
     //It will also print java.lang.Integer
     System.out.println(((Object)myInt2).getClass().getName()); }
}
```

```
***Demonstration 4.Local Variable Type Interpretation.***

The value in myInt2 is :1
The myInt1 is of type:
java.lang.Integer
The myInt2 is of type:
java.lang.Integer
```

Restrictions

Here are some important restrictions when you use var:

- You need to put both declaration and initialization together.
  For example:

  ```
  var myInt=1;//ok
  ```

  But the following line will raise a compile-time error:

  ```
  var myInt;//Error
  myInt=1;
  ```

- You can use a variable name as var. The compiler will not complain
  about the following declaration; that is, it is not treated like reserved
  keywords in Java:

  ```
  var var=12.5;//Till now , compiler allows it
  ```

- You can use var in the context of initializing local variables and for
  loops, but you cannot use them in method parameters or return
  types. For example, in the following code segment, both methods in
  MyClass will raise compile-time errors:

  ```
  //You can use 'var' in the context of initializing local variables
  //and for loops but you cannot use them in method parameters
  //or return type.
  ```

```
class MyClass {
    void myMethod1(var i) { // Compile-time error
    // some code
    }

    var myMethod2(int i) { //Compile-time error
    }
}
```

New String Methods from Java 11

From Java 11 onward, you'll get some new String class methods. In the following
example, you will see three of them—isBlank(), repeat(), and strip(). Let's see their
definitions:

- isBlank(): This method will return the Boolean value true if the
  string is empty or contains only white space codepoints; otherwise,
  false.

- repeat(int n): Returns a string whose value is the concatenation of
  this string repeated *n* number of times.

- strip(): This method returns a string with all leading and trailing
  white space removed.

Demonstration 5

Consider the following code:

```
class StringMethodsFromJava11 {

  public static void main(String[] args) {
      System.out.println("***Demonstration 5.Some new String methods from
      Java 11.***\n");
      String str1 = "A non-empty string.";
          System.out.println("The str1 is :"+ str1);
          System.out.println(" 'The str1 is a blank string'-This
          statement is "+ str1.isBlank());
```

```
        String str2 = "";
        System.out.println("The str2 is :"+ str2);
        System.out.println(" 'The str2 is a blank string'-This
        statement is "+  str2.isBlank());

        //Repeat the string
        System.out.println("\nRepeating 'str1' 3 times now.");
        System.out.println(str1.repeat(3));

        //Using strip() removing beginning and trailing whitespaces
        String str3 = " Hi, Readers! How are you? ";
        System.out.println("\nThe str3 is :"+ str3);
        System.out.println("After strip() operation, str3 is :" +
        str3.strip());
    }
}
```

Output:

```
***Demonstration 5.Some new String methods from Java 11.***
The str1 is :A non-empty string.
 'The str1 is a blank string'-This statement is false
The str2 is :
 'The str2 is a blank string'-This statement is true

Repeating 'str1' 3 times now.
A non-empty string.A non-empty string.A non-empty string.

The str3 is : Hi, Readers! How are you?
After strip() operation, str3 is :Hi, Readers! How are you?
```

Q&A Session

14.8 How is isEmpty()different from isBlank()?

The definition of isEmpty() says that if and only if the string length is zero, it will return true. The following block of code can illustrate the difference between these two methods:

```
//isBlank vs isEmpty
String nonEmpty=" ";//a tab space
System.out.println("The nonEmpty.length()="+ nonEmpty.length());
System.out.println(nonEmpty.isBlank());//true
System.out.println(nonEmpty.isEmpty());//false
```

When you execute this block of code, you will get following output:

```
The nonEmpty.length()=1
true
false
```

Since the length of nonEmpty is not zero, isBlank() returns true, but isEmpty() returns false.

14.9 How is **strip()** different from **trim()**?

strip() can detect Unicode whitespace. But trim() can remove the space that is less than or equal to \u0020. To see the difference, you can examine a string like the following:

```
//Medium Mathematical Space U+205F
String str1 = "\u205F \u205FThis is my test string with trailing
whitespace-END.\u205F \u205F";
```

Now if you call the trim() method and the strip() method on this string object, you will notice the difference. For example, if you test with the following lines of code:

```
String trimmedString = str1.trim();
String strippedString = str1.strip();
System.out.printf("'%s'%n", trimmedString);
System.out.printf("'%s'%n", strippedString);
```

you will see that strip() can recognize the initial and trailing whitespaces of the string and complete its job properly.

New switch Expression in Java 12/13

The switch expression appeared in Java 12 and was further refined in Java 13. But it is a preview language feature. Using this expression, an entire switch block can receive an input value. You can use lambda-style syntax to implement this. Using this feature, you implement a straightforward control flow that is free of "fall-through."

Note If you are not aware of a preview feature, you can refer to Q&A 14.1. And you saw the use of a lambda expression in Demonstration 2 in this chapter.

Demonstration 6

The following demonstration shows a simple use of this feature. For case 1 to case 5, it will print a common message (Your version is between 1 and 5), for cases 6 to 12 it will print another common message (Your version is between 6 and 12). If the version is 13, the example will show a different message (which is shown in the output). The example also includes a default case to print about the default version. For simplicity, the myVersion variable is "hard-coded" here. But you can always modify it to accept a different version or consider the user's input. My focus was on the main feature, so I'm ignoring the other fancy parts.

```java
class SwitchExpressionTest {
 public static void main(String[] args) {
  System.out.println("***Testing Switch expression in Java 13.***");
   System.out.println("Considering versions between 1 to 13.");
   int myVersion=13;//Your version.You can change here.
   testNewSwitchExpressionInJava13(myVersion);
}

public static void testNewSwitchExpressionInJava13(int version){
 switch (version) {
   case  1,2,3,4,5-> System.out.println(" Your version is between 1 and 5.");
   case 6,7,8,9,10,11,12-> System.out.println("Your version is between 6
   and 12");
```

```
case 13-> System.out.println("At present, 13 is the latest version. You
picked it.");
default -> System.out.println("You didn't pick between 1 and 13. Default
version is: 0");
            }
        }
}
```

Output:

```
***Testing Switch expression in Java 13.***
Considering versions between 1 and 13.
At present, 13 is the latest version. You picked it.
```

Running the Code

In a command-line environment, if the path is not set, to avoid a lot of typing (to mention the javac and java locations), you need to set the path. You can set it in your environment variable, or you can set the path like the following.

Normally, Java13 will be installed in this path. If you use a different path, mention that location only for the path variable. In Chapter 7, you saw how to troubleshoot some common errors in a command-line environment.

C:\TestClass\chapter14>**set path=C:\Program Files\Java\jdk-13\bin;**

To compile the code in this demonstration, you need to use the –enable-preview option. Here is a sample:

C:\TestClass\chapter14> **javac --enable-preview -source 13
SwitchExpressionTest.java**

Here is the immediate output:

```
Note: SwitchExpressionTest.java uses preview language features.
Note: Recompile with -Xlint:preview for details.
```

To run the program, you can try the following command, shown in bold:

C:\TestClass\chapter14>**java --enable-preview SwitchExpressionTest**

The output is already shown "" above.

Q&A Session

14.10 Why do I need to pass the additional parameters with `javac` or `java` when I compile or run this program?

This is still a preview feature. This simply means that, though the overall feature is complete, the final decision to include it in a mainline JDK has yet to be decided. To build confidence in a feature and to get maximum possible feedback, a feature can be tagged like this.

When you use a preview feature, you need to unlock it when you compile the program or run the program. This is why you used the `-enable-preview` option earlier to compile and run the program in this example (Demonstration6).

Summary

This chapter covered the following:

- Switch expression from Java12/13

- New `String` class methods from Java 11

- Local variable type inference from Java 10

- Private methods from Java 9

- Implementing functional interfaces with lambda expressions from Java 8

- Try-with resource-from Java 7

PART III

Explore Real-World Scenarios

CHAPTER 15

Introduction to Design Patterns

Design patterns are used to find common solutions when you design your software. In the initial period of software development, there was no standard to instruct software developers on how to design their applications. In an organization, each team had different mottos and followed their own style. When a new engineer joined an existing team, learning the architecture of the current system was a gigantic task. Senior or experienced members of the team would need to explain the current architecture precisely. They also needed to answer some common questions, like what the advantages of using the current design were, and why an alternative design was not considered. The experienced developer also trained the new developer on how to reduce future effort by simply reusing concepts already in place. Design patterns address this kind of issue and provide a common platform for all developers. So, you can think of them as the recorded experience of experts in the field. These patterns were meant to be applied in object-oriented designs, with the intention of reuse.

In 1994, Erich Gamma, Richard Helm, Ralph Johnson, and John Vlissides published the book *Design Patterns: Elements of Reusable Object-Oriented Software* (Addison-Wesley, 1994). In this book, they introduced the concept of design patterns in software development. These authors became famous and are currently known as the Gang of Four. I refer to them as the **GoF** throughout this chapter. The GoF described 23 patterns that were recorded through the common experiences of software developers over a period of time. Each pattern can have its own complexity, pros, and cons, but their intents are different. Nowadays, when a developer joins a new team, they are expected to know about these patterns.

© Vaskaran Sarcar 2020

V. Sarcar, *Interactive Object-Oriented Programming in Java*, https://doi.org/10.1007/978-1-4842-5404-2_15

The concept of a real-life design pattern originated from the building architect Christopher Alexander. During his lifetime, he discovered that many of his problems were similar in nature. So, he implemented similar solutions to those common problems. He said:

> Each pattern describes a problem, which occurs over and over again in our environment, and then describes the core of the solution to that problem, in such a way that you can use this solution a million times over, without ever doing it the same way twice.

The software engineering community started believing that though these patterns were described for buildings and towns, the same concepts could be applied to patterns in object-oriented design because, at their cores, patterns are solutions to common problems. As a result, the original concepts of walls and doors in the construction industry were substituted with instances of classes and interfaces in the software industry.

Lastly, it is important to note that the GoF discussed the original concepts of design patterns in the context of C++. But Sun Microsystems released its first public implementation of Java 1.0 in 1995, and then it went through various changes. (You may know that Oracle corporation acquired Sun Microsystems in 2010.) So, in 1995, Java was totally new to the programming world. But it grew rapidly and secured its place among the world's top programming languages within a short period of time and remains popular today. Remember, the concepts of design patterns are universal. So, if you can exercise these fundamental concepts of design patterns with Java, your knowledge and expertise will be enhanced, and you can announce yourself as a better programmer.

This is a Java book. This chapter focuses on the design patterns, but not on the latest features of Java. In fact, I have deliberately chosen simple examples that can be version independent so you can understand these concepts easily.

Key Points

Before you start, let's review some important points regarding design patterns:

- A design pattern describes a general reusable solution to a software design problem. While developing a software, you may encounter some common problems repeatedly. But you can always solve similar kinds of problems with similar kinds of solutions. Keeping this principle in mind, you can attack a problem with an already tested solution. At the same time, you should ensure the effectiveness of the solution. Ideally, a solution should be tested over a long period of time.

- In general, a pattern provides you with a template that helps you to solve a problem in many different situations. It should also help you to get the best possible design much faster.

- In simple words, these patterns are descriptions of how to create objects and classes and customize them to solve a general design problem in a particular context.

- The GoF discussed 23 design patterns. Each of these patterns focuses on a particular object-oriented design. Each pattern can also describe the consequences and tradeoffs of use. The GoF categorized these 23 patterns based on their purposes, as shown next.

Creational Patterns

These patterns abstract the instantiation process. You make the systems independent from how their objects are composed, created, and represented. In these patterns, you will have concerns like "Where should I place the new keyword in my application?" This decision can determine the degree of coupling of your classes. The following five patterns belong to this category:

- Singleton Pattern

- Prototype Pattern

- Factory Method Pattern

- Builder Pattern

- Abstract Factory Pattern

Structural Patterns

These patterns focus on how classes and objects can be composed to form a relatively large structure. At core, you generally use inheritance or composition to group different interfaces or implementations. You know that the choice of composition over inheritance (and vice versa) can affect the flexibility of your software. The following seven patterns fall into this category:

- Proxy Pattern

- Flyweight Pattern

- Composite Pattern

- Bridge Pattern

- Facade Pattern

- Decorator Pattern

- Adapter Pattern

Behavioral Patterns

Here, you will concentrate on algorithms and the assignment of responsibilities among objects. You also need to focus on the communication between them and how the objects are interconnected. The following eleven patterns fall in this category.

- Observer Pattern

- Strategy Pattern

- Template Method Pattern

- Command Pattern

- Iterator Pattern

- Memento Pattern

- State Pattern

- Mediator Pattern

- Chain of Responsibility Pattern
- Visitor Pattern
- Interpreter Pattern

Class and Object Patterns

The GoF made another classification based on scope, namely whether the pattern primary focuses on the class or its objects. You can guess that *class patterns* deal with classes and subclasses. These patterns use inheritance mechanisms, so these are static in nature and fixed at compile time. On the other hand, *object patterns* deal with objects that can change at runtime. So, object patterns are dynamic.

In this chapter, I'll pick one pattern from each category for this introductory discussion on design patterns. Each pattern is divided into six parts: a definition (which is basically termed as intent in the GoF's book), a core concept, a real-world example, a coding example, a sample program with output, and the Q&A Session section. As mentioned before, I have chosen simple examples so that you can pick up the basic ideas quickly. But you must think on it, keep reading and practicing, try to link with other problems, and then keep coding. This process will help you to learn the subject quickly.

Note   You can refer to my other book, *Java Design Patterns: A Hands-On Experience with Real-World Examples* (Second Edition), which is published by the same publisher, to learn other design patterns in depth.

Q&A Session

15.1 What are the differences between class patterns and object patterns?

Class patterns focus on static relationships, but object patterns focus on dynamic relationships. As their name suggests, class patterns focus on classes and their subclasses. Object patterns focus on the object's relationships.

The GoF further differentiated them as shown in Table 15-1.

Table 15-1. *Class Patterns vs Object Patterns*

	Class Patterns	**Object patterns**
Creational	Can defer object creation to its subclasses	Can defer object creation to another object
Structural	Focuses on the composition of classes (primarily uses the concept of inheritance)	Focuses on the different ways of composition of objects
Behavioral	Describes the algorithms and execution flows	Describes how different objects can work together and complete a task

15.2 Can I use multiple patterns in an application?

Yes. In real-world programming, this is common.

15.3 Are these patterns dependent on a particular programming language?

Programming languages can play an important role. But the basic ideas are the same. Patterns are just like templates, and they will give you some idea in advance of how you can solve a particular problem. In this book, I primarily focus on object-oriented programming with Java. But let's suppose, instead of any object-oriented programming language, you have chosen some other language (for example, C) that is not object oriented. In that case, you may need to think about the core object-oriented principles, such as inheritance, polymorphism, encapsulation, abstraction, and so on, and how to implement them. The choice of a particular language is always important because it may have some specialized features that can make your life easier.

15.4 Should I consider common data structures like arrays and linked lists as different design patterns?

The GoF clearly excludes those, saying that "they are not complex, domain-specific designs for an entire application or subsystem." They can be encoded in classes and reused as is. So, they are not your concern in this chapter.

15.5 If no particular pattern is 100% suitable for my problem, how should I proceed?

It is obvious that you cannot solve an infinite number of problems with a finite number of patterns. But there is the probability that someone else before you faced a similar problem and found a solution. You can always use those recorded experiences. So, if you know these common patterns and their trade-offs, you can pick a close match. Lastly, no one prevents you from using your own pattern for your own problem. But you have to tackle the risk from all possible dimensions.

15.6 Do you have any general advice before I jump into the topics?

I always follow the footsteps my seniors and teachers who are experts in this field. Here are some general suggestions from them:

- You should program to a supertype (abstract class/interface), not an implementation.

- You should prefer composition over inheritance.

- You should try to make a loosely coupled system.

- You should segregate the code that is likely to vary from the rest of your code.

- You should encapsulate the code that varies.

Let's jump into design patterns now.

Prototype Pattern

GoF Definition

Specify the kinds of objects to create using a prototypical instance, and create new objects by copying this prototype.

Concept

In general, creating a new instance from scratch is a costly operation. Using the concept of the prototype pattern, you can create a new instance by copying or cloning an existing instance. This approach can save both time and money.

Real-life Example

Suppose you have a master copy of a valuable document. One day you find that you need to incorporate some change into it. In this case, you can make a photocopy of the original document and make the changes to see the impact.

Consider another example. Suppose a group of people suddenly decides to celebrate the birthday of one of their friends, say, Ron. What will they do? They can go to a cake shop and order a ready-made cake. To make it special, they may request the seller to write something like "Happy Birthday to Ron." From a seller point of view, he is not making any new model. He already defined the model, and every day he produces many cakes (which all look the same) by following the same process, and finally he makes it special with some small changes.

Coding Example

Let us assume that you have an application that is very stable. In the future, you may want to update the application with some small modifications. You must start with a copy of your original application, make the changes, and analyze further. Surely, you don't want to start from scratch, so as to save you time and money. In real-world programming, when you add a new feature to your existing application, you may follow the same strategy.

The following note gives you a clue about how you can use this pattern in your application.

Note   In Java, you can consider the `clone()` method of the `Object` class as an example of a Prototype pattern. This method can create and return a copy of an existing object. (In this context, your class needs to be `Cloneable`.)

Illustration

Figure 15-1 illustrates a simple prototype structure, which I am going to follow in the following implementation.

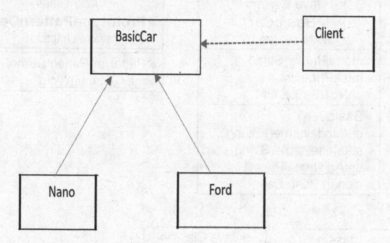

Figure 15-1. *A sample prototype structure*

Here, **BasicCar** is the basic prototype. **Nano** and **Ford** are the concrete prototypes, and they have implemented the **clone()** method defined in **BasicCar**. In this example, I have created these cars with some base price (in Indian currency). Later, I have updated the final price as per the model. `PrototypePatternExample.java` is the client in this implementation.

Class Diagram

Figure 15-2 shows the class diagram for the illustration of the Prototype pattern.

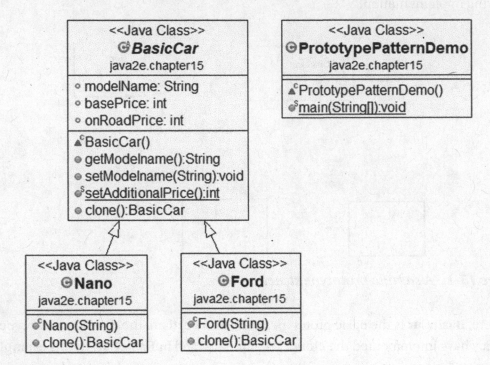

Figure 15-2.   Class diagram

Package Explorer View

Figure 15-3 shows the high-level structure of the program.

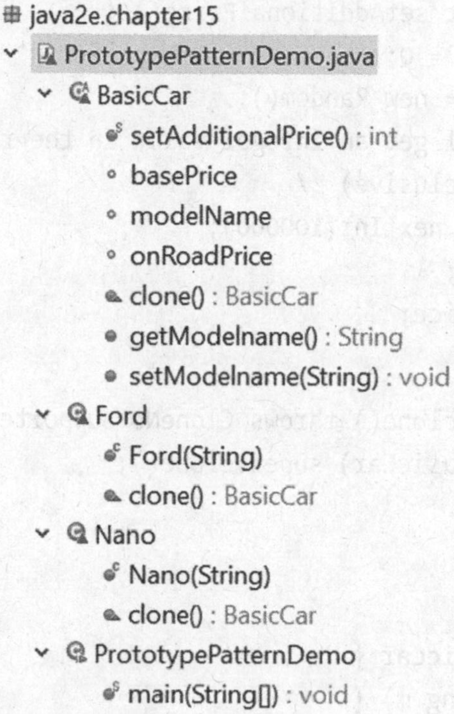

```
# java2e.chapter15
  ∨ 🔲 PrototypePatternDemo.java
      ∨ ⓒ BasicCar
          • setAdditionalPrice() : int
          ◦ basePrice
          ◦ modelName
          ◦ onRoadPrice
          ⬤ clone() : BasicCar
          • getModelname() : String
          • setModelname(String) : void
      ∨ ⓒ Ford
          • Ford(String)
          ⬤ clone() : BasicCar
      ∨ ⓒ Nano
          • Nano(String)
          ⬤ clone() : BasicCar
      ∨ ⓒ PrototypePatternDemo
          • main(String[]) : void
```

Figure 15-3. *Package Explorer view*

Implementation

```java
package java2e.chapter15;

import java.util.Random;

//BasicCar class
abstract class BasicCar implements Cloneable {
    public String modelName;
    public int basePrice, onRoadPrice;

    public String getModelname() {
        return modelName;
    }
}
```

```java
        public void setModelname(String modelname) {
                this.modelName = modelname;
        }

        public static int setAdditionalPrice() {
                int price = 0;
                Random r = new Random();
                /* We will get an integer value in the range 0(inclusive) to
                100000(exclusive) */
                int p = r.nextInt(100000);
                price = p;
                return price;
        }

        public BasicCar clone() throws CloneNotSupportedException {
                return (BasicCar) super.clone();
        }
}

//Nano class
class Nano extends BasicCar {
        public Nano(String m) {
                modelName = m;
                // Basic price for Nano
                basePrice = 200000;
        }

        @Override
        public BasicCar clone() throws CloneNotSupportedException {
                return (Nano) super.clone();
        }
}

//Ford class
class Ford extends BasicCar {
        public Ford(String m) {
                modelName = m;
```

```java
        // Basic price for Ford.
        basePrice = 500000;
    }

    @Override
    public BasicCar clone() throws CloneNotSupportedException {
        return (Ford) super.clone();
    }
}

class PrototypePatternDemo {

    public static void main(String[] args) throws
    CloneNotSupportedException {
        System.out.println("***Prototype Pattern Demo***\n");
        BasicCar nano = new Nano("Nano XT");
        BasicCar ford = new Ford("Ford Figo");
        BasicCar nanoClone,fordClone;
        // Making a copy of a Nano object
        nanoClone= nano.clone();
        System.out.println("Nano's base price is: Rs."+nanoClone.
        basePrice);
        //Making the change on the copied object.
        // Price will be more than 200000
        nanoClone.onRoadPrice = nanoClone.basePrice +
        BasicCar.setAdditionalPrice();
        System.out.println("In India, the final price of a " +
        nanoClone.modelName + " is Rs." + nanoClone.onRoadPrice);

        // Making a copy of a Ford object
        fordClone = ford.clone();
        System.out.println("Ford's base price is: Rs."+fordClone.
        basePrice);
        //Making the change on the copied object.
        // Price will be more than 500000
        fordClone.onRoadPrice = fordClone.basePrice + BasicCar.setAddi
        tionalPrice();
```

```
            System.out.println("In India, the final price of a " + -
            fordClone.modelName + " is Rs." + fordClone.onRoadPrice);
    }
}
```

Output:

```
***Prototype Pattern Demo***

Nano's base price is: Rs.200000
In India, the final price of a Nano XT is Rs.294803
Ford's base price is: Rs.500000
In India, the final price of a Ford Figo is Rs.595733
```

Note   You may notice a different price in your system, because I am generating a random price in the `setAdditionalPrice()` method inside the `BasicCar` class. But I have ensured that the NanoXT's final price is more than Rs 200,000, the Ford Figo's final price is more than Rs 500,000, and the price of a Ford Figo will be greater than that of a Nano XT.

Q&A Session

15.7. What are the advantages of using Prototype design patterns?

Here are the key advantages:

- Creating a new instance from scratch is a costly operation. Prototype patterns help you to create a new instance from an existing one. So, it is less expensive.

- You may need to face some complicated or boring process if you start from scratch. Instead, by using a Prototype pattern, you can focus on upcoming features only.

- You can include or discard products at runtime.

15.8. What are the challenges associated with using Prototype design patterns?

Here are the key challenges you may face when you use this pattern:

- You need to focus on the cloning or copying mechanism.

- Sometimes, creating a copy from an existing instance is not simple. For example, implementing a cloning mechanism can be challenging if the objects under consideration do not support copying/cloning at all or if there are circular references. For example, in Java, a class with the `clone()` method needs to implement the `Cloneable` marker interface; otherwise, it will throw a `CloneNotSupportedException`.

- In our example, I have used the `clone()` method that performs a shallow copy in Java. Following the convention, you obtained the returned object by calling `super.clone()`. If you need to get a deep copy that can be expensive.

15.9. Can you please explain different types of copying technique with examples?

You know that the `Object` (in the `java.lang` package) class is the super class for all classes. This `Object` class has a method called `clone()`, which supports the cloning operations. If you hover your mouse on the `Clone()` method in the Eclipse editor, you will see the following syntax:

```
protected native Object clone() throws CloneNotSupportedException;
```

The method description also says that this method "creates and returns a copy of this object. The precise meaning of 'copy' may depend on the class of the object."

When you use cloning, you will come to know about two different techniques of cloning, namely shallow copy and deep copy. Here is the key distinction between these two:

- Shallow copy is faster and less expensive. It is always better if your target object has primitive fields only.

- Deep copy is expensive and slow. But it is useful if your target object contains many fields that have references to other objects.

So, let's understand the theories behind them. Shallow copy creates a new object and then copies various field values from the original object to the new object. So, it is also known as field-by-field copy. If the original object contains any references to other objects as fields, then the references to those objects are copied into the new object (i.e., you do not create copies of those objects).

Let us try to understand the mechanism with a simple diagram. Suppose you have an object, X1, and it has a reference to another object, Y1. Further, assume that object Y1 has a reference to object Z1. Figure 15-4 demonstrates the same.

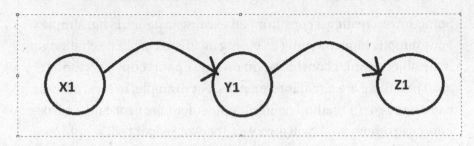

Figure 15-4. *Before: shallow copy of the reference(s)*

Now, with a shallow copy of X1, a new object, say, X2, will be created that will also have a reference to Y1. Figure 15-5 demonstrates the same.

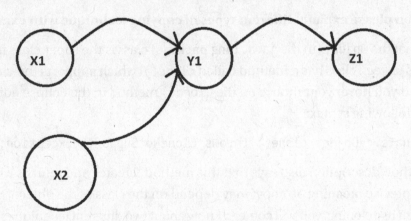

Figure 15-5. *After: shallow copy of the reference(s)*

But for a deep copy of X1, a new object, say, X3, will be created. X3 will have a reference to new object Y3, which is actually a copy of Y1. Also, Y3, in turn, will have a reference to another new object, Z3, which is a copy of Z1. Figure 15-6 demonstrates this.

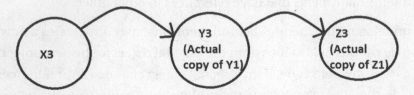

Figure 15-6. *After: deep copy of the reference*

458

In the case of a deep copy, the new object is totally separated from the original one, and any changes made in one object should not be reflected in the other one. In Java, to create a deep copy, you may need to override the clone() method and then proceed. Also, deep copy is expensive because you may need to create additional objects.

Shallow Copy Versus Deep Copy in Java

You can make a clone (or copy) using the clone() method in Java, but you need to implement the Cloneable interface because only the Java objects that implement this Cloneable interface are eligible for cloning. The default version of clone() creates a shallow copy. To create the deep copy, you need to override the clone() method.

Here are the key characteristics of the following program:

- In the following example, you have two classes: Employee and EmpAddress.

- The Employee class has three fields: id, name, and EmpAddress. So, you may notice that to form an Employee object, you need to pass an EmpAddress object. So, you will notice the line of code as follows: Employee emp=new Employee(1,"John",initialAddress);

- EmpAddress has only a field called address, which is a String datatype.

- In the client code (inside the main() method), you create a cloned object empClone using the built-in clone() method in Java. So, you will notice the line of code as follows: Employee empClone=(Employee)emp.clone();

- Then you change the field values of the emp object.

- But now you see a side effect of this change because you notice that the address of the empClone object also changed, which was unwanted.

```
class EmpAddress implements Cloneable {
    String address;

    public EmpAddress(String address) {
        this.address = address;
    }
```

```java
        public String getAddress() {
                return address;
        }

        public void setAddress(String address) {
                this.address = address;
        }

        @Override
        public String toString() {
                return this.address;
        }

        @Override
        public Object clone() throws CloneNotSupportedException {
                // Shallow Copy
                return super.clone();
        }
}

class Employee implements Cloneable {
        int id;
        String name;
        EmpAddress empAddress;

        public Employee(int id, String name, EmpAddress empAddress) {
                this.id = id;
                this.name = name;
                this.empAddress = empAddress;
        }

        public int getId() {
                return id;
        }

        public void setId(int id) {
                this.id = id;
        }
```

```java
    public String getName() {
        return name;
    }

    public void setName(String name) {
        this.name = name;
    }

    public EmpAddress getAddress() {
        return this.empAddress;
    }

    public void setAddress(EmpAddress newAddress) {
        this.empAddress = newAddress;
    }

    @Override
    public String toString() {
        return "EmpId=" + this.id + " EmpName=" + this.name + "
        EmpAddressName=" + this.empAddress;
    }

    @Override
    public Object clone() throws CloneNotSupportedException {
        // Shallow Copy
        return super.clone();
    }
}

class CloningTechniques{

    public static void main(String[] args) throws
    CloneNotSupportedException {
        System.out.println("***Shallow vs Deep Copy
        Demonstration.***\n");
        EmpAddress initialAddress = new EmpAddress("21, abc Road,
        USA");
        Employee emp = new Employee(1, "John", initialAddress);
        System.out.println("The emp details is as follows:");
```

```
            System.out.println(emp);
            Employee empClone = (Employee) emp.clone();
            System.out.println("The empClone details is as follows:");
            System.out.println(empClone);
            System.out.println("\n Now changing the name, id and address
            of the emp object ");
            emp.setId(10);
            emp.setName("Sam");
            emp.empAddress.setAddress("221, xyz Road, Canada");
            System.out.println("Now emp details is as follows:");
            System.out.println(emp);
            System.out.println("And empClone details is as follows:");
            System.out.println(empClone);
    }
}
```

Here is the output:

```
***Shallow vs Deep Copy Demonstration.***

The emp details is as follows:
EmpId=1 EmpName=John EmpAddressName=21, abc Road, USA
The empClone details is as follows:
EmpId=1 EmpName=John EmpAddressName=21, abc Road, USA

 Now changing the name, id and address of the emp object
Now emp details is as follows:
EmpId=10 EmpName=Sam EmpAddressName=221, xyz Road, Canada
And empClone details is as follows:
EmpId=1 EmpName=John EmpAddressName=221, xyz Road, Canada
```

Analysis:

Notice the last line of output. You can see an unwanted side-effect, because you notice the address of the cloned object is modified due to the modification to the emp object. This is because the original object and the cloned object both point to the same address, and they are not totally disjointed. Figure 15-7 can depict the scenario better.

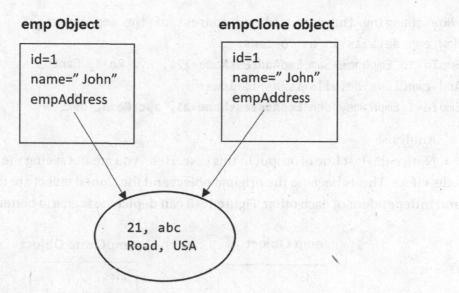

Figure 15-7. *Shallow copy scenario in prior example*

To implement a deep copy implementation, let's modify the clone() method of the Employee class as follows:

```
@Override
public Object clone() throws CloneNotSupportedException {
// Shallow Copy
// return super.clone();

// For deep copy
Employee employee = (Employee) super.clone();
employee.empAddress = (EmpAddress) empAddress.clone();
return employee;
}
```

Here is the modified output:

```
***Shallow vs Deep Copy Demonstration.***

The emp details is as follows:
EmpId=1 EmpName=John EmpAddressName=21, abc Road, USA
The empClone details is as follows:
EmpId=1 EmpName=John EmpAddressName=21, abc Road, USA
```

```
 Now changing the name, id and address of the emp object
Now emp details is as follows:
EmpId=10 EmpName=Sam EmpAddressName=221, xyz Road, Canada
And empClone details is as follows:
EmpId=1 EmpName=John EmpAddressName=21, abc Road, USA
```

Analysis:

Notice the last line of output in this case. Here, you are not seeing the unwanted side-effect. This is because the original object and the cloned object are totally different and independent of each other. Figure 15-8 can depict the scenario better.

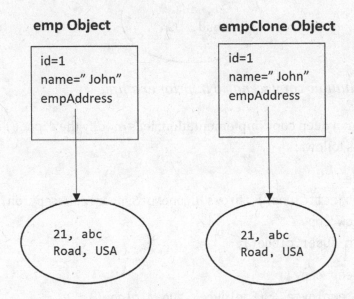

Figure 15-8. *Deep copy scenario in modified Demonstration*

15.10 When should you choose shallow copy over deep copy (and vice versa)?

Shallow copy is faster and less expensive. It is always better if your target object has primitive fields only.

Deep copy is expensive and slow. But it is useful if your target object contains many fields that have references to other objects.

15.11 In Java, if I need to copy an object, I need to use the clone() method. Is this understanding correct?

No, there are many alternatives. For example, you can use your own copy constructor. Apart from this, you can use the concept of serialization.

15.12 Does Java support a default copy constructor?

No, but you can define your own copy constructor. Chapter 3 demonstrates such an example.

Bridge Pattern

GoF Definition

Decouple an abstraction from its implementation so that the two can vary independently.

Concept

This pattern is also known as the **Handle/Body pattern**. In this pattern, you will see two different inheritance hierarchies—one for the abstraction layer and one for the implementation layer. You connect these two hierarchies using a bridge. But the role of the bridge is important. It connects them in such a way that these two hierarchies can change without affecting each other.

From a coding perspective, you can use either an abstract class or an interface for your abstraction and/or implementation, but when you implement the concept, the abstraction will contain a reference to the implementor, and you use composition to bridge the two hierarchies.

Real-life Example

In a software product development company, the development team and the marketing team each play a crucial role. The marketing team might do a market survey and gather the customer requirements, which may vary depending on the nature of the customers. The development team implements those requirements in their products to fulfill the customers' needs. Any change (say, in the operational strategy) in one team should not have a direct impact on the other team. Also, in the future, when new requirements come from a customer, that demand should not change how developers work in their organization. In a case like this, you can think of the marketing team as playing the role of the bridge between the clients of the product and the development team of the software organization.

Coding Example

A GUI framework can use the Bridge pattern to separate abstractions from platform-specific implementation. For example, it can separate a window abstraction from a window implementation for Linux or macOS using this pattern.

Note   In Chapter 13, you learned about JDBC. It acts as a bridge between your application and the database. For example, the `java.sql.DriverManager` class and the `java.sql.Driver` interface can form a Bridge pattern, where the first one plays the role of abstraction and the second one plays the role of implementor. The concrete implementors can be `com.mysql.cj.jdbc.Driver` or `oracle.jdbc.driver.OracleDriver`. (It is important to note that the class `com.mysql.jdbc.Driver` is deprecated. You need to use the new class, `com.mysql.cj.jdbc.Driver`.)

Illustration

Suppose you are a remote-control maker and you need to make remote controls for different electronic items. For simplicity, let us assume that you are presently getting orders to make remote controls for televisions and DVDs. Let us also assume that your remote control has two major functionalities—on and off.

Suppose you want to start with the design shown in Figure 15-9 or the one in Figure 15-10.

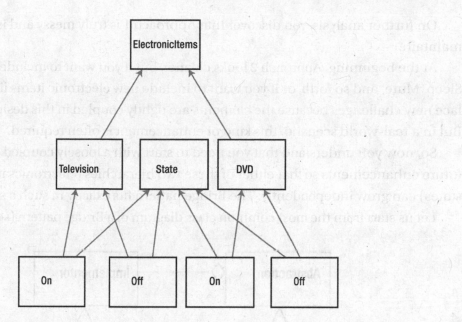

Figure 15-9. *Approach 1*

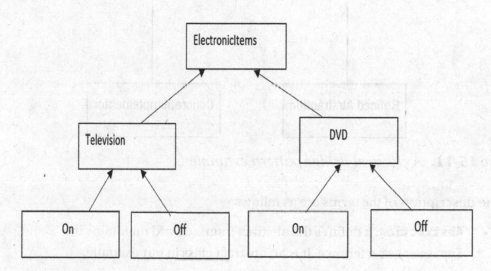

Figure 15-10. *Approach 2*

On further analysis, you discover that Approach 1 is truly messy and is difficult to maintain.

At the beginning, Approach 2 looks cleaner, but if you want to include new states like Sleep, Mute, and so forth, or if you want to include new electronic items like AC, you will face new challenges because the elements are tightly coupled in this design approach. But in a real-world scenario, this kind of enhancement is often required.

So, now you understand that you need to start with a loosely coupled system for future enhancements so that either of these two hierarchies (electronics items and their states) can grow independently. The Bridge pattern fits exactly in such a scenario.

Let us start from the most common class diagram of a Bridge pattern (see Figure 15-11).

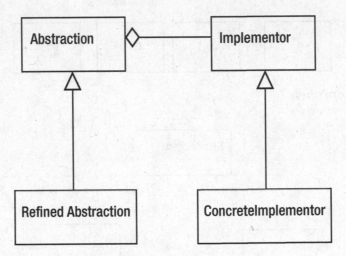

Figure 15-11. *A classical Bridge pattern example*

The description of the terms are as follows:

- **Abstraction**: It defines the abstract interface and maintains the Implementor reference. It is an abstract class in our example.

- **RefinedAbstraction**: It extends the interface defined by Abstraction. It is a concrete class in our example.

- **Implementor**: It defines the interface for implementation classes. It is an interface in our example.

- **ConcreteImplementor**: It is a concrete class in our example. It implements the Implementor interface.

I have followed a similar architecture in the following implementation. For your ready reference, I have pointed out all the participants in the following implementation with comments.

Class Diagram

Figure 15-12 shows the class diagram.

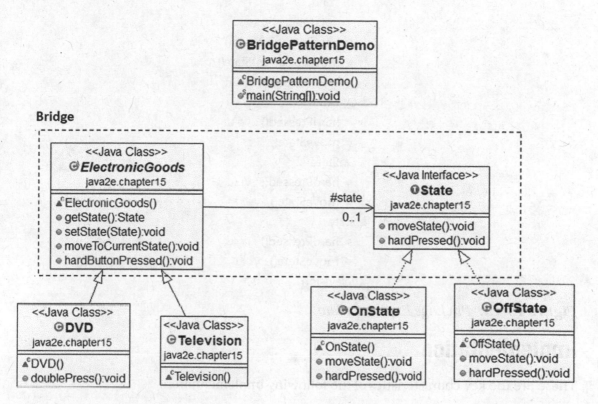

Figure 15-12. Class diagram

Package Explorer View

Figure 15-13 shows the high-level structure of the program.

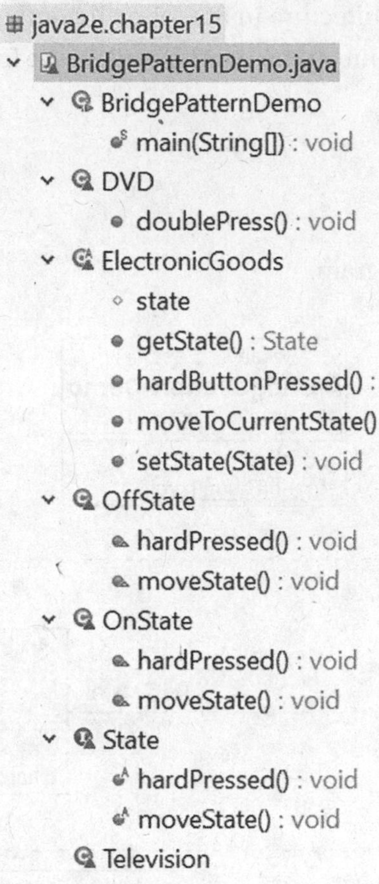

```
⊞ java2e.chapter15
  ˅  🗋 BridgePatternDemo.java
      ˅  🔾 BridgePatternDemo
          🔾ˢ main(String[]) : void
      ˅  🔾 DVD
          ● doublePress() : void
      ˅  🔾 ElectronicGoods
          ○ state
          ● getState() : State
          ● hardButtonPressed() : void
          ● moveToCurrentState() : void
          ● setState(State) : void
      ˅  🔾 OffState
          ● hardPressed() : void
          ● moveState() : void
      ˅  🔾 OnState
          ● hardPressed() : void
          ● moveState() : void
      ˅  🔾 State
          🔾 hardPressed() : void
          🔾 moveState() : void
      🔾 Television
```

Figure 15-13. *Package Explorer view*

Implementation

These are the key characteristics of the following implementation:

- The abstract class `ElectronicGoods` plays the role of abstraction, and the interface `State` plays the role of the implementor.

- The concrete implementors are the `OnState` class and the `OffState` class. They have implemented the interface methods `moveState()` and `hardPressed()` as per their requirement.

- The abstract class `ElectronicGoods` holds a reference of the implementor `State`.

- The abstraction methods are delegating the implementation to the
  implementor object. For example, notice that hardButtonPressed()
  actually is a shorthand for state.hardPressed(), where state is the
  implementor object.

- There are two refined abstractions: Television and DVD. The class is
  happy with the methods it inherits from its parent. But the DVD class
  wants to provide an additional feature. So, it implements a DVD-
  specific method, doublePress(). The method doublePress() is
  coded in terms of super class abstraction only.

```
package java2e.chapter15;

//Abstraction
abstract class ElectronicGoods
{
    //Composition - implementor
    protected State state;
    /*Alternative approach:
      You can also pass an implementor (as input argument) inside a
      constructor.
     */
    /*public ElectronicGoods(State state)
    {
        this.state = state;
    }*/
    public State getState()
    {
        return state;
    }
    public void setState(State state)
    {
        this.state = state;
    }
    /*Implementation specific:
      We are delegating the implementation to the Implementor object.
     */
```

```java
        public void moveToCurrentState()
        {
                System.out.print("The electronic item is functioning at : ");
                state.moveState();
        }
        public void hardButtonPressed()
        {
                state.hardPressed();
        }

}
//Refined Abstraction
//Television does not want to modify any super class method.
class Television extends ElectronicGoods
{

        /*public Television(State state)
        {
                super(state);
        }*/
}
/*DVD class also ok with the super class method.
In addition to this, it uses one additional method*/
class DVD extends ElectronicGoods
{

        /*public DVD(State state)
        {
                super(state);
        }*/
        /* Notice that following DVD-specific method is coded with super
        class methods but not with the implementor (State) method. So, this
        approach will allow to vary the abstraction and implementation
        independently.
         */
        public void doublePress() {
                hardButtonPressed();
```

```
                hardButtonPressed();
        }
}

//Implementor
interface State
{
        void moveState();
        void hardPressed();
}
//A Concrete Implementor.
class OnState implements State
{
        @Override
        public void moveState()
        {
                System.out.print("On State\n");
        }

        @Override
        public void hardPressed()
        {
                System.out.print("\tThe device is already On.Do not press the
                button so hard.\n");

        }
}
//Another Concrete Implementor.
class OffState implements State
{
        @Override
        public void moveState()
        {
                System.out.print("Off State\n");
        }
```

```java
    @Override
    public void hardPressed()
    {
            System.out.print("\tThe device is Offline now.Do not press the
            off button again.\n");

    }
}
class BridgePatternDemo {

    public static void main(String[] args) {
            System.out.println("***Bridge Pattern Demo***\n");

            System.out.println("Dealing with a Television at present.");

            State presentState = new OnState();
            //ElectronicGoods eItem = new Television(presentState);
            ElectronicGoods eItem = new Television();
            eItem.setState(presentState);
            eItem.moveToCurrentState();
            //hard press
            eItem.hardButtonPressed();
            //Verifying Off state of the Television now
            presentState = new OffState();
            //eItem = new Television(presentState);
            eItem.setState(presentState);
            eItem.moveToCurrentState();

            System.out.println("");
            System.out.println("Dealing with a DVD now.");
            presentState = new OnState();
            //eItem = new DVD(presentState);
            eItem = new DVD();
            eItem.setState(presentState);
            eItem.moveToCurrentState();

            presentState = new OffState();
            //eItem = new DVD(presentState);
```

```
        eItem = new DVD();
        eItem.setState(presentState);
        eItem.moveToCurrentState();

        //hard press-A DVD specific method
        //(new DVD(presentState)).doublePress();
        ((DVD)eItem).doublePress();

        /*If you uncomment the following line of code, it will cause
        error because a television object does not have this method.*/
        //(new Television(presentState)).doublePress();
    }
}
```

   Output:

Bridge Pattern Demo

Dealing with a Television at present.
The electronic item is functioning at : On State
     The device is already On. Do not press the button so hard.
The electronic item is functioning at : Off State

Dealing with a DVD now.
The electronic item is functioning at : On State
The electronic item is functioning at : Off State
     The device is Offline now. Do not press the off button again.
     The device is Offline now. Do not press the off button again.

Q&A Session

15.13 In this example, I see lots of dead code. Why are you keeping that?

Many engineers prefer constructors over getter/setter methods. You can see the
variations in different implementations. I am keeping those for your ready reference, and
you are free to use any of them.

15.14 You could use simple subclassing instead of using this kind of design. Is this understanding correct?

No. With simple subclassing, your implementations cannot vary dynamically. Though it may appear that the implementations may behave differently with subclassing techniques, in actuality, that kind of variation is already bound to the abstraction at compile time.

15.15 I recently learned the State pattern, and I am seeing lots of similarities. Is this understanding correct?

No. State patterns are not described in this book. They are described in detail in my other book, *Java Design Patterns*, Second Edition (Apress, 2019). You can refer to that book if you want. But if you are familiar with it, you will find that the State pattern falls into the Behavioral Pattern category, and its intent is different. In this chapter, I have shown an example where the electronic items can be in different states, but the key intent was to represent the following:

- How can you avoid the tight coupling between the items and their states?

- How can you maintain two different hierarchies, where both of them can extend without impacting each other?

- How do you deal with multiple objects where implementations are shared among themselves?

With this in mind, go through the comments that are attached to this implementation for a better understanding. I also want to draw your attention to the DVD-specific method `doublePress()`. Notice that it is constructed with super class methods, which in turn delegate the implementation to the `implementor` object (a state object, in this case). This approach will allow you to vary the abstraction and implementation independently, which is the key objective of the Bridge pattern.

15.16 What are the key advantages of using a Bridge design pattern?

Here are the key advantages when you use this pattern:

- Implementations are not bound to the abstractions.

- Both the abstractions and the implementations can grow independently.

- Concrete classes independent from the interface implementor classes—i.e., changes—in one of the hierarchies do not affect the other hierarchy. So, you can also vary the interface and the concrete implementations in different ways.

15.17 What are the challenges associated with this pattern?

Here are the key challenges when you use this pattern:

- The overall structure may become complex.

- Sometimes it is confused with the Adapter pattern. (You can remember that the key purpose of an Adapter pattern is to deal with incompatible interfaces only.)

15.18. Suppose I have only one state—either OnState or OffState. In this situation, do I need to use the interface State?

No, it is not mandatory for you. The GoF classified the case of not using a State interface as a degenerate case of the Bridge pattern.

15.19 In this example, an abstract class is used to represent an abstraction, and an interface is used for an implementation. Is this mandatory?

No. You can also use an interface also for the abstraction layer. Basically, you use either an abstract class or an interface for any of the abstractions or implementations. I have just used this format for better readability.

Observer Pattern

GoF Definition

Defines a one-to-many dependency between objects so that when one object changes state, all its dependents are notified and updated automatically.

Concept

In this pattern, there are many observers (objects), which are observing a particular subject (also an object). Observers register themselves to a subject to get the change notification from the subject. If any observer loses interest in the subject it can unregister from the subject. Sometimes this model is also referred to as the Publish-Subscribe model. The whole idea can be summarized as follows: *Using this pattern, an object (subject) can send notifications to multiple observers (a set of objects) at the same time.*

You can visualize the scenarios with the following diagrams. Let's assume there are three different types of observers (let's say observer1, observer2, and observer3) that show interest in a subject.

1. Observers are requesting to a subject to get notifications (see Figure 15-14).

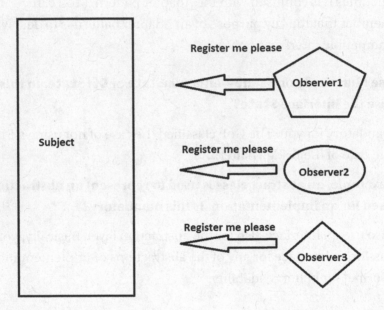

Figure 15-14. *Step 1*

2. Subject grants all the requests (i.e., connection established; see Figure 15-15).

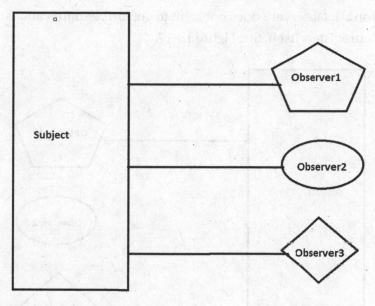

Figure 15-15. *Step 2*

3. Subject sends notifications to the registered observers (for example, a typical event occurs in the subject and it wants to notify its observers; see Figure 15-16).

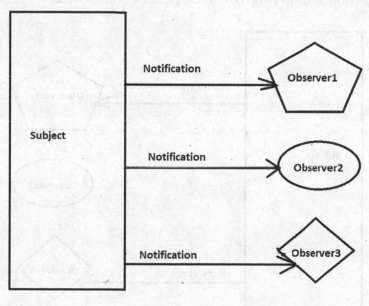

Figure 15-16. *Step 3*

479

4. **(Optional)**: Observer2 does not want to get further notifications. So, it unregisters itself. See Figure 15-17.

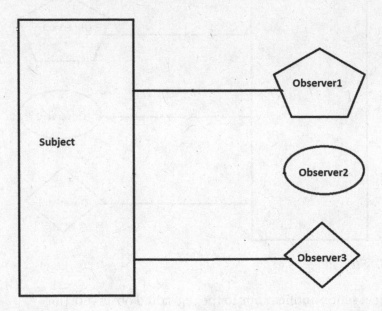

Figure 15-17. *Step 4*

5. From this point onward, only Observer1 and Observer3 will receive notifications from the subject. See Figure 15-18.

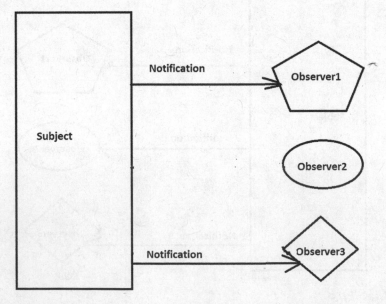

Figure 15-18. *Step 5*

Real-life Example

We can think about a celebrity who has many followers. Each of these followers wants to get all the latest updates from the celebrity. When they lose interest, they simply do not follow that celebrity. Here, you can treat each of these followers as an observer and the celebrity as a subject.

Coding Example

Consider a simple UI-based example where the UI is connected to a database. A user can execute search queries through that UI, and, after searching the database, the result is reflected in the UI. Here, you segregate the UI from the database in such a way that if a change occurs in the database, the UI should be notified, and it can update its display according to the change.

You can even simplify the preceding scenario. You can simply assume that you are the person responsible for maintaining a particular database in your organization. So, whenever there is a change made inside the database, most likely you want to get a notification so that you can take an early action if it is required.

Note   You may use this pattern in an event-driven software. Modern computer languages like Java and C# provide built-in support for handling events and make your life easy. Java event listeners are observers only. These observers can implement the Observer interface, which has an update() method: void update(Observable o,Object arg). This method is invoked whenever a change occurs in the observed object. You can call the Observable object's notifyObservers() method to notify the observers of the changes. The addObserver(Observer o) can add an observer, and the deleteObserver(Observer o) method can delete an observer. You can delete all the observers using the deleteObservers() method. These are similar to the register and unregister methods discussed earlier.

Illustration

Now, let us directly enter into our example. Here, I have created three observers and one subject. The subject maintains a list for all of its registered users. Our observers want to receive notifications when a flag value changes in the subject. With the output, you will discover that these observers are getting the notifications when flag values are changed to 5, 50, and 100, respectively. But one of them did not receive any notification when the flag value changed to 50 because at that moment it was not a registered user. But later he registered himself to get further notifications from the subject. At the end, all observers were unregistered, so, none of them got notification when flag value changed to 500 in the subject.

In this implementation, the methods `register()`, `unregister()`, and `notifyRegisteredUsers()` have their usual meanings. The `register()` method is used to register an observer in the subject's notification list; the `unregister()` method is used to remove an observer from the subject's notification list; and `notifyRegisteredUsers()` is used to notify all the registered users when a typical event occurs in the subject.

Class Diagram

Figure 15-19 shows the class diagram.

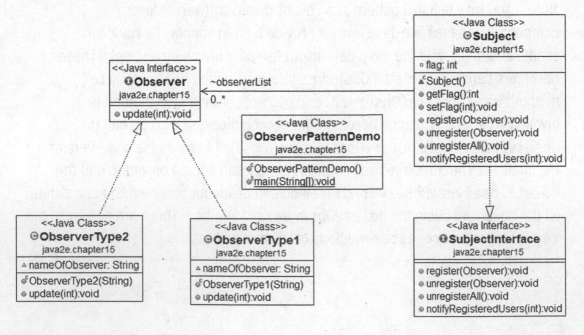

Figure 15-19. *Class diagram*

Package Explorer View

Figure 15-20 shows the high-level structure of the program.

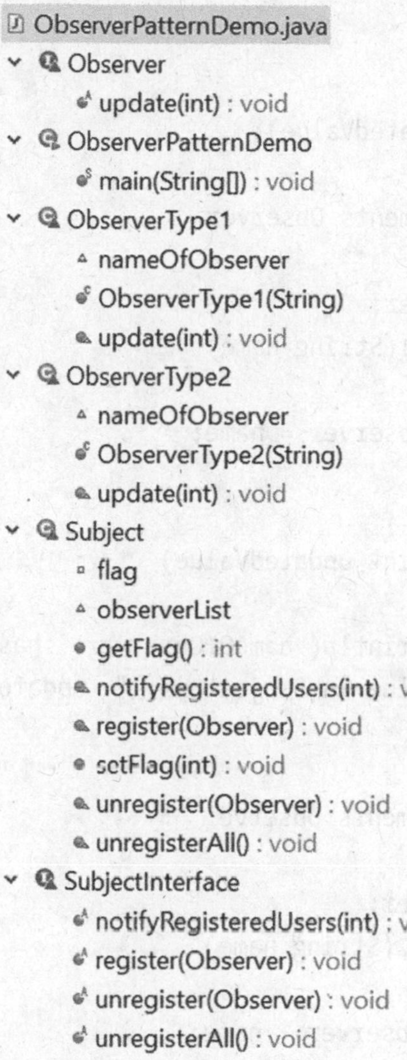

> ▣ ObserverPatternDemo.java
> - ⊻ ⊕ Observer
>   - ♪ update(int) : void
> - ⊻ ⊕ ObserverPatternDemo
>   - ♪ main(String[]) : void
> - ⊻ ⊕ ObserverType1
>   - ▵ nameOfObserver
>   - ♪ ObserverType1(String)
>   - ♠ update(int) : void
> - ⊻ ⊕ ObserverType2
>   - ▵ nameOfObserver
>   - ♪ ObserverType2(String)
>   - ♠ update(int) : void
> - ⊻ ⊕ Subject
>   - ▫ flag
>   - ▵ observerList
>   - ● getFlag() : int
>   - ♠ notifyRegisteredUsers(int) : void
>   - ♠ register(Observer) : void
>   - ● setFlag(int) : void
>   - ♠ unregister(Observer) : void
>   - ♠ unregisterAll() : void
> - ⊻ ⊕ SubjectInterface
>   - ♪ notifyRegisteredUsers(int) : void
>   - ♪ register(Observer) : void
>   - ♪ unregister(Observer) : void
>   - ♪ unregisterAll() : void

Figure 15-20. *Package Explorer view*

Implementation

```java
package java2e.chapter15;
import java.util.*;

interface Observer
{
    void update(int updatedValue);
}
class ObserverType1 implements Observer
{
    String nameOfObserver;
    public ObserverType1(String name)
    {
        this.nameOfObserver = name;
    }
    @Override
    public void update(int updatedValue)
    {
        System.out.println( nameOfObserver+" has received an alert:
        Updated myValue in Subject is: "+ updatedValue);
    }
}
class ObserverType2 implements Observer
{
    String nameOfObserver;
    public ObserverType2(String name)
    {
        this.nameOfObserver = name;
    }
    @Override
    public void update(int updatedValue)
    {
        System.out.println( nameOfObserver+" has received an alert:
        The current value of myValue in Subject is: "+ updatedValue);
    }
}
```

```java
interface SubjectInterface
{
        //Use it to register an observer
        void register(Observer anObserver);
        //Use it to unregister an observer
        void unregister(Observer anObserver);
        //Use it to unregister all observers
        void unregisterAll();
        //Use it to notify all registers users(i.e.observers)
        void notifyRegisteredUsers(int notifiedValue);
}
class Subject implements SubjectInterface
{
        private int flag;
        public int getFlag()
        {
                return flag;
        }
        public void setFlag(int flag)
        {
                this.flag = flag;
                //Flag value changed. So notify registered users/observers.
                notifyRegisteredUsers(flag);
        }
        List<Observer> observerList = new ArrayList<Observer>();
        @Override
        public void register(Observer anObserver) {
                observerList.add(anObserver);
                System.out.println("Currently, observerList.size()="+
                observerList.size());

        }
        @Override
        public void unregister(Observer anObserver) {
                observerList.remove(anObserver);
```

```java
            System.out.println("Currently, observerList.size()="+
            observerList.size());
    }
    @Override
    public void unregisterAll()
    {
            observerList.clear();
            //Or, use this
            //observerList.removeAll(observerList);
            System.out.println("Currently, observerList.size()="+
            observerList.size());
    }
    @Override
    public void notifyRegisteredUsers(int updatedValue)
    {
            for (Observer observer : observerList)
                    observer.update(updatedValue);
    }

}
public class ObserverPatternDemo {

    public static void main(String[] args) {
            System.out.println(" ***Observer Pattern Demo***\n");
            /*We have 3 observers- 2 of them are ObserverType1, 1 of them
            is of ObserverType2 */
            Observer myObserver1 = new ObserverType1("Roy");
            Observer myObserver2 = new ObserverType1("Kevin");
            Observer myObserver3 = new ObserverType2("Bose");
            Subject subject = new Subject();
            //Registering the observers-Roy,Kevin,Bose
            System.out.println("+Registering Roy.+");
            subject.register(myObserver1);
            System.out.println("+Registering Kevin.+");
            subject.register(myObserver2);
            System.out.println("+Registering Bose.+");
            subject.register(myObserver3);
```

```
            System.out.println(" Setting Flag = 5 ");
            subject.setFlag(5);
            //Unregistering an observer(Roy))
            System.out.println("-Unregistering Roy-");
            subject.unregister(myObserver1);
            //No notification for Roy this time, as he is NOT a
            //registered user now.
            System.out.println("\n Setting Flag = 50 ");
            subject.setFlag(50);
            //Roy is registering himself again
            System.out.println("+Registering Roy again.+");
            subject.register(myObserver1);
            System.out.println("\n Setting Flag = 100 ");
            subject.setFlag(100);
            System.out.println("Now unregistering all observers.");
            //Unregister all observers
            subject.unregisterAll();
            System.out.println("\n Setting Flag = 500 ");
            //At this stage, no one will get the notification from the
            //subject.
            subject.setFlag(500);
        }
}
```

   Output:

Observer Pattern Demo

```
+Registering Roy.+
Currently, observerList.size()=1
+Registering Kevin.+
Currently, observerList.size()=2
+Registering Bose.+
Currently, observerList.size()=3
 Setting Flag = 5
Roy has received an alert: Updated myValue in Subject is: 5
Kevin has received an alert: Updated myValue in Subject is: 5
```

Bose has received an alert: The current value of myValue in Subject is: 5
-Unregistering Roy-
Currently, observerList.size()=2

Setting Flag = 50

Kevin has received an alert: Updated myValue in Subject is: 50
Bose has received an alert: The current value of myValue in Subject is: 50
+Registering Roy again.+
Currently, observerList.size()=3

Setting Flag = 100

Kevin has received an alert: Updated myValue in Subject is: 100
Bose has received an alert: The current value of myValue in Subject is: 100
Roy has received an alert: Updated myValue in Subject is: 100
Now unregistering all observers.
Currently, observerList.size()=0.

Setting Flag = 500

Notice that initially all three observers—Roy, Kevin, and Bose—registered themselves to get the notification from the subject. So, in the initial phase, all of them received notifications. But in between, Roy was not interested in getting further notifications, so he unregistered himself. So, from this time onward, only Kevin and Bose were receiving notifications (notice the case when I set the flag value to 50). But Roy changed his mind and again registered himself to get notifications from the subject. So, when I set the flag value to 100, all of them were getting notifications from the subject. Finally, the subject does not want to send any notifications to anyone, so he clears the observer's (registered users) list. So, in the last case, when the flag value was set to 500, no one received any notifications from the subject.

Q&A Session

15.20 If I have only one observer, then I may not need to set up the interface. Is this understanding correct?

Yes. But if you want to follow the pure object-oriented programming guidelines, "Programming to the interface" is always considered as a better practice. In this case, it mandates any future observer to have the update() method, which reduces the chance of bugs and allows a clean code to write and understand. So, you should prefer interfaces (or abstract classes) instead of using a concrete class. Also, in general, you will have multiple observers and you want them to implement the methods in a systematic manner following the contract. So, you can benefit from this kind of design.

15.21 Can I have different types of observers in the same application?

Yes. Here, you have already seen three observers from two different classes. So, you should not assume that for each observer you need a different class.

Consider a real-world scenario. When a company releases or updates new software, both the business partners of the company and the customers who purchased the software get notifications. In this case, the business partners and the customers are two different types of observers.

15.22 Can I add or remove observers at runtime?

Yes. Notice that in our program, at the beginning, Roy was a registered user, and he was getting notifications from the subject. After some time, he was not a registered user and did not get notifications when the flag value was set to 50. But Roy was reregistered again and got notifications when flag value was set to 100 in the subject.

15.23 It appears to me that there are similarities between the Observer pattern and the Chain of Responsibility pattern. Is this understanding correct?

In an Observer pattern, all registered users get notifications at the same time, but in the Chain of Responsibility pattern, objects in the chain are notified one by one, and this process will continue until an object handles the notification fully. The following diagrams (Figure 15-21 and Figure 15-22) summarize the difference.

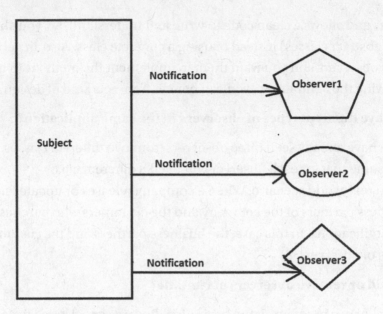

Figure 15-21. *The basic workflow of an Observer pattern*

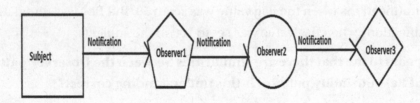

Figure 15-22. *The basic workflow of a Chain of Responsibility pattern*

15.24 This model supports one-to-many relationships. Is this understanding correct?

Yes. Since a subject can send notifications to multiple observers, you can say that this kind of dependency is clearly depicting a one-to-many relationship.

15.25 I have seen that Java supports this pattern and there are some built-in constructs to use. Then why are you writing your own code?

To change the ready-made constructs in your preferred way is not always easy. In many cases, you cannot change the built-in functionalities at all. But I believe that when you try to implement the concepts yourselves, you may have a better understanding that can help you to use those ready-made constructs in a better way.

Consider some typical scenarios:

- In Java, `Observable` is a concrete class and does not implement an interface. So, you can't create your own implementation that can work with Java's built-in Observer API .

- You need to remember that Java does not allow multiple inheritance. So, when you have to extend the `Observable` class, you have to keep in mind the restriction. So, it may limit the reuse potential.

- The signature of the `setChanged()` method in `Observable` is as follows:

```
protected void setChanged().
```

This means if you want to use it, you need to subclass the `Observable` class. This violates one of the key design principles that basically says to prefer composition over inheritance.

15.26 What are the key benefits of the Observer pattern?

Here are the key benefits:

- Subjects and their registered users (observers) make a loosely coupled system. They do not need to know each other explicitly.

- No modification is required in a subject when you add or remove an observer from its notification lists.

- You can add or remove observers at any time independently.

15.27 What are the key challenges associated with an Observer pattern?

Here are the key challenges:

- Undoubtedly memory leak is the greatest concern when you deal with any event-based mechanism. An automatic garbage collector may not always help you in this context. You can consider a case when you forget to unregister some events.

- The order of notification is not always dependable.

- Java's built-in support for the Observer pattern has some key restrictions, which we discussed earlier (I suggest you revisit the answer of Question 15.25 again), and one of them will force you to prefer inheritance over composition. So, it clearly violates one of the key design principles that always prefers the opposite.

Summary

This chapter discussed the following topics:

- Brief introduction to Gang of Four (GoF) design patterns

- Classification of GoF patterns and their usage

- Full implementation of Prototype Design pattern

- Full implementation of Bridge pattern

- Full implementation of Observer pattern

CHAPTER 16

Frequently Asked Questions

It is time to test your understanding. Here, I have listed some important and frequently asked questions, which are a very small subset of all the questions that have been discussed in the Q&A Sessions and in different theoretical discussions across the book. These questions can help you to review quickly. If there is any doubt, please go back to the respective chapter to find the answer.

1. What is a class?

2. What is an object?

3. How do you differentiate between an object and a reference?

4. Can you implement multiple inheritance in Java?

5. Can you implement hybrid inheritance in Java?

6. How do you differentiate between an abstract class and an interface?

7. How do you differentiate between method overloading and method overriding?

8. How can you implement dynamic polymorphism in Java?

9. What is JVM?

10. How do you differentiate between JRE and JDK?

11. What is an inner class?

12. How can you create a static class in Java?

13. How can you implement abstraction and encapsulation in Java?

© Vaskaran Sarcar 2020

V. Sarcar, *Interactive Object-Oriented Programming in Java*, https://doi.org/10.1007/978-1-4842-5404-2_16

14. How do you differentiate between a static binding and a dynamic binding in Java?

15. What is the use of super in Java?

16. What is/are the use/s of this in Java?

17. What is the use of default in Java?

18. Can you use an abstract class without an abstract method?

19. Can you inherit constructors?

20. What is the use of final in Java?

21. How do you differentiate between an instance method and a class method (static method)?

22. Can you create a static block? What is its use?

23. What is a package? Why is it important?

24. What is the default package in Java?

25. Why would you use import statements?

26. Which statement should appear first—a package statement or an import statement?

27. Can you have multiple package statements in a program?

28. "Package statement should always come on top"—is this true?

29. What is a default modifier?

30. Does Java support pointers?

31. What is an exception?

32. What is the super class of Exception?

33. What do you mean by checked exceptions?

34. What do you mean by unchecked exceptions?

35. How can you create your own exception?

36. What are some examples of an error condition?

37. What is the difference between throw and throws?

38. What will happen if you encounter an exception in a `finally` block?

39. What is the drawback of handling exceptions?

40. What is the advantage of handling exceptions?

41. What do you mean by chained exceptions?

42. What are the key methods associated with chained exceptions?

43. What is garbage collection? How does it work in Java?

44. How can you make an object unreachable?

45. Can you explain garbage collection with a simple program?

46. What is finalization? Why is it important?

47. How can you remove memory leak in Java?

48. What is the purpose of a constructor?

49. What are the different types of constructors?

50. How can you use getter-setters in your application?

51. What is an initialization block?

52. What are the different types of initialization blocks? How do they work?

53. What is a nested class?

54. What is an inner class? How is an inner class useful?

55. What is shallow copy? How is it different from deep copy?

56. What is a wrapper class? Why are wrapper classes important in Java?

57. How can you differentiate between a user-defined no-argument constructor and a default constructor in Java?

58. Can the use of a default method in the interfaces lead to the diamond problem in Java?

59. Java does not support multiple inheritance through classes, but C++ does. Do you treat it as an advantage or disadvantage of Java?

60. Can multiple variables reference the same object in memory?

61. What is the expected output if you use the following line of code?

    ```
    System.out.print(anObject);
    ```

62. What is constructor chaining?

63. How can you pass a variable number of arguments inside a method?

64. What is the difference between char in Java and char in C/C++?

65. What do you mean by automatic type conversion?

66. Do you treat Java as a purely object-oriented language? If not, why?

67. Can a constructor be private?

68. Can a constructor be final or abstract or static?

69. Differentiate among final, finally, and finalize.

70. What is the difference between a default constructor and a no-argument constructor?

71. Can you have both this() and super() in the same constructor? If not, why?

72. Can you have backward inheritance?

73. In an inheritance hierarchy, how can you decide a parent class or a child class?

74. What is a blank final variable? How can you use it in your program?

75. Can you override an overloaded method?

76. If you make the main() method final, will you receive any compile-time or runtime errors?

77. What are the advantages of a tagging interface?

78. Is there any alternative to marker interfaces?

79. Which one do you like—use of marker interfaces or use of marker annotations? Why?

80. How can you implement the concept of generalization/specialization in Java?

81. How can you implement the concept of realization in Java?

82. Is there any alternative to inheritance? What is that? When you can use that concept?

83. Does Java support structures? If not, why?

84. What is the basic difference between `String` and `StringBuffer`?

85. How you can distinguish a Java applet from a Java application?

86. What is the difference between `StringBuffer` and `StringBuilder`?

87. In which scenario do you prefer `StringBuilder` over `StringBuffer` (and vice versa)?

88. What is a thread? How does it differ from a process?

89. What are the different ways to create a thread, and which one do you prefer?

90. What are the benefits of multi-threading?

91. Can multi-threading improve performance in a multi-core system?

92. Name some `Thread` class methods and mention their usages.

93. How is `sleep()` different from `wait()`?

94. What is synchronization?

95. How can you implement synchronization in your application?

96. What is a deadlock? How can you detect a deadlock in your system?

97. What do you mean by interthread communication?

98. What is a thread pool?

99.   How do you make a "Monitor" in your application?

100.   What do you mean by a generic program? How is it better than its counterpart—a non-generic program?

101.   What is the use of wildcard types in a generic program?

102.   What do you mean by an upper bound and lower bound of a wildcard type?

103.   What is an unbounded wildcard type?

104.   Are List<?> and List<Object> the same? If not, why?

105.   What is a reifiable type?

106.   What is a raw type?

107.   What is a bounded type parameter? How can you use it in your application?

108.   How do wildcards differ from bounded type parameters?

109.   What is an erasure? How does it work?

110.   How can you use a diamond operator in your application?

111.   What is a bridge method?

112.   Can you mention some restrictions in generic programming?

113.   What do you mean by JDBC?

114.   How can you connect to a database?

115.   How can you pick your driver to connect a database?

116.   What is the use of Driver, DriverManager, Connection, and Statement in a JDBC program?

117.   What is a ResultSet? Why is it useful in a JDBC program?

118.   Are PreparedStatements faster than Statements? If so, why?

119.   Is passing parameters to PreparedStatement objects mandatory?

120.   How can you implement batch processing?

121.   What are the advantages of using a PreparedStatement object?

122.   When can you use a `CallableStatement` object?

123.   When should you prefer a `Statement` object over a
       `PreparedStatement` or a `CallableStatement`?

124.   What is a stored procedure?

125.   Can you use DDL, DML, and DCL statements in your Java
       application?

126.   What is a resource? How can you use a `try-with-resource`
       statement in your application?

127.   What is a functional interface? Why is it important?

128.   What is a lambda expression?

129.   How can you use lambda expressions to implement a functional
       interface method?

130.   Can you use a private interface method?

131.   Can you make a default interface method private?

132.   Can you make a private interface method static?

133.   What do you mean by local variable type inference?

134.   How does the `isEmpty()` method differ from the `isBlank()`
       method?

135.   How does the `strip()` method differ from the `trim()` method?

136.   What is a preview feature in Java? Can you give an example?

137.   What do you mean by design patterns? Why are they useful?

138.   Can you show some examples of design patterns?

APPENDIX A

Test Your Skill in Language Fundamentals

Before you jump into object-oriented programming in Java, let's review the language's fundamentals. This section is added to help you to better understand the discussions in the book. You can learn the advanced topics easily if you know these core concepts. In this appendix, you will see many code segments and I'm asking you to predict the output. Still, I am keeping the supportive comments in many places for your easy understanding.

SET 1

1.1 What will be the output?

```
package java2e.appendixa.set1;
class Q1 {
    static public void main(String[] args) {
        System.out.println("Hello World.");
    }
}
```

Output:

Hello World.

Analysis:

You can see that you can change the order. Instead of `public static void main(...)`, you can write `static public void main(...)`.

© Vaskaran Sarcar 2020
V. Sarcar, *Interactive Object-Oriented Programming in Java*, https://doi.org/10.1007/978-1-4842-5404-2

1.2 What will be the output if you pass some arguments through the command line (e.g., java Q2 John Sam Bob**)?**

```
package java2e.appendixa.set1;
class Q2 {
      public static void main(String[] args) {
            System.out.println("*** Testing Command-line arguments ***");
            //java Q2 John Sam Bob
            System.out.println(args[0]);
            System.out.println(args[1]);
            System.out.println(args[2]);
      }
}
```

Output:

```
*** Testing Command-line arguments ***
John
Sam
Bob
```

Analysis:

When you use command-line arguments like the following:

```
java <your program name> a0 a1 a2 ...
```

values will be assigned in the String array args as args[0]=a0, args[1]=a1, args[2]=a2, etc. Also note that you can choose any other name you want for your String array. For example, the following code :

```
public static void main(String myStringArray[]){
//Some code
}
```

is perfectly fine. (If you do so, change the args with myStringArray in corresponding places.)

For Eclipse users, you can enter arguments in the Arguments tab under Run Configurations, like this:

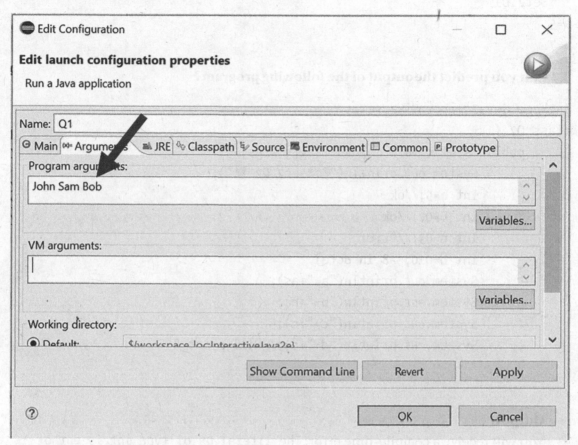

SET 2

2.1 Can you predict the output of the following program?

```java
package java2e.appendixa.set2;
class Q1 {
    public static void main(String[] args) {
        System.out.println("***Set2.Q1***");
        int a=5;//ok
        int b=07;//ok
        System.out.println("a="+a );
        System.out.println("b="+b);
    }
}
```

Output:

```
***Set2.Q1***
a=5
b=7
```

2.2 Can you predict the output of the following program?

```java
package java2e.appendixa.set2;
class Q2 {
    public static void main(String[] args) {
        System.out.println("***Set2.Q2***");
        int a=5;//ok
        int b=07;//ok
        int c=09;//Error
        int d=010;//8 in octal
        System.out.println("a="+a );
        System.out.println("b="+b);
        System.out.println("c="+c);
        System.out.println("d="+d);//Will print 8
    }
}
```

Output:

You will receive a compile-time error: The literal 09 of type int is out of range. Here is a snapshot from Eclipse IDE.

Description	Resource	Location
∨ ⊗ Errors (1 item)		
⊗ The literal 09 of type int is out of range	Q2.java	line 9

Analysis:

When you put a leading 0, Java treats it as an octal representation. So, in that case, the range it can support is 0 to 7. In this example, you have crossed that boundary. To print 8 using octal representation, you can code as follows:

```
int d=010;//ok. It will print 8
System.out.println("d="+d );
```

2.3 Can you predict the output of the following program?

```
package java2e.appendixa.set2;
class Q3 {
    public static void main(String[] args) {
        System.out.println("***Set2.Q3***");
        int c = 0x12;
        int d = 0x1E;
        int e = 0X1F;
        System.out.println("c=" + c);// 18
        System.out.println("d=" + d);// 30
        System.out.println("e=" + e);// 31
    }
}
```

Output:

```
***Set2.Q3***
c=18
d=30
e=31
```

Analysis:

When we prefix 0x or 0X, Java treats them as a hexadecimal integer literal representation. So, in this case, the range it can support is 0 to 15. A to F is used to represent the digits with values 10 to 15.

2.4 Can you predict the output of the following program?

```
package java2e.appendixa.set2;
class Q4 {
      public static void main(String[] args) {
            System.out.println("***Set2.Q4***");
            int a=5;
            double const=3.14;//Error
            System.out.println("const value is ="+const);//Error
      }
}
```

Output:

You will receive compile-time errors. Here is a snapshot from the Eclipse IDE.

Description	Resource	Location
˅ ⊗ Errors (2 items)		
⊗ Syntax error on token "const", invalid Expression	Q4.java	line 9
⊗ Syntax error on token "const", invalid VariableDeclaratorId	Q4.java	line 8

Analysis:

You cannot use keywords as identifiers in your program. As per JLS11, "The keywords const and goto are reserved, even though they are not currently used. This may allow a Java compiler to produce better error messages if these C++ keywords incorrectly appear in programs."

Note   In JLS11, these are the 51 keywords that you cannot use as identifiers. (See Table A-1.)

Table A-1. *Keywords in Java*

abstract	assert	boolean	break	byte	case	catch
char	class	const	continue	default	do	double
else	enum	extends	final	finally	float	for
if	goto	implements	import	instanceof	int	interface
long	native	new	package	private	protected	public
return	short	statics	strictfp	super	switch	synchronized
this	throw	throws	transient	try	void	volatile
while	_(underscore)					

SET 3

3.1 Can you predict the output of the following program?

```
package java2e.appendixa.set3;
class Q1 {
      public static void main(String[] args) {
            System.out.println("***Set3.Q1***");
            byte b1=127;//ok
            byte b2=128;//Error
            System.out.println("b1="+b1);
            System.out.println("b2="+b2);
      }
}
```

> **Output:**
> You will receive a compile-time error. Here is a snapshot from the Eclipse IDE.

Description	Resource	Location
⌄ ⊗ Errors (1 item)		
⌦ Type mismatch: cannot convert from int to byte	Q1.java	line 7

Analysis:

Range of a byte is -128 to 127.

3.2 Can you predict the output of the following program?

```
package java2e.appendixa.set3;
class Q2 {
    public static void main(String[] args) {
        System.out.println("***Set3.Q2***");
        byte b1 = 127;// ok
        int i1 = b1;// ok
        System.out.println("b1=" + b1);
        System.out.println("i1=" + i1);
    }
}
```

Output:

```
***Set3.Q2***
b1=127
i1=127
```

Analysis:

The two types—int and byte—are compatible, and here you can place the byte variable into an int variable. This is possible because the destination type is larger than the source type. So, the compiler is okay with this conversion.

3.3 Can you predict the output of the following program?

```
package java2e.appendixa.set3;
class Q3 {
    public static void main(String[] args) {
        System.out.println("***Set3.Q3***");
        byte b1=127;
        int i1=b1;//ok: small to big
        b1=i1;//Error: big to small
        System.out.println("b1="+b1);
        System.out.println("i1="+i1);
    }
}
```

Output:

You will receive a compile-time error. Here is a snapshot from the Eclipse IDE.

Description	Resource	Location
✓ ⊗ Errors (1 item)		
📄 Type mismatch: cannot convert from int to byte	Q3.java	line 8

Analysis:

Here, the destination type is smaller than the source type. So, the compiler is raising the concern.

SET 4

4.1 Can you predict the output of the following program?

```
package java2e.appendixa.set4;
class Q1 {
    public static void main(String[] args) {
        System.out.println("***Set4.Q1***");
        int i=2147483647;
        System.out.println("i="+i);
        int j=++i;
        System.out.println("Now i is="+i);
        System.out.println("j="+j);
        ++j;
        System.out.println("Now j is="+j);
    }
}
```

Output:

```
***Set4.Q1***
i=2147483647
Now i is=-2147483648
j=-2147483648
Now j is=-2147483647
```

Analysis:

The maximum value of an integer is 2,147,483,647, and the minimum value is -2,147,483,648. Here, in j (with post-increment of i), you have crossed the maximum limit of an integer.

4.2 Can you compile the following program?

```
package java2e.appendixa.set4;
class Q2 {
    public static void main(String[] args) {
        System.out.println("***Set4.Q2***");
        int i = 5;
        int j = i++;// j becomes 5, i becomes 6
        System.out.println("Now j=" + j);
        System.out.println("Now i=" + i);
        int k = ++j;// j and k both becomes 6
        System.out.println("Here j=" + j);
        System.out.println("Here k=" + k);
    }
}
```

Answer:

Yes. The program will compile and run successfully. Here is the output:

```
***Set4.Q2***
Now j=5
Now i=6
Here j=6
Here k=6
```

4.3 Can you compile the following program?

```
package java2e.appendixa.set4;
class Q3 {
    public static void main(String[] args) {
        System.out.println("***Set4.Q3***");
        int i = 260;
```

```
        byte b = (byte) i;
        System.out.println("b=" + b);
    }
}
```

Answer:

Yes, The program will compile and run successfully. Here is the output:

```
***Set4.Q3***
b=4
```

Analysis:

Here, you are trying to type cast a larger variable (int) into a smaller variable (byte). So, in this type of case, Java calculates the modulo of the larger variable by the range of the smaller variable. Our byte range is -128 to 127. So, the final result would be 260 % 256; i.e., 4.

4.4 Can you compile the following program?

```
package java2e.appendixa.set4;
class Q4 {
    public static void main(String[] args) {
        System.out.println("***Set4.Q4***");
        int i=65550;
        short s=(short)i;
        System.out.println("s="+s);
    }
}
```

Answer:

Yes. The program will compile and run successfully. Here is the output:

```
***Set4.Q4***
s=14
```

Analysis:

See the prior explanation (for Q3 in Set 4). The range for the short datatype is -32768 to 32767; i.e., the total range it covers is 65536. So, in this case, the values of s will be 65550 % 65536=14.

4.5 What will be the output?

```
package java2e.appendixa.set4;
class Q5 {
      public static void main(String[] args) {
              System.out.println("***Set4.Q5***");
              char c1 = 65;
              char c2 = 'a' + 3;
              System.out.println("c1=" + c1);
              System.out.println("c2=" + c2);
      }
}
```

   Output:

```
***Set4.Q5***
c1=A
c2=d
```

   Analysis:
   ASCII value of A *is 65 and ASCII value of* a *is 97.*
   97+3=100, which is the ASCII value of d.

SET 5

5.1 Why do you prefer **double** over **float**?

We use double for double precision, while float is for single precision. So, to maintain the accuracy of a calculation, double is a better choice over float.

5.2 What is the difference between **char** in Java and **char** in C/C++?

In C/C++, char is an integer type (8-bit wide). But Java uses Unicode (UTF-16) to represent them. In Java, char is of a 16-bit type.

5.3 What do you mean by Unicode?

Unicode defines a fully international character set that can be found in most of the world's human languages/writing systems. So, it is a unification of all those character sets. This allows us to encode, represent, and handle texts in those languages in a standard way.

5.4 What do you mean by automatic type conversion?

Two basic criteria must be followed for an automatic conversion:

- The destination type should be larger.

- The types must be compatible.

For example, the following conversion is automatic:

```
int i1=15;
double d=i1;//ok
System.out.println("d="+d);//15.0
```

But the following conversion is not allowed:

```
boolean b=true;
int i2=b;//error: Cannot convert from boolean to int
```

5.5 Why does Java not convert primitive types to objects?

Unnecessary overhead will be created due to these conversions, and it may lose efficiency.

5.6 Why do all Java primitive types have a fixed range?

To support portability, Java supports this concept.

5.7 What do we mean by the word portability?

In simple language, suppose you have developed an application in a machine. Now you want to reuse it in other environment (for example, in a different hardware/software platform or version or different operating system, etc.) without major rework (in ideal scenario: no rework). If you can do that, you can claim that your application is portable.

We also remember that JVM and bytecode make Java portable.

SET 6

6.1 What will be the output?

```
package java2e.appendixa.set6;

class Q1 {
    public static void main(String[] args) {
        System.out.println("***Set6.Q1***");
        int x = 10;
```

```
            int result = ++x * 5;
            System.out.println(" The result is: " + result);
        }
}
```

Output:

```
***Set6.Q1***
 The result is : 55
```

Analysis:

The ++ operator has a higher precedence than the operator *. So, ++x operation will be performed before the multiplication operation.

6.2 Can you predict the output of the following program?

```
package java2e.appendixa.set6;

class Q2 {
    public static void main(String[] args) {
        System.out.println("***Set6.Q2***");
        int x=5;
        System.out.println(" ~x is : "+ ~x);
    }
}
```

Output:

```
***Set6.Q2***
 ~x is : -6
```

Analysis:

5 is represented by 0000 0101. ~5 will make it 1111 1010, which is for -6.

To understand it better, represent 6 in binary: 0000 0110. Now 2's complement of it (inverting all bits first and then adding a 1 to that) will make it 1111 1010.

6.3 Can you predict the output of the following program?

```
package java2e.appendixa.set6;

class Q3 {
    public static void main(String[] args) {
        System.out.println("***Set6.Q3***");
        int x=21;
        int y=15;
        int z=x^y;
        System.out.println(" z is : "+ z);
    }
}
```

Output:

```
***Set6.Q3***
 z is : 26
```

Analysis:

- 21 in binary is 0001 0101.

- 15 in binary is 0000 1111.

XOR combines bits with the rule: if exactly one operand is 1, then the result is 1. So, our result becomes 0001 1010; i.e., 26.

6.4 Can you predict the output of the following program?

```
package java2e.appendixa.set6;

class Q4 {
    public static void main(String[] args) {
        System.out.println("***Set6.Q4***");
        int x=24;
        int y=11;
        int result= ++x * y--;
        System.out.println("Result is : "+ result);
        System.out.println("y is now : "+ y);
    }
}
```

Output:

```
***Set6.Q4***
Result is : 275
y now : 10
```

Analysis:

Pre-increment happened to x, but post-increment happened to y. So, prior to multiplication, x becomes 25, but y remains at 11.

6.5 Predict the output of the following program:

```
package java2e.appendixa.set6;

class Q5 {
    public static void main(String[] args) {
        System.out.println("***Set6.Q5***");
        int x=24;
        int y=11;
        int z=100;
        int result= ++x *--y %z;
        System.out.println(" Result is : "+ result);
        System.out.println(" y now : "+ y);
    }
}
```

Output:

```
***Set6.Q5***
 Result is : 50
 y now : 10
```

Analysis:

Pre-increment happened to x, and pre-decrement happened to y before the multiplication operation, which results in 250. Finally, the modulo operation results in 50 (250%100=50).

6.6 Predict the output of the following program:

```
package java2e.appendixa.set6;
class Q6 {

    public static void main(String[] args) {

        System.out.println("***Set6.Q6***");
        int x = 10;
        int y = 4;
        double result = ++y * x / y;
        System.out.println(" Result is : " + result);
        System.out.println(" y now : " + y);
    }
}
```

   Output:

```
***Set6.Q6***
 Result is : 10.0
 y now : 5
```

   Analysis:

   You must notice that y incremented first (because ++ has a higher precedence than * and /) and became 5. So, 5*10/5 becomes 10.0 because we are storing the result in a double datatype.

6.7 Predict the output of the following program:

```
package java2e.appendixa.set6;
class Q7 {
    public static void main(String[] args) {
        System.out.println("***Set6.Q7***");
        int a=7,b=12;
        System.out.println(a+b);//19
        System.out.println("a+b=" +a+b);//a+b=712
        System.out.println(a+b+"=a+b=" +a+b);//19=a+b=712
    }
}
```

Output:

```
***Set6.Q7***
19
a+b=712
19=a+b=712
```

Analysis:

You must note this behavior: once the string is encountered, we started seeing the concatenation instead of addition. That's why initially a and b are added and result in 19, but after that it encountered a string '=a+b', so from now onward it will start with string concatenation operations.

6.8 Differentiate between break vs continue, with an example

```java
package java2e.appendixa.set6;

class Q8 {

    public static void main(String[] args) {
        System.out.println("***Set6.Q8***");
        System.out.println("***break vs continue***");
        System.out.println("***Example : break***");
        for (int i = 0; i < 5; i++) {
            System.out.print("At entry, i is :" + i + "\t");
            if (i == 3)
                break;
            System.out.println("At Exit, i is :" + i);
        }
        System.out.println();
        System.out.print("***Example : continue***\n");
        for (int i = 0; i < 5; i++) {
            System.out.print("At entry, i is :" + i + "\t");
            if (i == 3)
                continue;
            System.out.println("At Exit, i is :" + i);
        }
    }
}
```

Output:

For a better visual, let's consider the snapshot of the output from Eclipse IDE.

```
***Set6.Q8***
***break vs continue***
***Example : break***
At entry, i is :0        At Exit, i is :0
At entry, i is :1        At Exit, i is :1
At entry, i is :2        At Exit, i is :2
At entry, i is :3
***Example : continue***
At entry, i is :0        At Exit, i is :0
At entry, i is :1        At Exit, i is :1
At entry, i is :2        At Exit, i is :2
At entry, i is :3        At entry, i is :4        At Exit, i is :4
```

Analysis:

From the preceding code, you can see that once you encounter `break` (at i=3), control comes out from the `for` loop block, but in case of continue, it just skips the remaining portion for that iteration (i.e., it did not print an `Exit` statement for i=3) and continues looping to the end.

Note   As per Oracle Java documentation, a "break can have two forms—labeled and unlabeled. An unlabeled break statement can terminate the innermost for, while, do-while, and switch statements, but a labeled break can terminate an outer statement." In case of a labeled break, the control flows to the statement that immediately follows the labeled (terminated) statement.

6.9 Predict the output of the following program:

```
package java2e.appendixa.set6;

class Q9 {
    public static void main(String[] args) {
        System.out.println("***Set6.Q9***");
        System.out.println("*** Conditional Operator Demo***");
```

```
            int a=10;
            int b=5;
            int c=a>b?a:b;
            System.out.println("Here c is : "+c);
        }
}
```

Output:

```
***Set6.Q9***
*** Conditional Operator Demo***
c is : 10
```

This is a very common use of the conditional operator. It simply says, if a>b, then c=a else c=b. Since the condition :a >b is true here, c is taking the value of a which is 10. If this condition becomes false, c will take the value of b which is 5 in this case.

6.10 What will be the output?

```
package java2e.appendixa.set6;

class Q10 {
      public static void main(String[] args) {
            System.out.println("***Set6.Q10***");
            System.out.println("*** ConditionalOperator.Demo-2***");
            int a=10;
            int b=5;
            //Error:Cannot convert from int to String
            String result=a<0?"Negative":a;
            System.out.println("result is : "+result);
      }
}
```

Output:

Compilation error. Here is a snapshot from Eclipse IDE:

Description	Type	Location
˅ ⊗ Errors (1 item)		
⊡ Type mismatch: cannot convert from int to String	Java Problem	line 12

Analysis:

You cannot put an integer inside a string. So, be careful of the following type of comparison:

expression1? expression2: expression3

expression 2 and expression3 must be same.

For example, the following code segment can work for you:

```
String str="hello";
String result;
result=str.equals("hello")?"Correct Match":"Doesn't match";
System.out.println(result);
```

SET 7

7.1 What is an array?

An array is a container object that can hold a fixed number of a particular type. If an array can contain *n* number of elements, it is called an array of length *n*.

It is important to note that when you write something like int[] myIntArray; you are declaring an array of int only, but after this declaration, when you write something like the following:

```
myIntArray=new int[5];
```

or, if you simply write something like this:

```
myIntArray={ 0,1,2,3,4};
```

you allocate space for array elements.

7.2 Write a simple program to demonstrate an array and display the contents inside it.

```
package java2e.appendixa.set7;

class Q2 {
    public static void main(String[] args) {
        System.out.println("***Set7.Q2***");
        System.out.println("Creating an  integer array which can
        contain 5 integers.");
```

```
            int[] myIntArray=new int[5];
            for(int i=0;i<5;i++)
            {
                    myIntArray[i]=i;
                    System.out.println("Inserted "+ i +" in
                    myIntArray["+ i + "]");
            }
            System.out.println("Displaying the contents of the Array:");
            for(int i=0;i<5;i++)
            {
                    System.out.print("\t"+myIntArray[i]);
            }
        }
}
```

Output:

```
***Set7.Q2***
Creating an  integer array which can contain 5 integers.
Inserted 0 in myIntArray[0]
Inserted 1 in myIntArray[1]
Inserted 2 in myIntArray[2]
Inserted 3 in myIntArray[3]
Inserted 4 in myIntArray[4]
Displaying the contents of the Array:
        0       1       2       3       4
```

7.3 In the previous program, can I declare the array like the following?

```
int myIntArray[]=new int[5];
```

Yes. You can use either of these forms: int[] myArray or int myArray[].

7.4 How can you alter the size of an array ?

As per JLS11, "Once an array object is created, its length never changes. To make an array variable refer to an array of different length, a reference to a different array must be assigned to the variable."

So, once you learn ArrayList, you know that ArrayList is a better choice in a case like this. But there is a workaround. You can make an array of your desired size, and then you can copy the elements from the old array to the new array using the copyOf() method, as follows:

```
//Increasing the size of the array
int[] myBigArray=Arrays.copyOf(myIntArray,6);
//Putting a new value in newly added location
myBigArray[5]=6;
```

Note   Once you see the definition of the Arrays.copyOf() method, you'll see this:

```
public static int[] copyOf(int[] original, int newLength) {
        int[] copy = new int[newLength];
        System.arraycopy(original, 0, copy, 0,
                        Math.min(original.length, newLength));
        return copy;
    }
```

This simply means that Arrays.copyOf() is actually using the System.arraycopy() method to perform the job.

7.5 Can you shorten the code size in Q&A 7.2?

You can directly initialize the array like this:

```
int  myIntArray[]={0,1,2,3,4}; //it is also ok
```

7.6 Can you compile the following code segment?

```
int[] myIntArray=new int[3];
myIntArray[0]=10;
myIntArray[2]=20;
myIntArray[3]="Thirty";
```

Answer:

No. You cannot put a string into an integer array. You will receive a compile-time error saying Type mismatch: cannot convert from String to int.

7.7 Will the following code compile?

```
package java2e.appendixa.set7;

class Q7 {
    public static void main(String[] args) {
        System.out.println("***Set7.Q7***");
        int[] myIntArray=new int[3];
        myIntArray[0]=10;
        myIntArray[2]=20;
        System.out.println("Contents of Array:");
        //Runtime error will occur for the following block of code
        for(int i=0;i<5;i++)
        {
            System.out.println("\t"+myIntArray[i]);
        }
    }
}
```

Answer:

Yes. There is no compilation error, but you'll encounter a runtime exception because you are trying to access locations beyond the boundary (notice that the array size is 3 only). You'll see the discussion on exceptions in Chapter 10 in this book.

```
***Set7.Q7***
Contents of Array:
    10
    0
    20
Exception in thread "main" java.lang.ArrayIndexOutOfBoundsException: 3 at
java2e.appendixa.set7.Q7.main(Q7.java:14)
```

7.8 In the previous output, I can see MyIntArray[1] is printed as 0, but you have not supplied 0 in it. Is this array initialized with default values?

Answer:

Yes. Default value for integers is 0.

7.9 Can you predict the output of the following program?

```
package java2e.appendixa.set7;

class A {
    int i;
    A(int i) {
        this.i = i;
    }
}

class Q9 {
    public static void main(String[] args) {
        System.out.println("***Set7.Q9***");
        A[] myArray = new A[5];
        myArray[0] = new A(10);
        myArray[2] = new A(25);
        System.out.println("Contents of Array:");
        for (int i = 0; i < 5; i++) {
            System.out.println(myArray[i]);
        }
    }
}
```

Output:

```
***Set7.Q9***
Contents of Array:
java2e.appendixa.set7.A@15db9742
null
java2e.appendixa.set7.A@6d06d69c
null
null
```

Analysis:

You can see that all object references are initialized to their default values; i.e., null. Here, you did not provide values for indexes 1, 3, and 4. So, those locations are holding null.

7.10 How can you modify the prior program to see the values stored inside the objects?

Let us modify the body of the for loop, which is as follows:

```
for (int i = 0; i < 5; i++) {
//System.out.println(myArray[i]);//in Q9
//Modification for Q10 in Set 7
  if(myArray[i]!=null) {
            System.out.println("myArray["+ i+"] : "+myArray[i].i);
            }
}
```

Output:

Here is the modified output for the mentioned change:

```
***Set7.Q9***
Contents of Array:
myArray[0] : 10
myArray[2] : 25
```

Analysis:

Notice that you put in an extra guard to do a null check inside the for loop. Otherwise, you'll encounter a NullPointerException because some of the values inside the array are null.

7.11 Can you write a simple array-handling program where you need to supply four integers between 1 and 5 (no repetition is allowed)? Then, your program needs to respond back to you saying which number you have not used.

```
package java2e.appendixa.set7;

import java.util.Scanner;

class Q11 {
      public static void main(String[] args) {
            System.out.println("***Set7.Q11***");
            System.out.println("Type any 4 integers between 1 and 5 (no
            repetition is allowed and do not provide null values).");
            int[] myStore = new int[5];
            int accumulatedSum = 0;// To sum up the numbers you have entered
```

```
        for (int i = 0; i < 4; i++) {
                Scanner in = new Scanner(System.in);
                int input = in.nextInt();
                myStore[i] = input;
        }
        System.out.println("You have entered:");
        for (int i = 0; i < 4; i++) {
                {
                        System.out.println("myStore[" + i + "] : " +
                        myStore[i]);
                        accumulatedSum = accumulatedSum + myStore[i];
                }
        }
        int expectedSum = 5 * (5 + 1) / 2;// Formula to calculate sum
        //of 1 to 5 integers=n*(n+1)/2;
        int missingNumber = expectedSum - accumulatedSum;
        System.out.println("The missing number is : " + missingNumber);
    }
}
```

Output:

```
***Set7.Q11***
Type any 4 integers between 1 and 5 (no repetition is allowed and do not
provide null values).
2
4
5
1
You have entered:
myStore[0] : 2
myStore[1] : 4
myStore[2] : 5
myStore[3] : 1
The missing number is : 3
```

Analysis:

Sum of *n* numbers = $n*(n+1)/2$. Replace *n* with 5 for 5 integers to get the sum of 5 numbers (expectedSum). Now you sum up the four numbers you have entered through the keyboard (accumulatedSum). So, the difference between expectedSum and accumulatedSum is the missing number in this case.

Note   For simplicity, null checking is omitted in this example. Also, we have ignored the case where a user provides an unintended value by mistake.

SET 8

8.1 Will the following code compile?

```
package java2e.appendixa.set8;
class Q1 {
    public static void main(String[] args) {
        System.out.println("***Set8.Q1***");
        int myNumber = 6;
        switch (myNumber) {
        case 1:
            System.out.println("one");
            break;
        default:
            System.out.println("Default");
        case 2:
            System.out.println("Two");
            break;
        }
    }
}
```

Answer:

Yes. We'll get the following output:

```
***Set8.Q1***
Default
Two
```

Analysis:

You may note that you can put a default case anywhere in the switch block. And also, if there is no break statement, control will continue to fall through until a break statement is encountered or the end of the block is reached, whichever be the case.

8.2 Can you compile the following program?

```
package java2e.appendixa.set8;

class Q2 {

    public static void main(String[] args) {
        System.out.println("***Set8.Q2***");
        System.out.println("***Discussions on Switch ***");
        int myNumber = 6;
        switch (myNumber) {
        case 1:case 5:
                System.out.println("One or Five");
                break;
        default:
                System.out.println("Default");
                break;
        case 2:case 6:case 8:
                System.out.println("Two or Six or Eight");
                break;
        }
    }
}
```

Answer:

Yes. Here is the output when you run the program:

```
***Set8.Q2***
***Discussions on Switch ***
Two or Six or Eight
```

Analysis:

Multiple case labels are possible like this in a switch statement.

8.3 Can you compile the following program?

```
package java2e.appendixa.set8;

class Q3 {
    public static void main(String[] args) {
        System.out.println("***Set8.Q3***");
        System.out.println("***Discussions on Switch ***");
        char myChoice = 'e';
        switch (myChoice) {
        case 'b':
                System.out.println("b");
                break;
        default:
                System.out.println("Default");
                break;
        case 'a':
                System.out.println("a");
                break;
        }
    }
}
```

Answer:

Yes. Here is the output when you run the program:

```
***Set8.Q3***
***Discussions on Switch ***
Default
```

Analysis:

It is not necessary that, in the switch statement's expression, we put integers only. Other built-in data types like byte, short, char, and enums are also supported here. Java 7 or above can support String objects inside those expressions.

8.4 What will be the output when you compile the following program?

```
package java2e.appendixa.set8;

class Q4 {
    public static void main(String[] args) {
        System.out.println("***Set8.Q4***");
        System.out.println("***Discussions on Switch ***");
        boolean value = true;
        switch (value) // compile-time error
        {
        case true:
                System.out.println("true");
                break;
        case false:
                System.out.println("false");
                break;
        default:
                System.out.println("Default");
                break;
        }
    }
}
```

Answer:

You will receive a compile-time error: Cannot switch on a value of type Boolean. Only convertible int values, strings or enum variables are permitted. Here is a snapshot from the Eclipse IDE:

⊗ Errors (1 item)

⊗ Cannot switch on a value of type boolean. Only convertible int values, strings or enum variables are permitted

Analysis:

The output is self-explanatory: the Boolean variables cannot be used in such a way with `switch` statements.

8.5 When should we prefer `switch` over `if-else`?

There is no universal rule. It depends on the situation or demands of your program. But you may remember that `if-else` can test conditions or a range of values, while `switch` works on an integer, enum, or `String` object.

8.6 Name the different types of iteration statements in Java.

- `while` loop
- `do...while` loop
- `for` loop
- `for-each` loop (From J2SE5)

8.7 Why do we need these statements?

To create loops. Alternatively, you could say that to execute a segment of code up to some specified number of times repeatedly, you need these statements.

8.8 What is the key difference between a `while` loop and a `do...while` loop?

In case of `do...while`, the condition is checked at the end of the loop. So, even if the condition is false, a `do...while` loop executes at least once.

Consider the following program. Note that I am checking whether the value of *j* is less than 10 in the *while* part. Still, I'm able to print the statement in do{..}.

```
package java2e.appendixa.set8;

class Q8 {
    public static void main(String[] args) {
        System.out.println("***Set8.Q8***");
        System.out.println("***do...while Demo***");
        int j=10;
        do
        {
            System.out.println("j is now: " + j);
            j++;
```

```
        } while (j < 10);
    }
}
```

Output:

Here is the output when you run the program:

```
***Set8.Q8***
***do...while Demo***
j is now: 10
```

8.9 Can you compile the following program?

```java
package java2e.appendixa.set8;
class Q9 {
    public static void main(String[] args) {
        System.out.println("***Set8.Q9***");
        int x=10;
        //compile-time error
        while(x){
                System.out.println("I am inside the loop");
        }
    }
}
```

Answer:

No, you will receive a compile-time error: Type mismatch: cannot convert from int to Boolean. Here is a snapshot from Eclipse IDE:

Description	Resource	Location
∨ ⊗ Errors (1 item)		
📑 Type mismatch: cannot convert from int to boolean	Q9.java	line 8

Analysis:

In Java, boolean and int are not compatible. In the preceding case, we need to use a Boolean variable inside the while loop.

SET 9

9.1 Predict the output.

```
class Q1 {
    public static void main(String[] args) {
        System.out.println("***Set9.Q1***");
        System.out.println("***String vs StringBuffer***");
        String str1="Hello";
        str1.concat("World");
        System.out.println(str1);//Hello

        StringBuffer str2=new StringBuffer("Hello");
        str2.append("World");
        System.out.println(str2);//HelloWorld
    }
}
```

Output:

```
***Set9.Q1***
***String vs StringBuffer***
Hello
HelloWorld
```

Analysis:

String is immutable—i.e., cannot be modified—but StringBuffer is mutable. For the String object, when you are concatenating "World," a new object is actually created inside memory. But for StringBuffer, the value of the object is modified. To see it properly, you can do a simple test—check their hash codes. So, I have added some lines of code to the previous program to analyze the output once again.

Once you execute the program, you'll see that for the String object, you get different hash codes, but for the StringBuffer object, you get the same hash code.

```java
package java2e.appendixa.set9;

class Q1Modified {
    public static void main(String[] args) {
        System.out.println("***Set9.Q1-Analyzing the Modified
        Program***");
        System.out.println("***String vs StringBuffer***");
        String str1="Hello";
        str1.concat("World");
        System.out.println(str1);//Hello
        System.out.println("The str1.hashCode()="+ str1.hashCode());
        System.out.println("The str1.concat(\"World\").hashCode()=
        "+ str1.concat("World").hashCode());
        StringBuffer str2=new StringBuffer("Hello");
        str2.append("World");
        System.out.println(str2);//HelloWorld
        System.out.println("The str2.hashCode()="+str2.hashCode());
        System.out.println("The str2.append(\"World\").hashCode()="+
        str2.append("World").hashCode());
    }
}
```

Output:

Here is the output of the modified program:

```
***Set9.Q1-Analyzing the Modified Program***
***String vs StringBuffer***
Hello
The str1.hashCode()=69609650
The str1.concat("World").hashCode()=439329280
HelloWorld
The str2.hashCode()=366712642
The str2.append("World").hashCode()=366712642
```

The value of the hashcode() may differ in your system.

535

9.2 What is the fundamental difference between StringBuffer and StringBuilder?

StringBuffer is synchronized, so in a multi-threaded environment it is much preferred over StringBuilder. You can learn about multi-threading and synchronization in Chapter 11.

On the other hand, Java Oracle documentation says that if speed is the primary concern and synchronization is not important, then StringBuilder is preferred over StringBuffer.

9.3 What is the difference between applets and applications?

The easiest distinction is that an application contains the main() method and requires JRE. In an applet, you'll not see main(). An applet needs a browser (for example, Chrome). An applet should be executed in a secured environment, whereas an application does not need as much security as an applet. In this book, I have focused only on applications.

APPENDIX B

Getting Started with Java

In 1990–91, Sun Microsystem decided to start a new closed-door project initiated by Mike Sheridan and Patrick Naughton. The project was called "Green Project," and it was headed by James Gosling.

The project started with only a few members (some sources say it was initially a thirteen-member team). The "Green Team" wanted to develop something new and interesting, but their initial objective was different. They wanted to anticipate and plan for the "next wave" in computing. After some initial discussions, they decided to focus on consumer electronic devices, particularly for the digital cable television industry.

The concept was too advanced for the team at that time, but it was perfect for the emerging internet.

The team members wanted a name that would be unique in nature and at the same time reflect the essence of upcoming technologies. So, they picked up names like "Dynamic," "Revolutionary," "Silk," "Jolt," "DNA," and so forth.

Java was initially called Oak, after an oak tree that was visible from Gosling's office. But because of some legal problems, it was renamed to Java. Who first proposed the name Java? Different sources say different things.

Some other sources say that Greentalk was the initial name, which became Oak, and then finally it was renamed to Java. James Gosling later said that Java was one of the top choices, along with Silk. But finally they selected Java.

Sun Microsystems released Java 1.0 in 1996. Java became open source on November 13, 2006. Sun finished the process by making all of Java's core code available under free software/open-source distribution terms (aside from a small portion of code to which they did not hold the copyright) on May 8, 2007.

Later, Oracle Corporation purchased Sun Microsystems, and the acquisition process was finished on January 27, 2010. At the time of this writing, Java 12 is the latest version, which was released on March 19, 2019.

V. Sarcar, *Interactive Object-Oriented Programming in Java*, https://doi.org/10.1007/978-1-4842-5404-2

These qualities were the primary focus area for Java:

- Simple, object-oriented, and familiar programming style

- Robustness and security

- Architecture-neutral and portable

- High-performance capabilities

- Interpreted, threaded, and dynamic

Basic Terms

When you learn Java, you will see some basic terms get used in different contexts. Let's review some of them.

JVM

- It stands for Java Virtual Machine. When you compile the Java file, you get a .class (not an .exe) file. This file contains Java byte code, which is interpreted by JVM. JVM is responsible for loading, verifying, and executing the code. We say that JVM is platform dependent because it converts the bytecodes into the machine language for the specific computer (or machine).

JRE

- It stands for Java Runtime Environment. It contains the JVM, the library files, and the other supporting files. To run a Java program, the JRE must be installed in the system. So, you can simply say JRE=JVM+ some packages.

JDK

- It stands for Java Development Kit. It provides the tool that you need to develop Java programs and the JRE. This tool contains javac.exe, java.exe, etc. When you launch a Java application, it will open the JRE and load the class, and then, in turn, it will execute the main method. So, you can conclude that JDK=JRE+ development tools. At the time of this writing, the latest version of JDK is 12 (commonly known as Java 12).

Bytecode

- Bytecodes are the machine language of the JVM. They provide the instruction set for a JVM. In simple words, it is a virtual machine language in which Java code is compiled. JVM comes into the picture because it stands between these bytecodes and your physical machine.

Platform

- We use the term *platform* to mean where the program will run. It can be your machine, your fully developed OS, etc. When we say a language is platform independent, we mean that the code of a programmer will not vary across different platforms.

Once you compile a Java program, you get the bytecodes. The bytecode format is the same for every platform (Windows/Linux/Solaris/etc.). So, you need an interpreter that will interpret these bytecodes and then produce the machine-specific codes. At this stage, JVM comes into the picture. In Java, these bytecodes are interpreted by JVM, which is available for all operating systems. So, to port the Java program into a new platform, you need to port the Java interpreter. As a result, you can say that the pair—JVM and bytecode—make Java portable.

Note   The bottom line is that the trio—JVM, JRE, and JDK—are platform dependent (because of the OS dependence), but Java is platform independent.

You may remember this simple fact: any machine language is dependent on the OS of the machine. So, if your program has a dependency on the machine-specific OS, the program is not platform independent. Java is platform independent because once the source code is compiled into standard bytecodes, those bytecodes are platform independent. Because of this facility, Sun Microsystems created the slogan WORA (Write Once, Run Anywhere) for Java. But the hard truth is true platform independence is a theoretical concept because even after your best effort you may encounter with surprises when you deal with a platform that is tightly constrained, for example, consider the case of maximum length of a filename and similar constraints. But still we can say, Java is very close to support the true platform independence.

IDE

- It stands for Integrated Development Environment. A standard IDE provides the facilities for software development. In general, these IDEs are very smart—they provide us with an intelligent code-completion technique. If there is a typo in your code, they can also highlight (or suggest) different kinds of possible fixes. An IDE should have a source editor, a debugger, and the automation tools to build the application. IDEs, in general, contain a compiler or an interpreter (or both). Eclipse IDE contains both of these.

Installation

Initially, to start coding, you may need the following things:

- JDK
- IDE

Download JDK

To get the JDK, you can visit the official Oracle page:

`https://www.oracle.com/technetwork/java/javase/downloads/index.html`

Or, to download JDK, directly go here:

`https://www.oracle.com/technetwork/java/javase/downloads/jdk12-`
`downloads-5295953.html`

You may see the following contents in the page mentioned earlier.

Java SE Development Kit 12.0.2

You must accept the Oracle Technology Network License Agreement for Oracle Java SE to download this software.

◯ Accept License Agreement   ⦿ Decline License Agreement

Product / File Description	File Size	Download
Linux	155.14 MB	⬇jdk-12.0.2_linux-x64_bin.deb
Linux	162.79 MB	⬇jdk-12.0.2_linux-x64_bin.rpm
Linux	181.68 MB	⬇jdk-12.0.2_linux-x64_bin.tar.gz
macOS	173.63 MB	⬇jdk-12.0.2_osx-x64_bin.dmg
macOS	173.98 MB	⬇jdk-12.0.2_osx-x64_bin.tar.gz
Windows	158.63 MB	⬇jdk-12.0.2_windows-x64_bin.exe
Windows	179.57 MB	⬇jdk-12.0.2_windows-x64_bin.zip

Note   In this book, our focus is on looking at fundamental concepts in depth, not on the latest features. Most of the programs in the book will run on Java 8 onward. But it is recommended that you download the latest version based on your system configuration (e.g., 32 bit/64 bit, Windows/Linux, etc.).

An Important License Update from Oracle

Oracle's new license is substantially different from its prior JDK licenses. The new license still permits personal use and development at no cost, but it is recommended that you go through the license agreement prior to installing the JDK. I offer a snapshot from the official Oracle page about this recent change:

Important Oracle JDK License Update

The Oracle JDK License has changed for releases starting April 16, 2019.

The new Oracle Technology Network License Agreement for Oracle Java SE is substantially different from prior Oracle JDK licenses. The new license permits certain uses, such as personal use and development use, at no cost -- but other uses authorized under prior Oracle JDK licenses may no longer be available. Please review the terms carefully before downloading and using this product. An FAQ is available here.

Commercial license and support is available with a low cost Java SE Subscription.

Oracle also provides the latest OpenJDK release under the open source GPL License at jdk.java.net.

Download Eclipse

To download the Eclipse IDE, visit here:

https://eclipse.org/downloads/

Note   Like in the previous case, at this time, the link is working fine, but it may be altered in future.

As mentioned earlier, try to download the latest version based on your system configuration. At the time of this writing, Eclipse IDE 2019-06 is the latest version. So, you may notice the following segment when you want to download the Eclipse IDE for your computer:

Naming Conventions

Following the developer guidelines, these are the naming conventions that I'll follow in this book:

- **Class**—A class should start with an uppercase letter and should be a noun; e.g., MyClass, String, etc.

- **Interface**—An interface should start with an uppercase letter and should be an adjective; e.g., Runnable, Remote

- **Method**—A method should start with a lowercase letter and in most cases, this is a verb; e.g., print(), draw(), run(), runQuickly(), showMyMethod(), etc.

- **Variable**—A variable should start with lowercase letter; e.g., myIntegerValue, myDoubleValue, myName, etc.

- **Package**—A package should be in all lowercase letters; e.g., mypackage, java2e.chapter1, etc.

- **Constant**—A constant should be in uppercase letters; e.g., MY_CONSTANT, etc.

Final Comments

These conventions are recommended for coding practice only. In short, you should choose some meaningful names that are easier to read and understand. If you are ever confused, just open the original implementations in Java to get an idea. For example, to get your desired output, in most of the applications you will use System.out.println("Some message");.

Now, let's open the declaration in Eclipse IDE, which shows the following:

```
public void println(Object x) {
    String s = String.valueOf(x);
    synchronized (this) {
        print(s);
        newLine();
    }
}
```

You can see that println(), newLine(), etc. are methods. x is a method parameter in println(Object x).

Now, go through a containing class, which is as follows:

```
public class PrintStream extends FilterOutputStream
    implements Appendable, Closeable{..}
```

Here, you can see `PrintStream` is the class and `Appendable` is an interface.

Also, go through a package declaration:

```
package java.lang;
```

From all these constructs, you can see that both a class name and an interface name start with uppercase letters, a method and its parameters start with lowercase letters, and package names are all in lowercase letters.

APPENDIX C

Installing MySQL and Testing SQL Commands

Here I present you with step-by-step instructions on how to install MySQL on a Windows 10 Home operating system. The instructions were initially written for MySQL community server 8.0.16, but at the time of this writing it has been upgraded to the version 8.0.17. Ideally, these steps should not vary in upcoming versions, but there is no guarantee. So, it is recommended that you always visit the official home page at `https://dev.mysql.com/downloads/mysql/` prior to installation. From this page, you can also get the installer for other operating systems (for example, Debian Linux, Ubuntu Linux, Fedora, macOS, Oracle Solaris, etc.).

Note   The installation steps for different operating systems are also available at `https://dev.mysql.com/doc/refman/8.0/en/installing.html`.

Step 1: Download the latest MySQL Community server from the official site at `https://dev.mysql.com/downloads/mysql/`. For me, it was 8.0.16, but now it has been updated to 8.0.17. It is suggested that you always try to install the latest version.

You get the following screen.

© Vaskaran Sarcar 2020
V. Sarcar, *Interactive Object-Oriented Programming in Java*, https://doi.org/10.1007/978-1-4842-5404-2

Select your operating system (Microsoft Windows) and click on **Go to Download Page**. It will redirect you to the actual download page for Windows MySQL server.

Step 2: Now you will see two different installers. Choose the installer with the bigger size; i.e., **mysql-installer-community-[latest version].msi**.

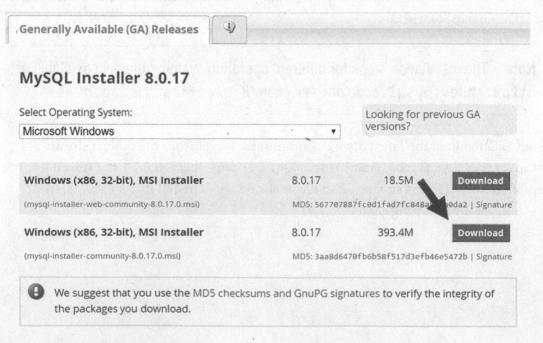

Step 3: Now it asks for credentials. You can either log in or sign up. I opted for the **No thanks, just start my download** option. It downloads the selected MySQL in the local machine.

⊕ MySQL Community Downloads

Login Now or Sign Up for a free account.

An Oracle Web Account provides you with the following advantages:

- Fast access to MySQL software downloads
- Download technical White Papers and Presentations
- Post messages in the MySQL Discussion Forums
- Report and track bugs in the MySQL bug system

Login » using my Oracle Web account	Sign Up » for an Oracle Web account

MySQL.com is using Oracle SSO for authentication. If you already have an Oracle Web account, click the Login link. Otherwise, you can signup for a free account by clicking the Sign Up link and following the instructions.

 No thanks, just start my download.

Step 4: Go to your Downloads folder and locate the `mysql-installer-community` file. Double-click the installer. (Or you can right-click on that file and choose the Install option.)

mysql-connector-java-8.0.16	06-08-2019 09:36	File folder	
mysql-connector-java-8.0.16	19-05-2019 10:40	WinZip File	4,395 KB
mysql-installer-community-8.0.16.0	19-05-2019 09:34	Windows Installer Pa...	3,82,340 KB

mysql-installer-community-8.0.16.0	19-05-2019 09:34	Windows Installer Pa...	3,82,340 KB

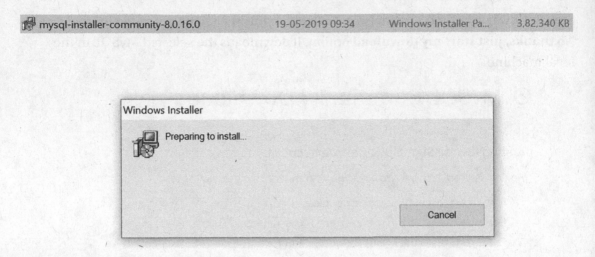

Step 4.1: During the installation process, it may ask you for permission to change your computer settings or firewall confirmation. Once you accept those, it will proceed, and it may take some time to configure the installer.

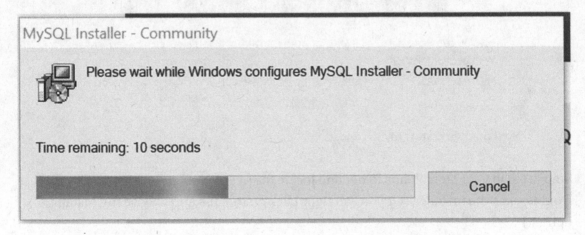

Step 5: Read the license agreement. To proceed further, you need to accept the license terms. Then click **Next**.

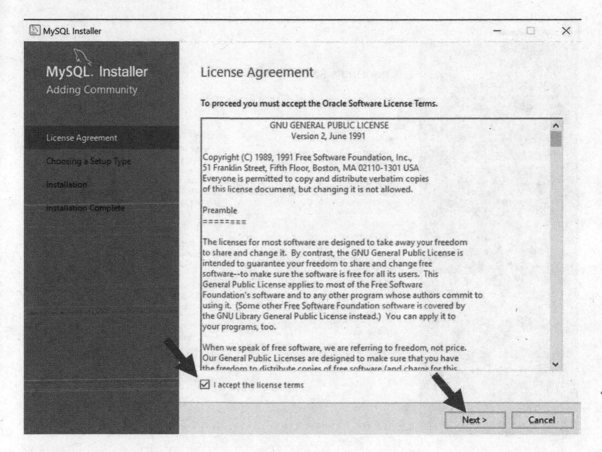

Step 6: Now, you'll get various options. I have chosen the **Developer Default** to serve my needs. Click on **Next**.

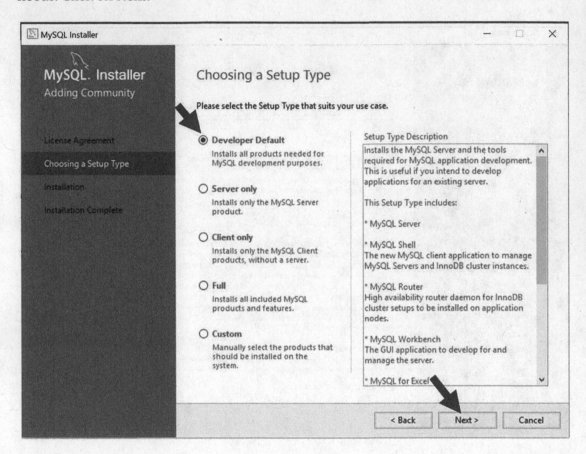

Step 7: Now you will notice any failing requirements. It depends on the current configuration of your system. Click **Next**.

Step 7.1: For example, before I installed Visual Studio 2019 on my system, I got the following screen.

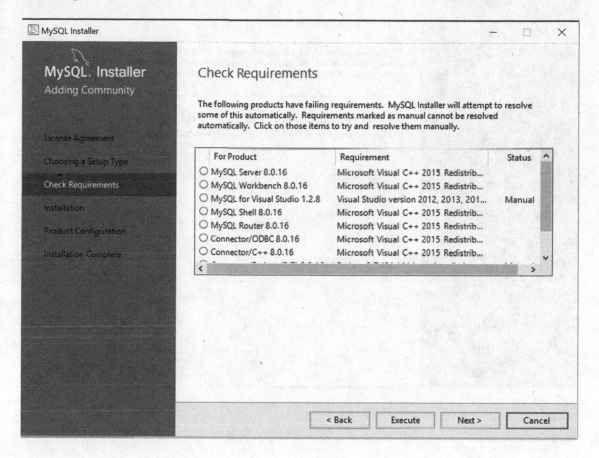

Step 7.2: But once I installed Visual Studio Community 2019 on my system, I got the following screen.

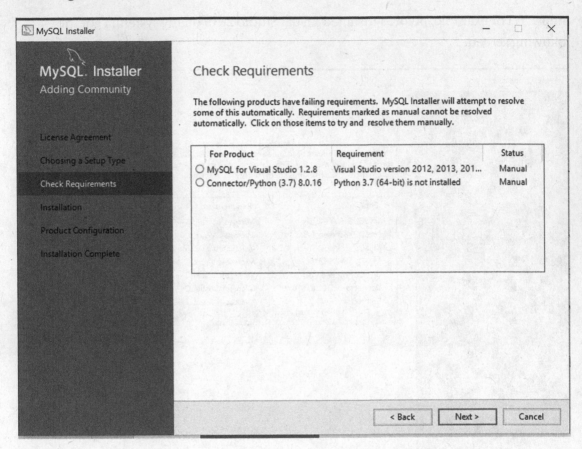

Step 8: So, based on the current Windows configuration, it may prompt you that "One or more product requirements have not been satisfied." Click **Yes** and then **Next**.

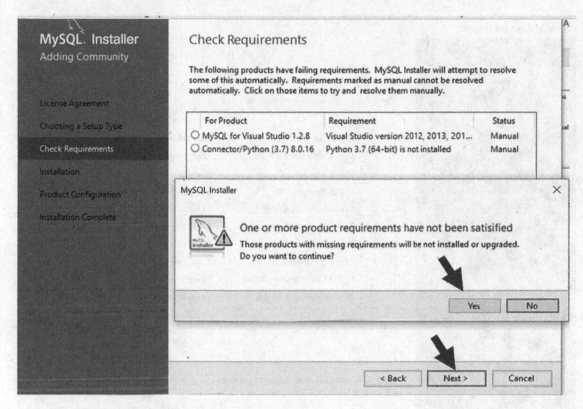

Step 9: Now, you may get a screen similar to the following screen. (As said before, it is dependent on your current configuration.) Press **Execute**.

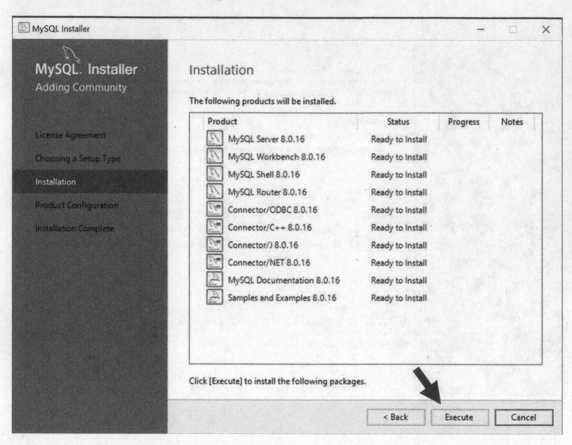

Step 10: You will get a similar screen.

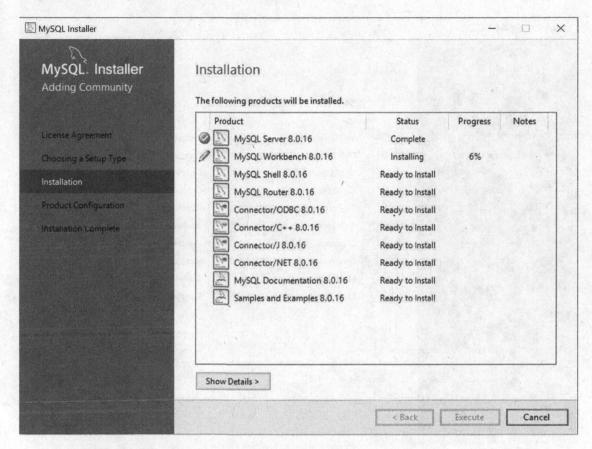

Step 11: Once everything installed, you will see the following screen. Click **Next**.

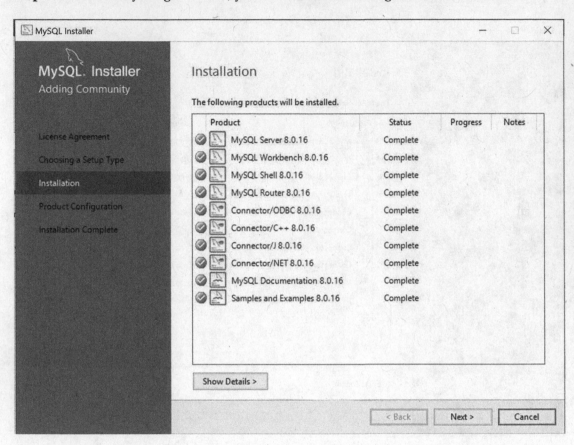

Step 12: Now MySQL suggests that you configure the server settings. Click **Next**.

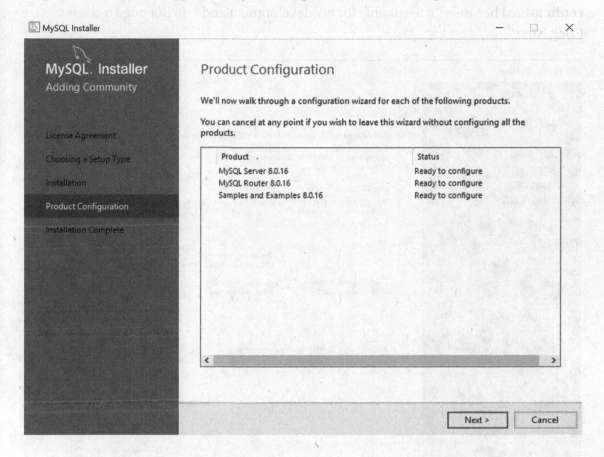

Step 13: I opted for the default settings (**Standalone MySQL server/Classic MySQL replication**) because I'll use it only for my development and I do not need a cluster. Click **Next**.

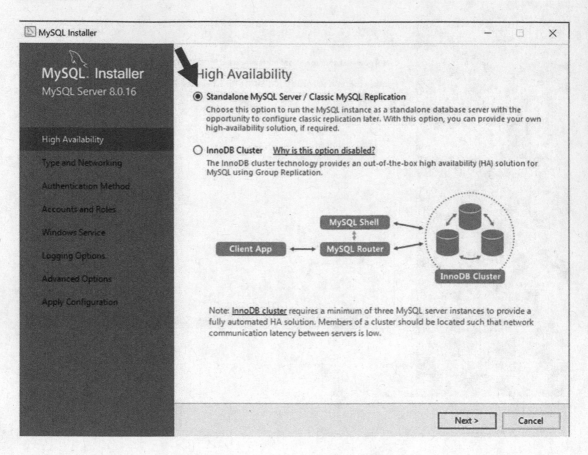

Step 14: Keep everything as default; i.e., I chose **Development Computer**. You can choose other options as per your needs. Click **Next**.

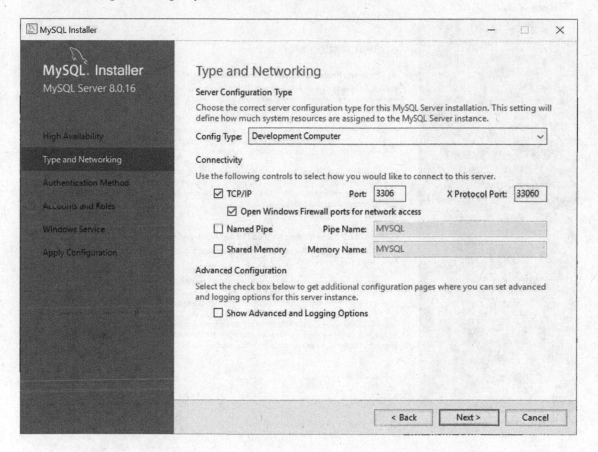

Step 15: Choose the default recommended method and click on **Next**.

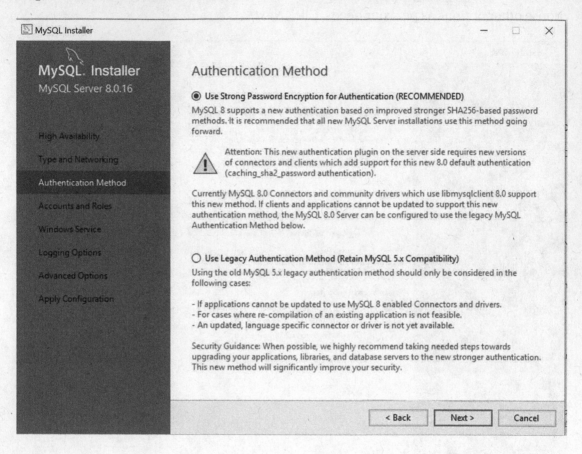

Step 16: Set the MySQL root user password and then click **Next**.

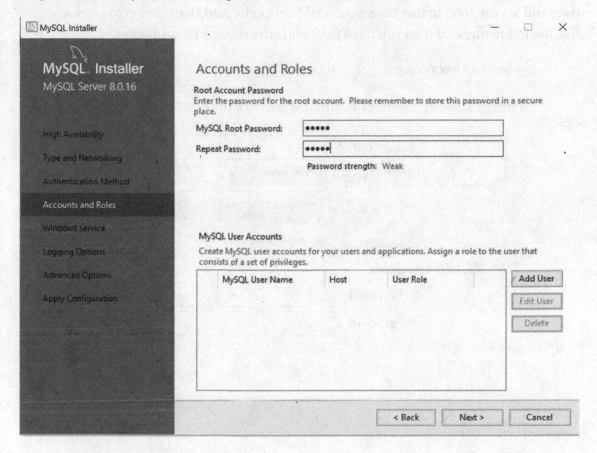

Step 16.1: For now, I am not creating any new users. But you can always create a new user and set the role. In that case, you need to click the **Add User** button to get a screen like the following, and then you need to provide the required information.

Step 17: I kept all the default settings. Click **Next**.

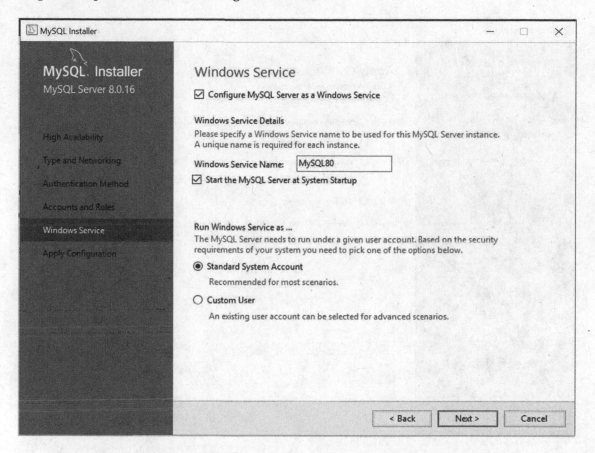

Have you noticed the service name **MySQL80**? Remember that I have used the version **8.0**.16.

Step 18: Click **Execute** to apply the configurations from the previous step.

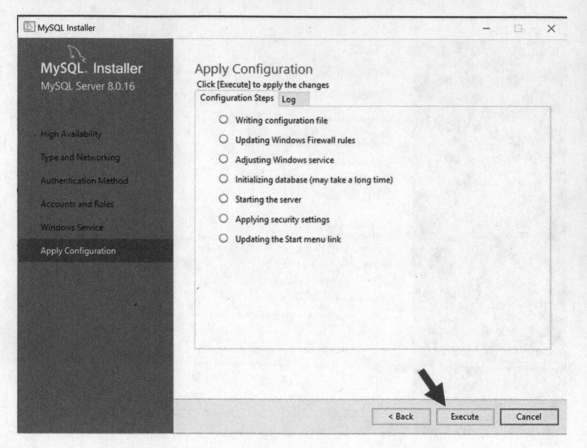

Step 19: Upon execution, you may see a screen similar to the following.

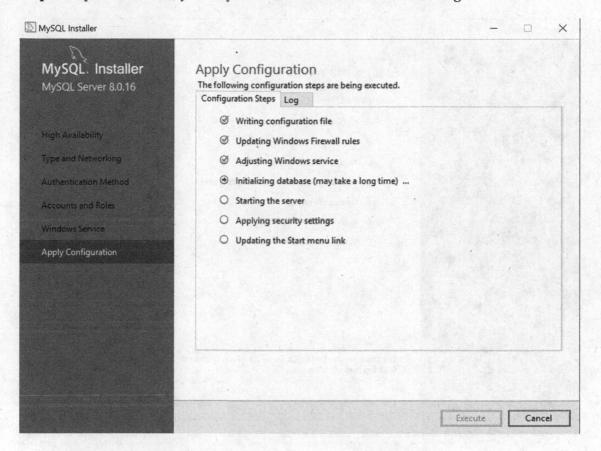

Step 20: Once everything is installed, you will see the following screen. Click **Finish**.

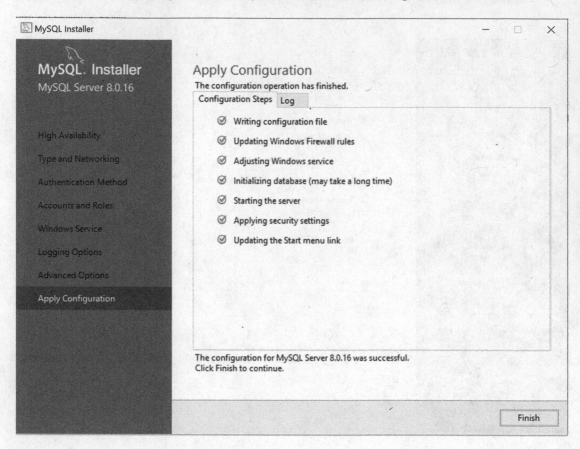

Step 21: Now you will get the following screen. Click **Next**.

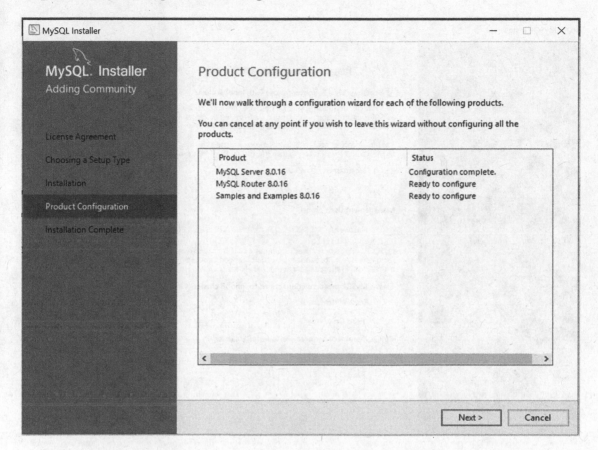

Step 22: You do not need to set up the router information for now. Click **Finish**.

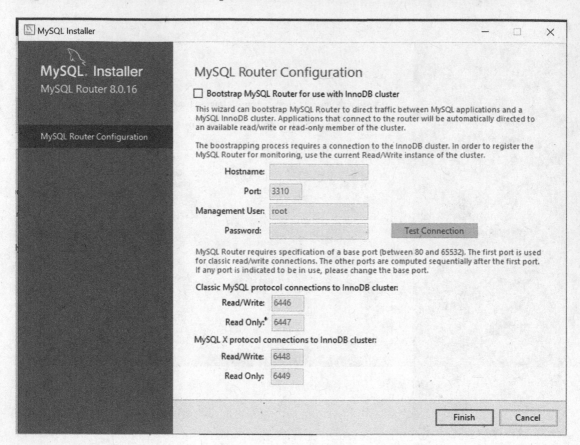

Step 23: Notice that since you did not provide any settings, *"Configuration not needed"* appeared for MySQL Router 8.0.16. Click **Next**.

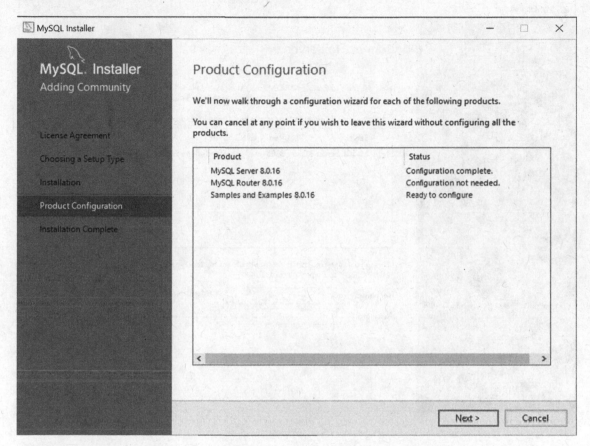

Step 24: Supply password for root user.

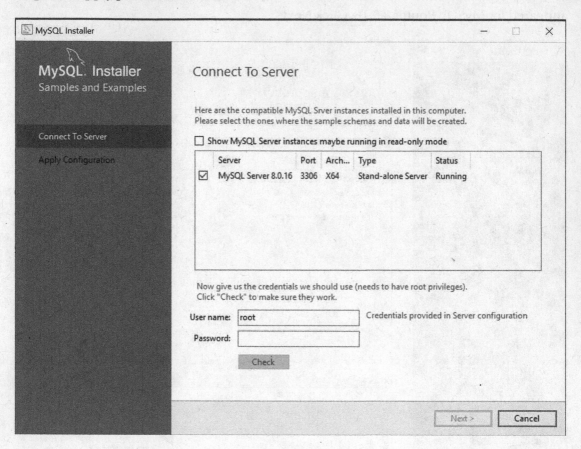

Step 25: Press the **Check** button and then click **Next**.

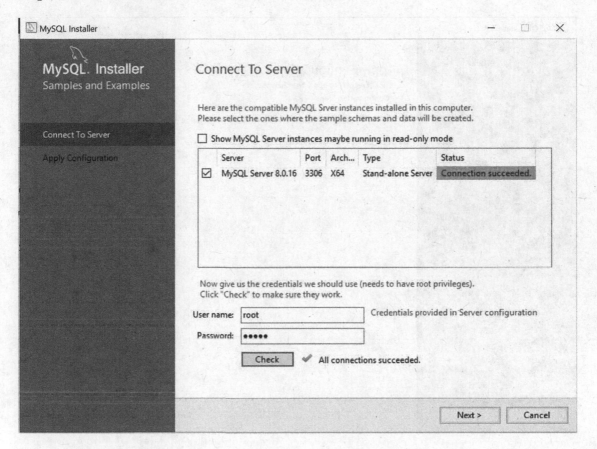

Step 26: The following screen will appear. Press **Execute**.

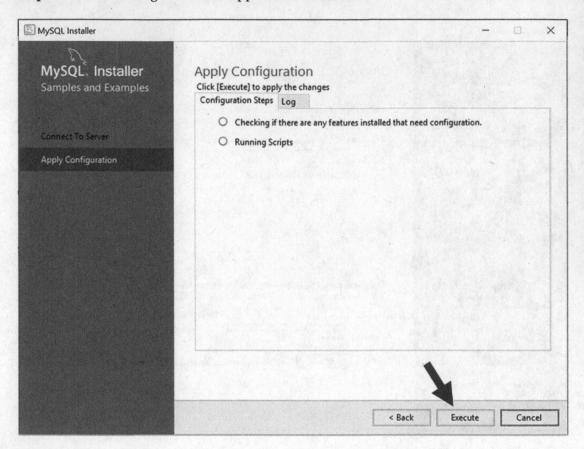

Step 27: Once everything is applied, you will get the following screen. Click **Finish**.

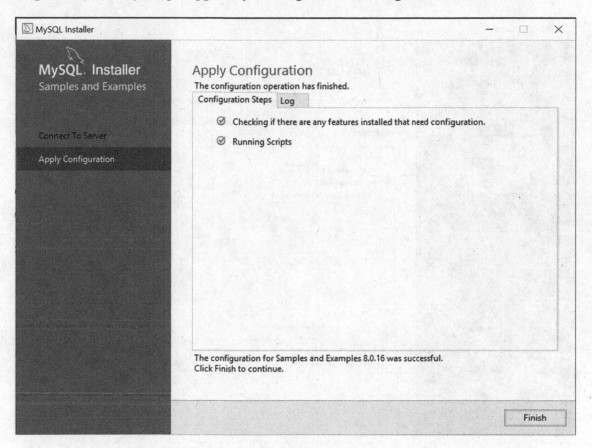

Step 28: The following screen will appear. Click **Next**.

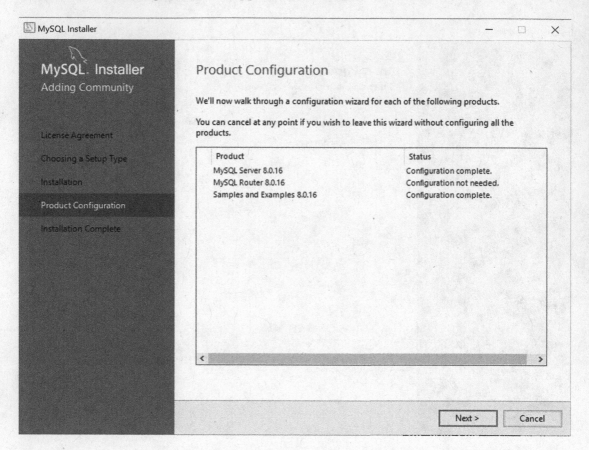

Step 29: Receive the Installation Complete message. Click **Finish**.

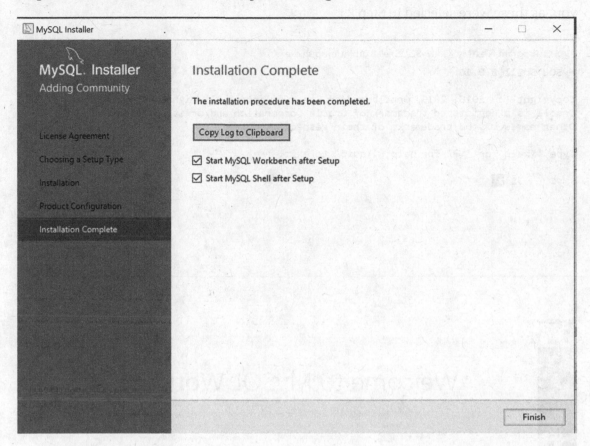

Step 30 (optional): Both MySQL Workbench and the MySQL Shell prompt will open for you, as these were selected in Step 29.

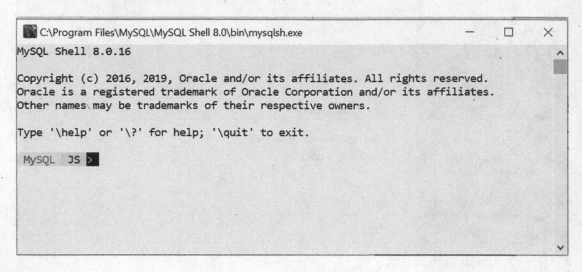

Let's test the installation and execute simple SQL statements. Here are some sample SQL queries/statements for your reference. These statements were exercised with a MySQL database using the command prompt.

Enter password: *****

Welcome to the MySQL monitor. Commands end with ; or \g.

Your MySQL connection id is 8

Server version: 8.0.16 MySQL Community Server - GPL

Copyright (c) 2000, 2019, Oracle and/or its affiliates. All rights reserved.

Oracle is a registered trademark of Oracle Corporation and/or its affiliates. Other names may be trademarks of their respective owners.

Type 'help;' or '\h' for help. Type '\c' to clear the current input statement.

```
mysql> show databases;
+--------------------+
| Database           |
+--------------------+
| information_schema |
| mysql              |
| performance_schema |
| sakila             |
| sys                |
| world              |
+--------------------+
6 rows in set (0.30 sec)

mysql> create database test;
Query OK, 1 row affected (0.23 sec)
mysql> show databases;
+--------------------+
| Database           |
+--------------------+
| information_schema |
| mysql              |
| performance_schema |
| sakila             |
| sys                |
| test               |
| world              |
+--------------------+
```

```
7 rows in set (0.00 sec)
mysql> use test;
Database changed
mysql> create table employee(EmpId Integer primary key,Name Varchar(10),Age
Integer not null,Salary Double);
Query OK, 0 rows affected (1.06 sec)

mysql> insert into employee values(1,'Amit',25,1200.5);
Query OK, 1 row affected (0.31 sec)
mysql> insert into employee values(2,'Sam',23,1000.25);
Query OK, 1 row affected (0.22 sec)
mysql> insert into employee values(3,'Bob',30,1500);
Query OK, 1 row affected (0.14 sec)

mysql> select * from employee;
+-------+------+-----+---------+
| EmpId | Name | Age | Salary  |
+-------+------+-----+---------+
|     1 | Amit |  25 |  1200.5 |
|     2 | Sam  |  23 | 1000.25 |
|     3 | Bob  |  30 |    1500 |
+-------+------+-----+---------+
3 rows in set (0.00 sec)
```

Here is a snapshot for a compact view:

```
mysql> select * from employee;
+-------+------+-----+---------+
| EmpId | Name | Age | Salary  |
+-------+------+-----+---------+
|     1 | Amit |  25 |  1200.5 |
|     2 | Sam  |  23 | 1000.25 |
|     3 | Bob  |  30 |    1500 |
+-------+------+-----+---------+
3 rows in set (0.00 sec)
```

```
mysql> desc employee;

+--------+-------------+------+-----+---------+-------+
| Field  | Type        | Null | Key | Default | Extra |
+--------+-------------+------+-----+---------+-------+
| EmpId  | int(11)     | NO   | PRI | NULL    |       |
| Name   | varchar(10) | YES  |     | NULL    |       |
| Age    | int(11)     | NO   |     | NULL    |       |
| Salary | double      | YES  |     | NULL    |       |
+--------+-------------+------+-----+---------+-------+
4 rows in set (0.17 sec)
```

Here is a snapshot for a compact view:

```
mysql> desc employee;
+--------+-------------+------+-----+---------+-------+
| Field  | Type        | Null | Key | Default | Extra |
+--------+-------------+------+-----+---------+-------+
| EmpId  | int(11)     | NO   | PRI | NULL    |       |
| Name   | varchar(10) | YES  |     | NULL    |       |
| Age    | int(11)     | NO   |     | NULL    |       |
| Salary | double      | YES  |     | NULL    |       |
+--------+-------------+------+-----+---------+-------+
4 rows in set (0.17 sec)
```

```
mysql> create function total(firstNumber double,secondNumber double)
returns double deterministic return firstNumber+secondNumber;
Query OK, 0 rows affected (1.03 sec)
```

```
mysql> create table NumberTable(FirstNo Double, SecondNo Double);
Query OK, 0 rows affected (2.77 sec)
```

```
mysql> show tables;
+----------------+
| Tables_in_test |
+----------------+
| employee       |
| numbertable    |
+----------------+
2 rows in set (0.08 sec)
```

```
mysql> insert into numbertable values(12.3,15.7);
Query OK, 1 row affected (2.12 sec)

mysql> insert into numbertable values(32.3,25.3);
Query OK, 1 row affected (0.13 sec)

mysql> insert into numbertable values(25,75);
Query OK, 1 row affected (0.08 sec)

mysql> select * from numbertable;
+---------+----------+
| FirstNo | SecondNo |
+---------+----------+
|    12.3 |     15.7 |
|    32.3 |     25.3 |
|      25 |       75 |
+---------+----------+
3 rows in set (0.08 sec)
```

Index

E, F

Printed in the United States
By Bookmasters